From the RENAISSANCE
to the COUNTER-
REFORMATION

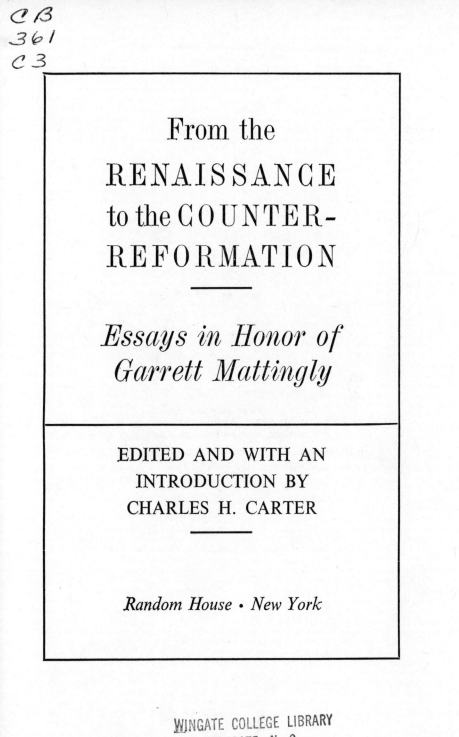

From the
RENAISSANCE
to the COUNTER-
REFORMATION

*Essays in Honor of
Garrett Mattingly*

EDITED AND WITH AN
INTRODUCTION BY
CHARLES H. CARTER

Random House • *New York*

FIRST PRINTING

*Manufactured in the United States of America
by The Book Press, Brattleboro, Vermont*

Designed by Hermann Strohbach

Library of Congress catalog card number: 65–11281

CONTENTS

v

From the RENAISSANCE
to the COUNTER-
REFORMATION

INTRODUCTION

This *Festschrift* originated in three separate such projects which were merged in a committee composed of Robert Webb, Robert Kingdon, De Lamar Jensen, David Hicks, and myself. We should like to thank those who have assisted directly in this project, those who have given invaluable indirect support, and still others who have set aside separate plans so that a single memorial volume could be achieved. It is sincerely hoped that it will adequately represent the esteem not only of those whose names appear herein but also of the great many friends, colleagues, and former students whose names do not.

To make a more adequate memorial, it was felt that the proper number of contributions was twenty—as large a collection as seemed possible, while still of properly substantial individual length, without making the volume too large to reach as wide an audience as the memory of so fine an historian deserves. As is usual in such matters, more than that number were invited, to allow for those predictably unable to participate even on such an occasion as this; the response was so remarkable—a tribute that must be recorded here—that had insuperable circumstance not intervened for some,* this optimum scheme would have been demolished. In the event it was not; one hopes that a proper balance of length and number has been achieved.

Inevitably the reader will think of names that might well have appeared here, not all of them covered by the above passage. One sought an adequate institutional spread; participation by both

---

* For example, the essay conceived for this volume by Hans Baron and interrupted by illness will be expanded to cover a longer period and published as a book, dedicated to Professor Mattingly.

American colleagues and former students; a substantial British representation; Pieter Geyl for the Continent; and a variety of subject matter to correspond to the wide range of the historical interests of the man being honored. Even with these guide lines, however, reducing the list for the single round of invitations was a painful task; the committee as a whole should be credited with inclusions, I alone blamed for omissions.

Very special gratitude is due Dr. Morris Philipson, not only for his customary editorial acumen, but for his remarkable patience in seeing the undersigned through some unforeseen problems in preparing this volume.

As editorial bystander, it seems to me wholly appropriate that these commemorative essays should so strongly emphasize re-examination and exploration, fresh sources and fresh subject matter. It was the kind of history Garrett Mattingly preferred. The nature of the man, in fact, has dictated the nature of the volume: its essential unity lies in its intentional span of Professor Mattingly's period, from the fifteenth to the seventeenth centuries; in its attempt to reflect through variety the amazing breadth of his interests and erudition—political, diplomatic, intellectual, cultural, and other aspects of history; and perhaps most of all in the refusal of these memorial essays to be grouped in watertight categories any more readily than Garrett Mattingly's historical vision was capable of subdivision into disconnected pieces.

For this reason they are presented here not in neat compartments but in a chronological order modified slightly to allow greater kinship with their neighbors. For the reader who may wish to know *bref* what lies therein, a few words about their contents may be in order. After the personal appreciation by Leo Gershoy and the scholarly appreciation by J. H. Hexter, the next half dozen essays deal with society and culture in the fifteenth and sixteenth centuries. In the first of these, Joan Gadol draws (among other sources) upon her own researches in depth on Leone Battista Alberti in arguing the unity of the Renaissance. Paul Oskar Kristeller, through the example of Bartolomeo Facio, illustrates the rich store of unused manuscript sources awaiting historians on figures outside the ortho-dox canon of Renaissance history (especially welcome to this editor, who believes studies of the minor but ignored now contribute far more than do continual retreads of the major figures). David Hicks's contention that corporativism was virtually dead in Siena by the mid-fifteenth century is based upon research in the Siena archives so fresh it was still going on at deadline for this volume.

Denys Hay, sallying onto the almost unexplored ground of the Italian Renaissance outside Italy, points out the crucial changes in both the Italian and English settings which determined the early lack and later presence of Italian influence in England. John Hale discards a wagonload of old chestnuts about the material and ethical influence of gunpowder, and shows how quickly resistance to its use disappeared. Gerald Strauss describes the publication history of Sebastian Münster's *Cosmography* to illustrate the fund of knowledge available in its time—far larger, and absorbed by a much greater part of the population, than we patronizing moderns often suppose.

The volume having proceeded into the Counter-Reformation, Robert Kingdon illuminates one of the most significant questions of sixteenth-century political thought: the manner in which Catholic writers adopted their Protestant enemies' justifications for rebellion. Monsignor Philip Hughes, making original use of the correspondence of John Lingard—rightly called our first scientific historian—goes behind the scenes of John Allen's public attack on his revisionary account (which became the accepted view) of the St. Bartholomew's Day Massacre. De Lamar Jensen draws on his long researches on the subject to trace the workings of Franco-Spanish diplomacy in the Armada crisis.

Pieter Geyl develops more fully a thesis he has put forward briefly before—but never so completely, and never in English—that the 1587 document which provided the keystone for generations of Dutch constitutional thought has strangely been misinterpreted for all that time. Frank Smolar describes commercial activity during the "decline of Antwerp," and offers alternative explanations for both the continued prosperity and the eventual demise of Antwerp commercial houses. In my own contribution I have attempted to trace the main patterns of diplomatic representation in early modern Europe and to examine their implications.

Christopher Hill, by letting villains and their betters speak at length about each other, fills in an important element in political thought and attitudes in the reigns of Elizabeth and the early Stuarts, and in the process leaves beyond repair whatever remained of the myth of social harmony in Merrie England. G. R. Elton re-examines the "Form of Apology and Satisfaction" of 1604 to illustrate a revolutionary proposition of great insight: that in early Stuart England, even as late as 1640, "the one thing quite out of the question was a civil war."

Through an examination of Blackloism, Father Robert I. Bradley demonstrates the lack of any practical possibility of England's being recovered for Rome in the seventeenth century—long supposed to be a real danger. Sister Joseph Damien complements this on the lay side of recusant history, describing in the person of Dorothy Lawson the English Catholics' struggle to preserve the faith in adversity.

C. V. Wedgwood describes the reaction in European capitals to the execution of Charles I and the conspicuous gulf between words and action to define the extent and limits of the influence in practical affairs of the sanctity of kingship. Herbert Rowen closes the volume with a reassessment in context of early modern Europe's basic political institutions and concepts, which have been badly distorted through a modern prism.

The authors individually and collectively dedicate these essays to a truly great scholar and a most excellent man, and hope that this book may be found at least a partially satisfactory tribute to his memory.

C H A R L E S   H .   C A R T E R
Tulane University
October, 1964

GARRETT MATTINGLY:
A PERSONAL
APPRECIATION

L E O G E R S H O Y
New York University

No one can replace Garrett Mattingly in the hearts of his friends. When he was with us, we inclined affectionately before him. We now treasure the memory of a man of rare personality and gifts, recalling in sorrow but with pride the generosity of his spirit, his endearment, and his ripe wisdom. To all who cherished him deeply, his loss is irreparable.

It is fitting that a memorial volume honor him as a distinguished scholar who had risen to the summit of his profession. Happily he did not have to wait for posterity to win recognition for his achievements: he had gained it in his lifetime. When he died on December 18, 1962, he had already taken his place among the illustrious of his time. Fellow workers in his own field and all students acquainted with his writings hailed him as an outstanding authority who embodied with exemplary mastery the highest attributes of the historian's craft.

Though fully abreast of the specialized research of other scholars, to which he applied the same exacting criteria that he demanded from himself, he worked mainly from original sources, both published and archival. He did so, he stated in the Preface to *The*

7

Armada, not because he attached "a higher purity" to that procedure, "but because that is the way I enjoy working." The disclaimer need not be taken literally. He preferred to visit or re-visit the places he wanted to talk about and to use primary sources, because working that way did in fact ensure "a higher purity." The disclaimer, one would like to believe, with its oblique thrust at the more literal-minded worshipers at the shrine of research, was deliberately contrived to indulge an ironic warning. Research, he seemed to be intimating in that passing aside, was no sacred "Thing in Itself." It was indeed the *sine qua non* of scholarship, but it was not sacrosanct. It was no autonomous activity or goal enjoying an independent existence.

It was the means to an end, the end of faithfully reconstructing the past and presenting it in a rich and meaningful narrative. Taking it for granted that all good scholars did make the required and demanding effort to master the sources, he preferred to have his research implicit in his writing. An instinct of workmanship, a sense of artistry, would not permit him to have the scaffolding obstruct his completed structure from view. So with unobtrusive skill and a mastery seemingly effortless he made his way through the sources that he so conscientiously utilized. He moved through the thickets of official documents and dispatches and in and out of the morasses of political debates. He diligently combed the contemporary press and with meticulous patience searched diaries, letters, and memoirs for the valuable and revealing traces they would yield about the thinking and the acts of participants.

He wrote much, and everything he wrote, books, articles, reviews, was written with care. Everything bears his stamp, even brief notices for learned journals and fugitive reviews that he published in periodicals intended for a larger audience. It all reflects the facets of his broad cultural interests and the authority of a well-stocked mind.

Three great books, *Renaissance Diplomacy, Catherine of Aragon,* and *The Armada,* are the testament of his being. In structure and style they are the embodiments of the intellectual distinction and the engaging charm that captivated his readers for many years. The style was lean and economical in *Renaissance Diplomacy,* where every sentence advanced thought and every thought was the product of hours of concentrated consideration and reflection. He cast a compelling spell upon all who read his moving *Catherine of Aragon*. He held them enthralled in the richly brocaded *Armada,* with its superb portraiture and its dramatic reweaving of the strands of conflict in the culminating moments of the duel for mastery between the two great powers of Europe.

Students who worked for advanced degrees in his seminars at Columbia University had the close and conscientious guidance of a friend, a guidance imbued with sympathetic understanding of their problems and directed by solicitude for their progress. They were privileged, too, those who heard him as he stood on the lecture platform, talking with verve and color and eloquence, with kindly irony or, as the occasion warranted, with biting wit, distilling the essence of his great learning. Most privileged of all were those who saw and heard him at more intimate gatherings when, happily relaxed, he showed himself at his most dazzling Renaissance.

For he was indeed a man of the Renaissance, steeped in its values, living in the twentieth century. Head cocked, eyes sparkling, his smile benign, he talked in a flow of words, witty, gay, and serious, about poetry and drama and novels, about music he loved dearly, about tapestries and paintings he admired, about rich wines and fine food that few appreciated with equal discrimination. He loved, too, to talk about explorers whose voyages he could so fully trace, and about their sailing ships, how they were built and manned and how navigated.

As he talked, so radiantly, in the vein of his living and his writing, there was no separating the man from the historian. It was that organic fusion of personality with professional standards and responsibilities that won him the admiration of the many thousands of readers whom he had never seen or met. Unknown to him and they not knowing him, he nevertheless had impressed himself firmly on their thoughts and feelings. They were shocked and instinctively saddened by his death, regretful that they had not met him.

If we ask why it was that those men and women of his larger audience felt that something greatly treasured had been taken from them, that a sounding board of their values and ideals was muted, the answer surely is not difficult to find. His audience beyond the circles of academic life understood, great scholar that he was, that Garrett Mattingly had not been swallowed by the canons of the historians' craft. Professionalism had not stolen his life. It had imposed upon his large human and humane outlook no myopic vision. Man and historian, he remained vitally absorbed by the vagaries of existence, its grandeurs and its smallness. He deplored the setbacks that life inflicted, and he hailed the triumphs that man gained over adversity. His readers grasped with sensitive intuition his own deeply felt consciousness of the existentialist world in which men lived, a world not to be explained solely by scholarly precision or by logical clarity of analysis. In the stuff of life, consequently of history, he knew, there was much beyond precision and logic. There were rationalities and deep layers of irrationalities. There were appetites and wants and interests. There were tensions and drives, hopes not to be realized, yearnings not to be requited.

If, like Tocqueville, he accepted necessity in the affairs of men, he also made allowance for the contingent and the accidental. Distinguishing however between determinism and irresistibleness, he refused to believe that the future could proceed against the wills that created it. Not the force of things but man, sometimes with and sometimes against forces, decided his destiny, wisely or not, on the basis of his knowledge and understanding. To attain knowledge and understanding and then act upon them "luck and ingenuity" were needed, as he put it in an unpublished lecture.* Most of all man needed the aid of the historian. History was perhaps not the unique *magistra vitae* that Cicero held it to be, but it was still the best available counselor and guide at man's disposal. Hence the responsibility of the historian in his writing and his teaching was paramount. The historian was the custodian of the social memory, and the writing of history—here Mattingly was one with Ranke—was a matter of conscience.

It was a matter of conscience with him, because he was almost passionately convinced that the indifference, ignorance, apathy, and prejudices of citizens decisively fashioned and limited policy decisions of responsible leaders. He chose on that occasion to discuss those basic weaknesses in the conduct of our foreign relations, but all his life he also fought to eradicate their ugliest manifestations in

---

* "A Sample Discipline—The Teaching of History," read at the Princeton Bicentennial Conference on The University and its World Responsibilities, February 20, 1947.

our domestic affairs. With deeply felt words, he presented a series of concrete suggestions for the teaching of history in the universities. He made a plea for the establishment of a global frame of reference in our teaching so that we would be able to live knowingly with all our associated fellow nation-states. To the historians who were his listeners, he deprecated the distorted and parochial instruction that isolated our national experience from its European background and setting. The North Americans of the United States, he maintained, were "Western Europeans . . . a subsection of a great society called Western Civilization," and that civilization was itself part of the greater society of mankind.

This was the identity that Garrett Mattingly wished us to recapture, the identity of our past and present with the total tradition of the West, the identity of being moved by the same forces and moving toward a common destiny. "If man's destiny," he concluded, "is still partly in his own hands; if human intelligence and human will can change the course of events; if our enemy is really human folly and not inexorable fate, then upon the scholars and teachers of the West, now living, and particularly upon the scholars and teachers of the United States, is laid a responsibility we dare not ignore or palter with." He often stated that he would like to write a book on that theme. It is a pity he was not spared long enough to realize the wish.

Readers, then, not known to him and for whom he had become a counselor and a conscience, admired his matchless style, but they also grasped that it was the vehicle and the substance of his person. Style was integral with being. It was no cloak that he chose to put on or take off. It was the conscious and controlled expression of himself, the sacrament of what he held dear and defended with the ardor of lofty partisanship. For he was a partisan. His faith was one with his love of life, the life of dignity and civility that man could live but had rarely been permitted to do, the life of refined distinction of thought and artistic expression.

It was life and the world of man that he loved. Life often dejected him; it never dismayed him. He was no sentimentalist weeping over the ills of humanity. He was warm-hearted but tough-minded. Expansive and generous in his sympathies, he responded to and encouraged the best in people. The pretentious, the arrogant, and the intolerant he roundly condemned, and he fought valiantly against the cruelties of prejudices and tabus wherever he found them, in the market place or in the highest social and scholarly strata. He was tender and compassionate. He treasured the mediation of men of good will, for he himself had wisdom and forebearance and long vision. Perhaps most of all, he cherished what he so amply possessed, what so possessed him—profound honesty and courage. It was delight to be his friend. And an honor.

The warm feelings of readers whom he did not know and the deep affection of those on whom his personal impact was great are being transmuted into endearing oral legend; and that legend is fusing with the brilliant record he left. In that blend of admiration, respect, and love, Garrett Mattingly assuredly will have the immortality befitting the gallant man that he was.

LEO GERSHOY
New York University

GARRETT MATTINGLY,
HISTORIAN

J . H . H E X T E R
Yale University

Some historians are by temperament or preference or natural gifts writers of articles, some of essays, some of monographs, some of full-scale comprehensive books. Garrett Mattingly was a writer of books; he wrote three of them. Of these the one known best and to the widest public is *The Armada;*[1] it is that rarity, a book by a professional historian and admired by professional historians which nevertheless became a best seller. Only slightly less well known is his biography of Catherine of Aragon.[2] Both enjoy the current form of literary apotheosis, publication in paperback; and they will surely survive in that pantheon when thousands of volumes currently occupying a niche there have vanished. Mattingly's third book, *Renaissance Diplomacy,*[3] did not directly reach so many readers as the other two, and it probably never will; but historians of early modern Europe tend to regard it as his crowning effort. The story of a great naval battle, the biography of a Spanish-born English Queen, and an account of the origin and growth of a highly specialized institution—in the hands of most professional historians these would be appropriate subjects for a typical form of academic history, the monograph. In Mattingly's hands they became not monographs but full-scale histories. They are so, because Mattingly had the wide-range panoramic vision of the book writer. Whether

13

he wrote about the Armada, or Catherine, or Renaissance diplomacy, he saw them in their relation to the complex, richly textured pattern of this society they belonged to. He dealt lovingly with the detail of each of his subjects, and he was a master of the enlivening detail. There is the young Henry VIII, with his irrepressible passion for adolescent pageantry, showing off his fleet, "clad in a sailor's smock and trousers all of cloth of gold, and blowing on a silver whistle 'so loud it was like a trumpet.' "[4] And the peace of Good Queen Bess:

> In the midst of a Europe torn by foreign and civil war [the English] remained placidly at peace. No royal taxgatherers took from their pockets the fruits of their industry. Prices were high, business was good, money was plentiful; and the profits could be confidently plowed back into land and shipping and the growing production of textiles and metals in which, for the first time, England was beginning to take a notable place in the world. No soldiers clanked through the streets except those home from fighting in foreign quarrels, and a sudden knock on the door at night would be only a neighbor or a carter.[5]

And Henry III's preparations for the assassination of the Duc de Guise:

> There were still some complicated arrangements to make. The François Ier wing of the castle, where the king slept, was a rabbit warren of twisty little stairways and unexpected passages. Two doorways, usually open, had to be blocked, and one door, always locked, had to be opened, so that some of the necessary actors could arrive on the scene unobserved. The king saw to everything himself.[6]

But in Mattingly's books the detail stood out from a complexly patterned background. He did not amputate the subjects he wrote about from the larger society to which they belonged, Latin Christendom mainly in the age of the Renaissance. The Renaissance he defined broadly as "the critical phase of the transition from the unified, hierarchically ordered, spiritually oriented society of Latin Christendom, to the heterogeneous, secularly oriented society of autonomous sovereign states which made up modern Europe."[7]

Although Mattingly wrote three books, his name also appears on the title page of a fourth, to which he used to refer to wryly as his *magnum opus*. In the literal sense, indeed it was, since it almost outweighed the other three taken together. The cover of that book—in the conservative drab-green buckram of the *Calendars of State Papers,* the ancient, honorable, and now archaic uniform of the Public Record Office Calendars—reminds us that the editor of the volume, Garrett Mattingly, was among other things a meticulous, precise, inordinately painstaking researcher; that he had technical equipment and proficiency unequaled by any other scholar of his generation for the kind of work he undertook; that underpropping all three books he wrote was an unsurpassed familiarity with the sources, printed and archival; that his writing only sampled and distilled, never exhausted, but sometimes almost perversely concealed his massive knowledge.

And this points to a paradox in Mattingly's historical work. The formidable patient scholar of the *Calendar* was indispensable to the witty, urbane, and brilliant author of *Catherine of Aragon* and *The Armada,* and yet the two were in a sense at war with each other. Indeed, the marks of the battle appear in both *Catherine* and the *Armada*. Both books are extremely careful and accurate and enormously erudite. But the traces of care, accuracy, and erudition are either carefully concealed or utterly obliterated. In vain will other historians seek in the place where it ought to be, at the foot of the page, for the guidance provided by that proper and useful instrument of their shared labors, the footnote. In *Catherine* the notes are somewhat shamefacedly tucked away at the end of the book, and they are so set out as to maximize the inconvenience of anyone seeking to find a particular note. In *The Armada* there are no notes at all, only sketchy bibliographical remarks on each chapter, again stacked at the end of the book, and the remarks on any given chapter are infuriatingly hard to find. Yet a reasonably full documentation, satisfying both scholarly convention and scholarly convenience, need in no way have affected the pace of either book or even involved the alteration of a word of the text. The omission was wholly gratuitous. It is as if the popular author of *Catherine* and *The Armada* were thumbing his nose at the scholarly editor of the *Further Supplement to Letters, Despatches, and State Papers, relat-*

ing to the Negotiations between England and Spain, preserved in the Archives at Vienna and Elsewhere [*1513–1542*], "edited by Garrett Mattingly, Ph.D." Actually the case was that of a superb and accomplished professional giving its come-uppance to a pedantic professionalism in a way which unfortunately imposed both inconvenience and sheer loss on his fellow historians.

The principal losers in the conflict, however, those that suffered from it most, were *Renaissance Diplomacy* and Garrett Mattingly himself. Mattingly suffered because he felt that somehow the best history ought to have a broad popular appeal. But the book to which he gave his most earnest thought and his most intense effort did not have it. *Renaissance Diplomacy* simply could not have such appeal; it was not that kind of book. No history of the growth of an institution in an age as remote from ours as the sixteenth century has achieved popularity within my memory; and I doubt if one ever will.

Considering that it incorporates a lifetime of the experience and the learning of a man at once erudite and wise, *Renaissance Diplomacy* is a short book. It is considerably shorter than either *The Armada* or *Catherine,* although its limits are wider, the problems it deals with more difficult to expound, the ideas involved more intricate. It is, indeed, too short; in a few places it is unduly elliptical, bearing the mark of an excessive compression. It should be longer; and in fact it was once a good deal longer. It ran into publishing troubles early. The American house to which Mattingly first sent the manuscript rejected it. Presumably on the grounds of its length and its limited appeal that publisher suggested he submit it to a university press, and surely at the time any of a number of university presses would have regarded it as an honor to issue the original manuscript of *Renaissance Diplomacy* with scarcely a modification. Mattingly would have none of it. To him the university press was the very symbol of that withdrawal of history into the academic citadel which he deplored and distrusted. He said that rather than turn his work over to a university press he would tear it up. Happily, he did not do that. Unhappily, he took the publisher's judgment seriously. He did not want to consign his most exacting study to the sterile wilderness haunted by the ghosts of unread historical treatises. He cut *Renaissance Diplomacy* by a third and destroyed the original draft. He never fully reconciled himself to the inevitable fact that no amount of cutting and revising could make his most remarkable intellectual achievement a popular book. It is perhaps a measure of that achievement that the *Renaissance Diplomacy* which historians read with such admiration is not as good as Mattingly could have made it; it is, indeed, not as good as he had made it. Even so, it remains one of the finest historical works of the past half century.

If any amount of skill could have made *Renaissance Diplomacy* a popular book, its author had the skill; but the cards were stacked against him. Yet as it stands *Renaissance Diplomacy* is a magnificent achievement. It scintillates with flashes of wit superbly phrased. Thus the Renaissance image of the "perfect prince" is neatly characterized and caricatured—a "shadowy figure cast by medieval idealism on the vapours of humanistic rhetoric."[8] Or, with respect to the diminishing employment of clerics as ambassadors:

> Among the later writers, the instances, modern and classical, which came most readily to hand, all seemed to indicate that priests sometimes served another master than their natural sovereign. The oblique glance was, of course, at the Counter-Reformation papacy. That an ambassador who was a priest might be embarrassed by his allegiance to a Master even more exacting than the pope seems not to have occurred to anybody.[9]

In a line or two Mattingly pricks the balloon of one of the most absurdly overinflated reputations of the age—that of Louis XI. In his reign

> Guienne, ducal Burgundy, Provence, Anjou and Maine fell in, providing the main acquisitions of a king who, however much his statecraft was admired by his contemporaries, was successful chiefly by surviving his relatives.[10]

Far from being the last word in diplomatic shrewdness

> Louis was too suspicious, too devious, and too parochial to grasp all the uses of diplomacy. He could conceive of no negotiations not inspired by malice and conducted by deception.[11]

Beside the detailed and total dismemberments of conceptions—
the balance of power, nationalism, the economic or rational political
motivation of early modern wars—which too long have cluttered the
historians' view of the age, *Renaissance Diplomacy* is full of incisive two-sentence wrap-ups of subjects on which many historians
would spend pages with less to show for their verbiage. Thus, on
the impact of England's defeat in the Hundred Years War:

> By the loss of its French dependencies, England had gained
> freedom of diplomatic manoeuvre. Secure behind its seas, Eng-
> land could now take as much or as little of any war as it liked.
> No commitment was more than tentative, no alliance irrevocable,
> and at each new shuffle in the diplomatic game the other players
> had to bid all over again for England's friendship or neutrality.[12]

Or on the medieval law of nations:

> In making and sustaining the law of nations, reason, revelation
> and custom were held to be collaborators, not competitors.
> Therefore the Bartolists were able to assimilate the decrees of the
> Church and the practices of existing governments into what they
> regarded as Roman Law, and, reinforcing it by the only authority
> left to the Roman Republic, the authority of its law schools,
> make *jus gentium* a living common law for Western Europe.[13]

To get so much meaning and so many ideas into so few words requires an astonishing gift for compression; but it also demands more
of the reader in concentration than most amateurs of history are
willing to give, and more in background knowledge than all but a
very few amateurs possess. More than that, there are a half dozen
chapters in *Renaissance Diplomacy* that for sheer brilliance, for
depth of insight, for concise easy statement of complex and fundamental truths about the age they deal with, have few peers in historical literature. Yet only scholars immersed in the history of that
age, able therefore to compare Mattingly's work with other men's,
will recognize the sheer virtuosity of his performance in those chapters; the general reader is not likely even to realize that a performance to admire is in progress.

Although by all his predispositions Mattingly was a book writer,
during his life he published in the learned journals a number of

articles. They are not the work of a man for whom the learned article is his natural métier, as for example it is for H. J. Habakkuk. They do not—as the most successful articles do—focus on a neatly limited area and so deal with that area as to suggest or make needful the rethinking of matters of larger and more general concern. Several were *pièces d'occasion;* others were skillful, well-wrought scholarly exercises, exact (it goes without saying) in their scholarship. One of these was a virtuoso piece—a masterful and erudite investigation of the date of Shakespeare's 107th Sonnet.[14] Alone among Mattingly's writings this essay directly reflects one quirk of his career. As an undergraduate at Harvard he had concentrated in History and Literature, and for many years he taught courses in English as well as in History. The care he lavished on the seemly writing of history was the fruit of this early and long concern with literature. In a couple of other essays he made a bold foray into the region of Machiavelli studies, and from it he emerged somewhat less bashed-up than most of us who have ventured onto that dark and bloody ground of learning where muddled armies clash by night.[15]

His one essay on historical writing dealt with the labors of historians on the political history of the Renaissance in the century after Burckhardt.[16] There, Mattingly, whose public pronouncements on some of the highly touted members of his craft were milder than his private judgments, for once let himself go in a hilarious *essai à clef.* The piece turns on the way historians have handled three of the major political crises of the Renaissance era—the collapse of the Italian states, the motives of French policy from 1494 to 1559, and the causes of the revolt and division of the Netherlands. Most of the recent historians whom Mattingly mentions by name—Baron, Romier, Zeller, Geyl, Valeri, Palmarocchi—come off with good marks. The piece is an *essai à clef* because of the eminent historians of several nations who appear anonymously as "some distinguished names," or "deeper thinkers," or "the vanguard," or even more facelessly as "it has been discovered," or "we hear." Anyone who has worked in the field of Renaissance politics, however, will recognize most of the gentlemen so discreetly disguised. Some of them chased the hare Machiavelli started and found the source of Italy's disaster in moral decline, papal intrigue, and the use of mercenaries; others found the roots of French policy in nationalism and rational political or economic objectives; yet others asserted the inevitability of a split between the north Netherlands and the south Netherlands as the outcome of ancient national differences. And they were all wrong, quite wrong. Who got the story straight? Not only the recent historians Mattingly names; but Burckhardt and, in essentials at least, those targets-of-choice of up-to-date historians, Michelet and Motley. Of all people! They got the essentials right, because whatever their prejudices they did not let them rule their judgment when they sat face-to-face with the pertinent documents. If they rode their hobbies a bit, at least they did not let their hobbies (under the alias of "new and daring interpretations") ride them.

Mattingly's earliest scholarly publication, appearing in 1932, was "A Humanist Ambassador."[17] It cleared up a number of details about the life of Eustache Chapuys, Charles V's resident in England. From then on most of Mattingly's contributions to learned journals were in the nature of engineering operations on the way to or from writing books, path clearing to ease the passage of the big battalions or tidying up after they had gone by.[18] And yet to understand what sort of historian Mattingly was and why he was among the very best of that sort, we do well to examine carefully one of his articles —"The Reputation of Dr. de Puebla," which appeared in the *English Historical Review* in 1940.[19] The article was on the way not to just one but to two of Mattingly's books. Dr. de Puebla held two firsts in Renaissance diplomacy: he was the first resident ambassador in England and the first Spanish resident outside Rome, and so he had a place in Mattingly's study of that diplomacy. He also negotiated the marriage between Henry VII's elder son and Catherine of Aragon. When the death of Prince Arthur brought that union to a premature end, he negotiated the marriage treaty which was fatefully to link Catherine and Henry VII's younger son, Prince Henry; so he had a place in the biography of that unfortunate princess. Still, these days Dr. de Puebla does not cut a very great figure in the history of his time; in the best recent survey of the Tudor period he rates one index entry and one sentence, and the judgment or valuation thus implied does not seem unreasonable.

Mattingly offered an explanation, but not a complete or wholly satisfactory explanation, for his painstaking inquiry into de Puebla's reputation. He said that he undertook it because de Puebla's "cor-

respondence is an invaluable source for the period, [and] our judgment of his character must affect our judgment of the negotiations
he conducted and our evaluation of his reports."[20] But the further
one follows him into the assessment of the evidence about de Puebla,
the more obvious it becomes that the initial motive ceases to be the
sole and sufficient reason for the loving care, the concentrated
thought that Mattingly put into his investigation. The reputation of
de Puebla before Mattingly undertook to reassess it was that of

> an abject, pettifogging rascal, a shady trickster, scrabbling to-
> gether sordid gains, and living, through avarice, in squalor; a
> shabby and deformed little cripple, mean, boastful, treacherous,
> shameless, the butt and the aversion of all he met, without any-
> thing to commend him to the rulers of Spain and England except
> servility, low cunning, and a complete lack of moral scruples.[21]

He emerges from Mattingly's examination the butt of a few men of
his time and certainly of his aristocratic rival, Don Pedro de Ayala,
boastful no doubt, devious by both necessity and temperament, cold,
somewhat narrow in outlook, sensitive to slights, living meanly
because his pay was too low and always heavily in arrears. He also
emerges as energetic, shrewd, and patient, for over twenty years a
faithful servant of the Catholic Kings, who had no appetite for being
ill served, and who requited his service with trust, but little else. He
was a successful negotiator when success was possible, a resourceful
one even when the course his master required him to follow doomed
his efforts to failure, a man of honor, not by the standards of a
sixteenth-century aristocrat but by the standards of the new profession of diplomacy of which he was a pioneer. In the end by deed or
word or both, all those who knew most about him and who had no
sinister interest in blackening his name—Henry VII, Ferdinand,
Catherine, even Fuensalida, his successor, who ruined what little the
old man wrought in the hard days of his and Henry's and Ferdinand's old age—vindicated him against all his detractors.

Vindication, of course, is the heart of the matter. Technical professional requirements may have led Mattingly to reassess de Puebla
as a source of information; but somewhere along the line of inquiry
the source of information became a man, the victim of an ancient
and enduring wrong that needed to be set right. But why so much

bother to vindicate a man really rather obscure, wholly forgotten by all but about .0000001 of men now living, dead now nearly half a millennium? To this question Mattingly had an explicit answer which brightly illuminates his own traits and his excellence as a historian. That answer does not appear in "The Reputation of Dr. de Puebla," but in *The Armada,* written two decades later. It directly has to do with another Spaniard whose qualities were better than his luck, and better than the judgment posterity long passed upon him: the grandee who commanded the disastrous enterprise against England, the Duke of Medina Sidonia.

> There is a tendency of late to speak more kindly of Medina Sidonia . . . to recognize his courage and his administrative ability, but no one has yet said he could not have done better. It is at least arguable, however, that no one could. . . . Not that such a judgment would have been much comfort to Medina Sidonia. Whatever he did, it was not enough. Nor does it matter at all to the dead whether they receive justice at the hands of succeeding generations. *But to the living, to do justice, however belatedly, should matter.* [Italics added.][22]

This casual remark, which Mattingly dropped in the course of his story, implies a whole general view of what history ought to be. Mattingly does not expound this general view in ponderous pronouncements about the nature of historical reality. As it should be with a historian, his view is immanent in the whole body of history that he wrote, and it is there that we must seek it. In the first place Mattingly believed that although history may be about any number of things—barrel staves and prevailing winds and cannons, canon law and the speed of posts and cryptography—it is also, perhaps it is mainly, about men and women and children, sometimes of necessity considered as aggregates, but often also considered as persons. But if a historian deals with men as persons, he must concern himself with human character. He must bring to play on the understanding of men of whom, in the nature of things historical, the record grants him only fragmentary glimpses, all the resources afforded him by his systematic knowledge, his experience of life, his introspection, and such wisdom as God gave him.

The historical record which is all too exiguous is also paradoxi-

cally all too full. In order to make human character stand clear of the clutter of routine action which filled the lives of Renaissance men as it fills ours, Mattingly had to practice the art of discerning and reporting the telling detail, the illuminating incident, the revelatory remark. To do this he was especially hard-pressed in *The Armada* and *Catherine of Aragon,* where the historical scene was jammed with men whose motives and natures had to be rendered intelligible quickly, lest the reader be trapped in a bewildering shuffle of wholly unmemorable names. Mattingly's judgment in such matters was immaculate. He showed it in the big set pieces—the contrasting encounters of Henry VIII with the vain Francis I and the modest Charles V;[23] Catherine's grandeur and dignity and pathos before the court that her husband had maneuvered into existence to rid himself of her;[24] Mary, Queen of Scots, magnificently playing out the last act of her life, not only before she laid her head on the block but even after the executioner had done his work.[25] But he showed it to even greater advantage in the unobtrusive detail. There is the account of de Puebla's interview with young Catherine, in which that necessarily devious old man, straightforward for once in his life, with mingled fear and anger, exposed and shattered the plot laid by Catherine's trusted duenna and her brother to undermine Ferdinand's position in Castile.[26] There is the Duke of Medina Sidonia in a short cloak, because he had given his great cloaks to a friar and a wounded boy, leaning wearily on the taffrail of his flagship as his battered fleet ran northward before the wind from the foredoomed failure of his mission in the Channel to the more terrible disaster of the long voyage home.[27] There is Philip II, who, after learning the full dimensions of that disaster, read the incorrigibly optimistic report of his ambassador in Paris, Bernardino de Mendoza, whose energy did so much to forward the great enterprise, and, having read, with his "weary pen scrawled in the margin, 'Nothing of this is true. It will be well to tell him so!' "[28]

Mattingly's way of treating human character has two notable traits. It would not be quite accurate to say that he always disliked winners—he admired Elizabeth, who almost never lost.[29] Yet he had a warm spot in his heart for those against whom the deck of life was stacked, for losers, especially for losers, who, having used every reputable resource at their disposal and without flinching given all they had to gain their end, met defeat as men—and women—of valor without display or self-exculpation or self-pity. Second, Mattingly does not confront his readers with a series of posed portraits interjected into a narrative at more or less random intervals. The characters he portrays are people in action. In Mattingly's books character reveals itself in what men do and say as they follow out the lines of their lives.

How was Mattingly's own work as a historian—and implicitly his view of his calling—affected by his habitual vision of the past as men acting or suffering? In practice he treated his job as that of telling a story about people. He was not dogmatic enough to say that that was what all historians ought to do, much less that it was all that historians ought to do. Yet he loved what he was doing well enough and knew that it was enough worth doing to hold in mild derision the "new wave" historians who were somewhat patronizing to him in their pride at being not narrative but analytical historians,[30] or, as some of them put it, writers of "why" history rather than "how" history. (This last widely current formulation is of such massive and stupefying naïveté that of itself it might suggest to its proponents the wisdom of deploying their powers on matters less arcane.) Indeed, in *Renaissance Diplomacy,* Mattingly himself produced the *reductio ad absurdum* of the notion that history ought to be divided into two non-communicating compartments, one labeled "Narrative" with "childish" painted on top, the other labeled "Analytical" with "grown-up" painted on top. For *Renaissance Diplomacy* is a masterful analysis of an institutional complex centered around a new Renaissance phenomenon—the resident ambassador. One may suppose that it answers "why" questions—whatever they are—since it answers very nearly all the serious questions that a curious mind is likely to raise about the institutions of diplomacy from the fifteenth century to the Peace of Westphalia. Yet never, one suspects, in so few pages of analytical and institutional history have so many people (not mere names) showed up, and never has so much happened. This is so because *Renaissance Diplomacy* is both narrative and analytical history.

This is as it should be. In the best writing of history, analysis and narrative do not stand over against each other in opposition and contradiction; nor do they merely supplement each other mechanically. They are organically integrated with each other; to separate them is not an act of classification but of amputation. It is an act the frequent performance of which stands a good chance of killing history altogether. Mattingly was too modest to say that whenever the historical work in progress permits, analysis and narration *ought* to be inseparably unified as they are in *Renaissance Diplomacy* and (for the benefit of the myopic, we may add) in *Catherine of Aragon* and *The Armada;* but that is of course the fact of the matter. I suspect that had he lived a few years longer Mattingly might have enjoyed the experience of others like him who dug in their heels on historical issues such as these, while their more modish colleagues marched off in the pursuit of the most recent will-o'-the-wisp. Somehow in the end the marchers come full circle, so that simply by standing still one eventually finds oneself in the vanguard.

Mattingly's uncommon concern for the losers has been ascribed to a pro-Catholic bias; and in support of such an allegation one can cite his affection for Catherine, his admiration of Medina Sidonia, his generosity extending even as far as Philip II. But against this view stands the most despicable figure in Mattingly's whole gallery, about whom "there is no mystery . . . except how so shallow an egotist attracted so many people. He was the type of the adventurer relying on a bold front and a calloused conscience, the gambler playing for stakes beyond his means."[31] Such was Henry, Duc de Guise, the idol of the French Catholics and chief of the Catholic League. Whatever biases Mattingly had were not cut along the line separating Protestant from Catholic. It just happened that the hard-pressed people living at the center of the stories Mattingly told were Catholics; had he happened to choose stories revolving around William the Silent and Henry of Navarre, no suspicion of pro-Catholic bias would have risen. It was not ideological nostalgia for a medieval dream world that moved Mattingly; it was admiration for men and women, true to themselves and their calling, responsible men and women, people of honor and courage, capable of dedication, people whose centers, as it were, lay somewhere outside themselves. Because the traits he admired are most fully tried by adversity he seemed to have a special fondness for losers. His actual predilections, however, are clearly marked in his judgment of the three great monarchs of Christendom in the earlier sixteenth century. He despised the frivolous playboy Francis I, who never grew up; he cared not much more for Henry VIII, who somehow managed the transition from reckless egocentric youth to harsh megalomaniac old age with hardly a pause for responsible adulthood. In contrast was the stolid, pedestrian Charles V. He bade farewell to youth before he was twenty; he worked with all his personal resources at the thankless, unmanageable task of husbanding the sprawling cumbersome congeries of dominions that God or chance put in his hands; and with all his congenital and political handicaps he proved a better steward of what had been entrusted to him than did either of his more brilliant rivals. Charles was a man to suit Mattingly's tastes.

Those tastes were themselves a sharp though inexplicit comment on a couple of the fashions prevailing in recent decades in the small world of professional historians. Mattingly had no use for the Big Battalion view of history in any of its manifold guises. Whether as proponents of a theory of progress, or manifest destiny, or the tide of democracy, or the self-realization of the spirit, or dialectical materialism, or the rule of the master race, historians who take the Big Battalion view of history always perceive the past in the light of their current notion of what constitutes the wave of the future. Losers are of little importance in this view of history; they are just inevitable, usually faceless, casualties of the historical steamroller, crushed because of their malice, or their stupidity, or their failure to pick the winner, or because—in one of the most callous and revolting aphorisms ever taken up by men who called themselves humanists—"you can't make an omelet without breaking eggs." There was nothing in Mattingly's way of perceiving the past to attract him to this peculiarly vulgar form of the worship of success.

Nor could the man who wrote, "To the living, to do justice, however belatedly, should matter," ever delude himself that history could or ought to be, as some historians insist, altogether non-valuative, wholly *wertfrei*. This does not mean that Mattingly, one of the least naïve of all historians, believed that he should assume the posture of a Divine Sunday School Teacher handing out gold stars to the good boys of history and demerits to the naughty ones.

It does mean that he knew that the vocabulary we ordinarily use in writing about men carries an ancient load of value-packed connotation. To discard that vocabulary is simply to discard what little capacity for judgment the cumulative experience of a great civilization has afforded us. To use that vocabulary with measure and care along with whatever means of testing the evidence and knowing the facts he can master in order to deal justly with the past is at once the historian's duty and his privilege. To do otherwise is to surrender history's proper claim to being a practical, humane, and moral science in order to chase the foolish, fond hope of transforming it into a theoretical one. On this view of the matter it is no puzzle at all to know why a fine historian like Mattingly, in mid-career toward two splendid books, paused to write a long vindication of poor old obscure Dr. de Puebla. It was just the right thing for him to do.

N O T E S

1. *The Armada* (Boston, 1959), published in England as *The Defeat of the Spanish Armada* (London, 1959; paperback edition, Boston, 1962).

2. *Catherine of Aragon* (Boston, 1941; London, 1942; paperback edition, New York, 1960).

3. *Renaissance Diplomacy* (London and Boston, 1955).

4. *Catherine of Aragon*, p. 133.

5. *The Armada*, p. 12.

6. *Ibid.*, p. 381.

7. "Some Revisions of the Political History of the Renaissance," in Tensley Hilton, ed., *The Renaissance* (Madison, 1961), pp. 3–23.

8. *Renaissance Diplomacy*, p. 223.

9. *Ibid.*, p. 216.

10. *Ibid.*, p. 130.

11. *Ibid.*, p. 133.

12. *Ibid.*, p. 129.

13. *Ibid.*, p. 285.

14. "The Date of Shakespeare's Sonnet CVII," *PMLA*, 48 (1933), 705–21.

15. "Machiavelli's *Prince:* Political Science or Political Satire," *American Scholar*, 27 (1958), 482–91; "Machiavelli," *The Horizon Book of the Renaissance* (New York, 1961), pp. 57–64.

16. "Some Revisions," pp. 3–23.

17. "A Humanist Ambassador," *Journal of Modern History*, 4 (1932), 175–85.

18. "The First Resident Embassies: Medieval Italian Origins of Modern Diplomacy," *Speculum*, 12 (1937), 423–29; "An Early Nonaggression Pact," *Journal of Modern History*, 10 (1938), 1–30; "William Allen and Catholic Propaganda in England," *Bibliothèque d'humanisme et renaissance*, 27 (1957), 333–38. Mattingly's essays on Machiavelli (see note 15 above) are in a sense of a similar character. They reveal the substance of thought behind what looks like a very casual *obiter dictum* in *Renaissance Diplomacy*, pp. 116–17.

19. "The Reputation of Dr. de Puebla," *English Historical Review*, 55 (1940), 27–46.

20. *Ibid.*, p. 28.

21. *Ibid.*, p. 27.

22. *The Armada*, p. 375.

23. *Catherine of Aragon*, pp. 208–19.

24. *Ibid.*, pp. 285–87.

25. *The Armada*, pp. 2–5.

26. *Catherine of Aragon*, pp. 76–77.

27. *The Armada*, p. 340.

28. *Ibid.*, p. 363.

29. *Ibid.*, pp. 9–13.

30. Note his wickedly funny vignette of the history of history writing in America since 1900 in "Some Revisions . . . ," p. 9.

31. *The Armada*, p. 386.

THE UNITY OF THE RENAISSANCE: HUMANISM, NATURAL SCIENCE, AND ART

J O A N   G A D O L

The City College of New York

Among the many currents of thought that make up the intellectual life of the Renaissance, two especially distinguish themselves as characteristic products of Renaissance culture—humanism and that combination of mathematics and empirical research that marks both the artistic and scientific work of the age. This twin birth of humanism and mathematical-empirical science has long seemed right and proper. Historically, the humanistic ideal of moral autonomy has emerged and thrives only in a rationally oriented culture, and independent scientific inquiry endures only when man recognizes his right to shape the intellectual world by his own powers. Earlier historians of the Renaissance such as Michelet and Burckhardt spoke quite readily, therefore, of its simultaneous and harmonious "discovery of the world and man."

Yet, curiously enough, subsequent research has hardly sustained this view. In place of an almost inevitable bond between the two developments, a deep and apparently irreconcilable opposition has been exposed, particularly by historians of science such as George Sarton and Lynn Thorndike. As they see it, humanism failed to follow the scientific directives contained in the ancient mathematical and scientific texts which it restored, and it even impeded the emergence of a scientific attitude toward natural phenomena by taking the written works of Greco-Roman culture as ends in themselves and submitting to their authority. Scientific thought had to throw off this weight of the past to come into its own; it had to turn from the words of authorities to the works of nature.

Here is a conflict of intellectual purpose of which the humanists and scientists themselves seem to have been quite conscious. At the very inception of the humanist movement, Petrarch expressed hostility toward the Scholastic learning of his day and toward all natural knowledge in general. And Montaigne, at the culmination of Renaissance humanism, continued to belittle the "useless" pursuit of mathematical and natural studies, particularly astronomy, in his essay on education. For the Renaissance humanist, it was the literature of antiquity, its poetry, history, and moral philosophy, that constituted the basis of genuine learning. But scientific knowledge, as Galileo pointed out, requires arguments and demonstrations, "not texts and authorities," for science is concerned with "the sensible world and not one on paper."[1]

The overt opposition between humanistic and scientific learning voiced in statements like these should not obscure for us, however, the several underlying and complex connections that unite the two. It is true that the relations between humanistic and scientific thought cannot be reduced to a simple and "natural" harmony, but neither are they fully defined by this conflict over the primacy of sensory experience or that of literature. Apart from their differences in themes, methods, and materials, humanism and science share two fundamental standpoints. Both maintain that reality is to be understood rationally and that its principles of explanation are immanent to it. The unity of Renaissance thought is to be looked for in the formation of this intellectual orientation.

The expressions of opposition to the "other" kind of learning, in which Renaissance humanists and scientists alike indulged, sprang from the awareness on both their parts of the distinctive ways in which they were responding to a common intellectual task: the task of determining the methods and objectives proper to their respective disciplines. The Renaissance surely did not "discover" the world of nature and that of man, but during the Renaissance there emerged two kinds of science, in the broad sense of the word, through which the outer and inner worlds, nature and man, came to be newly construed.[2] Both the newly forming natural and cultural sciences were at this time determining their basic perspectives; determining, that is, their specific objects of thought according to their own indigenous rational principles and procedures, and thereby the concepts of objective and subjective reality alike came to be disentangled from the religious and metaphysical contexts of thought in which they had hitherto been elaborated. Each of these two modes of inquiry defined its method and object by contrasting them with those of the other, but in the working out of their common rational aim, humanistic and empirical thought nonetheless contributed, in several instances, to each other's development; and in the distinctive ways in which they pursued this aim, they disclose their fundamental, dialectical connection.

1. The "science" that the early humanists spurned consisted, in their day, of Scholastic dialectics and of systematic philosophy and theology. With regard to speculative theology, they displayed a devotional conservatism which also prevailed among the contemporary philosophical opponents of the Scholastic "rationalism" that sought to rise to the doctrinal truths of Faith by means of logic and Aristotelian metaphysics. Both Petrarch and Lorenzo Valla saw in the presumption of this kind of philosophizing the source of heterodoxy. Yet even if motives of piety are at work in this rejection of philosophy, they did not lead to an irrationalist position. Humanistic scepticism, its mistrust of systematic philosophy and theology as a rational means of arriving at, or confirming, religious "truths," accords well with the "positivism" of the fourteenth-century Terminists and the emerging empirical attitude of the Renaissance artists and technicians. It is anti-metaphysical, not anti-rational.

In his *De libero arbitrio* (c. 1440), Valla claims that Boethius was too warm an admirer of philosophy to please God, but his charge against this philosopher, and through him against all philosophy, is that of vainly seeking to know what transcends human experience. The point at issue in this work, as in so many of the writings of Petrarch, Erasmus, and Montaigne, is that reason must be restrained from pursuing problems beyond her powers so as to be restored to the human concerns and literary style natural to her. Not theology but human wisdom is proper to man, and the "natural" expression of a sound intelligence is more reasonable than the "artificial" Scholastic treatment of subjects. Consequently, although nothing new in content is added to the traditional problem of free will and God's omnipotence in Valla's dialogue, the treatment is radically changed. The question is wrested out of the Scholastic-Aristotelian system of thought and becomes a subject discussed by two cultivated laymen. Their new philological and historical learning is brought to bear upon the texts involved, but their reasonable discourse respects its natural bounds. Thus the problem of the coexistence of divine omniscience and human freedom is resolved, but not that of divine omnipotence and free will. "Let us therefore shun greedy knowledge of high things," Valla concludes, "condescending rather to those of low estate."[3]

Turning away from theological and metaphysical issues, the humanist displays the same desire to restrict the pursuit of knowledge to "natural" problems as, for example, Leonardo does within the context of the new kind of mathematical-empirical scientific thought.[4] Yet this other current of empirical lay learning, which Leonardo represents, forms no more an integral part of the humanistic studies than did Scholastic "science." Knowledge of nature does not serve the humanist's intention any better than speculative theology, for it contributes nothing to human wisdom, as Petrarch and Montaigne so often pointed out. It was the ways of the human spirit, not the movements of the spheres, that the humanist wanted to study, and for this he turned to literature rather than to the natural sciences.

The primary accomplishment of humanism was its new appreciation of the humanities, of poetry, history, and moral philosophy, as intellectual instruments by which to attain and express a knowledge of subjective reality. And this methodic insight, for which Petrarch was primarily responsible, bore immediate fruit. In their historical and ethical writings, inspired by the literary examples of antiquity, the humanists were to bring about a new theoretical vision of the inner world. The herald of this development, and its first cultural manifestation, was a new conception of historical life and change.

In historical writing, Leonardo Bruni's biography of Petrarch is one of the early examples of this dual achievement. Following the course marked out by Petrarch, Bruni helped to restore the genre of the lives of illustrious men in his *Vite di Dante e Petrarca,* and by this very act he grasped the significance of Petrarch as the initiator of a turning point in the history of culture. Petrarch's revival of the Ciceronian style served Bruni as a means for understanding and categorizing in historical terms the development of culture from antiquity to his time. Taking linguistic style as his criterion, he periodized and evaluated cultural change, so that a period of decadence is seen to set in with the Empire and one of "renaissance" with Petrarch's imitation of Ciceronian Latin.

Simple as this system of periodization may seem, it represents a marked advance in historical thought. For a medieval chronicler like Giovanni Villani (who wrote his *Croniche Fiorentine* around 1300) history exhibits a temporal sequence in which there is continuity but no change. One event stands next to another in a schema which orders all occurrences according to their position before or after the birth of Christ, but in this succession there is no genuine development. From the time of Noah to the present, man is what he is and always has been. There is no fundamental diversity in human culture and no development in man's understanding of the world and of himself. Here we find a peculiar mode of regarding the past comparable to that which Panofsky has noted in Gothic art, where Virgil and other ancient personages are depicted in twelfth- or thirteenth-century garb, and contemporary figures given the attributes of ancient ones. There is no recognition of an historical difference between "then" and "now," so that Romans can appear like feudal knights to Villani, who blandly speaks of Julius Caesar's "chivalry."

It was Petrarch's literary sensitivity that first introduced a sense of movement into this static scheme of things.[5] His appreciation of the language and style of the classics made possible a discrimination between the linguistic and literary expression of Roman antiquity and that of the ages that followed. Enamored as he was of a past which he could now recognize as really "past," as vanished, Petrarch could conceive of the idea of a literary and cultural "renaissance." Of course, the scheme of periodization which he and the humanists after him introduced was hardly one that allowed for gradations or for a dispassionate historical appraisal of the past. There is the golden age of Greco-Roman antiquity, in which all preceding developments culminated; there is the present which seeks to restore the cultural achievements of that classic past; and there is the age that lies between, the Middle Ages, in which all those accomplishments lay hidden in the darkness of barbarism. Still, this is a genuine system of historical periodization, because it was intended to represent what the humanists took to be major turning points in the culture of man. What is important here is that these turning points are not introduced from without by an eternal, Divine plan, but are immanent to human history. They symbolize humanity's development: its virtue, its decadence, and its revival.

As an historical idea, the notion of "renaissance" provided a vantage point for the new representations of the human past which began to appear in historical writing. But this idea had moral implications as well. It provided orientation for the present, as well as a way of evaluating the past, by setting up an ideal toward which the present should move. The ethical writings and educational program of humanism also drew inspiration and vitality, therefore, from the recognition that a change in cultural forms, and in the power and sway of civilizations, manifests an inner, spiritual development. As an ethical idea, an awareness of cultural development found its most pregnant expression in the conviction that emulation of the forms of ancient thought would restore to man his natural virtue and excellence. Out of this conviction was born that union of *virtù e lettere* which defined the humanistic program: the pursuit of classical, literary studies as a means of cultivating what is specifically human.

The *studia humanitatis,* founded upon the study of the poets, historians, and moral philosophers of antiquity, aimed at renewing the forms of virtue known to antiquity. It aimed at forming the cultivated man:

> What the Greeks called "paideia" we call "studia humanitatis."
> For learning and training in virtue are peculiar to man; therefore our forefathers called them "Humanitas," the pursuits, the activities, proper to mankind.[6]

"A good education," wrote Montaigne, "affects the judgment and character." Through the educational aim and program of humanism, the historical process itself was affected. The *studia humanitatis* transformed the historical idea of "renaissance" into the cultural and moral imperative of the age. As such, the ideal of renaissance vivified almost all currents of thought and life, including the artistic envisagement of space which was to be so momentous in the formation of the scientific concept of nature and natural law.

2. While Renaissance art owes its inception to the humanistic attitude toward antiquity, what accounts for its distinctive style is not the mere desire to renew the forms of classical art, but rather the manner in which those forms were approached and appropriated. The archeological researches of Brunelleschi and Donatello in Rome in the beginning of the fifteenth century lie behind the marked changes which appear in Florentine art of the 1420s and 1430s: the reappearance of the classical orders in architecture, the flexibility and anatomical differentiation of the sculpted form, and the new sense of spatial depth in the painting of Masaccio, a friend of Brunelleschi who incorporated in his work the architect's ideas on painter's perspective.

It was not so much the external appearances of classical architecture and sculpture that were imitated in these new works of *quattrocento* art, as it was their inherent proportions. Brunelleschi and Donatello took measurements of the classical works they examined; what inspires their work, and Masaccio's, is a common attentiveness to the proportional structure of the specific sensuous forms they are creating. They penetrated to the spatial logic of the classical orders and sculpted form, a logic that Brunelleschi also extended to painting in his perspectival attempts to create the semblance of proportionally receding spatial intervals on the two-dimensional picture plane.[7] These first representatives of the artistic "renaissance" could appreciate the principles of classical art as they did, and apply them anew in their own works, because of their new, mathematically inspired spatial vision. And this same spatial vision also accounts for the union of art and science during the Renaissance, often allowing its artistic works to merge into scientific ones, and vice versa.

The intimate connections between Renaissance art and humanistic scholarship on the one hand, and between art and scientific developments on the other, are exhibited most fully in the person and works of Leon Battista Alberti. By means of his writings on the principles of the three visual arts, we can follow the logical evolution of this new spatial intuition as it affects painting, sculpture, and architecture, and then broadens into a general theory of nature which grounds and supports the mathematical investigation of empirical reality.

Of his three books on the arts, the one on painting was written first, in 1435. In the Preface to the vernacular version of *Della pittura,* which he dedicated to Brunelleschi, Alberti expresses high enthusiasm for the new Florentine artists in whom nature seemed to have restored the vigor of the ancients. There was one problem in the new painting, however, which Brunelleschi and Masaccio together had not been able to solve (although Alberti was too gracious, and too indebted to Brunelleschi to say just that), and to this problem Alberti addressed himself in the greater part of the work. As he explicitly noted, the accurate depiction of three-dimensional objects upon a two-dimensional plane had never been perfectly achieved, either in antiquity or in modern Florence. The key to that accurate representation of nature was to be provided by geometry, but a new kind of "visual geometry" that would be applied to physical objects.

His first step, therefore, was to present sensible objects as geometric forms, as made up of visible or corporeal points, lines, angles, and planes. By imaginatively "seeing" objects as composed of measurable surfaces, the problem of depicting them, and the changes in their appearance as they are placed closer or farther away from the spectator, could be solved by geometric methods. This is the basic idea of the system of painter's perspective which Alberti here developed. What is important for our purposes, however, is not the rules of perspective themselves, but the implicit and subtle change in the view of nature which they brought about.

The theory of pictorial representation which Alberti took for granted in *Della pittura* was the mimetic one. Painting is to imitate nature, and, specifically, it is to represent a visual image. By means of the rules of perspective, the painting is constructed in such a way that the plane on which it is drawn seems to the spectator to be transparent, a pane of glass through which the spectator looks onto the (painted) scene. The painted scene appears as an actual one viewed through a window, for it is constructed so that it continues the spectator's actual line of sight. But if the picture is meant to "imitate" a visual image of the actual world, then the way in which it is constructed implicitly reveals the way we think nature is constituted. This is exactly what happened in Alberti's works, and in the view of nature expressed by Renaissance art in general.

Granted that the painted scene is constructed so as to continue the spectator's line of sight, what of the size of the picture and of the persons and objects it contains? If they are much smaller or larger than life-size, will this not destroy the illusion of an imitation of nature? No, said Alberti, for if everything in the world were reduced to half its size, no one would notice the change. The painter need not reproduce absolute dimensions; he is concerned only with relative ones, with ratios. If he keeps proportions constant—if he gives objects the sizes relative to each other that they have in actuality, and if he proportions these relative sizes to the distance from which the spectator sees them—his picture will seem to be an actual, visual image. The panel can become "an open window through which we see what is painted,"[8] because its picture imitates nature by means of "analogy," in the geometric sense of that word. In short, the perspectival picture is a proportional or geometric picture of nature, representing not so much the sensory "stuff" of visual experience as the proportional structure of what is viewed.

This same principle of proportional imitation Alberti also applied to sculpture, giving rules, in his *Della statua,* for measuring the various parts of the body in relation to its length. Once more, he measures not absolute size but proportions. Consequently, the statue which represents a certain figure or model can be of any size; for an accurate representation, the sculptor need only reproduce the proportional structure of his model.

Thus far, the concept of imitation as "proportional representation" may seem innocent enough. The picture imitates nature by representing a visual image, the statue by representing the organic body, and both represent their objects by means of analogy. But when we come to architecture, the difficulties in this procedure become apparent. The question of what the building represents in its imitation of nature Alberti sought to answer in terms of a comprehensive idea of nature as a whole, not in terms of any one of its single parts. Thus, in his great *De re aedificatoria* (c. 1452), as he moved from the geometrization of pictorial and sculptural form to that of architecture, he had to appropriate and develop more of the theoretical aesthetic ideas of antiquity than he did in the two earlier, more technical works.

The building, Alberti says, is like a body in that it has both matter and form or design. The purely formal design, the composition, constitutes the "work" of architecture; hence it is the design that is to represent nature taken as a whole. Since the building is like a body, its form is also a proportional structure; but here, no one body is represented or imitated. The design of the building is composed of the "natural proportions" by which nature forms all her creations. It is because of this idea of an imitation of "natural proportions" that Renaissance architecture revived the classical orders. For the first time since Vitruvius, the rules for the Doric, Ionic, and Corinthian orders were stated once more, in Alberti's *De re aedificatoria,* because the architecture based upon them is precisely an architecture of proportions. Each order has a fundamental ratio, that of the column's length to the diameter of its base, and the entire building built in a determinate order is proportioned in agreement with this. Once again, the rules of classical architecture, like those of perspectival painting, arise from and express a certain envisagement of nature, for what the proportional design of the building represents is the design of the cosmos. It "imitates" the structure of the House of the World, the universe.

The architect, Alberti wrote, must seek beauty in his imitation of nature, for "nature consults beauty in a manner to excess, in everything she does. . . . If beauty is therefore necessary in anything, it is so particularly in a building."[9] And since the design of the building is a proportional form, beauty quite aptly, even inevitably, comes to be defined by Alberti in terms of the classical idea of congruity, the perfection of a proportional or relational whole. Beauty (*concinnitas*) "is a harmony of all the parts, in whatsoever subject it appears, fitted together with such proportion and connection that nothing could be added, diminished, or altered, but for the worse."[10] Thus the artist comes to "imitate" nature in two senses, and in each sense, as Alberti formulates them, we can see a new image of art and a new understanding of nature emerge. On the one hand, the artist is likened to nature insofar as both seek this beauty of *concinnitas* in the production of their works. Since the artist is a conscious, creative agent, nature, too, by an illicit slip to be sure, is conceived as a conscious and rational creative force. For Alberti, nature becomes "the greatest artist of all manner of compositions"; for Leonardo the term "formative nature" will convey this same idea of *natura naturans*. Secondly, since beauty has come to be understood as a universal law which guides nature in the creation of her forms much as it guides the artist in the composition of his, the architect must reproduce in the design of his work not any arbitrary proportions he happens to hit upon, but only those by which nature achieves her aesthetic aim. He must discover and embody in his buildings those regular or lawful proportions which are exhibited in her manifold works and which lead to the harmony of the whole of nature, as *natura naturata*.

These regular and hence "natural" proportions Alberti found in the harmonic intervals, the musical ratios which the Pythagoreans and Plato had long ago believed to be expressive of the lawfulness of nature and of its structural harmony. As Vitruvius had done before him, he transposed the proportions of aural harmony to the visual forms of architecture, "convinced of the truth of Pythagoras' saying, that nature is sure to act consistently and with a constant analogy in all her operations. From whence I conclude that the same numbers, by means of which the agreement of sounds affects our ears with delight, are the very same which please our eyes and our mind."[11] The one lawful order of nature which is grasped in the harmonies of sound reappears in the proportional design of the building, for it is this universal order that Renaissance architecture set out to represent. The restoration of the Pythagorean-Platonic metaphysics, according to which the essence of nature consists of an immanent, rational order governed by the overriding law of harmony, was thus an integral moment in the artistic "renaissance." All its technical rules of perspective and proportion were but the means whereby art made manifest this one mathematical, spatial intuition through which the proportional character of nature and her beauty appears.

3. The metaphysical principles of Renaissance art, together with its geometric analysis and construction of spatial form, had a direct impact upon the most significant scientific developments of the age. A new ideal of knowledge was implicitly contained in this aesthetic outlook, one which we can recognize as the animating principle in all the diverse works of Leonardo. His great genius seized upon and developed all the methodic implications of the mathematical view of nature that could be realized on the intuitive level of vision. His dedication, as a painter, to visual form and to the determination of form as proportional structure he carried over to his studies in optics, anatomy, botany, zoölogy, geography and geology, and mechanics. And it was by his very faithfulness to his painter's vision that he brought about such remarkable developments in each. His striking powers of visual observation bound him to the sensory world, to that "experience" which became, for him, the only mediator between man and nature.

But by the same token, that experience which interprets nature to man also teaches him that nature is formed and governed by "necessity." *La neciessità* is the theme and the eternal rule of nature,[12] and it is her regular, theoretic structure which is to be sought in things if the mind is to have a true knowledge of them. Almost all of Leonardo's studies were directed, therefore, by this quest for rules, as we find it formulated in this passage on perspective: "Find out how much a man diminishes at a certain distance and what the length of that distance is; and then at twice that distance and at three times, and so make your general rule."[13]

The rule by which we capture this "necessity" of nature is the rule of a proportional correlation. It presupposes, therefore, that mathematical determination of the form of sensible objects which constitutes the stylistic distinction of Renaissance painting, sculpture, and architecture. Whether it is an anatomical or botanical description Leonardo gives us, whether it be graphic or verbal, we always find the same penetrating visual discrimination which "sees" in visual experience the rational structure of "natural" form. His painter's eye measures as it observes the leaves of the elm tree, for example: The space from one leaf on a branch to the next "is half the extreme length of the leaf or somewhat less, for the leaves are at an interval which is about one-third of the width of the leaf."[14] In his description of the walnut, he gives us a proportional correlation in verbal terms: The leaves on the new shoots are more numerous, and farther apart from each other, "in proportion as the branch, from which this shoot springs, is a young one. And they are inserted more closely and fewer in number when the shoot that bears them springs from an old branch."[15] Mind and eye work as one in determining the rule whereby observed proportions vary—with the age of the walnut branch, in this example, with distance in the study of perspective, with the motions of the body in his studies of human proportion. Even his mechanical investigations, as well as his anatomical ones, have their origins in Leonardo's artistic studies of the human body.[16] "Formative nature" and man both make "machines," and the laws of motion are the same in each. Organic and mechanistic terms are interchangeable in his descriptions of the mechanism of moving bodies, of wealth and dearth of muscles and of levers and counter-levers which regulate, by their action, the changing proportions of the whole.

It is because of the clarity with which Leonardo grasped this one aim, and the consistency with which he carried it out in his manifold investigations, that Cassirer found him to be the first thinker to have determined with precision the methodic foundations of experimental science.[17] His quest for the proportions of sensory phenomena and the rules that govern them contains implicitly the scientific idea of natural law. Convinced that the Book of Nature, as Galileo would put it, was written in mathematical symbols, Leonardo knew that there could be no scientific certitude save where mathematics is applied to experience. The study of the sensible world without geometry had become impossible, and once this methodic idea was recognized, the empirical scientist had to make his appearance on the historical stage as *filosofo geometra*.[18]

4. This new conception of science, which combined an empirical interest in the phenomenal world with mathematical techniques of measurement and analysis, allowed for the re-establishment of direct relations between natural knowledge and humanistic learning. The humanists not only restored many of the ancient texts which contributed greatly to the development of mathematics, empirical science, and physical speculation in the fifteenth, sixteenth, and seventeenth centuries, but they also stimulated a new interest in authors like Euclid, Ptolemy, and Archimedes among those who, like themselves, stood outside the university tradition of natural philosophy. Humanist scholars like Alberti introduced Euclid to painters by demonstrating that the "natural" (*i.e.,* perspectival) principles of their art were mathematical. On the other hand, painters, like Leonardo, Bellini, and Raphael, applying the idea of a mathematically constructed space outside the domain of painting, soon appeared as cartographers; and to construct their town-plans and regional maps they combined their art with the surveying and mapping techniques of antiquity.

Many of the humanists themselves participated in this work of understanding and applying afresh the principles of the sciences of applied mathematics and the technical knowledge gained from ancient sources. Alberti, Puerbach, and Regiomontanus, for instance, were inspired by Ptolemy's example and were immersed in the construction of mathematically schematized maps of the earth and the heavens based upon fresh observations. Alberti, who joined his friend Toscanelli in making astronomical observations, shared the Italian scientist's geographical interests as well. Imitating Ptolemy's *Geography* in his *Descriptio urbis Romae,* Alberti laid down the rules for mapping small areas and drew, in his map of Rome, one of the earliest known town-plans to be based upon a mathematical survey. The short-lived Puerbach, a lecturer on the Latin classics at the University of Vienna, made the same kind of astronomical observations as Alberti and Toscanelli, besides planning an epitome of the *Almagest* which Regiomontanus completed. Regiomontanus, himself an outstanding classical scholar, also constructed almanacs for navigational use.

The advent of humanism thus contributed greatly to that fusion of abstract or intellectual methods with manual ones, that interpenetration of mathematical ideas with technical practice, which characterizes the scientific developments of the fifteenth and sixteenth centuries. Although the conquest of natural phenomena by mathematical means was not the aim of humanistic study, a number of the humanists extended their ideal of lay learning to mathematical and empirical research, thus including in their notion of "renaissance" the principles of scientific thought, as well as those of the literary and artistic works of antiquity. The vital interrelations among the humanistic, artistic, and scientific currents of the Renaissance are, however, nowhere so readily apparent as in the most outstanding scientific accomplishment of the age, the Copernican Revolution.

There is a direct line of continuity between the renewed humanistic interest in the principles and techniques of Ptolemaic astronomy and cartography, and the work of Copernicus. As his disciple Rheticus saw it, Copernicus had accomplished the "renaissance" of the work of Ptolemy, even while departing from his fundamental geocentric hypothesis. In good humanistic fashion, Rheticus claimed that Copernicus had rescued Ptolemy from the obscurity in which he had long lain. In this, Copernicus was continuing and perfecting the work of the humanist Regiomontanus; but "I rather compare Copernicus with Ptolemy," Rheticus went on,

> not because I consider Regiomontanus inferior to Ptolemy, but because my teacher shares with Ptolemy the good fortune of completing, with the aid of divine kindness, the reconstruction of astronomy which he began, while Regiomontanus . . . departed this life before he had time to erect his columns.[19]

Indeed, from Ptolemy stemmed the key idea of all the spatial sciences of the age, the idea that underlies perspectival painting as well as Copernicus' "reconstruction" of astronomy: namely, that the system of the world is to be understood and represented as an interpretation of a geometric model or system. Hence truth was to be ascertained in exact measures by Copernicus, and his hypothetical-empirical method of establishing the "laws" of astronomy consists, much as Leonardo's did, in assuming hypotheses from which mathematical deductions can be made and which can be checked by observations.

These are the methodological principles of Ptolemy; but whereas Copernicus could call upon two thousand years of observations, Ptolemy's data covered scarcely a quarter of that period. Copernicus therefore chose as fundamental hypotheses not those of a geocentric system but those of a heliocentric one—which would better conform to sense-experience and reason, as Rheticus explained. We know, however, that Copernicus, although he intended his system to be accurate, personally made very few observations. His primary consideration centered in the conviction that the world was more harmoniously constructed than the Ptolemaic system could allow, complicated as that system was by the geometric devices of epicycle, deferent, and eccentric circle which were needed to "save the appearances." As Rheticus understood it, "The chief cause of all the uncertainty in astronomy was that the masters of this science fashioned their theories and devices for correcting the motion of the heavenly bodies with too little regard for the rule which reminds us that the order and motions of the heavenly spheres agree in an absolute system."[20] In establishing the harmony of the motions of the heavenly bodies, he thought, the astronomers should be like musicians who do not seek to correct one false string, but rather to regulate the tones of all of them in relation to each other. This, Copernicus had done. When he described his heliocentric system in his *De revolutionibus orbium caelestium* (1543), Copernicus justified the daring innovation of his work, not by empirical considerations, but in terms that echo the aesthetic, metaphysical ideas of *concinnitas* which Alberti had formulated in his work on architecture a century earlier. The new system seemed to him to confirm the harmonious perfection of the world, for "it so bound together both the order and magnitude of all the planets and the spheres and the heaven itself, that in no single part could one thing be altered without confusion among the other parts and in all the universe."[21]

Convinced of the simple, rational, and organic order of the cosmos which accords with the artistry of "the best and most systematic builder of all,"[22] Copernicus broke through the confines of the hierarchical world-order which had set the heavenly bodies in their "superior" places, imparting to them a radiance and the perfect, circular motion denied to the base, dark, and immobile earth. He rejected the Aristotelian and medieval belief in the heterogeneity of diverse bodies and places, and replaced the earth-centered Ptolemaic system with a relatively simple and uniform intellectual pattern which was taken to underlie and govern the motions of all the planets. The new spatial intuition that first expressed itself in and through Renaissance art finally transformed astronomy as well.

5. If humanism played a part in restoring the Pythagorean-Platonic view of nature which dominates the aesthetic and scientific outlook of the Renaissance, the new artistic and scientific ideas of outer or objective reality also had implications for the humanistic view of man. The source from which humanism drew its enthusiasm for culture as well as its basic historical and ethical ideas was the recognition of the original creativity of the human spirit. As Alberti put it, man was born *per stare facendo,* for through his work he forms both his "self" and his culture. This humanistic sense of the dignity of man and his work was greatly enhanced by the new conception of nature as a homogeneous organic whole, the rational structure of which could be grasped and reconstituted by human art and knowledge. In man's ability to recognize and reformulate nature's underlying regularity, the humanist's faith in the creative power of man found its confirmation.[23] Thus it was that Alberti discovered and grounded the spontaneity of the mind in the idea of objective beauty which brings the artist into fundamental accord with the basic law of the cosmos. The mind which responds to beauty does not derive its idea of harmony from sensible objects; it "recognizes" in sensible objects the exemplifications of its own ideal norm. The idea of beauty does not "arise so much from the body in which it is found, or any of its members, as from itself and from nature, so that its true seat is in the mind and in reason."[24]

This idealistic insight, which permeated the thought of the Florentine Academy in the latter part of the fifteenth century, is what gave the Renaissance artist his *divinità*. At one and the same time, it established his creative independence and his innate bond with "nature, the greatest artist of all forms."[25] Then, as the mathematical character of man's scientific knowledge of the world came to be understood, science added its voice and authority to this high evaluation of the mind and its works. As reason spontaneously recognizes beauty in its natural and artistic embodiments, so it recognizes the necessity of natural law. The necessary *ragioni* of things are known *da per sè,* as Galileo demonstrates in the Socratic exercises through which he brings Simplicio to "recall" the scientific concepts he is after in his *Dialogue Concerning the Two Chief World Systems.* Natural truth, being mathematical, is grasped by an autonomous act of the human mind. And by such acts, the mind attains knowledge of necessity, which places it on a par with the Divine Mind in the certitude, if not the comprehensiveness, of its understanding.[26]

This grounding of the idea of creativity is not the only point of contact, however, between the new scientific conception of the outer world and the concept of subjectivity which emerges from humanistic thought. Even the features of homogeneity and immanent law that characterize the scientific knowledge of nature find their counterparts in the humanistic understanding of the spiritual principle of man and his culture. The idea of a unitary spiritual content contained in man's literary works was first expressed, as Cassirer has pointed out, through the traditional allegorical theory of literature.[27]

By means of this theory, the early humanists hoped to effect a reconciliation of ancient poetry with Christian doctrine, maintaining that poetic literature sets forth no literal (discursive) ideas, but expresses through its fictions one fundamental and ineffable theological "truth." Much as this belief—that all mythopoeic literature symbolically conveys one spiritual truth—had the effect of leveling differences of intrinsic doctrinal value, so the strictly didactic theory of prose literature, which accompanied the development of the allegorical justification of poetry, gave rise to a secular version of this same tendency toward universality. The conviction that the historical life and ethical teachings of antiquity were relevant to the contemporary quest for virtue gave support to the idea of a unitary human or moral nature. In this secular context of thought, however, the notion of spiritual universality was to take on a dynamic character which was lacking in the allegorical-theological view.

The very conception of a *studia humanitatis* contained the fundamental notion of the formative nature of the human spirit, for it was founded upon the idea that the learning derived from classical, literary studies is intimately bound up with the development of the moral life of man. In the expression of their ideas on education, the humanists tended to focus attention upon the work of the soul, and the spiritual principle of man came increasingly to be viewed as a process of self-formation.

This "work" by which the spirit composes its own form is precisely what constitutes the dignity of man in Pico della Mirandola's famous *Oratio de hominis dignitate* (1486). Here, the new unitary conception of the spirit voiced by Pico in his theory of the allegorical nature of all the world's literature and teachings finds a parallel in his poetic image of man's universal spiritual task. But this image of spiritual formation, endowed with creative movement, explicitly wrests the idea of the soul out of its traditional metaphysical frame of reference. As Pico resolves the substantival notion of the soul into pure act, into a dynamic spiritual function of knowing and forming, he liberates man from his "place" in the fixed ranks of being. As long as man was held to have a determinate nature, the angels were assuredly "superior" to him and were to be recognized as such. The true and distinctive worth of man appeared to Pico only in his realization that man has no fixed model or form. He *has* no nature; he *is* spirit, a spirit that makes and molds the "self." It is by means of this activity of self-creation that man achieves his destiny, and by this means he approaches the Divine even more closely than those pure spiritual beings who, though pure spirit, are nonetheless created "as they are," with their own determinate form.

The humanistic idea of spiritual creativity prepared, in this way, a completely secular and functional concept of the soul, delivered from the hierarchical order of substances that makes up the medieval view of reality. In this form, the idea of subjectivity was taken up by the historical and ethical thought of the sixteenth century which could now seek to define the universal, immanent laws by means of which this spiritual life develops.

6. The "new path" that Machiavelli opened by his great *Discorsi* led to the discovery and formulation of general political rules that are exemplified in diverse historical events, rules which account for past events happening as they did, and which thereby allow contemporary affairs to find their historical analogues and their "law." Machiavelli presupposed, in taking historical examples of statesmanship and politics as models for action, that men have not changed "the order of their motions and power," that they are no different from what they were in ancient times.[28] But this ahistorical notion of a constant human nature was not really pertinent to his objective task. It was his conception of universality as an immanent universality of *law* that stamps the Machiavelli of *The Prince* and *The Discourses* as the first political scientist, and this is the methodic

idea which he also brought to bear upon the writing of history proper.

Medieval history had had its own kind of universality, the unity of a single, temporal order which allowed the chronicler to fit his particular history into the context of a general history of man. In the genealogical attempt to order events in this one simple schema of "before" and "after," however, less attention was paid to the events themselves than to their interconnections, which were established by uniting the origins of each series to each other. Giovanni Villani thus traced the founding of Florence, Rome, and Greece to the three sons of King Atlas who descended from Noah. All his "authorities" were uncritically accepted—the Bible, Virgil, the Arthurian romances—because of this overriding aim of establishing one unbroken series out of them.

The humanist historian, on the other hand, generally detached his work from the context of universal history. He abandoned the mythic quest for "origins," and distinguished legendary from historical accounts. But in the events he did describe, he found a new, universal concept of spiritual life which underwent genuine historical change. This historical concept of subjective life is the material of Machiavelli's *Istorie Fiorentine,* and by means of his quest for its inner, ideational form, he raised the historical study of man initiated by the humanists to a new scientific and artistic level.

Machiavelli's history is not scientific in the historiographic sense of critique of sources. To be sure, he rejected the legendary features of Villani's history, but otherwise he was bound by the limitations of his age; he did not even trouble to report conflicting accounts of particular events, as Leonardo Bruni had done a century earlier in his history of Florence. But in Machiavelli, to a far greater degree than in the fifteenth-century humanist historians, history is presented as a theoretical unity. Its events are not *disjecta membra;* they become the integral parts of a relational whole by the way in which he establishes their "reasons."

In his reflections at the beginning of Book IV, for example, Machiavelli sums up the preceding account of the tyranny of the Duke of Athens and the revolt of the Ciompi by a general theory of the relation of liberty to law. Neither the tyranny of the nobility nor the license of the people can maintain liberty and stability in the state, for both create powerful opposing factions, and both depend upon the *virtù* of persons for their continuation and well-being. Sound republican government and its fruit, liberty, rest upon subjection to law, not to persons. Here the inner logical bond between the Duke's tyranny and the rule of the Ciompi is disclosed, and the historical outcome of the two series of events is, at the same time, explained and evaluated.

This quest for a general pattern of law in the *accidenti vari* of historical experience, which led Machiavelli to the formulation of rules in *The Prince* and *The Discourses,* directed him in his historical work toward those genuinely dynamic laws which are causally operative in the chief events of Florentine history and which those events, in turn, bring about and further. This is what gives to his *Istorie Fiorentine* the unity and organicity of a tragedy: through its events we "see" the unfolding of a fate, a "living" fate which is character. The factionalism of Florentine political and social life, the key to Machiavelli's conception of Florentine history, appears as a theme, therefore, only as the Florentines themselves begin the shaping of their history. Until 1215 Florence suffered the domination of others, but in the very moment that she asserted herself as an historical entity, Machiavelli sees her bring about in her own life the social dissension from which the rest of Italy suffered. The Guelph-Ghibelline dispute is the "first division" which struck like a disease her newly independent republican life. The course of Florentine domestic history from that point on is cursed by the progressive spread of that corruption through its different stages. From the strife among the factions of the nobility to the struggle of the *grassi* against the *grandi,* and the rise of the *popolo minuto* against the *grassi,* the events of Florentine history are so presented as to illustrate and create that fate whereby Florence destroys her own power to maintain liberty and independence. Yet scientific import is not second to literary integrity in this work of historical synopsis. It is one with it, for the factionalism of Florence, which is the unifying theme of the work, is at the same time the "true cause" of the failure of republican life which presented itself to Machiavelli as the primary problem of Florentine history.

This perfect fusion of artistic and scientific unity-in-diversity gives Machiavelli's *Istorie Fiorentine* its distinctive character. This is what makes it a great piece of historical literature, and yet the historical work is itself but the symbol and vehicle of the new conception of spiritual life that Machiavelli has articulated through it. In the unfolding fate of Florence, he has created an unforgettable image of historical being which is dissolved into a spiritual becoming and nonetheless has form, the dynamic form of its own innate laws of development. In this image of a dynamic yet lawful spiritual life, the humanistic insight into the nature of subjectivity finds one of its most complete expressions. Another was to be provided by Montaigne. This same insight which Machiavelli developed through his presentation of historical process, Montaigne brought to fulfillment in the context of the personal rather than the social "self."

Montaigne also understood history as the study of a unitary human nature. In history, man as a whole is presented more fully and vividly than in any other form of literature. But Montaigne preferred to study man's personal actions rather than the public ones over which fortune has more sway; he sought motives rather than deeds, inner rather than outer happenings. Consequently, among historians Plutarch satisfied this requirement best for him, but better than all historical or biographical study was the unique method of introspective inquiry which he developed in his *Essais*. Montaigne became the student of his own inner being, and it was in this study that he discovered that lawful process of subjective life which Machiavelli had portrayed in history.

Turning toward the analysis of his "self," Montaigne found the lines of his self-portrait to vary and change continuously, for what he encountered was passage, not being. The image of the soul that he gives us is one ever in motion, in act. The mind "stirs itself and makes trial of its strength, exercising its power of handling a subject . . .; it steadies, moderates, and strengthens itself."[29] Indeed, from this conception of the mind "making trial of itself" springs the originality of the literary form as well as the content of the *Essais:* "Could my mind find firm footing, I should not always be making *essais,* but should come to conclusions; it is, however, always in its apprenticeship and on trial."[30] The pursuit of truth rather than its possession consequently becomes the proper business of the mind for him, because soul itself has become a process, a principle of vital, rational life rather than a "thing." But by objectifying the trials of his mind in his *Essais,* Montaigne hoped to clarify and fix those reflexive ideas which became the chief maxims of his conduct, thereby bringing a consistency into the flux of his opinions and behavior. By the examination of his inner life, he sought "to shape his soul." His lifelong task thus became the formation of a life, molded by the rules imposed by his own judgment.[31]

The intellectual *telos* that Montaigne struggled toward, then, was law, as was the case with Machiavelli. Through a self-analysis as pitilessly "objective" as Machiavelli's analysis of history and politics, he sought a rule of life which, as his *Apologie de Raymond Sebond* indicates, had been entirely obscured by the religious conflicts of his day. That which was falsehood for the people on the other side of the mountains could be no "natural" truth. Reason by her own efforts had, therefore, to discover how to live, and to live "according to nature," in the fulfillment of which maxim Montaigne was eventually to see the sovereign good. "We seek other conditions," he wrote, "because we do not understand the proper use of our own, and go out of ourselves because we do not know what is within."[32] As he had attained self-knowledge in his study of man through history, so Montaigne found "the complete pattern of human nature" in his examination of the passage and formation of his unique self. That universal rule of life which lies hidden beneath the layers of convention and custom that separate men from each other he discovered in the very process of self-examination and self-formation; and this he came to regard as mankind's fundamental and noblest "work." It is living itself that is our goal. Our life is our masterpiece, sufficient unto itself because of the lawful form imposed upon it by our own judgment.

7. The justification of the human world of culture which had begun with the allegorical and didactic theories of literature finds its completion here. Initially, the study of that single spiritual and moral teaching contained in the literary works of antiquity had been proposed, by Petrarch and the early humanists, as "another path" toward the transcendent goal of Christian life. But gradually, as the humanistic ideal of *virtù e lettere* allowed for the development of the idea of self-formation, culture became the only path toward man's true end. Through culture, man does not merely approach divinity;

he achieves it. As "maker and molder of thyself," Pico's God tells man, "thou shalt have the power, out of thy soul's judgment, to be reborn into the higher forms [of life] which are divine."

The final step in this steady secularization of the idea of man's spiritual work was left to Montaigne. With him, mortality itself, the very negate of the divine, is recognized as necessary to the unique work and worth of human life. His *essais* at honestly portraying his own experience and discovering therein the abilities and limitations of human nature demanded this final admission.

> *D'autant est tu dieu comme*
> *Tu te recognois homme.*

At the culmination of the humanistic movement, it is Socrates, not Jesus, who emerges as the true model of *humanitas*. Human life is seen to have attained its perfect form in him, a form shaped by reason, not by the pious hope of immortality; a form made possible precisely because Socrates was a mortal.[33]

In its conception of the soul as the formative spiritual principle of human life, humanistic thought thus touches once again the achievement of Renaissance science, bringing about in its way a reconciliation with the natural world similar to that effected by art and empirical research. The explicit rejection of a transcendent goal for an immanent one, the acceptance of living itself as the aim of life, has been made possible only by the realization that life is shaped by its own inner law. In this realization, the Renaissance idea of subjective reality finds its fundamental accord with the idea of objective reality that emerged in art and science. Both spring from the same idealistic outlook, and both humanism and science have brought about an unhesitating acceptance of nature by this recognition that both human life and empirical knowledge are products of the formative process of the human spirit.

If humanism and science appear to us as necessarily opposed to each other, we can plainly see in this historical development that they are opposed only as the termini of a dialectical relation. Since the Renaissance, the idea of subjectivity has been determined primarily by the humanities or cultural sciences, as that of objectivity has been chiefly determined by the natural sciences, but even in their very movement toward differentiation and scientific autonomy, these two modes of rational inquiry were bound by a common orientation of thought. The humanities and mathematical-empirical inquiry discovered their distinctive scientific tasks only as they recognized in phenomenal reality the mind's constructive and rational work. In their appreciation of the ideal lawful order of physical and human nature, each found the grounds for its reconciliation with the world. Here, too, are the grounds for their reconciliation with each other.

NOTES

1. *Dialogo sopra i due massimi sistemi del mondo, Tolemaico e Copernicano* (Firenze, 1632), Giornata seconda.

2. The classic study of the subject-object relation in Renaissance thought, to which this essay is greatly indebted, is Ernst Cassirer's *Individuum und Kosmos in der Philosophie der Renaissance* (Leipzig and Berlin, 1927).

3. "Dialogue on Free Will," trans. Charles Edward Trinkaus, Jr., *The Renaissance Philosophy of Man* (University of Chicago Press, 1948), p. 181.

4. "O stoltitia umana . . . e vuoi poi colla moltitudine de' soffistichi ingannare te e altri, sprezzando le matematiche scienzie, nelle qual si contiene la verità, notitia delle cose che in lor si contengono; e vuoi poi scorrere ne' miracoli e scrivere ch'ài notitia di quelle cose, di che la mente umana non è capace, e non si possono dimostrare per nessuno esenplo naturale . . . ," in *The Literary Works of Leonardo da Vinci,* ed. Jean Paul Richter, (2 vols, London, 1883), II, no. 1210.

5. Eduard Fueter, *Histoire de l'Historiographie Moderne,* trans. Emile Jeanmarie (Paris, 1914), pp. 1–6.

6. Battista Guarino, "De ordine docendi et studendi," in William Harrison Woodward, *Vittorino da Feltre and Other Humanist Educators* (Cambridge, 1897), p. 177.

7. The fundamental work on the spatial form of Renaissance art is H. Wölfflin's *Principles of Art History* (New York: Dover, n.d.). Just as fundamental for perspective and the study of proportions are Erwin Panofsky's "Die Perspektive als 'Symbolische Form,'" *Vorträge der Bibliothek Warburg* (1924–25), pp. 258–330; *Renaissance and Renascences* (Uppsala, 1960); "The History of the Theory of Human Proportions as a Reflection of the History of Style," *Meaning in the Visual Arts* (New York: Doubleday, 1955), pp. 55–107.

8. *Della pittura* (Firenze, 1950), p. 70.

9. *De re aedificatoria libb. X* (Florentiae, 1485), IX, 5.

10. *Ibid.*

11. *Ibid.*

12. "La neciessità è maestra e tutrice della natura. La neciessità è tema e inventrice della natura e freno e regola eterna." Richter, I, 22.

13. *Ibid.*

14. *Ibid.*, I, 413.

15. *Ibid.*, I, 414.

16. Erwin Panofsky, "Artist, Scientist, Genius: Notes on the Renaissance-Dämmerung," *The Renaissance: Six Essays* (New York: Harper and Row, 1962), pp. 123–82.

17. *Das Erkenntnisproblem,* I (Berlin, 1906), pp. 24–53.

18. This is Galileo's term for himself: *Dialogo sopra i due massimi sistemi,* Giornata seconda.

19. "Narratio prima," trans. and edited by Edward Rosen, *Three Copernican Treatises* (New York: Dover, 1959), p. 109; see also pp. 132–33.

20. *Ibid.*

21. Dedicatory Letter to Pope Paul III, quoted by E. A. Burtt, *The Metaphysical Foundations of Modern Physical Science* (New York: Doubleday, 1955), pp. 49, 50. Burtt's view, which I have adopted here, is that the Pythagorean-Platonic current of thought provided an "alternative background besides Aristotelianism, in terms of which . . . metaphysical thinking might go on, and which was more favorable" to the development of the new astronomy. See p. 52 in particular.

22. Copernicus, *ibid.*

23. See Cassirer, *op. cit.,* pp. 149 ff.

24. *De re aedificatoria,* IX, 5: "necque in toto corpore aut partibus viget magis concinnitas quam in se ipsa atque natura: ut eam quidem esse animi rationisque consortem interpreter."

25. *Ibid.*

26. Galileo, *Dialogo sopra i due massimi sistemi,* Giornata prima.

27. *Das Erkenntnisproblem,* I, pp. 155 ff.

28. *Discorsi sopra la prima deca di Tito Livio,* Proemio.

29. *Essais,* III, 3.

30. *Ibid.,* III, 2.

31. "Il m'est advis que [la morte] est bien le bout, non pourtant le but, de la vie; c'est sa fin, son extremité, non pourtant son obiect: elle doibt estre elle mesme à soi sa visee, son desseing; son droict estude est se regler se conduire...." *Ibid.,* III, 12.

32. *Ibid.,* III, 13.

33. *Ibid.,* III, 12. The line, "You are a god only insofar as you know yourself to be a man," Montaigne quoted in III, 13, from Amyot's translation of Plutarch's *Life of Pompey.*

THE HUMANIST
BARTOLOMEO FACIO
AND HIS UNKNOWN
CORRESPONDENCE*

PAUL   OSKAR

KRISTELLER

Columbia University

T he widespread view that the intellectual history of the Renaissance is well known, and that its literary sources have been fully explored, does not correspond to the facts. Many texts, printed and manuscript alike, have long been known to exist, but never have been studied or edited. Moreover, a more systematic exploration of the manuscript collections, now made possible by greater facilities for travel and microfilming, continues to bring to

*This study was made possible by grants for travel and microfilms received from the American Philosophical Society and from the Council for Research in the Social Sciences of Columbia University. I am indebted for information and microfilms to many librarians, and especially to Drs. P. Ortega Lamadrid and M. Nieves Alonso-Cortés (Valladolid) and to Dr. Ugo Baroncelli (Brescia), Drs. Irma Merolle Tondi and Dr. D. Corsi (Lucca), B. Righini (Florence), Dr. M. T. Escoffier (Genoa), Dr. C. E. Wright (London), Dr. Ingeborg Stolzenberg (Marburg), Mme. D. Bloch (Paris), Dr. Lelia Sereni (Udine), the Rev. J. Lopez de Toro (Madrid), and the Rev. Alfonso Raes, S.J. (Vatican), as well as to Mr. Michael Baxandall (London) and to Mrs. John D. Gordan (New York).

light new texts that help to correct the findings offered by previous historians.

The manuscript sources of Italian humanism are still partly concentrated in Italian libraries, but a sizable number of Italian Renaissance manuscripts is now scattered in other countries. Due to the close political and cultural relations between the two countries, the libraries of Spain are especially rich in Italian manuscripts. An important part of the manuscripts collected by the Aragon kings of Naples during the fifteenth century is now in Valencia. The Italian manuscripts collected by the Marquess of Santillana, by Fernando Colombo, and by Philip II are now in Madrid, Seville, and the Escorial, and the manuscripts collected in Italy by Cardinal Zelada are in Toledo. Smaller groups of Italian manuscripts found their way to Barcelona, Salamanca, Zaragoza, and other libraries. Thus it is not surprising that several important manuscripts of Bartolomeo Facio, a scholar who lived for many years at the court of Alfonso of Aragon, should be found in Spanish collections. The most interesting of them, which yields some fifty-odd unpublished and previously unknown letters, is found in the University Library of Valladolid.

I found this manuscript from a distance, as it were. I wrote to the library for information on its manuscripts, received a microfilm of its rare printed catalogue, and obtained additional descriptions and microfilms of the manuscripts which attracted my special interest. Among them was the manuscript of Facius' letters which will supply much of the content of this paper.[1] I hope the topic may seem suitable for my tribute to the memory of a cherished friend whose own scholarly interests included the history of Italy and Spain during the Renaissance, and whose advice and personal connections were of great help to me when I visited Spanish libraries in search of Renaissance manuscripts.

Bartolomeo Facio is a significant, if not an important figure, who has been of interest to many students of Italian humanism, on account of his own life and writings, and because of his relationship to many contemporaries more famous than himself. Since he is mentioned in many comprehensive studies and has been the subject of a few articles, it would be quite wrong to call him a neglected figure. I hope a brief account of his life and works, supplemented and corrected with the help of the newly found letters, may acquaint the reader with a characteristic representative of Italian humanism, and help dispel some current misconceptions about that complex movement.

Since the letters are our chief source for Facio's life, let us begin with them. Until recently, sixty letters of Facius had been known from miscellaneous manuscripts in Florence, Venice, and the Vatican, and thirty-two of them have been published.[2] This count does not include the prefaces and covering letters of Facius' other works, or the letters addressed to him, and it also excludes a group of twenty-five letters found in Vat. lat. 5197 and partly attributed to Facio, but either apocryphal or dubious.[3]

To this we must now add the letters contained in the Valladolid manuscript. It now has the number 227 and belongs to the collection of the old Colegio Mayor de Santa Cruz, founded by Cardinal Pedro González de Mendoza around 1490. The manuscript was written on paper in the fifteenth century by an Italian humanistic hand, and consists of fifty-seven written folios, one of which (f.44) is blank. Whereas all other manuscripts containing letters of Facius are miscellaneous, this is the only compact collection of his correspondence that has come down to us. It has the following original title (f.1): *Bartholomei Faccii Genuensis ad amicos eius ac familiares epistole incipiunt.* Another manuscript containing Facius' letters and orations was once in the Escorial, but was destroyed in the fire of 1671.[4] The fact that Facius collected his own letters had been known from one of his published letters,[5] and is now confirmed by the Valladolid manuscript.

The manuscript contains seventy-seven pieces, beginning with Facio's Latin version of a novella of Boccaccio (f.1–2v), and ending with his own story of the origin of the war between France and England (f.45–57). This last text is separated from the letters by a blank folio, and has a title of its own. The collection of letters, without the two stories, consists of seventy-five pieces. If we deduct eight letters to Facio and one letter which appears in double copy (f.37v and 43), this leaves sixty-six letters of Facio, of which fifty-two had been previously unknown. Thus the total of his known letters is brought to 112. This is still only a part of the letters written and collected by Facio, for in the letter mentioned earlier he speaks of a hundred fifty letters.[6] Perhaps some of the additional letters were contained in the lost Escorial manuscript.

The letters of the Valladolid manuscript, and most of the others, were edited by the author and are now undated. Only some of the letters may be dated from their content, and the Valladolid collection clearly does not follow a chronological sequence. Only the letters in the Florentine manuscript are mostly dated and apparently unrevised, but in turn contain many obscure allusions to unidentified persons and events.

Our author's name was probably Bartolomeo Faccio, but I shall follow the prevailing practice and call him Facio (or Facius) rather than Faccio or Fazio. He was born in La Spezia before 1410[7] and belonged to a family of notaries. He seems to have been the youngest son of Ser Paolino who died before 1428. For several years Bartolomeo was the student of Guarino in Verona, and probably he had just finished his training when he went to Florence in 1429 to improve his Greek. He probably stayed there until the next year. From January, 1431, to January, 1434, Facio was in Genoa, living in narrow circumstances and occupied with family business.[8] From August, 1434, to December, 1435, he held a position in Lucca as a tax and customs official. After his return from Lucca, he seems to have lived in or near Genoa, but nothing definite is known about this period of his life. He may have held some minor offices and he may have been in the service of several noble families. He probably knew the Fieschi since 1436,[9] and appears to have been a tutor to Carlo Lascari, Count of Ventimiglia during the following years.[10] In a document of 1441, Facio appears as the chancellor of Francesco Spinola, and around the same period he must have served as a tutor to his son Gian Giacomo.[11] In 1441, he served as a notary to Raffaele Adorno; when the latter became Doge of Genoa in 1443, it was probably his influence that caused Facio to be named, on September 20, 1443, the official envoy of the Genoese Republic to King Alfonso of Aragon, with the task of negotiating a truce in the war that had been going on for a number of years. Facio met the King between Fermo and Ascoli, probably in October, carried out his negotiations, and returned to Genoa before November 8. On February 6, 1444, when the Republic sent ambassadors to the king for the signing of a peace treaty, Facio was sent with them to Naples to draft the treaty, and received the title of a chancellor of the city of Genoa, but without a salary.

It appears from the family letters of the Florentine manuscript that Facio, while staying in Naples with the Genoese ambassadors, also served as a tutor to Gian Giorgio, son of the Doge Raffaele Adorno, and to the son of another high Genoese official, and that with them he joined the retinue of the royal prince and future king, Ferrante. It was in this capacity that Facio remained in Naples after the Genoese ambassadors had gone home. When the Doge, instead of giving to Facio a position at home, asked him to stay with his son, Facio refused, and thus lost the favor of the Doge, who sent another person to replace him, but recommended him to the Neapolitan court. But only in July, 1445, was Facio taken into the service of King Alfonso. In December of that year, he received a salary payment from the King that enabled him to rent a house and to pay most of his debts. It is also evident that Facio received this salary for instructing Prince Ferrante, and that he retained the title of a Genoese chancellor, which was officially taken from him only on May 31, 1446.

It is quite probable that Facio assumed other functions at the court of Alfonso, for during the following years he was in constant touch with the King and his officials, participated in the readings and interpretations of Livy before Alfonso, and dedicated several of his writings to the king. Facio's appointment as royal historiographer, with an annual pension of 300 ducats, may have taken place as early as 1446, but is more definitely documented for October, 1448.[12] The latter date seems preferable, for we know that in 1447 and 1448, after the election of Nicolaus V, Facio made some efforts to be called to Rome. When Facio had finished the history of Alfonso, which he had been commissioned to write, he received an extra gift of 1,500 guilders, and while he composed other works for Alfonso, his pension was not only continued, but increased to 500 ducats in June, 1457. In contrast with the poverty of his earlier years in Genoa, Facio thus became a wealthy man, able to help his relatives, to make valuable gifts to his friends at court, and to order expensive cloth and pewter vessels from England.[13] He even had a gold-decorated glass bowl made to order in Venice, to keep his wine cool during the summer.[14] The Valladolid letters tell us some important facts about Facio's personal life that had been unknown: he married the daughter of Ambrosius de Nigro in Salerno,[15] and had a son, Giovanni, who grew old enough to receive Latin instruction and to show scholarly promise.[16] Facio, who was of small stature and whose portrait has been preserved in an illuminated manuscript, died in November, 1457.

Among Facio's acquaintances, the first place belongs to his teacher Guarino, whom he always mentioned with sincere affection. Facio tried to express his gratitude by helping Guarino's sons, Girolamo and Manuele. He also introduced Guarino as a chief character in his dialogue *De felicitate,* sent a copy of the work to Guarino, and was pleased to receive his comments.

Another humanist who played an important part in Facio's life was Antonio Panormita, who, as early as 1429, had recommended Facio to some of his friends in Florence. When Facio came to Naples in 1444, Panormita had been in the service of Alfonso for many years and it is evident from their correspondence and other sources that Panormita helped Facio at every stage of his career, and that their friendship remained close until the end of Facio's life. To the eight letters of Facio to Panormita that had been published from a Vatican manuscript, the Valladolid manuscript adds three more,[17] as well as many references to Panormita in letters written to others.

Facio's bitter controversy with Valla is well known. It was caused by their rivalry at court, and by the bitter enmity between Valla and Panormita. Apparently, they were never reconciled, but it appears from Valla's own words that they had been friends before the outbreak of the controversy. In his invectives against Valla, Facio refrained from personal insults, and many years later he wrote a laudatory biography of Valla, without alluding to their feud.

Facio's friendly relations with Poggio Bracciolini were based partly on their common antipathy against Valla, and we do not know whether they ever met. A number of letters exchanged between them has been published, and it appears that Facio encouraged Poggio to dedicate his translation of Xenophon's *Institution of Cyrus* to Alfonso, and that after the peace of 1455 Faccio personally recited at court a laudatory letter of Poggio to the King, and had it copied and distributed. The Valladolid manuscript contains two more letters to Poggio concerning the same topics.[18] In one of them Facio asks Poggio for a list of his writings and of those of Bruni, Manetti, and Traversari, evidently for his *De viris illustribus*.

Facio evidently met Enea Silvio Piccolomini in 1456, when the latter came to Naples as an envoy of Siena. Enea Silvio mentions Facio in his notes on Panormita's *De dictis et factis Alphonsi regis* (1456), and we know a rather cordial exchange of letters between them that must belong to the year 1457. The Valladolid manuscript adds another letter of Facio to Piccolomini, his original congratulation sent after the latter had been made a cardinal in December, 1456.[19]

An exchange of letters between Facio and Francesco Barbaro had long been known. Our manuscript adds a variant text of Facio's letter,[20] and in a letter to another person, Facio's regret's upon the death of Barbaro in 1454.[21] A letter from Biondo to Facio had been published, substantially a request for topographical information.[22] Facio's reply is not preserved, but the Valladolid manuscript contains the letter of transmission.[23] An exchange of letters between Facio and Prospero Camulio, dealing with some obscure business and political affairs, is known from a Vatican manuscript, as is a letter to Carlo Marsuppini.[24] Facio was in friendly relations with Jacopo Curlo, who succeeded him as Genoese chancellor in Naples, and is mainly known as a copyist. Although there are no direct letters, other acquaintances are mentioned in Facio's correspondence or elsewhere: Aurispa, Porcellio and Manetti, Lorenzo Bonincontri and Antonio Cassarino, as well as Nicolaus Sagundinus, a Byzantine exile, who included a warm eulogy of Facio in a letter written shortly after his death. The Valladolid manuscript adds some interesting names to the list of Facio's correspondents: Cardinal Giorgio Fieschi, who may have been Facio's pupil;[25] Cardinal Domenico Capranica, who was interested in Facio's writings;[26] Federico da Montefeltro, Count of Urbino, who sent Facio a mule to thank him for a friendly mention in his history of Alfonso;[27] Cosimo de'Medici, to whom Facio sent a complimentary copy of his *De viris illustribus;*[28] several members of Alfonso's court, such as Arnaldo Fenolleda, Francisco Martorell or Frater Ludovicus Podius (Luis Despuig), who served, along with Panormita, as Alfonso's ambassador to Venice and other

Italian governments; Gregorius Tifernas, whom Facius congratu-
lates upon his appointment as papal secretary under Nicolaus V,[29]
and Petrus Perleo, who was then teaching in Genoa, and whom
Facius compliments upon his translation of Isocrates.[30] A letter addressed to a namesake from Palermo removes any doubt about the
identity of that Barthomeus Faccius who was named administrator
of the cathedral of Cefalù in 1457.[31] A letter of transmission to
Dalmao de Mur, Archbishop of Zaragoza, preserved in a manuscript in the Escorial,[32] shows that Facio courted the favor of this
powerful prelate who was also in correspondence with Poggio. We
cannot give here a complete list of Facio's less prominent correspondents, but it is obvious from the preserved letters and other testimonies that Facio, at least during the later years of his life, was
widely known and respected, and that he had few enemies, if we
except the controversy with Valla and perhaps some earlier episodes.

Facio's writings cover many different areas of humanist literature, and may best be surveyed by genres. Two of his works, *De
differentiis verborum* and *Synonyma,* are short elementary treatises
on grammatical subjects. They are dedicated to Gian Giacomo
Spinola and belong to Facio's Genoese period, reflecting his experience as a tutor. They appear in a number of manuscripts and
early editions, and hence must have enjoyed a certain popularity.[33]
Another grammatical work, composed for Alfonso and entitled
De verborum priscorum significatione, was apparently much more
extensive, but has not been preserved.[34] Questions of Latin grammar
are also discussed in one of the letters, on the basis of passages Facio
had collected from classical authors.[35]

Facius did not write about rhetorical theory, but several of his
works may be classified as oratory or literary prose. In this category
we may place his letters which were carefully collected and edited
by the author, as we have seen, and hence considered as literary
compositions, in accordance with a well-known humanist tradition.
Another favorite humanist genre, the Latin oration, was surely
much cultivated by Facius, and we have reason to believe that he
composed many more formal speeches than have come down to us.
We have two short speeches in praise of Prince Ferrante and of
King Alfonso, composed in 1444 or 1445.[36] The speech addressed
by Facius to Alfonso, when he first met him as a Genoese envoy,

and inserted in his history of Alfonso probably represents an edited version of the original oration.[37] To this we may add the other speeches which Facio included, after the model of ancient historians, in his historical work.

A special kind of orations are Facio's invectives against Valla, written in 1446. Although they aroused the interest of several contemporaries, they survive in but few manuscripts and in their complete text have been published only once, and not too well.[38] The main purpose of Facio's invectives was to criticize Valla's history of Ferdinand of Aragon along grammatical and stylistic lines, and he also attempted to set up standards for the historian. Whether Valla's history deserves Facio's criticism, I must let those decide who have read it, rather than those who admire him on other grounds. It might also be helpful to read the invectives of Facio as well as Valla's reply before siding with the latter. The fact that Valla was the greater man does not in itself prove that he was right in this particular controversy, or that his opponent was altogether lacking in merit.

To the genre of oratory also belongs the only vernacular translation undertaken by Facio. It is a version of Isocrates' speech *Ad Nicoclem*. It has been preserved in the dedication copy in Valencia,[39] and is preceded by a Latin preface to Prince Ferrante at whose request it was made. From the preface we learn that Facius made his version from the Latin translation of Bernardo Giustiniani, rather than from the original Greek text. In trying to excuse his undertaking, Facius cites the precedent of numerous vernacular translations of the Latin classics which he had seen during his stay in Florence. The passage suggests that Facius intended to render Isocrates into Tuscan prose, but the actual nature of the vernacular he used has not yet been analyzed.

In view of the large place Latin poetry occupies in the work of many Renaissance humanists, it seems worthy of note that Facio apparently never composed any verse. A poem to Campanus once published under his name is clearly by another writer,[40] and the claim that there existed a poetic version of one of his shorter historical works is based on a misunderstanding.

The most important part of Facio's work as a writer belongs to the genre of historiography. Two short pieces, *De bello Veneto Clodiano* and *Aliud parvi temporis bellum Venetum*, were com-

posed during Facio's Genoese period and dedicated to Gian Giacomo Spinola, but were revised and published after his arrival in
Naples. Facio used some Genoese annals for his source, and probably
considered it his main task to present the same facts in elegant
Latin. The short works had a limited circulation and are of interest
chiefly as his first attempts in a field in which he was to excel. A
history of the wars between Genoa and the Catalans, if ever completed, remained unpublished and has not been preserved. Facio's
history of Alfonso, *De rebus gestis ab Alphonso primo libri X,*
is his largest work and the one for which he is most widely known.
It was probably begun after October, 1448. We know that by
September, 1451, he had completed the first seven books and was
working on the eighth, whereas in April, 1455, he was in the middle
of the last book. He probably finished the work before the end of
the same year.

Some historians have dismissed Facio's history with a few deroga-
tory remarks about its rhetorical and courtly character, but to my
knowledge it has never been carefully studied. In his style, Facius
was known to his contemporaries as an imitator of Caesar, and what
I have read of the work impresses me as rather concise. The work
describes the actions of a king, but the author disclaims any intention of writing his eulogy or biography.[41] Nobody has ever denied
that Alfonso deserved at least a part of the praise he received from
Facius and others, and Facius knows very well the difference between a good king and a tyrant. There is no indication that Facius
neglected the chief duty of the historian—to present the facts without
distortion to the best of his knowledge—and I see no harm in it if
he also aimed at dignity and stylistic purity. Among Facio's contemporaries, the history of Alfonso had considerable success. It
remains one of the more detailed and reliable narrative sources of
Neapolitan history for the period it covers.[42]

To the genre of history belongs also the only translation from the
Greek that Facius ever attempted, that of Arrian's history of Alexander the Great. Facius' knowledge of Greek was apparently limited,
and his repeated statements that original compositions are more important than translations sounds like an admission of his weakness.
It is definitely known that Facio made this translation at the request
of Alfonso; that he based it largely on the earlier translation of

Vergerio, a copy of which had been sent to Alfonso by Enea Silvio Piccolomini, and that he considered it his main task to improve upon the style of this earlier version; that he was aided by the advice of better Greek scholars, especially of Theodore Gaza and Nicolaus Sagundinus; that he spent three years on this translation and had revised only a part of it at the time of his death; and that the translation was copied and edited by Jacopo Curlo for Arnaldo Fenolleda some time after the death of Alfonso in 1458. The earliest printed edition of this translation (1508) seems to have been further revised by Ludovicus Odaxius.[43] Later classical scholars passed a harsh judgment on this translation, but a close comparison of Facius' version with that of Vergerius and with the Greek text has not yet been made, as far as I know.

To Facio's historical works we may add his *De viris illustribus,* a collection of contemporary biographies, which he composed in 1456 after the completion of the history of Alfonso. This work has also been criticized for the brevity of its presentation, but it serves as a precious early source for many of the persons it covers; it is reliable, and often based on first-hand information for many of its data; and in covering not only princes, but also citizens, humanists, other scholars, and artists, both Italian and Northern, the work reflects the range of human achievements that seemed important to the author and his time.[44]

Another type of narrative literature to which Facius contributed was the Latin short story or *novella.* His *De origine belli inter Gallos et Britannos historia* belongs to this genre, rather than to that of history proper. It was dedicated to Count Carlo of Ventimiglia, and hence belongs to Facio's earlier years. In the preface, Facio states that he used for his story a vernacular source, but such a source has never been identified. The work was printed only in the eighteenth century, but the number of its early manuscripts suggests that it was one of Facio's most popular compositions during his own time.[45]

To the same genre belongs a Latin version Facio made of Novella X 1 of Boccaccio's *Decameron.* This version was published from a single manuscript in Florence, together with a short epilogue addressed to a member of Alfonso's court.[46] In the Valladolid manuscript, the same text appears with a preface to Ludovicus Podius.[47] In this preface Facius cites the precedent of Leonardo Bruni for his attempt at turning Boccaccio into Latin. It appears from another letter of Facius to the same Podius that this translation was made after Facius had been appointed as a royal historiographer, probably in order to solicit a delayed payment of his salary.[48]

Aside from a few lost or doubtful writings, this leaves us with two more works of Facio that have established for him a modest place in the history of Renaissance thought.[49] The first of these moral treatises, *De humanae vitae felicitate,* was written in 1445 or 1446 and dedicated to Alfonso.[50] It has the form of a dialogue and takes for its subject "the condition of human life." Of the three speakers, Lamola, who is supposed to defend the active life, praises in turn different human advantages and forms of life: wealth, princely and civic power, the life of the courtier, of the soldier, of the farmer, pleasure, the life of the priest, and the knowledge of the arts and sciences. Guarino argues point by point that none of these forms of life contains happiness. In the second part, Panormita undertakes to defend the contemplative life, cites the definitions of the supreme good given by ancient philosophers and Christian theologians, and concludes that happiness consists in the enjoyment and contemplation of God and in the eternal life, and hence cannot be attained on earth. Guarino then confirms this conclusion, and describes in detail the pleasures of the future life. It appears from Facio's citations that he is better acquainted with Cicero and other Latin writers than with the Greek philosophers, and that he also knows Lactantius and Augustine. In his introduction, Facio characteristically apologizes both for himself and for the speakers of his dialogue on account of their interference in a subject that properly belongs to the philosophers and theologians. Some contemporary readers felt that Lamola yielded too easily to the objections of Guarino, a charge against which Facio defended himself in a letter to Roberto Strozzi,[51] and also in his invectives against Valla, who was to repeat this criticism. Some modern critics have found the treatise, on account of its emphasis on the afterlife, out of tune with the spirit of Renaissance humanism. Yet it may be their conception of this spirit that is at fault, and they seem to forget that even Valla's *De vero bono* concludes with an enthusiastic description of heavenly bliss. Facio's dialogue surely does not show much philosophical acumen or originality, but it does present the advantages of earthly life with some force, before rejecting them, and it has some interest for the moral thought of the author and of his time.[52]

Facio's other treatise, *De excellentia ac praestantia hominis,* has attracted even greater attention as the earliest humanist work entirely concerned with the dignity of man. It was dedicated to Nicolaus V in 1447 or 1448.[53] An interesting detail concerning its origin has been overlooked by most students of the subject. Facius was asked by Antonius Bargensis, a Benedictine monk with humanist interests and connections, to write about the dignity and excellence of human life, and even received a draft of the treatise from Antonius.[54] In discussing his subject, Facio first gives some reasons why God created man, and places his dignity mainly in his reason and his immortality. After a brief praise of man's achievements in government and civilization, in the arts and sciences, there is a long digression on the immortality of the soul. Man's dignity is placed in his future life, and the entire later part of the work is concerned with the joys and blessings of this future life. Facio repeatedly refers to his earlier treatise on happiness, and mentions at one point Thomas Aquinas with a note of cautious criticism.[55]

Nobody will wish to consider Facio as a great philosopher on the basis of his two treatises. He probably did not even mean to be original, and considered it his duty as a good Christian and citizen to lend his elegant style to the expression of worthy and approved ideas. He was, however, among the first humanist writers to deal with such important subjects as the dignity of man or the immortality of the soul that were to be treated more effectively by some of his more famous successors.

Facio's letters do not yield much additional information about his thought. In a letter of sympathy, Facio insists that we should expect help from reason rather than from time,[56] and in writing to the teacher of his son, he asks him to put greater stress on morals than on learning.[57] The letters are more instructive for Facio's classical interests. Latin writers such as Cicero, Virgil, and Juvenal are quoted frequently, and we also learn that he lent or borrowed manuscripts of less famous authors, or asked his friends to search for them. One letter contains an explanation of a passage in Suetonius, an author who seems to have been one of his favorites.[58]

In typical fashion, Facio admired antiquity and despised the barbarism of later centuries, and praises Guarino and other Italian humanists for having revived eloquence and the other humanities, regretting the fact that foreign nations, especially the French, have failed to participate in this revival.[59] Yet in spite of his admiration for things ancient, he considers it a worthy task to write about contemporary events and persons.

Facio kept his friends informed about his writing, and his letters tell us a good deal about the genesis and diffusion of his various works. He saw to it that his friends received the copies they had requested, and would lend his own manuscript to a person who was to transcribe it. In an urgent letter to a friend who was apparently in charge of supervising the transcription of his history of Alfonso, Facio sent several passages which he wanted inserted in the text,[60] and our printed text of the work shows that he succeeded. When Facio had completed the draft of one of his writings, he usually submitted it to the judgment of learned friends, and then turned it over to his copyist to be transcribed, making constant corrections as the parts of the manuscript were returned to him by the copyist. Apparently he took great care in correcting the copies transcribed for his friends. A passage in one of his family letters is of interest to students of paleography. Facius had one of his younger relatives trained as a scribe, and insisted that he should learn to write after the ancient manner, using some beautiful model, since this style is more beautiful, and now most frequently used in the chanceries.[61]

I hope this brief survey of Facio's life and work may illustrate some, if not all, of the typical interests of Italian humanists during the early fifteenth century. Facio did not contribute to poetry or to political thought, and his knowledge of Greek was scanty; but he was a good Latin scholar and prose writer, a competent grammarian, orator, and novelist, an honest moralist interested in ancient philosophy and even in patristic theology, and a prominent historian and biographer. The extent to which we have been able to reconstruct his life from previously unknown letters, and to estimate the diffusion of his previously known works from the number and distribution of their extant manuscripts, may point up the extent to which the study of Renaissance humanism may still benefit from

4. G. Antolín, *Catálogo de los códices latinos de la Real Biblioteca del Escorial,* vol. V (Madrid, 1923), p. 385.

5. Mittarelli, *op cit.,* pp. 372–73.

6. *Ibid.*

7. Mazzini and Sabbadini (whom I shall follow on many biographical and bibliographical details) have him born around 1400. Yet in a letter to Carlo Marsuppini (Vat. lat. 2906, f. 52) Facio says: "quum essem adolescencior Florencie." This visit took place in 1429 (F, f. 161–62).

8. See the letters in F.

9. F, f. 165.

10. Vat. lat. 2906, f. 53–55; *Vall.* f. 35v–36v.

11. That Gian Giacomo was the son of Francesco, I gather from *Vall.* f. 35–35v and 41–42.

12. T. De Marinis, *La biblioteca napoletana dei Re d'Aragona,* Vol. II (Milan, 1947), pp. 243–44, doc. 174. Cf. Vol. I (1952), p. 2.

13. *Vall.,* f. 35–35v and 41–42.

14. *Ibid.,* f. 42v–43.

15. *Ibid.,* f. 5v–6.

16. *Ibid.,* f. 28v–29; 32v–33v; 35v–36v.

17. *Ibid.,* f. 15v–16; 23v; 34v–35.

18. *Ibid.,* f. 18v–19; 27v.

19. *Ibid.,* f. 2v–3.

20. *Ibid.,* f. 25v–27

21. *Ibid.,* f. 36v.

22. *Scritti inediti di Flavio Biondo,* ed. B. Nogara (*Studi e Testi* 48, Rome, 1927), pp. 165–66.

23. *Vall.,* f. 8.

24. Vat. lat. 2906, f. 52–52v; 58v–60.

25. Vall., f. 3 and *passim.*

26. *Ibid.,* f. 3v and *passim* from Trinkaus, Saitta, and Di Napoli.

27. *Ibid.,* f. 8v–9.

28. *Ibid.,* f. 9v–10.

29. *Ibid.,* f. 33v–34v.

30. *Ibid.,* f. 30v–31.

31. *Ibid.,* f. 31v–32v.

32. Cod. f. IV 13. Another letter is in Madrid, Academia de la Nistoria, ms. 12-11-1, f. 122v–23.

33. For the editions, see Mazzini, p. 432–36; *Gesamtkatalog der Wiegendrucke* (GW) nos. 7033–7037. I used the copy of an undated edition (GW 7036) at the Morgan Library.

34. *Vall.,* f. 34v.

35. *Ibid.,* f. 38v.

36. Valencia, Biblioteca Universitaria, cod. 727, f. 17v–23.

37. Barth. Facius, *De rebus gestis ab Alphonso primo* . . . (*Raccolta di tutti i più rinomati scrittori dell'Istoria generale del Regno di Napoli,* IV (Naples, 1769), pp. 179–81.

38. R. Valentini, "Le invettive di Bartolomeo Facio contro Lorenzo Valla . . . ," *Rendiconti della Reale Accademia dei Lincei, Classe di Scienze Morali, Storiche e Filologiche,* Ser. V, Vol. V (1906), pp. 493–550, 660–62. He used one complete ms. (Oxford, Balliol 131) and two fragmentary ones (Vat. lat. 7179 and Angelica 1374). Another complete ms. in Berol. lat. oct. 176 in Marburg and a fragment in Vat. lat. 6850, pp. 74–86.

39. cod. 727, f. 1–17v.

40. Jo. Christ. Amadutius, *Anecdota Litteraria ex manuscriptis codicibus eruta,* vol. III (Rome, 1774), p. 431–36 (from ms. Savignano 68, f. 77). For the true author, Baptista Lunensis, see P. Parroni, "Il cod. Oliv. 23 di Marziale e il suo copista Battista Lunense," *Studia Oliveriana,* XI (1963), pp. 15–22.

41. See the letter to Francesco Barbaro (Mehus, pp. 93–96).

42. For Facio's relations with Alfonso and his court, see A. Soria, *Los humanistas de la corte de Alfonso el Magnanimo* (Granada, 1956).

43. I used a copy of this edition at the Morgan Library. The data I give are derived from the letters of Facio, Curlo, and others contained in this edition.

44. Mr. Michael Baxandall is preparing a new edition of the section that deals with artists. Aside from Vat. lat. 13650 (of which Mr. Baxandall reminded me), I know the following manuscripts: Berol.

lat. oct. 179 (fragm.) in Marburg; Brescia A III 2 (perhaps the ms. used by Mehus); Rome, Biblioteca Nazionale, ms. Vittorio Emanuele 854.

45. A. Ciaconius, *Bibliotheca,* ed. F. D. Camusat (Amsterdam-Leipzig, 1744), col. 893–902. I know at least 16 mss. containing this work, including Venice, Marc. lat. XIV 107 (4708) copied by Pietro Cennini in 1469 from Facio's autograph. Cf. A. Neri, "Intorno alla novella di Jacopo di Poggio Bracciolini e all' original testo latino di Bart. Fazio," *Il Propugnatore,* Vol. VII, part I (1874), 129–137; C. Braggio, "Giacomo Bracelli e l'umanesimo dei Liguri al suo tempo," *Atti della Società Ligure di Storia Patria* XXIII (1890, 5–206), 231–257; L. Di Francia, *La Novellistica,* I (Milan, 1924), 317–322.

46. C. Braggio, "Una novella del Boccaccio tradotta da Bartolomeo Fazio," *Giornale Ligustico,* XI (1884) 379–87 (from Magl. XXV 626).

47. f. 1–2v.

48. f. 6v–7.

49. L. Thorndike, *Science and Thought in the Fifteenth Century* (New York, 1929), pp. 185–7; G. Gentile, *Il pensiero italiano del Rinascimento* (third edition, Florence, 1940), pp. 91–92; Charles Trinkaus, *Adversity's Noblemen: The Italian Humanists on Happiness* (New York, 1940), pp. 20–21 and *passim;* E. Garin, *Filosofi italiani del Quattrocento* (Florence, 1942), pp. 210–21 (with selected passages in Latin and Italian); Garin, *La filosofia* (Milan, 1947), I, 252–55; Garin, *Der italienische Humanismus* (Bern, 1947), pp. 61–62; G. Saitta, *Il pensiero italiano nell'umanesimo e nel rinascimento,* vol. I (Bologna, 1949), pp. 465–69; G. Di Napoli, " 'Contemptus mundi' e 'dignitas hominis' nel Rinascimento," *Rivista di filosofia neoscolastica* (48, 1956, 9–41) at pp. 16–18; Di Napoli, *L'immortalità dell'anima nel Rinascimento* (Turin, 1963), pp. 86–90.

50. The work was printed four times. I cite from the third edition (in Felinus Sandeus, *De legibus Siciliae et Apuliae,* Hanau, 1611, pp. 106–48). I know almost thirty manuscripts containing this work which also served as a model for Juan de Lucena's *Libro de vita beata* (Soria, p. 91).

51. This letter is found in the manuscripts and editions of the dialogue,

and was also published by Mehus (pp. xxxiv–xxxvi) and De Marinis (vol. I, 1952, p. 25).

52. On the whole, Facio receives a friendlier treatment from Trinkaus, Di Napoli, and Saitta than from the other historians cited in note 49 above.

53. I cite from the only edition of 1611 (pp. 149–68). I know of only three mss.: Berol. lat. oct. 179 (in Marburg); Laur. 90 sup. 45; Vat. lat. 3562 (the dedication copy); Urb. lat. 227, pp. 150n.–69.

54. Antonii Bargensis *Chronicon Montis Oliveti,* ed. Placidus M. Lugano (Florence, 1901), pp. xxxv–xli; Mazzini, pp. 427–31. The manuscript used by Lugano is still at Monte Oliveto Maggiore, as I was informed by the Rev. Romualdo M. Zilianti AC Gen. Antonius Bargensis was also acquainted with Giannozzo Manetti (Vespasiano da Bisticci, *Vite di uomini illustri del secolo XV,* ed. L. Frati, Vol. II [Bologna, 1893], pp. 161–62).

55. *Ibid.,* p. 165.

56. *Vall.,* f. 40v.

57. *Ibid.,* f. 32v.

58. *Ibid.,* f. 43, cf., Vat. lat. 2906, f. 60.

59. Mittarelli, col. 376: haec enim eloquentia vix unquam extra Italiae claustra penetrare potuit. . . .

60. *Vall.,* f. 36v–37v.

61. F, f. 166–166v: vellem autem disceret scribere antiquorum more si quod pulchrum exemplar aliquunde haberi posset, quoniam forma illa litterarum magis placet viris doctis et certe prestantior est et in cancellariis nunc maxime usitatur.

THE SIENESE STATE
IN THE RENAISSANCE*

D A V I D   L .   H I C K S

New York University

"**P**ower aggregates" Garrett Mattingly called them (some, less accurately, call them "states"), and the theme of their birth and early years runs through everything he wrote and said about European history. He believed their appearance marked the end of the Middle Ages and the beginning of modern times. In *Renaissance Diplomacy,* he set forth his argument best, demonstrating the fragmentation of the Respublica Christiana by examining the origins of international relations and of modern diplomatic machinery. In articles, and particularly in lectures, he drew more general conclusions. Always his emphasis was on Italy of the quattrocento, for there he saw the source and the prototype of much that the North would later become.

The decade of the 1450s, when the Italian powers signed the Peace of Lodi, had a particular significance for Mattingly. By then Italian states had emerged, omnicompetent, egocentric, power hungry, for practical purposes sovereign with respect to each other.[1] But it was only the relationships among these states that time permitted him to study. Their domestic affairs, commerce, society,

* Most of the research for this article was done while the author was recipient of grants from the American Philosophical Society and New York University.

constitutions, he was obliged to leave to others. Not that he was without ideas! He clearly preferred republics—Florence above all—to dictatorships, and though he deeply admired Jacob Burckhardt, he was certain that the republican state was the true "work of art" of Renaissance politics. The validity of his belief is now being proved. Though the Burckhardtian tradition is dying hard (witness the titles of the two most recent general works in Italian on the subject[2]), dying it is as more and more scholars are getting down to work in the archives.

Florence has stimulated the most interest. What seems now to have become clear is that the Renaissance there, whatever else it may have been, was a time when the medieval Florentine commune with all its myriad corporations was transformed into a species of unitary government, when corporate groups as political—and indeed as social and economic—powers began to give way, when most separate jurisdictions and special privileges were replaced by a more impersonal and egalitarian fiscal and judicial authority, when men began to take on the appearance of citizens in the eyes of a state. It is also clear that this evolution was well advanced by Mattingly's critical 1450s. The Parte Guelfa had withered, victim of relentless pressure by a hostile government. The barbarian habits of duel and vendetta practiced by its pretentious members with an eye on Northern chivalry had been repressed by courts which refused to recognize spurious noble "rights." The Church was now supervised closely, its appointments, its income, its charities government business, its clerics subject to civil taxation and trial, its lay confraternities weakened by unsympathetic legislation. Long before, the companies of citizen militia, army of the corporate *popolo,* had abandoned the field to a state army of mercenaries. Though the government's debt was huge in the mid-fifteenth century, it was funded, and taxes, among them a kind of income-property tax, were collected without reference to an individual's social position. And one of the largest sources of revenue was the Florentine *contado,* whose subject areas and communes were controlled with surprising effectiveness from the great city at its center. For Florence was no longer merely a city—but a *territorial*-state.[3]

It hardly needs saying that the transformation of Florence from commune to state was not complete. Whatever fundamental changes had taken place in the practice of government and in attitudes toward law and civic responsibility, the constitution preserved the medieval republican form, its priorate, its councils, its elaborate electoral machinery, its guild flavor. Nor should one conclude that simply because commissions called *balìe* were often appointed to get a job done with efficiency and dispatch or because elections were rigged that the old constitution did not continue to operate. Furthermore, the Florentine people had not yet entirely abandoned their old loyalties to family, to guild, to *consorteria,* to ecclesiastical foundation.[4] A highly complex blending of the old and the new was perhaps most characteristic of the Florence of the 1450s. A great deal of detailed study is necessary before the exact proportions in this blend can be known.

The story of Florence's southern neighbor, the Republic of Siena, is in some ways less complex but follows a similar theme. For the second great Tuscan republic also progressed toward statehood, and the 1450s were a time of culmination.

The crucial facts of Sienese history during the quattrocento were the character of its economy and the consequent socio-political situation. In material ways, Siena compared unfavorably with Florence. Although its *contado* was nearly as large, its population was much smaller, under 15,000 in the city throughout the century.[5] The difference in wealth was as great. Siena's days of gold and grandeur were the thirteenth and early fourteenth centuries, when its bankers were known throughout Europe and its merchants traded in the North, in Spain, and in the Levant. By the second half of the fourteenth century, the Sienese economy was in crisis and undergoing a profound reorientation. Bank failures of the 1340s, the Black Death (though perhaps not so catastrophic as some have thought), the unsympathetic government in the middle decades of the century, the ruin brought on by invasion and prolonged occupation of the *contado* by *compagnie di ventura* in the 1360s and '70s, the huge sums extorted by these *compagnie* from a helpless government: all contributed to the destruction of large-scale commerce and banking.[6] The less important cloth industry suffered as well. And recovery never came, for Siena lacked a foundation on which to rebuild: no seaport worth mention, limited water for clothmaking, little surplus capital to lend. By 1400 or thereabouts, the city had become from an economic standpoint what it would forever remain —the center of a flourishing agricultural area, with local trade, local banking, local industry, and no real hope of anything more. The fruitful Tuscan soil, if left untouched by marauding armies, kept poverty from Siena's door. The half century before 1450 was a time of rising prosperity on this new basis, slow at first, quite rapid at the end.[7]

During that time, the Sienese began investing heavily in land, and less heavily but at an expanding rate in the government.[8] Some gave up urban business entirely. The middle classes, high and low, were transformed into a class of *rentiers*. It became more and more difficult to draw social distinctions except in terms of capital investment. The new *rentiers* were in substance a class of pseudo-aristocrats among whom wealth was becoming the chief measure of social status. The full significance of this is not appreciated until one realizes that the previous social structure was founded to a large degree on trade or profession, and that this structure was preserved in tradition by associations of families called *monti*. There were five of these *monti,* each the heir of an oligarchic or semi-oligarchic regime of the thirteenth and fourteenth centuries, and each in origin a fairly exact representation of an economic class. The *Gentiluomini* had been the petty landed nobility. The *Nove* sprang from the patricians (merchants, bankers, cloth manufacturers, an alliance of rich commoners and former petty nobility) who had led Siena to greatness in the three generations before 1355. The forebears of the *Dodici* were the middle guildsmen who overthrew the *Nove* in 1355 and were themselves overthrown by the *Riformatori* in 1368–69. The *Riformatori* and *Popolari,* at their birth in the decade and a half after 1368 were composed mostly of artisans and shopkeepers, with possibly a sprinkling of disenfranchised noblemen and middle guildsmen.[9] By the 1450s all that had changed. The *monti* remained, but their social meaning was altered. A new social structure was emerging—and being accepted—which cut straight across family and *monti* lines.[10]

The effect on political life was profound, for the *monti* were also the basis of representation in the government. Although there were five, since 1403 only three, joined in a coalition regime, bore the major burden of rule. These were the *Nove,* the *Riformatori,* and the

Popolari. In 1450, these *monti* shared the seats in the chief executive magistrature and in one of the two large legislative councils equally. Three representatives, one for each *monte* from each *Terzo* of the city, met together with the *Capitano del Popolo,* the three *Vessiliferi* (standard bearers) of the Terzi, and other officials as the *Concistoro* or Priorate. The *Concistoro*—a new one was elected every two months—initiated legislation, which after passage by the councils it also implemented.[11] The *Consiglio del Popolo,* whose role in the government is somewhat obscure, was composed of *residuti,* those citizens who had served in the *Concistoro.*[12]

At this point, the coalition lost some of its perfect tripartite character. The *Riformatori* were limited in their representation so far as some offices were concerned, notably the much sought-after *podesterie* and *vicariati* in the *contado,*[13] while a fourth *monte,* the *Gentiluomini,* received a bit of recognition. The *Consiglio generale,* chief law-making council of the commune and source of all communal authority, accepted these old noblemen in considerable numbers.[14] *Gentiluomini* were also permitted to sit as fourth members on such important administrative bodies as the *Provveditori di Biccherna* (the treasurers), the *Esecutori di Gabella,* the *Consoli di Mercanzia,* and the *Regolatori* (the state auditors and guardians of the statutes), and were regularly selected for a few posts in the *contado.*[15] This left only the *Dodici* without a place. They had wasted themselves in the century after their founding. Admitted as partners to the first coalition of 1385, they had foolishly rebelled in 1403 and lost all political privileges. Possibly some of them were accepted into other *monti* thereafter (a check of names shows them as *Riformatori*), but the others remained disfranchised.

But even without the *Dodici,* the Sienese government was broadly based, representing in terms of population probably close to half the city.[16] No other Italian city of Siena's size or larger had so numerous a body of governors. Furthermore, the door to political rights was as yet ajar. In the first half of the century a quite sizeable body of new men was permitted to run for office and be enrolled in a *monte,* almost always the *Popolari.*[17] With each new man went his descendants to the furthest generation. The entire situation had a unique democratic quality about it. Indeed, if Leonardo Bruni or some other contemporary with an eye to Aristotle had observed he might have concluded that a fairly close approximation of the master's ideal had been achieved.

The institution of the *monti*, then, gave a special character to Sienese political life. *Monti* members were citizens, equals in law, whose function was to serve the state. Indeed, the sole purpose of a *monte* was to supply such service; it had no other. In this most important way it differed from other groups in the commune, all of which had functions not connected with politics, and all of which were corporate in essence. Hence, by their very nature, the *monti* encouraged a sense of public responsibility which worked against the traditions of private law and special privilege. The *monti* also provided the means by which the Sienese could learn the arts of government, could gain the necessary administrative skills and broaden their political experience. And a great many Sienese took advantage of the opportunity, for throughout their lives members of the *monti* were primarily political men, applying most of their interest and energy to governing. The character of the Sienese economy made it easier for them to find time to devote to politics and gave them an added motive for advocating a well-ordered, soundly financed, peace-loving state.

The picture was not entirely without flaws. Historians of Siena have traditionally named "factionalism" as the citizens' worst political vice, and they have charged it to the *monti*.[18] Certainly, a tendency was always present for the *monti* to become ends in themselves and for the ends of the state to take second place. If the *monti* encouraged public responsibility, they also bred fierce loyalty to themselves. Such loyalty could be blind and dangerous, and several times was the strongest force behind revolt. But in the fifteenth century, wiser and leveler heads prevailed more often than not. In 1403 when the *Dodici* challenged the coalition, in 1456 when a small group of *Nove* did the same, and even in the chaotic years after 1480 when rational government seemed to have broken down completely, a spirit of compromise remained alive.[19] Most Sienese saw the advantages of cooperative government, and knew that they outweighed family and individual ambition. That Pandolfo Petrucci founded his regime on a new coalition in the 1490s—the broadest in more than a century—and thereby brought civic peace back to Siena is evidence of that.[20] Perhaps the lessons drawn from Aristotle and well illustrated by Lorenzetti's *Good and Bad Government* and with less felicity by the sometime chancellor and public speaker, Agostino Dati, implanted themselves in the Sienese mind.[21] Certainly a common interest encouraged cooperation. Certainly, too, fear of the greater states to the north and south bound the governors together.

And with reason. By the third quarter of the fourteenth century, Siena had become a second-rate Italian power. It could neither mount nor sustain a policy of adventure. Indeed, its aim was peace, with or without honor, for its citizens had neither the money for war nor the strength to bear the inevitable injury to their small trade and their agriculture. But there was no escape. All the powers sought their friendship: the Sienese purse was fat enough to buy a few troops, and more important the Sienese *contado* was a natural roadway between north and south. Even when neutral, Siena was prey to war. The depredations of the *compagnie di ventura* were followed by the War of the Eight Saints, in which Siena was allied to Florence. In the 1380s, Siena signed a pact with Milan, finally accepting Giangaleazzo Visconti's *signoria* in return for his protection—a cheaper choice in the long run than that of Florence, whose citizens stood fast for "liberty." In the teens of the new century, King Ladislas of Naples sent his army almost to the city gates and did much damage to the *contado*. In the next decades, the long struggle between Milan and Florence resumed, and despite efforts to stay aloof, in the 1440s and '50s the Sienese once more found Neopolitan troops on their doorstep. War and rumors of war were constant for close to a century.[22] Even self-defense demanded, besides financial outlays of considerable size, an expeditious and efficient government and a unity of purpose and effort among the citizens.

This unity of purpose and effort among the citizens was achieved in the face of necessity. Effective government came partly as a response to necessity and partly through simple evolution. As a result, Siena was better able to meet the last of the threats than the first of them. From the time of the establishment of the coalition regime in the 1380s, and especially after its stabilization in 1403, Siena moved steadily from medieval commune to modern territorial state. The economy and society, the government by *monti,* and the character of the coalition itself provided a congenial setting. Fear, and perhaps a certain patriotic pride in protecting republicanism, acted as goads to make the citizens amenable to institutional change. In a general way, the Sienese experience was like the Florentine. The relationship between city and *contado* was regularized, the tendency being to standardize the territorial administration and draw the lines of authority more tightly to the center. In the city itself, vestiges of special privilege and private or semi-private law were virtually eliminated. The Sienese—at least those who could claim (if not be granted) full political rights—became citizens in the eyes of an impersonal public authority. Justice and taxation were applied more systematically and with greater equity. At the same time, the machinery of government, though it remained in fact republican and in appearance communal, was transformed by the increasing use of special executive committees called *balìe*. In the 1450s, the "*Magistrato* (or "*Ufficio*") *della Balìa*" became for practical purposes permanent and Siena's chief executive organ. Much more archival research is necessary before all the details of this general description are known. Yet, to any but the most casual eye, the picture is clear.

The consolidation of the *contado* had gone forward in fits and starts since the twelfth century. By the first years of the fifteenth century a more concentrated, rational program was under way. At last the surviving family of great feudal nobility, the Aldobrandeschi, was subjugated and arrangements made for its small domains.[23] Apparently to simplify territorial administration while perhaps flattering the *contadini* and attracting prospective office holders, a series of laws in the 1420s upgraded most of the smaller communes to *podestarie*.[24] Many, both large and small, received new or revised *statuti*.[25] Though the local governments were permitted to retain a traditional flavor, the statutes were written with the help of Sienese, usually in the Sienese image. In every case, the Sienese official in residence, whether *podestà, vicario, capitano,* or *castellano,* was delegated great authority. Sometimes he sat as chief executive magistrate, and always he and his Sienese *giudice* dispensed high justice.[26] The Sienese *Concistoro* and courts acted in cases of appeal.[27]

Indeed, the central government seems to have made a serious

effort to see that its agents did well. Men wishing to be considered for *contado* posts were required to have some previous administrative experience, and residence during the six-month term of office was insisted upon.[28] When they left office, their performance was reviewed by their *contadini* and by the governors of Siena. For all this, however, Siena was interested first of all in the revenues the *contado* produced. These were of some size, as the account books show, but they seem to have been reasonable under the circumstances, and relief was granted when justified.[29] The financial affairs of the communes were watched with care. When it was found, for example, that local debts were mounting, the *Camarlingo di Biccherna* was ordered to step in and do something about it.[30] How well the entire system worked is suggested by the fact that it lasted with only minor modifications until the eighteenth century.[31]

In their own bailiwick, the Sienese governors were most concerned with problems of law and finance. Public order, loyalty to the state, and fiscal integrity they looked upon as the pillars of a good society. An extreme legalism, amounting almost to an obsession, was heir of the medieval tradition but was now in the process of evolving into something more. The governors broadened the scope and meaning of justice and tied it to the idea of a unitary and omnipotent state. Their point of view was expressed in the preamble to an edict of 1419 establishing the office of *maggior sindaco:*

> *In prima.* Considering that in the past many statutes, orders and reforms have been made which have not been observed. Desiring that this not occur in future, but that each man be under the yoke of reason and live correctly in honor and usefulness to the commune and the present regime. . . .[32]

The edict provided that the new magistrate have "full authority, jurisdiction, and responsibility for seeing that all statutes, orders and reforms, existing and future, be observed."[33] He was to be a foreign doctor of laws (local men were still considered untrustworthy) appointed for a year, and his right to impose a fine would extend to all but a few high elected officials.[34] Another edict of a generation later went even further, quadrupling the fine and expanding the law to include persons criticizing "by mouth or in writing" communal officials, among whom judges are specifically named, or teaching disrespect for the statutes.[35]

This effort to gather all Sienese under the legal wing of the state extended also to more mundane crimes. By the 1450s, Siena had a judge and a court for every sort of case, civil and criminal.[36] All were active, and there is little evidence that the stipulation contained in every prohibitive law, that it be applied without regard "to grade or condition," was often violated.[37] Civil matters such as petitions for tax relief seem also to have been handled without favoritism.[38] Yet, there must have been abuses, particularly in the treatment of second-class citizens, those who in Florence were called *miserabili*. Furthermore, administrative error, however unwitting, may well have led to abuses up and down the line, for jurisdictions overlapped, procedures were sometimes arbitrary, and enforcement spotty. That the Sienese were aware of these problems there can be no doubt. They continually sought a better, more certain embodiment of their legal ideal. Indeed, their reformist proclivities gave the judicial system a somewhat patchwork and impermanent air. In 1451, for example, they found it advisable to introduce two additional *giudici di riformagioni* and shortly thereafter to nominate a triumvirate of the *Balìa* (the *Tre Segreti*) to investigate political crimes.[39] Judicial legislation was ground out regularly almost till the end of Siena's independent history.[40]

The other main focus of the governors' attention was administration and finance. Here the Sienese showed themselves more sophisticated than in law, building a reasonably orderly and well-managed system, with a numerous, trained bureaucracy.[41] The foundations had already been laid. Siena's sources of income and its system of administering them were old ones, but they were flexible enough to keep up with the changes in the economy. The sources consisted chiefly of several *gabelle*, duties and tolls of various kinds in city and *contado*, and the *Lira*, an ancient tax on real and personal property similar to the Florentine *catasto*.[42] They were administered by some half dozen offices, staffed by managers, clerks, and notaries chosen by the usual electoral system. New legislation aimed at tightening administrative procedures to eliminate fraud and discrimination and to get full value for every *soldo* received. The *Biccherna*, principal office of collection and disbursement, received a lay *camarlingo* in place of a cleric, and its *Provveditori* continued to assume functions many of which had been left before to corporations. Indeed, by this time, the *Provveditori di Biccherna* had many duties more closely related to urban services than finance.[43] Some years before, auditing of all financial records had been made obligatory by the introduction of an accounting office, the *Regolatori*.[44] This became one of the busiest and most prestigious administrative bodies in the course of the fifteenth century. The volume of its accounting work was large: every official or office that handled public money presented his figures to be checked and to receive confirmation that the statutes had been adhered to. Like the *Provveditori*, the *Regolatori* were involved in many non-financial affairs as well.[45] The effect was further to centralize the Sienese government, while expanding its role in the lives of the citizens and *contadini*.

But good management of a prospering economy was not enough to support Siena's emergency needs. This required sound public credit and extraordinary financial demands of the citizens. Already in existence was the *Monte de' Paschi e Sale,* a kind of state bank which accepted sums for investment and paid a yearly dividend. The funds, of course, were used for public business, interest being paid out of the rents from the state-owned pasture lands and the salt *gabella* of city and *contado*.[46] In 1429, the *Monte* underwent a major reform. The new law, citing numerous abuses, created a *camarlingo* and a bookkeeping staff, ordered severe penalties for trafficking in shares or for using shares as business collateral, and set the dividend rate at 5 per cent annually.[47] Thereupon, the *Monte* began a new era of growth. Investment and confidence rose steadily, and the *Monte* became the central institution of the Sienese economy. The greater reliance on forced loans, called *preste,* to raise cash quickly may be attributed in part to the good health of the *Monte*—as may the good health of the *Monte* be attributed in part to greater reliance on *preste*.[48] These loans were treated as regular investments, earning dividends at the regular rate. They were an eminently fair—indeed democratic—sort of tax and a worthy companion to the *Lira*. As with the *Lira,* they were adjusted wholly to individual wealth, were not excessive, and drew something from every Sienese property owner in city and *contado,* however small.

Again, new procedures and new policies led inevitably to greater centralization of government, while forging a stronger bond between government and people.

Even with the frequent *preste* and increased voluntary investment, the Sienese *Monte* funds never approached the size of the Florentine.[49] The proportion of investors to the total population, however, was very much larger. The records of 1480 contain the names of more than three thousand investors, all but a few with shares worth less than a thousand *lire,* none with shares worth more than about forty thousand *lire.*[50] This represents a steady growth in numbers of shareholders and a more modest but still marked increase in the size of investments over the course of the century.[51] As suggested earlier, Siena became from an economic standpoint a city of large and small *rentiers.* The political effect was also significant, for most Sienese now had some kind of financial stake in Siena's future. It was in their own interest to encourage equal justice and efficient administration, to pay for defense, and even to respond positively to changes in the constitution.

One must not suppose that the Sienese studied their constitution and set about reordering it according to some rational plan. That the constitution had structure they were well aware. But it was a structure produced by long organic growth, hardly something to be swept cleanly away in favor of another. The idea would have puzzled and shocked them; even the revolutionaries of the thirteenth and fourteenth centuries held fast to the essential form if not the spirit of the regimes they overthrew. But at the same time, the Sienese were willing to experiment a bit, to patch up places they considered weak, to add an institution or take one away. Such an addition was the *balìa*. This may be defined as an extraordinary committee, invariably composed of leading citizens, appointed for a short term by the councils with "full and ample" authority in a closely restricted sphere.[52] *Balìe* were occasioned by emergencies, most often wars, when money had to be raised, troops hired, and the machinery of diplomacy set quickly in motion. The aim was to circumvent the councils and the *Concistoro,* whose responsibilities were already great, whose methods were slow and sometimes unsure, and whose point of view was fundamentally corporate. A second aim was to involve the city's elder statesmen in major policy decisions, to commit them and their followers to a course of action. *Balìe* served, in a sense, as republican substitutes for tyranny, providing unity, authority, and efficiency on a temporary basis, and most republics had them. Only at Siena, however, did the institution reach maturity. From being at first an occasional, expedient tool of the regular governing bodies, it became an essential adjunct to them, and finally replaced them altogether. They remained in existence, but pale shadows of their former selves, the permanent *Magistrato della Balìa* having gathered all important legislative and executive functions into its hands. Nothing better illustrates the triumph of statehood over communalism at Siena.

The crucial decade was the 1950s. For some years, the Sienese had been under the heavy pressure of war. Resources were running low, and a few of the governors were flirting with the King of Naples. In July, 1455, the councils created a *balìa* of fifteen, five from each of the dominant *monti,* to finish the war and arrange a peace.[53] The men selected were heads of their *monti,* respected, experienced.[54] They were granted authority equal to that of the *Concistoro* and for the first time met apart from it. Though their term of office was stated as two months, they in fact continued to sit for more than a year, at which time they were replaced by fifteen others much like themselves.[55] Never again was Siena without a *balìa.*

The accretion of legislative and executive power by the now-permanent *Magistrato della Balìa* began before the 1450s were out. Earlier *balìe* had been forbidden to interfere in all but clearly specified affairs of state.[56] The orders given to the *Balìa* of 1456 allowed for greater freedom of action. This *Balìa* was elected "for the safety of the city, *contado,* and the men and jurisdiction of Siena, and for the conservation of peace and liberty."[57] It was prohibited only from "laying hands on the *Monte del Sale* [*sic*] . . . [or] imposing any ordinary forced loan. . . ."[58] Other government business could and most did come under its purview; the contrast between its activities and those of its predecessors is striking.[59] What had before concerned the *Concistoro* now concerned the *Balìa.*[60] The councils, though retaining the right to re-elect the *Balìa* periodically, gave its day-to-day work their stamp of approval with little question.[61] Again, the process was unplanned. Once the Sienese found an answer to their chief constitutional problem, they simply let cir-

le compagnie di ventura nella seconda metà del secolo XIV (Civitanova-Marche, 1898).

7. The economic history of Siena has not yet been written, and generalizations of this kind are tentative at best. This one is drawn from an examination of the city's income (*entrata*) recorded in the books of the treasurers' office and of various *gabelle* for the years 1390, 1402, 1406, 1409, 1419, 1425, 1435, 1439, and 1444. See Archivio di Stato di Siena (hereafter ASS), *Biccherna*, Nos. 277, 288, 293, 301, 308, and 313; and *Regolatori*, Nos. 6, 8, and 9.

8. The conclusion about landownership is based on a study of several hundred *denunzie*, real and personal property reports, for the last quarter of the fifteenth century. For details, see the author's "Sienese Society in the Renaissance," *Comparative Studies in Society and History*, II, 4 (July, 1960). On investment in the government, see notes 50, 51, and 52.

9. There is no study of the *Gentiluomini*. On the *Nove*, see particularly W. Bowski, "The *Buon Governo* of Siena (1287–1355)," *Speculum*, XXXVII (1962), and on the *Dodici*, G. Luchaire, *Documenti per la storia dei rivolgimenti politici del Comune di Siena dal 1354 al 1369* . . . (Lyons, 1906). A contemporary calls the *Riformatori* "all artisans"; *Cronica di Paolo di Tommaso Montauri* in the new edition of L. Muratori, *Rerum Italicarum Scriptores*, Tome XV (Bologna, 1939), VI, 709. Events surrounding their origin demonstrate that the bulk of the *Popolari* were of similar economic and social condition.

10. For a fuller analysis, see the author's article cited in note 8. Wealth was not, of course, the only criterion. Ancient lineage and a tradition of public service also counted. The situation was not too different from the Florentine, though the spread within the governing class was narrower; see Martines, *op. cit.*, chapter II.

11. On the *Concistoro*, see the *Inventario* of the *Archivio del Concistoro*, edited by the Sienese archivists (Rome, 1952).

12. The acts of the *Consiglio del Popolo* are included with those of the *Consiglio generale*. Usually the two councils took joint action, though a few special duties fell to the former, selecting candidates for posts in the *contado*, for example. Not all *residuti* sat in the *Consiglio del Popolo*, the number being set at 190 in 1448; see ASS, *Regolatori*, No. 1, p. 200.

13. The selections for *podestà* in October, 1453, listed eight *Nove*, eight *Popolari*, and only four *Riformatori;* see ASS, *Consiglio generale*, No. 222, pp. 155–56bis. In the treasury reform of 1429 (see note 42), it was ordered that the new office of *Camarlingo* would be filled only by *Nove* and *Popolari;* see ASS, *Lira*, No. 437, p. 1. There are other examples.

14. In the *Consiglio generale* nominated by the *Concistoro* in January, 1455, there were ninety-five *Gentiluomini*, and sixty-eight each of *Nove*, *Riformatori*, and *Popolari;* see ASS, *Consiglio generale*, No. 226, pp. 294bis–96. The proportion had been set in 1426; see ASS, *Consiglio generale*, No. 211, p. 31 ff.

15. ASS, *Consiglio generale*, nos. 226, p. 123 and 222, pp. 155–55bis.

16. This is probably a conservative estimate. The only figures one has to work with are the total population, between 13,000 and 15,000, and the number of men who had sat in the *Concistoro*, 460 in 1447 (ASS, *Regolatori*, No. 1, p. 200). Adding the active *monte* members who had not yet sat in the *Concistoro*—certainly more than 460— to wives, children (political majority was twenty-five years), dependents, and retainers, the number of "constituents" must have come to more than 5,000.

17. Some seventy-six new families were accepted between 1385 and 1425. After 1425, the number is smaller, only twenty-one, for example, between 1440 and 1480. See A. Aurieri, *Raccolta di notizie riguardante le famiglie nobili di Siena* (manuscript in ASS at A.15), *passim*.

18. See the three chief narratives: R. Langton-Douglas, *A History of Siena* (New York, 1902); F. Schevill, *Siena, the Story of a Medieval Commune* (New York, 1909); and E. G. Gardner, *The Story of Siena and San Gimignano* (New York, 1926).

19. The revolts of 1403 and 1456 have not been studied; see O. Malavolti, *Historia de' fatti e guerre de' Senesi* . . . (Venice, 1599). On the events after 1480, see the author's unpublished Ph.D dissertation, "The Rise of Pandolfo Petrucci at Siena" (Columbia University, 1959).

20. *Ibid.*

21. On the paintings, see N. Rubenstein, "Political Ideas in Sienese Art," *Journal of the Warburg and Courtauld Institutês*, XXI (July–December, 1958). Dati's political ideas are best expressed in his

orations to newly elected *signori;* see *Augustini Dati Senensis Opera* (Siena, 1503).

22. Again, Malavolti, *op. cit.,* is the best published source for Siena's involvement in Italian affairs.

23. U. Morandi, *I. Giusdicenti dell'antico Stato Senese* (Rome, 1962), p. 29. (This is no. 17 of the "Quaderni" of the "Rassegna degli Archivi di Stato.")

24. See ASS, *Regolatori,* no. 1, 124bis, 125bis ff.

25. See the listing of statutes with their dates in the *Guida-Inventario,* Sienese archivists, ed. (Rome, 1951), I, 77 ff.

26. See, for example, the *statuti* of Asciano, Montalcino, and Sarteano; ASS, *Statuti delle citta, terre, e castelli,* nos. 8, 69 and 169.

27. See, for example, ASS, *Consistoro,* no. 1591, *passim.*

28. ASS, *Regolatori,* No. 1, pp. 127bis, 190.

29. The accounts are conveniently available in the books of the *Regolatori,* at ASS, *Regolatori,* Nos. 6, 7, and 8. Many petitions are contained in ASS, *Consiglio generale,* Nos. 225, 226, and 227 for the 1450s.

30. ASS, *Regolatori,* No. 1, pp. 227bis–28.

31. Morandi, *op. cit.,* is an excellent study of the legal arrangements of the Sienese *contado.*

32. "In prima. Connosia cosa che per lo passato sieno stati facti molti statuti ordini et riformagioni e quali non sonno stati observati. Volendo per l'avenire non si faccia per simile modo, ma ciascuno stia sotto el giogo dela ragione et viva correctamente per honore et utile di comune et del presente reggimento. . . ." ASS, *Regolatori,* No. 1, p. 101.

33. ". . . piena auctorita jurisdictione et officio di fare observare tucti li statuti ordini et riformagioni facti et quelli che si farano per l'avenire . . ."; *ibid.*

34. *Ibid.*

35. ASS, *Regolatori,* No. 1, p. 210bis.

36. A brief description of each of the courts and magistrates is contained in the Sienese archivists' *Guida-Inventario,* previously cited.

37. The usual phrase was "nessuna persona di qualunque stato et conditione"; see the copies of edicts contained in ASS, *Regolatori,* No. 1,

pp. 164, 207bis., and ASS, *Ufficiali di Custodia*, No. 1, May 23, 1460. The point may be illustrated by two mid-century cases of slander. In the first, Pietro di Nanni di Dominico Bandini was fined 10 *lire* for calling Minocio di Mariano de Minocio Panilini "uno latroncello." Both were *monte* members of little consequence, Panilini being a *Popolare* and a "new man." In the second case, Antonio di Naddo Colombini, of an ancient and wealthy family of *Nove,* was fined 300 lire for saying to Antonio di Tuce, his social inferior, "Tu sie [*sic*] uno latroncello, ponitor di taglie, et sei uno robatore." See ASS, *Capitano di giustizia*, No. 44.

38. See the references cited in notes 28 and 29. Petitions for tax relief are to be found in the *deliberazioni* of the *Concistoro* and *Consiglio generale.*

39. ASS, *Regolatori,* No. 1, p. 210 and *Balìa,* No. 4, pp. 5–5bis.

40. The *Auditori di Rota,* for example, were created in 1503 to replace the *Podestà;* Morandi, *op. cit.,* p. 9.

41. There were perhaps a hundred bureaucrats at work in Siena in the 1450s (see the salary list at ASS, *Regolatori,* No. 1, pp. 215–216). Technically they were elected in the usual way, but skill and experience seem to have counted, and many of them spent their lives going from one office to another.

42. The *Lira* dates from about 1200. For its history see L. Banchi, "Gli ordinamenti economici dei comuni toscani nel Medioevo, e segnatamente del comune di Siena," *Archivio storico italiano,* IV, III (1879), and the same author's "La Lira, la Tavola delle possessioni, e le Preste nella Republica di Siena," *Archivio storico italiano,* III, VII (1868).

43. See the *Inventario* of the *Archivio della Biccherna* edited by the Sienese archivists (Rome, 1953), pp. xii–xiii.

44. This office was founded in 1363, but it took some decades to establish itself, and its important work dates from the early fifteenth century; see the *Guida-Inventario,* I, p. 287.

45. The multifarious non-financial interests and duties of the *Regolatori* are recorded in ASS, *Regolatori,* no. 1. They ranged from enforcing the sumptuary laws to acting as a court in cases involving the Jews to supervising the fountains.

46. A brief discussion of the *Monte* may be found in the *Guida-Inventario,* I, pp. 238ff.

47. The law is contained in ASS, *Lira,* no. 437.

48. On the *preste,* see the *Guida-Inventario,* I, pp. 267 ff., and the article by Banchi cited in note 42.

49. For information about the Florentine *Monte,* the author is indebted to Marvin B. Becker and Richard Goldthwaite. The only published study is L. Marx, "The Financial Oligarchy in Florence under Lorenzo," in E. F. Jacobs, ed., *Italian Renaissance Studies* (London, 1960).

50. The "creditors" of the *Monti* in 1480 are listed in ASS, *Lira,* Nos. 448, 449, and 450. Their "credits" are entered in *lire.* There were four *lire* to a florin.

51. This conclusion is based on a comparison of earlier and later books listing "creditors." A particularly rapid increase in numbers seems to have taken place between 1460 and 1480: the book for the *Terzo* of San Martino contains about five hundred names for the first date and about eleven hundred for the second. See ASS, Nos. 444 and 449.

52. The best thing on the subject is the "Introduction" to the Sienese archivists' *Inventario* of the *Archivio di Balìa* (Rome, 1957).

53. ASS, *Consiglio generale,* No. 227, p. 61bis.

54. The list of members is contained in ASS, *Balìa,* No. 1, p. 1.

55. ASS, *Balìa,* No. 2, p. 4bis.

56. A typical set of restrictions is the one for the *balìa* of September 1392 (ASS, *Regolatori* No. 1, p. 38bis).
Non possono fare impresa di guerra.
Non possono vendere o impegnare terre del comune di Siena.
Non possono ribandire alchuno sbandito del comune di Siena.
Non possono concedere licentia di portare arme.
Non possono concedere alchuna immunita o franchigia.
Non possono concedere arbitrio ad alchuno Rectore di Siena.
Non possono rifirmare alchuno Rectore, o officiale del Comune di Siena.
Non possono conducere soldati da pie o da cavallo.
Non possono fare provisione ad alchuno cittadino o contadino senza el Consiglio Generale.
Non possono fare contra lo stato del Signore misser lo conte [di Virtu Siena was a *"signoria"* of Giangaleazzo Visconti at this time].
The restrictions for the last of the old *balìe* of early 1455 are not

much different; see C. Paoli, "Del Magistrato di Balìa nella Republica di Siena," *Atti della . . . R. Accademia dei Rozzi* (Siena, 1879), doc. 1.

57. ". . . per la salute della citta, contado, et li homini et jurisdictione di Siena et per la conservatione della pace et liberta"; see ASS, *Balìa*, No. 2, p. 30.

58. ". . . non potendo tocchare per alcuno modo il monte del sale . . . et non possino ponere alcuna presta ordinaria per alcuno modo ala citta . . ."; *ibid.*

59. See ASS, *Balìa*, No. 2, *passim*, which may be compared with ASS, *Balìa*, No. 1.

60. One should compare the record books of the *Concistoro* before and after 1455. ASS, *Concistoro*, Nos. 500–530 with 540–560, for example.

61. The books of the *Consiglio generale* may also be compared; ASS, *Consiglio generale*, Nos. 225 and 226 with Nos. 227 and 228, for example.

THE EARLY RENAISSANCE
IN ENGLAND*

D E N Y S   H A Y

University of Edinburgh

L ewis Einstein wrote in the preface of his *Italian Renaissance in England:* "The history of the Italian Renaissance in the countries of Europe outside of Italy still remains a subject half explored." He wrote this in 1902; sixty years later it is still broadly true for England and perhaps for other parts of Europe. There is no book to which one can turn for a general and authoritative survey of the Renaissance in England, apart from Einstein's own book, which has many of the structural faults of a pioneering venture and is marred by frequent errors of fact. It is true that what one may call the prehistory of the English Renaissance has been written, by W. F. Schirmer in 1931, and, even more completely for the fifteenth century, by Roberto Weiss (1940; new edition 1957). For a survey of the full flowering of the Tudor period we must consult Douglas Bush's little book, a quite remarkable performance if we remember it was composed of lectures delivered in 1939, but strongest on the Continental side and on Milton and in any case not pretending to be systematic or thorough. And ten years ago we had the brilliant, perverse volume contributed by the late C. S. Lewis to the Oxford History of English Literature, with its cumbersome

* A draft of this essay was read to the Renaissance Conference at Austin, Texas, in April, 1964.

title, *English literature in the XVI century excluding drama* (1954)
—a title which conceals what by any reckoning is one of the finest
pieces of critical writing of this century.

It is noteworthy that the authors cited are literary men: Schirmer,
Bush, and Lewis are historians of English literature; Weiss is a
professor of Italian. Now this monopoly of English Renaissance
studies by scholars of literature is not quite entire: if we were to
list monographic studies of various aspects of the Renaissance in
England, various articles and books devoted to individual humanists,
we would find a sizeable number of studies by historians of art, of
ideas, of religion, of institutions. Even a few scholars who are
historians *simpliciter* have made modest contributions. But they
have done so, one might say, rather by the way, leaving any attempt
at generalities to their literary colleagues. It is of course true that
no one could accuse either Professor Bush or Professor Lewis of
neglecting ideas. One can, however, accuse them fairly enough of
neglecting the historical background and this, to my way of thinking, is a serious defect in their work. Lewis's history as such will
be found on pp. 56–59: three and a half pages of the 558 pages of
his text. Historians are more generous: Mackie's volume on the
early Tudors has a whole chapter devoted to "The achievement of
the Age," and so has J. B. Black in his volume on Elizabeth's reign.
Oxford editors, it seems, have been firmer with their historians than
with their *belles lettristes*. What is so depressing in all this is, however, the divorce between civilization and the changing public situation. The literary specialist and the historian each gives a guilty
acknowledgment that his world is only part of the world, and then
proceeds as if it were the world in its entirety.

If one compares this with the way the Renaissance in Italy has
been treated the contrast is striking. One may feel (I do myself
feel) that Burckhardt's history is somewhat oddly conceived, and
that it fails in some respects to be integrated with the body of his
book. But it is there, big and plain, as the first section of his book.
Since then there has been a steady acknowledgment of the necessity
of associating history pure and history cultural in discussions of the
Renaissance in Italy—especially when written by non-Italians. You
will hardly need to be reminded of the brilliant way politics and
ideas have been woven together by Hans Baron. More recently others

have followed the same path who are, or who would regard it as an honor to be, counted as his disciples.

A short essay is not the best occasion on which to try to remedy the position with regard to the English Renaissance, even when it is only the early period, down to 1535 or thereabouts, which is under review.[1] What follows is a mere sketch. I shall begin by a short assessment of the political and social scene in the fifteenth and early sixteenth centuries and then go on to consider this as a framework for the reception and development of Renaissance concepts and practices.

C. L. Kingsford characterized the Lancastrian and Yorkist period as one of "prejudice and promise" and at first sight one is inclined to regard the prejudice as more noticeable than the promise. It is traditionally regarded as an age of war: Henry IV seized the throne and murdered the deposed Richard II; similar brutal changes of monarch occurred in 1471, 1483, and 1485; Henry V died of camp fever and only Edward IV died in his own bed. The domestic strife engendered during Richard II's reign lasted till the invasion of France in 1415. Then there was war abroad till 1453. By that time the country was in the thick of the disorders, local and central, which are collectively termed the Wars of the Roses. These were to double the rate at which noble families were normally extinguished from natural causes and to encourage the gentry to the dubious and often fugitive loyalties of "bastard feudalism."

Yet it would be wrong to regard the fifteenth century in England as a period of anarchy. We can apply to the whole period the judicious judgment of Bishop Stubbs on the dark days of the 1440s and 1450s: "The kingdom . . . was exhausted, improverished, and in disorder, but it was not unconstitutionally ruled."[2] Much of the exhaustion and improverishment was, we should remember, the product not of kings and lords but of general economic processes which, from the early fourteenth century, had clouded the whole European scene. It can, indeed, be argued that the violence of aggressive Englishmen on the Continent under Edward III and, later, the bitterness of the civil war in the next century, reflect economic pressures on the gentry and nobles, who found it harder to live comfortably off their manors than they had in the boom days of Henry III and the Lord Edward.

At any rate, in all the troubles of the fifteenth century legitimism prevailed; the dynasty was never at stake, and so the Crown was, in an important sense, above the battle. More than that, the magnates and their supporters were now turning to the King in ways which would have seemed inconceivable a century earlier. From the King flowed the captaincies and the keeperships, the honors and the perquisites of government. And, in a paradoxical way, the very acts of rebellion and war against the King made a stronger man of his successor, for the attainders and forfeitures of his discomfited rival's party offered a cozy way of keeping them obedient—a cumulative process, from which the Tudors were greatly to benefit, as Dr. J. R. Lander has demonstrated.[3] Of one thing there can surely be no doubt: by the 1470s the English King was stronger than he ever had been before. If we compare Edward IV or Richard III or Henry VII with Edward III or even Edward I we can see that whatever else the Wars of the Roses did, they did not weaken monarchy.

The foreign wars and the domestic wars, together with the economic troubles which were their concomitants if not their causes, not only did not seriously hamper the developing authority of the King, but they may even have provoked some of the more interesting innovations of the period. Foreign war stimulated diplomacy; domestic war strengthened a more modern notion of the court, while the council, permanent and professional, buttressed the administration by even bigger bastions of paper. In each of these spheres— diplomacy, the court, and the council—we see, of course, the King, but we also see the secretary.[4] The major administrative developments, the main new factors in the constitutional scene of later medieval England, were the inventive use of household machinery for government, the chamber as an exchequer, the signet as the most lively of the seals, and, though dimly enough at first, the secretarial maid-of-all-work who was to become, by the middle of the sixteenth century, the chief dynamo in the administrative machine. The court, the council, and the secretary, whose operations constituted the basis of Tudor government, were all present in the fifteenth century.

There is no doubt of the cultural consequences of the mounting tide of conciliar activity under Henry VII and Henry VIII; equally the diplomatic activity of the early Tudor Kings made imperative demands on the country's intellectual resources. Why do we not find an earlier adoption of Italian methods, manners, and attitudes which were obviously capable of responding so admirably to the new needs of government and which were to come in rapidly in the sixteenth century? Why do we not find in the fifteenth century the indigenous "professional" humanist (to use Roberto Weiss's useful term)? Why is there no Thomas More at the court of Edward IV? Part of the answer to this lies, I believe, in the inaccessibility of *early*-fifteenth-century Italian innovations, enveloped as they were in the bourgeois republicanism of Florence. It was not until the second half of the fifteenth century that Italian courts adopted, and to some extent modified, the message of Salutati, Bruni, and the rest. It is significant that the Englishmen who were customers of Vespasiano da Bisticci were for the most part aristocrats: Gloucester, Tiptoft, Grey;[5] their tastes were for what was solid, old-fashioned in Renaissance scholarship, and for what married most happily with the established hierarchies of Church and State, with the moral and educational traditions of Northern Europe. This leads to the real reason for the sluggishness of the English: the relative success with which the ancient arrangements coped with the slowly evolving social and cultural situation.

The rise of the gentry in England, about which we have heard so much in recent years in connection with the Elizabethan and Jacobean periods,[6] is a long story. Whether we can see it happening in the twelfth century, as Professor R. W. Southern has recently argued,[7] may be debated but there is no question about the fourteenth and fifteenth centuries. English public affairs at this time are incomprehensible if we do not take account of the thrusting ambitions of hundreds of small landowners, rising and falling like the handful of peers and, in much the same way, adding to their properties by marriage and purchase. They cling to the great, they throng Parliament, they climb the ladder of preferment in Church and State.[8] And, not least, they increasingly go to school and university.

One of the silent revolutions of the later Middle Ages is the way the old fabric of ecclesiastical education—song schools, grammar schools, universities—housed a new lay clientele with no intentions of pursuing the traditional curriculum to its logical end. Boys learned their letters not to become priests but in order to become

more effective laymen, in order to enter the law or at any rate to
have a smattering of law so useful in a litigious society where titles
to property were nearly always confused and doubtful, in order to
perform the arithmetic of trade, commerce and estate management,
in order to staff the administration of King, nobles, and bishops who
were turning now more and more to the literate laity and away from
clerical servants. When I refer to a silent revolution I do not, of
course, mean that no new schools and colleges were founded. They
were, and in impressive numbers. I mean rather that new institutions
did not seriously alter old practices. The only change we can really
see is the development of the ideal of a devout laity alongside the
educational ideal of a well-educated clergy; and even this is hardly
evident before its explicit statement in Colet's foundation at St.
Paul's in 1512. The provision of facilities for an instructed and
religious laity was taken much further in other parts of Northern
Europe in the fifteenth century and is best seen in the educational
arrangements associated with the Brethren of the Common Life.
In England, although we do not have any organized and self-
conscious educational movement, just as we do not have any systematic group mysticism, something of the same spirit prevails.

How literate were the laity? In London, where there was relatively
plentiful provision of schools, Miss Thrupp reached the conclusion
that in "the merchant class . . . all the men read English and most
of them had some training in Latin";[9] a survey of a still bigger
section of the London population in the mid-fifteenth century suggests that about 40 per cent of males were literate.[10] Later still,
Thomas More's guess that "farre more than fowre partes of all the
whole divided into tenne, coulde never reade englishe yet" suggests
that something approaching 60 per cent could,[11] though we may
suspect that reading did not take writing with it. As for the country
at large, composed mainly of agricultural laborers, the literate were
doubtless in a tiny minority—perhaps the fraction of one per cent
of Bishop Stephen Gardiner's estimate in 1547.[12] This does not
mean, of course, that no peasants acquired education, though we
may suspect that those who did soon left the plough and that there
were not many others like Robert Wyllyams, who, at the time
Gardiner was writing his letter, demonstrated his literacy with an
inscription in a book he read, "Keppynge Shepe uppon Seynbury

Hill."[13] If literate shepherds were rare, however, it was quite a different matter with their masters. The papers of the Pastons, the Lelys, the Stonors show country gentlemen of an extremely articulate kind and C. L. Kingsford's judgment is well-founded:

> . . . Capacity to read and write was no longer an accomplishment confined to the clerical class. The wives and sisters of country gentlemen could often write as well as their husbands and brothers, and both they and their servants could and commonly did keep regular household accounts.[14]

Moreover, while a hack dominie was retained in such households to write letters and to teach the children, the menfolk of the family were sent seriously to school and to university, as we can see in the case of the Pastons, whose very rise was attributed by a malicious enemy to the borrowing of money by the husbandman Clement Paston to send his son, the future justice, to school. By the end of the century a Paston had gone to Eton, then in the process of becoming that mysterious English phenomenon, a public, that is a private, school.[15] Eton, Winchester, and other establishments had been intended for the middling gentry, and the middling gentry responded.

It is necessary to insist on the political, social, and economic background, because it goes far to explain the character of the English response to the new developments in Italy. There are many contacts between England and Italy in the fifteenth century but they are not really productive until the early sixteenth century, and even then seem gradual rather than dramatic.

Nonetheless there are some pointers in the fifteenth century to the course events later took. We find, for example, a few isolated cases of the royal secretariate responding to its duties in a novel way. In 1412 a diplomatic occasion provoked an English clerk to conscious effort at stylish Latinity as can be seen in two letters printed recently by Monsieur Pocquet du Haut-Jussé.[16] Much more impressive is the scholarship of Thomas Bekynton, who was royal secretary from 1438 to 1443 and who, we read, "conceived classical learning not only as an intellectual attainment but also as a thing of practical value."[17] Professor Weiss attributes to Bekynton's influence the "literary qualifications" of not fewer than six other royal servants and diplomats. In addition the secretaries of the fifteenth century number James Goldwell, later Ambassador to Rome and Bishop of Norwich,[18] whose remarkable collection of humanist manuscripts was bequeathed to All Souls.[19]

The secretaries demand scrutiny because it is obvious that theirs was a sphere of activity in which the Renaissance was relevant. The secretaries, even though they themselves were technically clergy, headed a department which was thoroughly lay: the signet clerks are laymen from 1437, "a change . . . in line with the general tendency of the period, but . . . the earliest and most complete example."[20] Lay professionalism like this involves continuities not least because it involved (as it did not do with the clergy who served the Crown) a notion of office as property. And in the secretaries and in the council to which they were more closely attached, continuity is what we find. A highly expert councillor was worth his weight in gold and we should not have been surprised, as perhaps some of us were, when Dr. Lander showed us how many men were common to the councils of Edward IV, Richard III, and Henry VII.[21] One such figure is Oliver King. King, a very well-educated man (Cambridge and Orléans), was French secretary (1475–80) and then secretary to both Edward IV and his son (1480–83) and to Henry VII (1487–95). He was the first secretary to become a bishop while in office and under him the office became in a sense one of state: it became "public."[22]

The last decade of the fifteenth century and the first decade of the sixteenth see these processes carried further and consolidated. The Poet Laureate is Bernard André, from early in the reign.[23] A Latin secretary makes his appearance in 1495.[24] Three years earlier we find the first appointment of a King's Librarian.[25] Oliver King is succeeded in 1500 by Thomas Ruthal, who could be described not only as a man of affairs, but as a man of letters, too, for he is (I think) the first secretary to be the subject of a dedication, by the Italian nuncio Pietro Griffo, of the oration he would have made to Henry VII if the King had not died.[26] The episode also shows how significant a figure the secretary had become by this date. Pietro Griffo's name reminds us that the Italians have come to town. Professor Weiss has listed them for the fifteenth century. By the early sixteenth they are establishing themselves: Henry VII makes Carmelianus his Latin secretary and invites Polydore Vergil to write the history of England. Even more important, the humanities are beginning to get into the schools. The first schoolmaster who can fairly be said to be a humanist is John Alnwykill, teaching grammar at Magdalen College School from about 1481,[27] the earliest of a remarkable series of teachers there.

This is not to suggest that with the Tudors there was a steady infiltration of Italians, bearing in their new civilization on platters, so to speak. Much that was both original and Continental came from Northern Europe: Erasmus directly owed little to Italy, and from his first visit in 1499 his was the most potent single influence on the humanities as such in England. The first two Royal Librarians were Flemings.[28] The Italians were in any case men of the second rank even when, like Vergil, they were pretty influential. What strikes one about the decades on either side of 1500 is a new mood of receptivity and an atmosphere propitious to the establishment of new ideas and practices. This can probably be positively demonstrated by the book-buying habits of libraries and private persons, a subject that has yet to be properly examined.[29] But that a fresh air was blowing through England is surely evident from the emergence of three men whom we can reasonably describe as really important native humanists: Richard Pace, Thomas More, and Thomas Elyot. Each of these remarkable men was very largely the product of an English environment—More and Elyot were so almost completely; each was involved, because of his talents, in public service; and each was a man of the old order.

It is this more general spirit of receptiveness which makes itself felt by the end of the fifteenth century. Scholars and clergy had visited Italy for centuries; many of those who went there in the early and mid-fifteenth century had acquired a taste for the new humanities.[30] But in the Yorkist period to some extent, and much more under Henry VII, the aptitude and abilities of the new type of scholar found support and encouragement in high places, and notably from prelates like Morton, Fisher, and Fox. Above all they were fostered at court. This is seen not only in the Italians like Carmelianus and Vergil but in more permanent ways—especially in the new foundations at Cambridge, for it was the circle round Henry VII's mother that was responsible for changes which, whether intended so or not, began to "humanize" the universities. André and Linacre,

appointed tutors to Prince Arthur, and Skelton, tutor to the future
Henry VIII, are the first of a continuous series of humanist instruc-
tors for the royal children of Tudor England.[31] One must always
take Erasmus with two grains of salt—one of the genuine problems
of early Tudor scholarship is that one is compelled to see so much
through Erasmus's spectacles—yet his enthusiastic picture of England at the turn of the century culminates with his meeting Prince
Henry at Eltham, and it carries conviction. It must indeed have
seemed to the humanists propitious that the Crown was to pass in
1509 into the hands of a boy brought up in the modern manner.

Henry VIII as King did not in fact spend much time in writing
Latin exercises or conversing with elderly scholars: his personal
letters and his spoken language were mostly "vulgar" in the technical sense of the term. Moreover, the humanists who had found
favor in his father's court gradually found themselves squeezed out
by a fresh group. But the new men were also humanists or humanist
trained and the processes by which the humanities were integrated
into the fabric of public life continued at an accelerated pace. In
1516 Richard Pace, trained by Langton and in Italy, experienced
as secretary to Cardinal Bainbridge in Rome, became the first
thoroughly trained humanist secretary of the King. At just the same
time Bishop Richard Fox's creation, Corpus Christi College, opened
its doors at Oxford—a *trilingue* on the same model as Busleyden's
great institution which was to begin the next year at Louvain.

But the interesting point about developments under both Henry
VII and Henry VIII is not their inherent originality. Colleges had
been founded earlier and so had schools. Pace, as we have seen,
had predecessors somewhat like him in background if less impressive
as scholars. What *is* remarkable is the way that the new type of
scholar found himself becoming indispensable. Colet's foundation
of St. Paul's (1510) was in many ways an orthodox and conventional step: the devout dean had as his aim the promotion of
Christian morality. But the men who became high masters there,
from William Lilly onwards, were humanist grammarians on the
Italian model and what struck one Italian writing in the 1530s was
not that St. Paul's had produced devotion but that the youth of
London who went there were "more civilized," *politior;*[32] fifteen
years earlier Pace had referred to the school in the same way.[33]

There was nothing particularly original about the statutes of Alcock's foundation of Jesus College at Cambridge, or Smith's of Brasenose at Oxford, though the same Italian linked them with Fisher's Christ's and John's and Fox's Corpus as part of the diffusion among the English of *bonarum artium ac disciplinarum studia*.[34] By the 1530s, one feels, the steps taken in Henry VII's reign and earlier seemed predestined to accomplish a revolution.[35] The Lady Margaret, one must say, looking at her severe face in St. John's hall, wrought better than she knew; and so, perhaps, did Fisher.[36]

Professor Zeeveld has underlined for us further consequences of these developments.[37] Not only did Wolsey, with the active support of his master, provide a further college at Oxford—and one intended in its way to be as innovating as Corpus—but in the household of his bastard Thomas Winter he supported on the Continent a number of young scholars, as did Henry VIII in the household of Reginald Pole. Wolsey, indeed, stands out well in any examination of the new learning at court. Ex-grammar schoolmaster as he was, he had the sense to admire and use Richard Pace, who repaid his master by a glowing page in the *De Fructu*;[38] and Wolsey (we sometimes tend to forget) picked out another man who had knocked about in Italy, Thomas Cromwell.

Pace's *De Fructu* came out of the press of Froben at Basle in 1516. The occasion for its composition is described by the author in his dedication to Colet. While traveling back from Rome some years earlier, he had met at dinner "one of those whom we call gentlemen (*generosos*)." This gentleman, hearing one of the party praise good education, burst into a tirade against scholarship. "What rubbish," he cried. "All learned men are paupers—even Erasmus complains of poverty. By God's body, I would rather my son was hanged than that he should be studious. Gentlemen's sons should be able to sound the hunting horn, hunt cunningly, neatly train, and use a hawk. The study of literature should be left to the sons of peasants." Pace is provoked into a sharp reply: when the King needs someone to reply to a foreign ambassador, he will turn not to the horn-blowing gentleman but to the educated rustic.[39] As Mr. Fritz Caspari says, this is why gentlemen sought education;[40] the point has been stressed, in a wider context, by J. H. Hexter in his paper on the education of the aristocracy.[41] Pace wrote in Latin. In 1531 Thomas Elyot published his *Governour* in English.[42] One might say the battle was won, for in addition to summarizing, in an English context, the doctrines of learned public service, the notion of "true nobility" and so on, which come out of the earliest stages of the Italian Renaissance, its Florentine and republican matrix, Elyot did more. He introduced the gentlemen of England to the Courtier: to *Castiglione's* courtier in particular but in a larger sense to the whole complex of the Italian Renaissance in its late-fifteenth- early-sixteenth-century state, when it had moved into an ambience of popes and princes, an ambience obviously compatible with the social situation in Northern Europe.[43]

The moment that letters could take a man to fame and fortune, of course, there arose another set of problems and it is an interesting comment on the Wolsey period that at least one of the Cardinal's protégés felt that this had already happened. Thomas Lupset, writing in 1529, complained that the scholar's ambitions have become no different from those of other men of affairs: "The same confusion is with us scholers: for our first study is to get promotion, to get these goodis, to live welthily."[44] This observation comes from the man into whose mouth Starkey, about 1535, put the observations that "every honest man . . . ought . . . first to make himself perfit, and then to commune the same perfection to other"; and "whosoever . . . drawn by the sweetness of his studies . . . leaveth the cure of the common weal and policy . . . doth manifest wrong to his country and friends."[45]

I have tried to point out in this brief survey how the political and social structure in England during the fifteenth century gradually found in Italian experience matters and methods which could easily fit into a situation in which the royal court had a prominence it had lacked in earlier centuries; the gentry and nobles, flocking to the traditional schools and universities, were ready for doctrines which would justify both their increasing literacy and their concentration of interest in the court. Much of this had happened by the mid-1530s and I have chosen to stop there for several reasons. The next steps consisted, I believe, in the rapid establishment of the grammar or public school as an institution. Italian influences pure and simple come into their own in the later sixteenth century, in educational theory, in courtly doctrine, in the incipient mystique of the Grand Tour. The two major figures of the early Renaissance in England, More and Elyot, owe very little to direct contact with Italy. By the Elizabethan period Italy was a very potent force in literature, art, and scholarship.[46]

In this later stage, in the full flowering of the English Renaissance, we move into an essentially vernacular world. The "golden English" of Professor Lewis's periodization, it may be suspected, owed far more than he allows to the fundamental influence of Latin grammar. Are there any signs that "golden English" is on the way before More's death? There is plenty of evidence that the matter preoccupied authors. If Elyot thought that classical Latin writers had "incomparably . . . more grace and delectation" than English permitted,[47] More disagreed:

> For as for that our tongue is called barbarous, is but a fantasy: for so is, as every learned man knoweth, every strange language to other. And if they would call it barren of words, there is no doubt but it is plenteous enough to express our minds in anything whereof one man hath used to speak with another.[48]

More has, of course, been acclaimed with some justification as himself the first embodiment of a modern and effective prose, and when R. W. Chambers argues, as he does,[49] that More's style follows the lead of devotional writings of the previous two centuries this is further evidence of the influence of the literate laity of whom I have spoken. What can, however, surely not be denied is that More and others of his generation who wrote English with a fair degree of vigor, economy, and variety, were to a man the products of Latin scholarship. It is as and when the grammar school education of a new type permeates English letters in the middle decades of the sixteenth century that a generation emerges ready to produce and enjoy the vernacular Renaissance of the late Tudor and early Jacobean period. Insofar as this was anticipated before the mid-1530s it was because a few men had enjoyed the full experience of Latin. A recent illustration of this can be seen in Professor Sylvester's edition of More's *Richard III*.[50] One may suspect moreover that as much was done for the language by conscientious composition and translation at a level below that of a genius like

Thomas More. In Elyot, for example, we find a deliberate attempt spread over a lifetime to make English prose adequate for its new task of being the omnicompetent vehicle for all literature. In his day history, science, and learned work generally could hardly be well or accurately written in English. Elyot's labors, and those of so many of his contemporaries, are not easy reading, but they are, as Professor John Butt has demonstrated,[51] the bedrock of later prose.

Prose, then, was on the way to its later grandeurs by the middle of the reign of Henry VIII. Poetry largely slumbered in its "drab" dreariness. Yet even here the odd ray of hope was shed by a grammarian. Some years ago I was delighted to come on this Shakespearean couplet:

> Ther be many lordes that cannot pley the lorde,
> But I that am none can pley it rially.

This was written in the reign of Henry VII by the anonymous teacher at Magdalen College School, whose *vulgaria* have been printed by Professor William Nelson.[52] It is, of course, part of a piece of prose. But it is also part of an impetus to write English rhythmically and well which was released by the Latin pedagogues who were becoming a necessary part of the English scene.

N O T E S

1. Since writing this essay I have read the useful survey of P. O. Kristeller, "The European Diffusion of Italian Humanism," *Italica*, XXXIX (1962). Attention should also be drawn to R. Weiss, *The Spread of Italian Humanism*, which has just been published (London, 1964).

2. *Constitutional History*, III, p. 155.

3. J. R. Lander, "Attainder and forfeiture, 1453–1509," *Historical Journal*, 4 (1961), pp. 119–51.

4. J. Otway-Ruthven, *The King's Secretary and the Signet Office in the XV Century* (1923); J. F. Baldwin, *The King's Council in England during the Middle Ages* (1913); A. R. Myers, ed., *The Household of Edward IV: the Black Book and the Ordinance of 1478* (1959). In general, cf. S. B. Chrimes, *An Introduction to the Administrative History of Medieval England* (1952), pp. 241–70 and refs.

5. See Weiss, *Humanism in England,* pp. 58, 88, 115 and cf. the same author's article on Tito Livio Frulovisi's *Humfroidos* in *Fritz Saxl Memorial Essays,* ed. D. J. Gordon (1957), pp. 218–27. On Grey see now the excellent account by R. A. B. Mynors, *Catalogue of the Manuscripts of Balliol College* (1963), pp. xxiv–xlv.

6. R. H. Tawney, L. Stone, H. R. Trevor-Roper, J. H. Hexter. The bibliography to 1960 is referred to in Hexter's devastating essay, now in *Reappraisals in History* (1961). One of the most curious features in the whole curious affair is the starting date of 1540.

7. "The Place of Henry I in English History," *Proc. Brit. Acad.,* XLVIII (1962), pp. 127–69.

8. For their prominence by 1500, cf. the first chapter of Fritz Caspari, *Humanism and Social Order in Tudor England* (1954). I find it difficult, however, to go along with Dr. Caspari in his argument that the English gentry felt a natural sympathy with "the ideas of the humanists" because they were derived from an antiquity in which "there was a definite similarity between the Roman and the English aristocracy."

9. Sylvia L. Thrupp, *Merchant Class of Medieval London* (1948), p. 161; cf. 157n3 for references to earlier studies.

10. *Ibid.,* pp. 156–57.

11. H. S. Bennett, *English Books and Readers 1475–1557* (1952), p. 28; J. W. Adamson, *The Illiterate Anglo-Saxon* (1946), chap. III, *passim.* The subject has more recently been surveyed in chap. XI of Raymond Urwin, *The Heritage of the English Library* (1964).

12. Bennett, *loc. cit.*

13. Denys Hay, *Polydore Vergil* (1952), p. 69.

14. *Prejudice and Promise,* p. 35.

15. See H. S. Bennett, *The Pastons and their England* (reprinted 1932), pp. 107–8.

16. "La Renaissance littéraire autour de Henry V," *Revue Historique,* CCXXIV (1960), pp. 329–38; cf. E. F. Jacob, "Verborum florida venustas," *Essays in the Conciliar Epoch* (second edition, 1953), pp. 185–206.

17. Weiss, *Humanism in England,* p. 74.

18. Secretary 1460, bishop 1472: Otway-Ruthven, pp. 175–76.

19. Weiss, *Humanism in England,* pp. 176–77.

20. Otway-Ruthven, p. 129.

21. "Council, administration and councillors, 1461–1485," *Bull. Inst. Hist. Res.,* XXXII (1959), pp. 138–80.

22. Otway-Ruthven, pp. 140, 178–79.

23. W. Busch, *England under the Tudors* (1895), I, p. 393 (only Vol. I was published).

24. Otway-Ruthven, pp. 190–91: "a conscious creation to meet the needs of a new age."

25. G. F. Warner and J. P. Gilson, *Catalogue of Western MSS. in the Old Royal and King's Collections,* I (1921), p. xiii.

26. Printed by Pynson in 1509 (S.T.C. 12413). On Griffo see a jejune paper by the present writer in *Italian Studies,* II (1938–39), pp. 118–28.

27. Weiss, *Humanism in England,* pp. 168–69.

28. Quintin Poulet, 1492, and Giles Duwes, 1509: Warner and Gilson, *op. cit.,* pp. xiii-xiv.

29. We have no studies of English purchases of foreign books as such at the start of the sixteenth century, but cf. *Catalogue of the Library of Syon Monastery, Isleworth,* ed. Mary Bateson (1898), p. viii. The valuable collection of material in Sears Jayne, *Library Catalogues of the English Renaissance* (1956) marks a great step forward.

30. Cf. George B. Parks, *The English Traveller to Italy,* I (to 1525), (1954).

31. For the career of another, John Palsgrave (tutor to Mary Tudor, 1513, and Henry Fitzroy, 1525), see *The Comedy of Acolastus,* ed. P. L. Carver (E.E.T.S. no. 202, 1937), pp. xi–xii, xxiv–xxxv.

32. Vergil, *Anglica Historia* (Camden Series, 1950), p. 147 collation.

33. R. Pace, *De Fructu* (Basle, 1517), dedication to Colet, pp. 13–14; "Tanta praeterea eruditio ut extrusa pene omni barbarie (in qua nostri olim adolescentes solebant fere aetatem consumere, et longissimo tempore, ut nihil boni discerent, laborare) politiorem latinitatem, atque ipsam Romanam linguam, in Britanniam nostram introduxisse uideatur."

34. Vergil, *op. cit.*, pp. 145–46 collation.

35. Professor Lawrence V. Ryan, who was kind enough to read and comment on a version of this paper, pointed out to me the significance of the revised statutes for St. John's College (1524, 1530): cf. J. B. Mullinger, *The University of Cambridge from the Earliest Times to the Royal Injunctions of 1535*, pp. 622–25, where Fisher's borrowings from the statutes of Fox's and Wolsey's Oxford foundations are discussed.

36. For his nervousness, cf. Mullinger, *loc. cit.*

37. W. Gordon Zeeveld, *Foundations of Tudor Policy* (1948).

38. Pace, *op. cit.*, pp. 112–13.

39. *Ibid.*, pp. 15–16. Pace's gentleman despising education existed: see Carver's introduction to *Acolastus*, pp. xxxi–ii: the competition between the courtier-gentleman and the courtier-scholar could provoke tension round a prince.

40. Caspari, *op. cit.*, p. 137.

41. Now reprinted in *Reappraisals in History* (1961), pp. 45–70.

42. See Stanford E. Lehmberg, *Sir Thomas Elyot, Tudor Humanist* (1960).

43. Cf. Denys Hay, *Italian Renaissance in its Historical Background* (1961), pp. 179–201.

44. "An exhortacion to young men," in *Life and Works of Thomas Lupset*, J. A. Gee, ed. (1928), p. 240; for date of composition, *ibid.*, pp. 124–25.

45. Thomas Starkey, *A Dialogue between Reginald Pole and Thomas Lupset*, Kathleen M. Burton, ed. (1948), pp. 22, 24.

46. George B. Parks, "The genesis of Tudor interest in Italian," *P.M.L.A.*, LXXVII (1962). I have to thank Professor Sears Jayne for drawing my attention to this.

47. *Governour,* I, p. 129. And cf. E. J. Sweeting, *Studies in Early Tudor Criticism* (1940), pp. 52–57.

48. *Dialogue concerning Tyndale,* W. E. Campbell, ed., introd. A. W. Reed (1931), p. 247.

49. *On the continuity of English Prose from Alfred to More and his School* (E.E.T.S.) (sep. reprint, 1950), pp. cxxi–cxli.

50. Yale edition of the Complete Works of Thomas More, 2, *The History of King Richard III,* Richard S. Sylvester, ed. (1963), see pp. lvi–lix.

51. "A plea for more English Dictionaries," *Durham University Journal,* n.s., XII (1951), pp. 96–102.

52. *A Fifteenth Century School Book,* W. Nelson, ed. (1956), p. 84 (no. 351).

GUNPOWDER
AND THE RENAISSANCE:
AN ESSAY IN THE
HISTORY OF IDEAS.*

J . R . H A L E

The University of Warwick

Few survivors remain from the spacious days of unchallenged
historical generalizations, but from time to time The Influence
of Gunpowder on Civilization can still be glimpsed, stalking
through the careful husbandry of modern historical writing. "Gunpowder blasted the feudal strongholds and the ideals of their owners,"
a modern military historian has stated. "By changing the character
of war, gunpowder changed the medieval way of life. The search for
the perfection of firearms and of defence against them gave birth
to a spirit of inquiry which soon embraced all things."[1]

The notion that gunpowder blasted feudalism at the behest of
the centralized state can be found in Hume, Adam Smith, and
Hallam. For Macaulay the invention of gunpowder was, with that

* I have included in this essay some material which has appeared in two
much briefer treatments of this subject: "The Cruel Art," *The Listener*,
April 19, 1956, pp. 454-6, and a paper read at a *Past and Present* conference on "War and Society 1300-1600," *Past and Present*, July, 1962,
esp. pp. 28-32. I am grateful to the editors of these journals for their
permission to do this.

of printing, one of the two greatest events which took place in the Middle Ages. For Carlyle it was one of the three great elements of modern civilization (the others were printing and the Protestant religion). In 1857 Buckle elaborated his thesis that firearms had led to the creation of a specialized military class: "The result was, that the European mind, instead of being, as heretofore, solely occupied either with war or with theology, now struck out into a middle path, and created these great branches of knowledge to which modern civilization owes its origin." From this it was a short step to the textbook quoted by Johan Huizinga which announced that "the rebirth of the human spirit dates from the discovery of firearms."

These claims are attractive, but the historian of Renaissance Europe will not find them easy to accept. An occasional rebellious baron may have been brought to heel by royal cannon, but the complex development of the feudal into the centralized state began before cannon became effective and can be explained without reference to firearms. The same is true of changes in the "European mind." The English bow and the Swiss and Spanish pike required as much training and discipline as the arquebus: the existence of a specialized military class in the non-feudal sense is the result not of a particular weapon but of the concept of a standing army and thus belongs to the seventeenth century.

The effects of firearms were specific and dramatic: they raised problems of tactics, equipment, and supply; wars cost more, new methods of fortification had to be devised, but they had little effect on the fortunes of campaigns as a whole or on the balance of political power. It is true that states which had guns were at an advantage over armies which as yet had none, or few: thus the Turks beat the Mamluks and the Spaniards found conquest easy in the New World. It is true that guns knocked down unreformed fortifications, and this gave the French an advantage over the English at the beginning of the fifteenth century and the Spaniards an edge on the Moors at the end of it. But by the second decade of the sixteenth century, when cannon and portable firearms first became really effective on the battlefield, they were owned by all the powers, and the rapid spread of the new fortifications meant that anything like a *blitzkrieg* was out of the question. Firearms may have decided the issue of a single battle, as at Ravenna in 1512, or the tactics of one—the Armada fight of 1588, so brilliantly described by Mattingly, is an example—but they cannot be said to have decided a war. Nor can they be said to have influenced the mounting diplomatic tension of the sixteenth century; for a surprise attack their striking power was neutralized by the cumbrous organization of their supply trains. Gunpowder, in short, revolutionized the conduct but not the outcome of wars.

If gunpowder did not hasten the "European mind" toward attitudes which we recognize as "modern," it did trouble that mind. Its use was accompanied, throughout the Renaissance, by considerable debate, *pro* and *contra,* and the purpose of this essay is to watch the conscience of Christendom adjusting itself to the use of a weapon of hitherto unprecedented destructive power and one commonly thought to have been brought into existence by the devil himself.

Firearms had been used in Europe from the end of the thirteenth century, but when humanist historians discussed the origin of gunpowder, they attributed its invention to a mid-fourteenth-century German, and its first use to the Venetians in their war of Chioggia (1378–81) against the Genoese. The first *locus classicus* for this opinion, endlessly quoted and requoted for the next two hundred years, was Flavio Biondo's *Roma triumphans,* written between 1455 and 1463, in which he spoke of bombards, "*machinae omnium impetuosissimae, quam anno nondum centesimo inventam fuisse docuimus, teutonicū munus Venetis delatum, quando Genuenses in Clugia clausi a Venetis obsidebantur.*"[2] Platina made the same point in his history of the popes (1474), and in 1493 Antonio Cornazano identified the German as an alchemist,[3] an opinion shared in the most influential of all early accounts of the origin of gunpowder, a passage from Polydore Vergil's *De Inventoribus Rerum,* first published in 1499. In the words of the English translation of this work, the first gun

was perceived by a certain Almain, whose name is not known, after this sort: it chanced that he had in a mortar powder of brimstone that he had heated for a medicine and covered it with a stone, and as he struck fire it fortuned a spark to fall in the powder. By and by there rose a great flame out of the mortar, and lifted up the stone wherewith it was covered a great height. And after he had perceived that, he made a pipe of iron and tempered the powder, and so finished this deadly engine, and taught the Venetians the use of it when they warred against the Genoese, which was in the year of our Lord MCCCLXXX.[4]

Similar accounts occur in two contemporary works, the chronicle of Rafael of Volterra[5] and the *Rapsodiae Historiarum Enneadum*[6] of M. C. Sabellico, both of which were frequently quoted by later writers. Under the influence of these works it was generally taken for granted in the sixteenth century that guns were first used in 1380.

This theory ran counter to an earlier one, mentioned by Petrarch,[7] that gunpowder had been known to the ancients and invented by Archimedes. For those humanists who believed that the ancients had anticipated everything, it was easy to read accounts of ancient sieges, especially those employing some form of Greek fire, in terms of guns. Pius II told Duke Federigo of Urbino that "in Homer and Virgil could be found descriptions of every kind of weapon which our age used"[8]—a reference to the machine made by Salmoneus to counterfeit the thunder of Jupiter and described in the sixth book of the *Aeneid*. In 1472 Roberto Valturio, in his *De re militari,* named Archimedes as the inventor of the gun, but by the end of the century the military engineer Francesco di Giorgio expressed the majority view when he asked: If the ancients had guns, why don't we find any traces of gun-ports in their walls? Why did they go on using rams and catapults?[9]

Spanish historians, it is true, said that gunpowder had first been used by the Moors against Alfonso XI in 1343,[10] and a number of writers believed that it had been invented by the Chinese. Buonaiuto Lorini, for instance, said it had been brought into Europe via Turkey by German merchants.[11] Raleigh accepted the Chinese thesis in his *History of the World* (1614),[12] but in the same year Camden discounted it in his *Remaines concerning Britaine*. He opted for the German alchemist (by now named as Berthold Swart, or Schwarz, and identified as a monk or Franciscan friar) as the inventor of the gun, but pointed out that firearms had been used from the early fourteenth century.

Nearly all the writers we have mentioned deplored the introduction of the new weapon. The Chinese and Moorish theories had the advantage of placing the responsibility on infidels, who could not be expected to know better, but preference was given to the most picturesque and shocking story. Men like to think that great inventions are the work of an individual whom they can imagine at work; this, the popular distrust of alchemists, and the Protestant dislike of monks, made the image of Swartz, pursuing his secret labors at the devil's prompting into one of the most compelling figures in the folklore of technology.

In the paper debate which accompanied the actual use of guns the bulk of the argument was provided by the opposition. The supporters of firearms were few. They lacked, of course, the spur of moral indignation, and in an age almost innocent of pacifism, war was thought to be necessary to the state and good for the individual, even when it included cannon. "Musk and civet have too long stifled us," says the captain in Shirley's *The Doubtful Heir*,[14] "there's no recovery without the smell of gunpowder." Guns were necessary for the defense of one's country, so Roger Ascham, an academic scholar with a passion for the longbow, could encourage men to practice with them,[14] and so could a cleric like Daneau.[15] In the right hands, guns were a guarantee of order. For Jean Taisnier they protected the individual and his household;[16] Sebastian Münster pointed out that by destroying the strongholds of brigands, cannon served the merchant and allowed trade to prosper.[17] On a bombard cast in 1404 for Sigismond of Austria is the motto, I AM NAMED KATRIN, BEWARE OF WHAT I HOLD; I PUNISH INJUSTICE;[18] and two hundred years later the English antiquarian historian Sir Henry Spelman could describe the gun as "*machina ad stabilienda Humana Imperia, potius quam ad delendum humanum genus. Execrantur pacis invidi hanc machinam: mihi autem semper visa est non sine Dei opt. max. providentia revelata.*"[19] Some authors claimed that the introduction of firearms had reduced casualties in battle, and Camden produced some dubious statistics in support. He contrasted the losses at the battle of Hastings (47,944 English killed) and Crécy (30,000 French killed) with those of battles where guns were used—Flodden, 8,000, Musselburgh, 4,000—and drew a drastically *post hoc, propter hoc* conclusion.[20] The commonest argument in defense of the gun, however, was that God had not armed man with fangs and claws like animals, but that He had given him the intelligence to invent weapons of his own; to render himself defenseless, especially unilaterally, against an enemy armed with guns would be an insult to the Creator and a neglect of His gifts. This argument occurs from the middle of the sixteenth century[21] and was used both by secular writers like Sir Walter Raleigh[22] and clerics; the Rev. J. Davenport defended the making of guns by saying—it is true, in a sermon to the Artillery Company of London—that man "can take . . . from within the bowels of the earth, what may serve for his use and benefit."[23]

Among the arguments against the use of firearms the least cogent was that they were less effective than the old familiar weapons. Very few men went so far as Montaigne in his opinion of the gun: "Except the astonishment and frighting of the ear, which nowadays is grown so familiar amongst men, that none doth greatly fear it, I think it to be a weapon of small effect, and hope to see the use of it abolished."[24] Some, like Sir John Smythe, complained that the effects of firearms were exaggerated, and that the bow should be retained as the most reliable and efficient missile weapon;[25] others, like the French soldier François de la Noue,[26] distrusted the more complicated firearms, especially the pistol. According to Du Bartas, when Henry IV of France was confronted by an enemy cavalryman:

> *Le courageux Henri lui porte tout à coup*
> *Le pistolet au front, il fait feu, non pas coup,*
> *Lors d'une voix colère: "O tromperesses armes,*
> *Je vous quitte" (dit-il); l'épée est des gendarmes*
> *La gloire plus insigne.*[27]

Most arguments, however, were based on the assumption that firearms were devilish and their use blasphemous, that they were unchivalrous and that they caused too much suffering.

From John Mirfield's mention in c.1390 of *"instrumento illo bellico sive diabolico quod vulgariter dicitur gonne,"*[28] the idea that gunpowder was a malicious patent of the devil became a commonplace. The title page of the 1489 Basel edition of Augustine's *De Civitate Dei* shows two walled towns—one manned by angels, the other by devils, one of whom is armed with a gun. Francesco di Giorgio, himself a designer of cannon, wrote that this weapon "*non senza qualche ragione da alcuni non umana ma diabolica invenzione è chiamata,*"[29] and the practical and sophisticated Francesco Guicciardini referred to guns in his *History of Italy* as "diabolical rather than human."[30] Erasmus made Peace exclaim: "O God immortal! With what weapons doth anger arm a man? Christians do invade Christian men with the engines of hell. Who can believe that guns were the invention of man?"[31]

Even a man like Vanuccio Biringuccio, who wrote the first detailed treatise on the making and use of cannon, could remark that "a great and incomparable speculation is whether the discovery of compounding the powder used for guns came to its first inventor from the demons or by chance."[32] An illustration in Munster's *Chronicle* did not share this doubt; it showed a devil leading the monk Schwarz toward a cannon,[33] and the point was made even more dramatically by a woodcut in Johan Stumpf's *Schwyzer Chronik* (1554) which showed monks at work in a laboratory; a small monster with a long tube-like snout is mixing powder for them, while a demon shaped like a flying goat is helping one of them grind it in a mortar.[34] Ben Jonson was only rephrasing an old tradition when he referred to the friar "Who from the Divels-Arse did Guns beget."[35] The supreme example of the devil-gun identification in English literature, however, is in book six of Milton's *Paradise Lost,* where Raphael tells Adam how, after his initial rout on the first day of his battle with the hosts of heaven, Satan invented the gun, so that batteries of them confronted the heavenly army on the second day:

> at each behind
> A Seraph stood, and in his hand a Reed
> Stood waving tipt with fire.

Before the linstocks could be applied, the good angels buried the cannon under mountains, and there they remained. But Raphael warns Adam lest

> haply of thy Race
> In future dayes, if Malice should abound,
> Some one intent on mischief, or inspir'd
> With dev'lish machination might devise
> Like instrument to plague the Sons of men
> For sin, on warr and mutual slaughter bent.

Such a rediscovery would not only serve the devil's end, but it would be blasphemy. *"Non erat satis de coelo tonantis ira Dei immortalis,"* asked Petrarch, *"nisi homuncio (O crudelitas iuncta superbiae) de terra etiam tonuisset?"*[36] God showed his wrath in thunder and lightning; it was not for man to imitate it.

The chivalrous contempt for firearms as a coward's weapon had been anticipated by a scorn for missile weapons that went back to the Greeks. In Euripides' *Hercules Furens* Lycus says scornfully of Hercules that his reputation for bravery is based on his combats with wild beasts. With men "he never seized a shield on his left arm or came close to the spear point but had bow and arrows, the most cowardly of weapons." Each new missile contrivance met with similar opposition. The Emperor Napoleon III cited "the well-known exclamation of Archidamus, King of Sparta, at the sight of the first catapult: 'This is the tomb of bravery!' "[37] Anna Comnena referred to the crossbow as "a really devilish contrivance."[38] A few Renaissance authors reported anecdotes of a generalized anti-missile sort: "What said the Laconian when wounded by a dart?" asked Henry Salmuth. " 'I am not,' quoth he, 'concerned at my death, but at my fall by a wound from a feeble archer,' "[39] but mostly they concentrated their scorn on the gun. From Polydore Vergil onwards there was a running fire of attack on the new weapon, thanks to which *"vera virtus bellica corrupta, et fere sublata sit."* All over Europe men were asking, with the anonymous eulogist of the French warrior Louis de la Tremouille, *"De quoy servira plus l'astuce des gensdarmes, leur prudence, leur force, leur hardiesse, leur preudhommie, leur discipline militaire, et leur desir d'honneur, puisqu'en guerre est permis user de telles invencions?"*[40] It is enough here to quote one example each from Italy, France, Germany, Spain, and England.

The most famous and influential of all attacks on gunpowder as unchivalrous came from Ariosto, in cantos nine and eleven of the *Orlando Furioso*. The poet tells how Orlando is begged by the daughter of the Count of Holland to avenge the death of her family, butchered by the King of Friesland, a vengeance all the more urgent in that they were not killed in fair fight but struck down at a distance by that cowardly new invention, the gun. Orlando accepts the charge and after defeating the evil king and his army, takes the cannon, together with its powder and ball, and sails away until his ship stands over the ocean's profoundest depths. There he has the accursed engines dropped overboard and sails away, thinking that the chivalrous virtues have been saved. But the respite is short. Two cantos later the grapnels go down:

> More than a hundred fathom buried so,
> Where hidden it had lain a mighty space,
> The infernal tool by magic from below
> Was fished and born amid the German race.[41]

And thence it spread from country to country, until the poet breaks out,

> How, foul and pestilent discovery,
> Did'st thou find place within the human heart?
> Through thee is martial glory lost, through thee
> The trade of arms becomes a worthless art:
> And at such ebb are worth and chivalry
> That the base often plays the better part.
> Through thee no more shall gallantry, no more
> Shall valour prove their prowess as of yore.[42]

Henry IV of France called the *Commentaries* of Blaise de Montluc "the soldier's Bible," and in them the fiery marshal, a veteran of nearly sixty years of war in Italy and France, said of guns: "Would to heaven that this accursed engine had never been invented. I had not then receiv'd those wounds which I now languish under [he had been shot in the face by an arquebus in 1562], neither had so many valiant men been slain for the most part by the most pitiful fellows, and the greatest cowards; Poltrons that had not dar'd to look those men in the face at hand, which at distance they laid dead with their confounded bullets."[43] In Germany, the most important and most frequently reprinted military book of the sixteenth century was the *Kriegs Ordnung und Regiment* of Leonhard Fronsberger, and he too was of the opinion that "many a time and oft it happens that a brave and manly hero is killed by a shot from a craven who would not dare look him in the face."[44]

Even more widely read were the words of a Spaniard who was tempted to give up knight-errantry altogether, because the gun prevented the battlefield from functioning as the finishing school for personal valor. "Blessed were the times," complained Don Quixote in his Curious Discourse on Arms and Letters, "which lacked the dreadful fury of those diabolical engines, the artillery, whose inventor I firmly believe is now receiving the reward for his devilish invention in hell; an invention which allows a base and cowardly hand to take the life of a brave knight, in such a way that, without his knowing how or why, when his valiant heart is full of furious courage, there comes some random shot—discharged perhaps by a man who fled in terror from the flash the accursed machine made in firing—and puts an end in a moment to the consciousness of one who deserved to enjoy life for many an age."[45]

English pride in her missile troops, the archers, meant that while Englishmen could condemn guns as being devilish or deride them as inefficient, few thought of them as cowardly. An exception was Samuel Daniel, who castigated men's use of guns in his poem *The Civil Wars* (1595):

> For, by this stratagem, they shall confound
> All th' ancient forme and discipline of Warre:
> Alter their Camps, alter their fights, their ground,
> Daunt mightie spirits, prowesse and manhood marre:
> For, basest cowardes from a far shall wound
> The most couragious, forc't to fight afarre;
> Valour, wrapt up in smoake (as in the night)
> Shall perish without witnesse, without sight.[46]

The suffering which firearms—the "crudel arte" of Ariosto—inflicted was also fairly widely deplored. After discussing the weapons used by the ancients, Pedro Mexia remarked that "*à todo esto vence en crueldad la invencion de la polvora y artilleria,*"[47] and the French surgeon Ambroise Paré, who devoted much of his career to treating gunshot wounds, made the same point and added that cannon are properly called basilisks and serpents, for they are as cruel among weapons as these among beasts.[48] For Biringuccio, too, guns were "horrible and fearful," so horrible, in fact, that he burned the manuscript of his treatise on artillery. But—and the force of all these anti-gunpowder arguments was reduced by a "but"—when in 1537 the rumor spread that Suleiman was preparing to move west, he wrote it out again and sent it to the printer: Christians must not be left at a disadvantage. And Paré, for all his protestations, was unable to resist having a gun turned on a party of "fourescore whores and wenches" waiting to draw water at a well outside the besieged Hesdin; "and at that shot fifteene or sixteene were kild, and many hurt."[49]

Similarly, the knightly class did not take a united stand against the use of guns. Froissart revised his account of Crécy by removing references to the English guns lest they should be offensive to the taste of his English readers,[50] but in thinking that the relish of victory would be soured by associating it with artillery he was showing an unusual deference to chivalrous ideals. The gap between these ideals and the actual conduct of war in the late Middle Ages needs no laboring.[51] The pageantry became more gorgeous, the values more cynical. At the end of the fourteenth century Eustache Deschamps portrayed a gathering of knights and squires at the Burgundian court. Were they discussing love or valor? No; on every lip was the question, *Et quant venra le Trésorier?* [When does the paymaster come?].[52] And a few years later his English contemporary Hoccleve admitted that "experience and art" were worth more in a battle than "hardinesse or force,"[53] a sentiment repeated in *Le Jouvencel,* the mid-fifteenth-century Burgundian romance in which Jean de Bueil described his ideal of the perfect knight: "One should take every advantage in war, for faults are always dearly paid for. And one should always accomplish one's purpose, if not by force, then by cleverness."[54]

One advantage was to make use of the new weapon. Christine de Pisan's translation (1408–9) of Vegetius' *Art of War* was written for knights and courtiers, but she interpolated a long section on the use of guns in siege-craft with no suggestion that this gave a mean or unchivalrous advantage. The use of guns is taken for granted in

Le Jouvencel. From the 1330s French nobles had been providing themselves with cannon,[55] and by the middle of the next century the artillery of chivalrous Burgundy was second to none in Europe for efficiency and inventiveness.[56] Aristocrats coveted the office of master of the ordnance for the prestige and the powers of patronage it offered. Princes took a growing interest in the techniques of gun casting. The illustrations to Maximilian I's *Weisskunig* make it clear that to this most self-consciously chivalrous of rulers a training in the manufacture and use of cannon was, with hunt and tilt, part of the routine training of the Christian knight.

It is true that much has been made of certain instances in which chivalrous complaint led to action being taken against the users of firearms. The most quoted instance is that of the late-fifteenth-century *condottiere,* Paolo Vitelli. "We read that Paolo Vitelli," wrote Burckhardt, "while recognizing and himself adopting the cannon, put out the eyes and cut off the hands of the captured *schioppettieri* of the enemy, because he held it unworthy that a gallant, and it might be a noble knight, should be wounded and laid low by a common, despised foot soldier."[57] Burckhardt is here following the *Elogia virorum bellica virtute illustrium* (1548) of Paolo Giovio. Now Giovio, historian and ecclesiastic, was a man with a romantic and antiquarian interest in knights and chivalrous deeds. It is from the same work that we get the assertion that Bartolommeo Colleoni was the first military leader to use guns in the field, instead of merely in siege operations, which is palpably false, and that when one of Colleoni's shot wounded Ercole d'Este the duke protested that Colleoni "had behaved evilly and barbarously, trying to kill with a novel and horrible storm of shot valiant men who fought with lance and sword in the name of honour and glory."[58] The duke's wound is mentioned by one of his contemporaries, the Florentine Vespasiano da Bisticci, without any comment at all.[59] And in the same way, Vitelli's conduct at Buti in 1498 was noticed *at the time* in two sources, one Pisan, the other Florentine, neither of which make any reference to Vitelli's attitude to firearms.[60] Nor did Guicciardini make any such reference when he dealt with the capture of Buti in his *History of Italy.* Not only do the sources before Giovio give no hint that gunners were discriminated against because of their weapon, but there were other considerations involved in Vitelli's action: the gunners were German mercenaries—his cruelty may have been a warning against employing more of them; the cruelty on this occasion was general—"yesterday," says the Pisan source, "our enemies took the Castello of Buti by force, employing their usual inhuman cruelty, taking prisoner and tormenting with divers tortures the men of the place, ejecting the women and violating some, and cutting all the bombardiers' hands off with such inhumanity that the barbarians and Turks could hardly use more." Giovio's facts are right, but it is very possible that his interpretation of them owes something to what he hoped, rather than knew, Vitelli's attitude to be. Certainly the practice current in Italy at the time of Buti was for captured *schioppettieri* to be pardoned or exchanged on the same terms as were other soldiers.[61] Montluc, it might be noted, used arquebusiers throughout his campaigning life and complained of firearms only when he had been wounded by one.

Gunpowder might well be a grievance for the horseman who had invested his fortune in his equipment and for the individual fighting for personal glory (rather than for a state or a cause), but it was accepted, however reluctantly, by the overwhelming majority of knightly soldiers. Guns were invented by the devil, de la Noue agreed, "howbeit, mans malice hath made them so necessarie that they cannot be spared. To the end therefore to profite by them. . . ," and he goes on to describe how they can be best put to use.[62] As Robert de Balsac, Sieur d'Entragues, had pointed out in his *Nef des Princes et des Batailles* (1502), a prince, before undertaking a war, must be satisfied that his cause is a just one; after that he must make sure that he has enough artillery. A good cause is God's cause, and "what can more encourage and strengthen soldiers who shall fight the battailes of God and our Prince," asked the English printer of an Italian treatise on artillery in his dedicatory epistle to the Earl of Leicester, "than skilfull shooting in great and small peeces of artillerie?"[63] Or as a clergyman told a soldier audience in the English Midlands, "As S. Paul gives a Christian in his welfare, the whole armour of God; a Sword to offend, a Shield to defend; so in this kind of Warre, we must improve all things whatsoever the bowels or face of the earth can affoord for our defence . . . [including] such an invention that many a brave spirit dies by the hand of a Boy, or as ignoblie as Abimelech, by the hand of a Woman. But seeing the

fierie disposition of our enemies, use this as all others to our annoyance, why may we not snatch those weapons out of madde mens
hands, and turne them into their own bosome?"[64]

This was not the first time that Christian society had been threatened by a new and cruel weapon. When the crossbow first inflicted
its jagged tearing wounds, the Church condemned its use. But this
did nothing to stop the acceptance of the crossbow, or its evolution
into an ever more precise and powerful killing machine. Why should
the Church now deprive herself, at a time when she was fighting her
own wars to regain prestige and power in Italy, of a weapon already
in her enemies' hands? Why should she emasculate the efforts of
archbishops to maintain the integrity of their sees?[65] Why should
she try to deprive Christians of a weapon that was in the hands of
the common enemy? The Infidels had guns, they battered down the
walls of Constantinople with them; why should not Christians have
them too? Necessity coated the speck of grit in Christendom's conscience, and the Church eased the process by supplying gunners with
a patron saint of their own, Saint Barbara.[66] Because her father,
who had denounced her as a Christian, was struck down by thunder
and lightning at the moment of her execution, she was connected
with explosions, and by the time Palma Vecchio painted her standing
over the muzzles of cannon for the Venetian association of *bombar-
dieri*, she was popularly invoked both by gunners (according to the
rules issued by Charles V to the artillery school in Burgos, the ar-
tilleryman was to call on the aid of Saint Barbara as he put the
ball into his weapon) and by soldiers praying for protection against
such missiles. Her image is thus found both on guns and on armor.[67]
As the popularity of her cult grew with the increased use of firearms, her powers were commemorated in cheap woodcuts and
ceramics as well as in paintings[68] to such an extent that Erasmus
could scoff at "the foolish but gratifying belief that . . . whoever
salutes an image of Barbara will come through a battle unscathed."[69]

The acceptance of firearms did not, of course, depend on the issue
of a debate. Fundamentally, guns came to stay because they worked;
they won battles, they demolished walls. But they were accepted,
too, because of their appeal at a less rational level. They appealed
because of their noise and violence, because they were modern and
ingenious, because they enlisted both national and professional pride.

A fascination with their violence can be traced throughout the battle descriptions and poems with military themes of the period. From an anonymous English cleric of the mid-fifteenth century comes this description of a battle at sea:

> The canonys, the bumbard and the gunne,
> Thei bloweth out the voys and stonys grete,
> Thorgh maste and side and other be thei runne,
> In goth the serpentyne after his mete;
> The colveryne is besy for to gete
> An hole into the top, and the crappaude
> Wil in; the fouler eek will have his laude.[70]

Sir Thomas Coningsby recorded his reaction at seeing a cannon ball discharged against Rouen in 1591, "where we might heare such ratling of houses, and see it fly through one house and grace upon the other, as were yt not for charytie it were pleasure to behold."[71] And typical of the frank pleasure found by a violent age in its most violent machine are these lines from *The Scottish Souldier* (1629): Away with silks and womanish conceits, cries the author, George Lawder,

> Let me still heare the Cannons thundring voice,
> In teror threaten ruin: that sweet noyse
> Rings in my eares more pleasing than the sound
> of any Musickes consort can be found. . . .
> Then to see leggs and armes torne ragged flie,
> And bodyes gasping all dismembered lie,
> One head beate off another, while the hand
> Sheaths in his neighbour's breast his bloodie brand,
> A Cannon bullet take a Ranke away,
> A Volley of small shot eclypse the day
> With smoke of sulphure, which no sooner cleares,
> Than death and honour everie where appeares.[72]

On the Elizabethan stage, the cannon—"Alarum, and chambers go off"—joined the drum in providing the atmosphere, frightening, yet thrilling, of war,[73] and patriotic poets called men to arms and to the music of Mars, "the roring Cannon, and the brasen Trumpe."[74] This same double music became part of the routine of celebration and salute. The announcement of the anti-French league of 1523 in Venice was accompanied by music and gunfire, and after the resulting victory at Pavia in 1525 the victorious ambassadors were allowed to draw gunpowder from the Venetian arsenal to commemorate it.[75] During the festivities in 1532, when Francis I—now free after his capture at Pavia—and Henry VIII came to Calais they "were saluted with great melody what with guns and all other instruments. . . . And at Boulogne, by estimation, it past not 200 shot but they were great pieces."[76] For the Moor it was not blasphemy that was in his mind but a consciousness of the thrill and terror of war when he bade farewell to its pride, pomp, and circumstance,

> And, O you mortal engines, whose rude throats
> Th'immortal Jove's dread clamours counterfeit,
> Farewell! Othello's occupation's gone!

And at a more trivially endearing level, fireworks, including set pieces showing mock battles, became a popular spectacle from the late sixteenth century.

From the fifteenth century, when men were only beginning to take sides in the Ancients *versus* Moderns controversy, the success of the new weapon was a key argument for those who felt that man could discover things unknown to the ancients, and that his intelligence should not be directed only to the rediscovery of ancient wisdom but to advancing, increment by increment, on what he could find out for himself about the physical world. The author of *Knighthode and Battaile* listed all the ancient siege weapons which could now be blown to bits.[77] The cult of the military methods of the ancients, which lasted well into the seventeenth century, after first attempting, with Machiavelli, to play down the effectiveness of firearms, contented itself with accepting the importance of the new weapon, but emphasizing that the really crucial lessons of ancient warfare, which above all concerned organization, discipline, and morale, were as relevant as ever. "I could heartily wish," Robert Barret made a captain say in 1598, "that, as neere as possible we might, we should reduce our selves with such armes as we now use, unto the forme, manner, and course of the auncient Romanes in their Militia and discipline of warre, although ages, seasons and inventions, have altered much and many weapons by them used."[78]

The growing scientific interests of the moderns welcomed the gun for what it revealed about ballistics and the laws of motion, and what its technology taught about metallurgy and the chemistry of explosives. Gunpowder manufacture was one of the industries that Francis Bacon recommended for study,[79] and it is no accident that on the title page of Bishop Thomas Sprat's *History of the Royal Society* Bacon, "Artium Instaurator," is portrayed pointing to a gun.

Another instinct the gun tapped was a love of ingenious devices and technical expertise. From the late fourteenth century men had toyed with the idea of putting the paddle boat and military machines described in the late classical manuscript *De rebus bellicis* into practice;[80] the illustrations to Valturio and, early in the sixteenth century, to editions of Vegetius, and the drawings of Renaissance artists like Francesco di Giorgio and Leonardo, to mention only the most famous, show elaborate and mostly impracticable devices: revolving turret guns, multibarrelled guns (a version of these was actually used), combination cannon and mortar and the like.[81] The taste for these inventions was satirized by Rabelais' description of the assault vehicle, "the great sow,"[82] and by Jonson in the *Staple of News,* where among other inventions, like submarines and the cork shoes which would enable Spinola's army to cross the Channel dry-foot, he mentions the Rosicrucians' notable discovery of "the art of drawing farts out of dead bodies."[83] Ingenious firearms, like the little gun carried at his girdle by Erasmus' friend Peter Falk, who was "curious about novelties in arts and machinery,"[84] appealed to collectors, and gunsmiths produced a wide range of combination weapons in which guns were combined with shields, war hammers, swords, daggers, even crossbows.[85] Though the simple matchlock proved the most practical military weapon, experiments were made with double- and triple-barrelled firearms, and the workmanship lavished on the locks and mountings of pistols and sporting guns put them among the most cherished of personal possessions.

The professional pride of the gunfounder comes out clearly from Biringuccio's remarks that he is not going to discuss mortars—the earliest guns were frequently of this type—"because they are not esteemed by us moderns,"[86] and Tartaglia boasts that he is dealing with

>   *... nuove invenzioni*
>   *non tolte da Platon né Plotino,*
>   *né d'alcun altro greco ovver latino,*
>   *ma sol da l'arte, misura e ragione.*[87]

Theorists of gunnery put their art on a par with that of music, medicine, astronomy, and mathematics,[88] and Captain Macmorris' outburst when he is not allowed to blow up the town of Harfleur splendidly expresses the involvement of the professional with his craft. "By Chrish, la, tish ill done; the work ish give over, the trompet sound the retreat. By my hand, I swear, and my father's soul, the work ish ill done; it ish give over: I would have blow'd up the town, so Chrish save me, la, in an hour: O, tish ill done, tish ill done; by my hand, tish ill done!"[89] Dekker's "Praise of the Shotte" in *The Artillery Garden* is a stirring eulogy of gunpowder and the deeds that are done with it:

>   Some say the Pouder is the Meale of hell. . . .
>   O shallow empty sculls, that under foote
>   Tread such a Mine, out of which growes the root,
>   Of all new warlike Discipline!

And he goes on to celebrate the gun as the bulwark of kingdoms, preserver of the world (for he too believes that battles had been more bloody in the Middle Ages), mother of inventions, the soldier's choicest music.[90] This pride in man's achievement was allied, in the case of Germans, to national pride. Smarting from the contempt shown them as barbarians by the sophisticates of Italy, the German retort was: "You may have studied the ancients longer than we have, but it took us to invent the most potent instrument in modern war." Toward the end of Jacob Wimpheling's *Rerum Germanicarum Epitome* (1505), where he explains why the Germans are such an admirable people, after chapters "On the Courage of the Germans," "On the Noblemindedness of the Germans," "On the Generosity of the Germans," there is one "On the offensive weapon, popularly called the Bombard, invented by the Germans." But the possession of an extensive park of artillery was a source of pride to all nations, and cities were proud of the guns which armed their new, bastioned fortifications. The cannon, in terms of national and civic politics, was one of the foremost status symbols of the Renaissance.

The appeal of guns was so strong, and they slipped into men's consciousness by so many insidious routes, that opposition was partly disarmed by familiarity. Early-fifteenth-century manuscript illuminations showed the armies of Alexander the Great and of the Crusaders conducting sieges with cannon. Cannon and handguns figure in the earliest illustrated printed editions of Livy: battles seemed unthinkable without gunpowder.[91] Guns were given names, and this helped to domesticate their terror. Pius II named two of his cannon Enea and Silvia after his own name, Eneas Silvius Piccolomini, and another after his mother, Vittoria.[92] They were named after birds and girls and animals, and both Charles V and Henry VIII had batteries known as the Twelve Apostles. From the time when Pisanello designed guns for Alfonso I of Aragon the menace of cannon was veiled by their beauty. Francesco di Giorgio's designs for large guns have an elaborate charm that diverts attention from their purpose; Biringuccio always added urns or heads of men or animals "to make the gun beautiful."[93]

Increasingly, wherever a man looked, he saw guns. The chivalrous battle scenes carved in 1489 for the choir stalls of Toledo cathedral showed cannon in action, or being hauled in oxcarts;[94] the elaborate marble monument sculpted before 1520 for Gaston de Foix by Agostino Busti (and now broken up) had panels where guns were introduced into piles of trophies *à l'antique*.[95] Guns appeared as trophies on the title pages of books from at least 1528.[96] Henry Peacham's *Minerva Britanna* (1612) illustrates the tag "*Quae pondere maior*" with a hand holdng a balance; in one pan are a pen and a laurel wreath, in the other a cannon; the gun had taken over from the sword as "Symbole of th'art Militar." And on the title page of the French translation (Rouen, 1627) of Giorgio Basta's *Il governo della cavalleria leggiera,* the figure of Bellum himself, though in one hand he flourishes a sword, in the other he holds a gun. Kings and princes exchanged cannon as tokens of respect—Charles V received one of "gold, silver and metal"—even as wedding presents.[97] Battle scenes showing artillery in action were embossed on armor from the middle of the sixteenth century.[98] Duke Federigo of Urbino, though he would not allow a printed book in his famous library, used a bomb as one of his *imprese,*[99] and Ariosto's own patron, Alfonso d'Este, bore the emblem of a flaming bomb-shell on his cuirass at the battle of Ravenna in 1512.[100] In this device the projectile symbolized not the horror of war but a praiseworthy moral quality, energy held in check until the critical moment, vigor tempered by a wise restraint. When Alfonso was painted by Titian he chose to be portrayed with his hand resting on the muzzle of a cannon: here I stand, he implies, a man of prudence, but capable, should the occasion demand it, of lethal activity.[101]

While guns were quietly taking their place among the iconographical clichés of statecraft, they were becoming still further domesticated by common use and usage. They were used as signals that processions or ceremonies were starting;[102] "gunshot" was used as a matter of course as a measurement of length in 1548;[103] and from the beginning of the seventeenth century the phrases "as sure as a gun," "right as a gun" appear.[104] When Isabella's brother vainly warns Bracciano to keep away from Vittoria in Webster's *The White Devil,* he warns him not with "We'll settle this by the sword" but "Wee'le end this with the Cannon."[105] The Spanish dramatist Veléz de Guevara wrote *La Serrana de la Vera* in 1613 in order that the most famous actress of her time could swagger about in it, shouldering an arquebus.[106] In early Stuart England gunpowder was used to cure toothache,[107] and the London bookseller Grismond disposed of his wares "at the signe of the Gun in Pauls Alley." Humor, too, helped to take some of the sting out of the lethal nature of artillery. Cannon balls were likened to tennis balls in Tudor ballads,[108] and when the tobacco controversy got under way at the goading of James I, Thomas Pestell defended it as the cheapest form of artillery with which to puff an enemy into subjection, and Joshua Sylvester attacked it as even worse than the gun,

> For Guns shoot from-ward, onely at their Foen;
> Tobacco-pipes, home-ward into their Owne
> (When, for the Touch-hole, firing the wrong end,
> Into our Selves the Poyson's force wee send).[109]

By 1620 water was spouting from the stone cannon of a fountain shaped like a galleon in the gardens of the Vatican,[110] and at about the same time the first miracle concerning small arms was recorded when a Dominican missionary turned a pistol with which he was being threatened into a crucifix.[111] From the middle of the sixteenth century, moreover, guns began to take their place in the symbolism of love. Naked *amori* shoot pistols at one another on an ivory powder flask,[112] a cupid is carved on the arm which sparks the flint and fires the pistol[113]—and in the Boar's Head tavern, Eastcheap, "Pistol's cock is up, And flashing fire will follow."[114]

English Renaissance drama shows that the gun took over from the sword as a virility symbol[115] at about the same time that it became a symbol of war itself, "Here, Pistol, I charge you with a cup of sack," says Falstaff. "Do you discharge upon mine hostess." "I will discharge upon her, Sir John, with two bullets."[116] In Beaumont and Fletcher's *The Honest Man's Fortune* the servants are discussing their mistress's new lover: "Ay, marry, boys! There will be sport indeed! There will be grappling! She has a murderer [a type of culverin] lies in her prow, I am afraid will fright his main-mast, Robin."[117] The medieval convention of describing love in terms of an attack by desire on the castle of chastity was revitalized by the use of guns and the elaborate outworks of the new bastioned fortification: ravelins, redoubts, half moons, horn works, and the rest. Modern siege imagery—used tenderly, as in Thomas, Lord Vaux' "The assault of Cupid upon the fort where the lovers hart lay wounded" (1585),[118] or crudely, as in Stephen Gosson's attack on corsets[119]—came to be used extensively in the drama, as in the scene in Beaumont and Fletcher's *The Woman's Prize* in which the heroine locks herself in her room, or the act in Shakerley Marmion's *Hollands leaguer* (1632) which passes in front of the "fort," a brothel.

This working of gunpowder imagery into the language of sex is a symptom of its acceptance by society at large, and literary men seized gratefully on the further opportunities it offered of freshening images concerned with speed, violence, and accuracy. Romeo begs for a poison that will spread through the body "As violently as hasty powder fired Doth hurry from the fatal cannon's mouth"; Falstaff is "afraid of this gunpowder Percy though he be dead"; Sir William Lucy expresses his anguish at the news of Talbot's death with "O, were mine eye-balls into bullets turn'd, that I in rage might shoot them at your faces!"; and when Juliet calls out for Romeo she weeps "as if that name, Shot from the deadly level of a gun, Did murder her."[120] Images were drawn from the whole range of artillery training and technology, from Friar Lawrence's attempt to dissuade Romeo from suicide, "Thy wit . . . Like powder in a skilless soldier's flask, Is set a-fire by thine own ignorance, And thou dismember'd with thine own defence," to Henry V's reference to the effect of ricochet, "Mark then abounding valour in our English, That being dead, like to the bullet's grazing, Break out into a second course of mischief," and Webster's "My friend and I, Like two chaine-bullets, side by side, will fly Thorow the jawes of death."[121] With "Invention flye in Fire, clap sulphery winges, Whilst every line like a ramde Bullet singes," Dekker likened gunpowder to literary inspiration itself.[122]

This service of gunpowder to imagery, and its heightening of atmosphere in the interest either of terror, as in Patten's description of the battle of Pinkie, [123] or of pathos, as in Drayton's poem on Agincourt[124] (an instructive contrast to Froissart's treatment of Crécy), meant that men met the gun in language as familiarly as in painting and sculpture, and this helped to reconcile them to meeting it in real life. And from the pulpit as from the stage: in his sermon for Trinity Sunday, 1535, Latimer warned his congregation that the devil "hath great peeces of ordinaunce, as mighty kinges and Emperours to shoote against Gods people. . . . He hath yet lesse ordinaunce, for he hath of all sortes to shoote at good christen men. . . . These be Accusars, Promoters, and slaunderers, they be evill Ordinaunce, shrewd handguns."[125] In a sermon at Paul's Cross in 1598 Gosson said that preaching itself :"is haile-shot; we send it among the thickest of you, desirous to hitte you all."[126]

With the intellectual debate *pro* and *contra* the use of gunpowder being, as we have seen, so inconclusive, and taking into account the powerful appeal of the new weapons both to the practical needs and the imagination of contemporaries, we must, I think, be careful not to give too much weight to the effect of the chorus of disapproval which accompanied the use of guns. It has recently been suggested that the effect of gunpowder might have been more terrible and destructive had it not been for the restraint imposed by moral and intellectual values and the diversion of inventive energy into decoration and display. Professor A. R. Hall has remarked that "the design of artillery remained essentially unchanged, less on account of the inability of science and industry to produce better weapons than of the absence of pressure to this end. Military opinion was happy in a surviving tradition of chivalry that close combat was more honourable than a long range bombardment between invisible foes."[127] And Professor Nef has referred to "the moral and intellectual scruples and the love of beauty which were still characteristic of Europeans in the early seventeenth century, and which bound them—scientists, artists, craftsmen, governors and statesmen alike—by a kind of voluntary servitude to make choices which seemed to them pre-eminently rational,"[128] *i.e.,* to restrict the effects of gunpowder.

When there were so many ways in which men could accommodate their consciences to the use of gunpowder it is, I think, very unlikely that in fact "the Christian sense of responsibility" moderated the use of firearms, or that the "concern of builders and craftsmen with beauty blunted the force of bullets, shot, balls and explosives."[129] Professor Nef takes the horror felt at the slaying by a cannon ball of Salisbury in *Henry VI, Part One,*[130] as an expression of contemporary anti-gunpowder feeling. The only support for this view, however, is Talbot's reference to "the treacherous manner of his mournful death," and this refers much more probably to the fact that Salisbury was killed not in combat but by a ruse—the covering by a gun of a vantage point in a tower used for observation purposes by the English. "Treacherous" in this situation would have suited a bowshot equally well. Here was a flower of English chivalry shot nastily to death ("One of thy eyes and thy cheek's side shot off," as Talbot observes) from a distance, and not even by a gunner but by a gunner's *boy,* and yet Shakespeare does not make any overt anti-gunpowder point. More revealing of contemporary opinion is Hotspur's contemptuous description of a gun-shy courtier:

> . . . he made me mad
> To see him shine so brisk, and smell so sweet,
> And talk so like a waiting-gentlewoman
> Of guns, and drums, and wounds—God save the mark!
> And telling me the sovereign'st thing on earth
> Was parmaceti for an inward bruise;
> And that it was great pity, so it was,
> This villainous saltpetre should be digg'd

> Out of the bowels of the harmless earth,
> Which many a good tall fellow had destroy'd
> So cowardly; and but for these vile guns
> He would himself have been a soldier.[131]

Certainly some inventors claimed to have discovered means of destruction so horrible that they suppressed them. Leonardo would not reveal his secret for destroying ships from under water (though he was prepared to cannonade and asphyxiate their crews from the surface);[132] Tartaglia would not reveal the composition of his noiseless powder;[133] John Napier said he had torn up the formula of a new explosive of terrifying power.[134] But we have no way of knowing if these things would have worked; the notion of silent gunpowder was pooh-poohed in 1601 by the English gunnery expert, Thomas Smith.[135] Moreover, other horrors were actually used: explosive shells, various forms of liquid fire, gasbombs, with which the Venetians were experimenting as early as 1482.[136] When Giambelli's explosive-packed infernal machine killed some five hundred of the besiegers of Antwerp in 1585, the European reaction was one not of outraged sensibility but rather of grudging admiration.[137] Nor was there any suggestion from the development of sporting guns— a competitive industry, unhampered by ethical considerations—that military weapons could have been made more lethal. Biringuccio's concern to beautify his cannon did not impede his desire to make them as effective as possible. There were alternative types of missile that caused more destruction than the spherical ball, but "because things cannot always be made according to desire, they often fail in operation."[138] The barrier to advance was not moral or esthetic, it was technological. More accurate guns had to wait until the use of machine tools in the nineteenth century; longer ranges awaited improvements in metallurgy; better explosives depended on advances in chemistry, a science still in its infancy in the Renaissance.

It is natural for modern historians, sickened by the arms race of their own day, to look back in nostalgia to an age when there is literary evidence to suggest that the race could be slowed by an appeal to men's better nature. This nostalgia, alas, is misplaced. By the early seventeenth century, ideals had given ground to the arguments of fact. Opposition to gunpowder retreated to one form of one weapon: the rifled musket, which, as a sharpshooter's weapon to pick off officers, was deplored as violating the code of war. But it was used, nevertheless.[139] Optimistic students of human nature can take little comfort from the reactions of their Renaissance ancestors to the greatest challenge to Europe's conscience offered by military technology before the atom bomb.

N O T E S

1. J. F. C. Fuller, *Decisive Battles of the Western World and their Influence upon History* (2 vols, London, 1954–5) I, p. 470.

2. (Basel, 1531), p. 132.

3. *Opera bellissima del arte militar* (Venice), book II, chap. 2.

4. Modernized from the translation by Langley, *An abridgement of the notable woorke of P. Vergile* (London, 1546), f. lxix[v].

5. *Commentariorum* (Paris, 1526), f. cccxxii[r].

6. (Lyons, 1535), Vol. II, p. 429.

7. In the *De remediis utriusque fortunae*, c. 1366. Quoted by H. Delbrück, *Geschichte der Kriegskunst im Rahmen der politischen Geschichte* (4 vols, Berlin, 1900–20) IV, p. 37.

8. *Commentaries*, book 5, F. A. Gragg and L. C. Gabel, eds., *Smith College Studies in History* (1947), p. 393.

9. *Trattato di architettura civile e militare*, Cesare Saluzzo, ed. (Turin, 1841), pp. 249–50.

10. For example, Pedro Mexia, *The Forest, or Collection of Histories*, trans. T. Fortescue (London, 1571), f. 15[r].

11. *Le Fortificationi* (Venice, 1609), p. 152.

12. Book I, chap. vii, note i.

13. Ed. 1629, pp. 202–4. There is no mention of artillery in the first edition of 1605.

14. *The Scholemaster* (London, 1570), ff. 19^v–20^r.

15. L. Daneau, *Brieve Remonstrance sur les Ieux de sort* (n. p., 1574), pp. 18–19.

16. His *Astrologiae* . . . *encomia* (1559) is described in Lynn Thorndike, *History of Magic and Experimental Science* (New York, 1923–58), Vol. V, p. 585.

17. *La Cosmographie universelle* (Basle, 1552), p. 545.

18. Musée de l'Arsenal, Paris.

19. Quoted by J. S. D. Scott, *The British Army: its Origin, Progress, and Equipment* (2 vols, London, 1868), II, p. 193.

20. *Remaines, ed. cit.*, pp. 202–3.

21. Vallo [Battista della Valle], *Du faict de la guerre et art militaire* (Lyon, 1554), ff. 5^v–6^r. This section does not occur in the earlier Italian editions.

22. "A discourse of . . . War," *Works* (8 vols, Oxford, 1829), VIII, p. 253:
"it is needful that against the wit and subtelty of man we oppose, not only the brute force of our bodies, (wherein many beasts exceed us) but, helping our strength with art and wisdom, strive to excel our enemies in those points wherein man is excellent over other creatures."

23. *A royall edict* . . . (London, 1629), p. 9.

24. *Essays* (trans. Florio), "Of steeds, called in French destriers."

25. The bow-*versus*-gun controversy is discussed in my edition of Smythe's *Certain Discourses Military* (1590), Folger Documents of Tudor and Stuart Civilization (Cornell, 1964).

26. *The Politicke and Militarie Discourses* (Eng. trans. London, 1587), p. 202.

27. *The Works of Guillaume de Salluste, Sieur Du Bartas* (Chapel Hill, 1940), p. 496.

28. Quoted from British Museum MS. Harleian 3,261, in C. Ffoulkes, *The Gun-founders of England* (Cambridge, England, 1937), p. 3 n.

29. *Trattato* . . . , *ed. cit.*, p. 245.

30. *History of Italy*, book I, chap. 3: "piuttosto diabolico che umano."

31. *Complaint of Peace*, W. J. Hirten, ed. (New York, 1946), p. 32.

32. *De la Pirotechnia* (Venice, 1540) trans. Smith and Gnudi (New York, 1943), book X, chap. 2.

33. (Basle, 1552), p. 544.

34. Reproduced in O. Guttmann, *Monumenta Pulveris Pyrii* (London, 1906), fig. 14.

35. "An execration upon Vulcan."

36. Quoted from *De remediis utriusque fortunae*, in Delbrück, *op. cit.*, IV, p. 37. Translated in *Phisicke against Fortune* (London, 1579), f. 126ᵛ.

37. *Political and Historical Works* (London, 1852), Vol. II, p. 246.

38. Quoted by A. Toynbee, *A Study of History* (10 vols, Oxford, 1934–54) III, p. 386.

39. Guido Camerarius *Nova Reperta*, with Salmuth's commentary (1602), (trans. 1715), p. 389.

40. *La Panegyric du chevalier sans reproche* (1527), quoted in Gladys Dickinson, The *Instructions sur le Faict de la Guerre of Raymond de Beccarie de Pavie Sieur de Fourquevaux* (London, 1954), p. xliv.

41. Trans. W. S. Rose (2 vols, London, 1858) I, canto xi, verse 23.

42. *Ibid.*, verse 26.

43. C. Cotton's English translation (London, 1674), p. 9.

44. Quoted by Delbrück, *op cit.*, IV, p. 39.

45. English trans. by J. M. Cohen (London, 1950), p. 344.

46. *Complete Works*, A. B. Grosart, ed. (n. p., 5 vols, 1885–96), II, book 6, stanza 40.

47. *Silva de varia lecion* (Valladolid[?], 1543), p. 41.

48. *La Methode de Traicter les Playes faictes par Harcquebutes . . .* (1545), English translation (1634) reprinted in *The Apologie and Treatise of Ambroise Paré . . . with many of his writings upon Surgery*, Geoffrey Keynes, ed. (London, 1951), p. 132.

49. *Ibid.*, p. 50.

50. H. W. L. Hime, *The Origin of Artillery* (London, 1915), p. 132.

51. For example, M. A. Gist, *Love and War in the Middle English Romance* (Philadelphia, 1947).

52. *Oeuvres Complètes,* Saint Hilaire, ed. (Paris, 1884), Vol. IV, p. 289.

53. *Regiment of Princes,* F. J. Furnival, ed. (E.E.T.S., London, 1897), p. 144.

54. Quoted in R. L. Kilgour, *The Decline of Chivalry* (Harvard, 1937), p. 325.

55. Napoleon III, *op. cit.,* p. 7.

56. C. Brusten, *L'armée bourguignonne de 1465 à 1468* (Bruxelles, 1953), p. 7.

57. *The Civilization of the Renaissance* (London, 1944), p. 62.

58. *Elogia,* Italian translation by Lodovico Dominichi (Florence, 1554), p. 173.

59. *The Vespasiano Memoirs,* translated by William George and Emily Waters (London, 1926), pp. 89–90.

60. *A Florentine Diary from 1450 to 1516 by Luca Landucci,* I. del Badia, ed. (London, 1927), p. 147 and 147n.

61. G. Canestrini, *Scritti Inediti di Niccolò Machiavelli risguardanti la Storia e la Milizia (1499–1512)* (Florence, 1857), pp. xxvi–xxvii.

62. *Op. cit.,* p. 199.

63. Niccolò Tartaglia, *Three bookes of Colloquies concerning the arte of shooting in great and small peeces of artillerie . . .* (London, 1588), f. 3^r.

64. Samuel Buggs, *The Midland Souldier* (London, 1622), pp. 26–27.

65. On the breech of a cannon cast near Coblenz, the residence of the Archbishop of Trèves, there is an inscription: "I am called the Griffon. I serve my gracious Lord of Trèves; where he bids me force my way, I cast down gates and walls." The gun is in the Musée de l'Arsenal, Paris.

66. S. Peine, *St. Barbara, die Schutzheilige der Bergleute und der Artillerie* (Freiberg, 1896).

67. For example, a superb cannon of Ferdinand II of Tuscany in the arsenal at Venice; horse armor in the Tower of London presented by Maxmilian I to the young Henry VIII in 1509.

68. For example, the broadsheet reproduced in P. Heitz, *Italienische Einblattdrucke* (Strassburg, 1933), Part I, No. 18; plaque in the

Museo Civico, Turin, which shows her standing above what looks like model cannon; a painting attributed to Jan or Hubert van Eyck which shows her in front of a tower (her usual attribute) in which is a statue of Mars, reproduced in Reinach, *Repertoire des peintures* (6 vols, Paris, 1905–23), Vol. II, p. 364.

69. *Praise of Folly*, trans. H. H. Hudson (Princeton, 1941), p. 56.

70. *Knyghthode and Battaile*, R. Dyboski and Z. M. Arend, eds. (London, E. E. T. S., 1935), p. 104.

71. *Journal of the Siege of Rouen*, J. G. Nichols, ed. (Camden Miscellany I, 1847), p. 40.

72. George Lawder, *The Scottish Souldier* (Edinburgh, 1629), f. A4^t.

73. See Paul A. Jorgensen, *Shakespeare's Military World* (University of California, 1956), pp. 15–17.

74. *A farewell, Entituled to the famous generalls of our English forces: Sir J. Norris & Syr F. Drake* (London, 1589), in D. H. Horne *The Life and Minor Works of George Peele* (2 vols, New Haven, 1952), I, p. 221.

75. *Calendar of State Papers, Venetian, 1520–1526*, nos. 736 and 942.

76. *The maner of the tryumphe at Caleys and Bulleyn* (London, 1532), modernized in E. Arber, *An English Garner* (8 vols, London, 1877–96) II, pp. 38–9.

77. *Ed. cit.* in note 70 above, p. 93. For examples of gunpowder being cited as a triumph of Modern over Ancient learning, see A. F. Jones, *Ancients and Moderns* (St. Louis, 1961), p. 12 and *passim*, and J. B. Bury, *The Idea of Progress* (London, 1920), p. 54.

78. *The Theoricke and Practike of Moderne Warres* (London, 1598), p. 32.

79. See Christopher Hill, *The Century of Revolution 1603–1714* (London, 1961), p. 94.

80. *A Roman Reformer and Inventor; being a new Text of the Treatise De Rebus Bellicis, with a Translation and Introduction by E. A. Thompson* (Cambridge, England, 1952), pp. 18 ff.

81. See, for example, G. Canestrini, *Arte militare meccanica medievale* (Milan, 1940).

82. *Gargantua and Pantagruel*, book 4, chap. 40.

83. III, ii.

84. F. M. Nichols, *The Epistles of Erasmus* (3 vols, London, 1907–17), II, pp. 335–56.

85. Specimens of all these varieties can be seen in the Metropolitan Museum of Art, New York.

86. *Pirotechnia, ed. cit.,* p. 227.

87. Quoted from *Quesiti e Invenzioni Diverse* (1546), by U. Forti, *Storia della Technica Italiana* (Florence, 1940), p. 294.

88. That is, Richard Rotheruppe's prefatory poem to Thomas Smith's *The Art of Gunnery* (London, 1600). On the use made of classical mythology to justify the use of gunpowder on the title pages of books on gunnery and fortification, see my "The argument of some military title pages of the Renaissance," *Newberry Library Bulletin* (March, 1964), pp. 61–102.

89. *Henry V,* III, ii.

90. f.D i[r-v].

91. For example, British Museum MSS., *Conqueste de Jerusalem* (15. E.1.ff.241[r] and 357[r]), *Roman de la Rose* (Harleian 4425, f. 139[r]), *Quintus Curtius* (Burn. 169, ff. 69[r] and 127[r]) and Livy: Venice, 1493, 1495, 1506; Mentz, 1505; Saragossa, 1506; Paris, 1514.

92. *Commentaries, ed. cit.,* p. 388.

93. On Pisanello's designs, see Canestrini, *op. cit.,* p. 232; Francesco di Giorgio's are in the manuscript of his *Trattato* in the National Library of Florence, MS. II. I. 141, f. 48[r]; Biringuccio, *ed. cit.,* pp. 243–44.

94. Preface by Walter Starkie to Ramón Menéndez Pidal, *The Spaniards in their History* (London, 1950), p. 43.

95. Giorgio Nicodemi, *Agostino Busti* (Milan, 1945), esp. pl. 20.

96. Battista della Valle, *Libro continente Appartenentie ad Capitanii* (Venice.)

97. Charles's cannon is referred to in *C. S. P. Venetian, 1520–1526,* no. 1021; Bashford Dean, *The Metropolitan Museum of Art. Handbook of Arms and Armor* (New York, 1930), p. 83.

98. Examples are: gauntlets of the Duke of Guise (1565) in the Metropolitan Museum, New York; gorget of Philip II in the Armory at Madrid.

99. G. F. Hill, *A Corpus of Italian Medals* (2 vols, London, 1930) I, p. 76.

100. Its significance is explained in Paolo Giovio, *Imprese* . . . (Lyons, 1574), p. 80. The motto that accompanied this device was *Loco et tempore.*

101. On this concept, see E. Wind, *Pagan Mysteries of the Renaissance* (London, 1958), pp. 95 ff.

102. As at the Field of Cloth of Gold in 1520. *C. S. P. Venetian, 1520–1526,* no. 67.

103. In Sir William Patten, *The Expedicion into Scotlande.*

104. In "Of Catesby, Faux, and Garnet," printed in Hyder Rollins, *Old English Ballads, 1553–1625* (Cambridge, 1920), p. 361, and John Fletcher, *The Prophetess,* I,iii.

105. II,i.

106. Starkie, *op. cit.,* p. 69.

107. *Duchess of Malfi,* III,ii, 17–19.

108. G. G. Langsam, *Martial Books and Tudor Verse* (New York, 1951), pp. 124 and 130.

109. *Complete Works,* A. B. Grosart, ed. (2 vols, London, 1880) II, p. 265. For Pestell, see *Poems,* H. Buchan, ed. (Oxford, 1940), p. 32, "On Tobacco."

110. Cesare d'Onofrio, *Le Fontane di Roma* (Rome, 1951), p. 147.

111. E. Mâle, *L'Art religieux après le Concile de Trent* (Second edition, Paris, 1951), p. 101.

112. H. J. Jackson and C. E. Whitelaw, *European Hand Firearms* (London, 1923), p. xv.

113. Pistol in Metropolitan Museum of Art, New York.

114. *Henry V,* II,i.

115. For the sword as a symbol of a swaggering kind of virility, see the overtly phallic treatment of hilts in engravings, painted glass, etc., especially German portrayals of *Landsknechte* in the early sixteenth century.

116. *Henry IV, Part Two,* II,iv.

117. V,iii.

118. *Poems,* ed. A. B. Grosart (Blackburn, 1872), pp. 39–40.

119. *Quippes for upstart newfangled gentlewomen* (London, 1595), p. 9.

120. *Romeo and Juliet*, V,i; *Henry IV, Part One*, V,iv; *Henry VI, Part One*, IV,vii, III,iii.

121. III,iii; IV,iii; *Challenge for Beauty*, quoted in Webster, *Works*, F. L. Lucas, ed. (4 vols, London, 1927), II, p. 189.

122. *The Artillery Garden, a poem* (Oxford, 1952), f. Bi^v.

123. Patten, *op. cit.*, esp. ff. G v^{r-v}.

124. *The battaile of Agincourt, Works*, J. William Hebel, ed. (five vols, Oxford, 1961) III, pp. 28–29.

125. *Fruitfull Sermons* (London, 1571), f. 2^r.

126. *The Trumpet of Warre* (London, n.d), f. G vi^r.

127. A. R. Hall, *Ballistics in the Seventeenth Century* (Cambridge, 1952), p. 9.

128. J. U. Nef, *War and Human Progress* (London, 1950), pp. 132–33.

129. *Ibid.*, p. 129.

130. II,iii.

131. *Henry IV, Part One*, I,iii.

132. Bern Dibner, "Leonardo da Vinci; military engineer," in *Essays in the History of Science and Learning offered . . . to George Sarton*, M. F. Ashley Montagu, ed. (New York, 1944), p. 104.

133. T. M. Spaulding in *Adams Memorial Studies*, J. G. McManaway, G. E. Dawson, E. E. Willoughby, eds. (Washington, 1948), p. 497.

134. Nef, *op. cit.*, pp. 121–22.

135. *Certain Additions to the Booke of Gunnery* (London, 1601), f. A2^r.

136. L. Simeoni, *Le Signorie* (2 vols, Milan, 1950), I, pp. 551 and 570.

137. L. Van der Essen, *Alexandre Farnèse* (5 vols, Brussels, 1933–37), IV, pp. 55 ff.

138. *Ed. cit.*, pp. 430–31.

139. For example, by Gustavus Adolphus' ally, the Landgrave William of Hesse-Cassel; Michael Roberts, *Gustavus Adolphus, A History of Sweden 1611–1632* (2 vols, London, 1953–58), II, p. 227.

A SIXTEENTH-CENTURY ENCYCLOPEDIA: SEBASTIAN MÜNSTER'S COSMOGRAPHY AND ITS EDITIONS

GERALD STRAUSS

Indiana University

Sebastian Münster's *Cosmography* was first published in 1544 and quickly became the most popular work of its kind. Although Münster's claim to a place in the scholar's pantheon rests most securely on his significance as a Hebraist[1] (his dictionaries, vocabularies, text editions, and translations were landmarks in the early phase of Hebrew studies), it was the *Cosmography* with which his name came to be principally associated in the minds of sixteenth-century readers. During the author's own lifetime (he died in 1552) the *Cosmography* went through eight printings. And after his death, revised and expanded versions continued to appear until 1628: thirty-five editions in all—twenty in German, five in Latin, six in French, three in Italian, and one in Czech,[2] plus several English epitomes and extracts.[3] Thirty-one of the full editions issued from Heinrich Petri's press in Basel; the others were printed in Paris, Cologne, Venice, and Prague.

Münster's *Cosmography*[4] belongs to the species of work that Jean

Bodin, in his *Methodus,* called "geographistory." In the course of a leisurely perambulation of the countries of Europe, the Near and Middle East, Asia, Africa, and the New World, the author reveals what he has been able to learn about the places traversed, about their inhabitants, their institutions, manners, cultures, ways of life. There was scarcely a limit to the amount and the kind of information that could be conveyed; everything was relevant, whether it pertained to the flora and fauna flourishing in a given region or to the operation of a secret judicial tribunal, ecclesiastical and political questions of the day, the latest news from Peru. A book of this sort was easily revised and augmented when it became expedient to do so, and the many successive editions of the *Cosmography* bear witness, in their increasing bulk as well as in the arrangement of what they contain, to the diligence with which editors tried to keep the volume informative and useful.

Even a cursory glance at a few of these editions shows an extraordinary abundance. Given the eager response to the book, the publisher decided to meet public interest not only by keeping the work up to date in its historical and geographical subjects, but by expanding it to contain all, or nearly all, that an inquisitive and imaginative person might wish to discover about the world. Even in its first German edition of 1544 the book ran to over 650 folio pages. In 1598 it had reached 1,461 pages, and in 1628, about 1,700. The Paris version of 1575, the work of François de Belleforest, the noted historian and anthologizer, was printed in two huge folio volumes of over 4,000 pages.[5] The Italian edition published at Cologne in 1575 ran to 1,237 large pages. Each editor included in his redaction such material as he thought his readers would expect. Thus the 1568 French edition expands Münster's scanty references to France in book two,[6] while Belleforest added to his version no fewer than 627 pages on the history and geography of his own country in order to balance the long third book on Germany which had formed the heart of Münster's original work. Many of these augmentations then found their way into subsequent German editions: the last of the editions of the *Cosmography,* that of 1628, devotes 190 large pages to France and 263 to Italy, compared to 61 pages and 123 pages, respectively, in 1559. Items of general interest on historical, geographical, cultural subjects were included as they became available. Illustrations, maps, plans, charts, portraits became profuse. The principle of this proliferation of facts and lore had been declared by Münster at the outset, and was reiterated by the editor of the last edition:[7] Nothing is stated in this volume that has not been previously written, in thousands of other books. But what elsewhere appears in fragments, and in scattered places, has here been brought together, "without any alterations or additions of our own." Sources are nearly always given. The best cure for disbelief in the book's trustworthiness, Münster notes, is to look up the sources cited. Taken all together, the editions of Münster's *Cosmography* constitute a chronicle of the taste, particularly the expanding taste, of the lay public in the second half of the sixteenth century. They have hardly been studied as such, even though the work's attractions strike one who merely turns the pages to look at the pictures. A book which, in less than a century, saw thirty-five editions and circulated as widely as the many surviving copies suggest, deserves close scrutiny.

To make a beginning, it might be interesting to explore one aspect of the *Cosmography* that impressed me as I traced some subjects through the editions: its character as a kind of encyclopedia of general knowledge.[7a] Münster's preface promises the prospective reader an exhaustive survey of all that is significant and interesting in his world. "The art of cosmography," he begins, "concerns itself not only with the countries, habitations, and lives of the various peoples of the earth, but also with many other things, such as strange animals, trees, metals, and so on, things both useful and useless, to be found on land and in the sea; [also] the habits, customs, laws, governments of men, . . . the origins of countries, regions, cities, and towns, how nature has endowed them and what human inventiveness has produced in them, [also] what notable things have happened everywhere. . . ."[8] But between preface and postscript, the fare is even richer than that. Far from drawing the contents of the work merely from his own learning and observations, Münster affirms that he shirked no effort to make the knowledge of others available to himself. "It is not possible nowadays that a man can see everything for himself. Life is too short, and there are too many perils to health and safety on the land." He has read, he says, histories and chronicles and other books without number, "and taken from each whatever suited my purpose." Moreover, "wherever I heard of a learned and travelled man, I wrote to him, told him about my project, and asked his help. And I found many who were willing to speed my work by sending a book or supplying a description."[9] This was the usual procedure for the production of books of this sort.[10] As Münster himself notes: "more often than not I give another's opinion rather than my own."[11] The resulting compilation did not have much unity of viewpoint[12] and could not pretend to balance and style, but it did bring together an extraordinary wealth of erudition of the most varied sort. Even today it is impossible to settle down to an hour's browsing in Münster without learning something. In the sixteenth century, the book brought knowledge and enlightenment to nearly three generations of readers.

What one calls an encyclopedic work is, of course, a matter of definition. Encyclopedias, in the proper sense of the word, existed at least since Roman antiquity.[13] Every age organizes its sum of knowledge in the way that suits it best, not necessarily in the dictionary order familiar to us now. The example from antiquity closest to the spirit of Münster's *Cosmography* is the elder Pliny's *Natural History,* a compilation made from the books of over four-hundred Roman and other writers, in nearly twenty-five hundred chapters on everything from astronomy to pharmacology, very unequal in both compass and quality. The *Natural History* was enormously popular in the fifteenth and sixteenth centuries. By 1544 more than forty printed editions had been published;[14] it was a treasure house of information for professional and lay readers alike. For other kinds of knowledge, one could, in Münster's day, look in Gregor Reisch's *Margarita philosophica,* first printed in 1503 and important especially as a popularization of natural science; Raffaele Maffei Volaterranus' *Commentarii rerum urbanarum,* published 1506, and, despite its title, a comprehensive encyclopedic work; Joachim Fortius Ringelberg's *Lucubrationes vel potius absolutissima kyklopaideia,* according to Gert Zischka the first book to use the word "encyclopedia" in a title, printed Basel, 1541; Paul Skalich's *Encyclopaedia seu orbis disciplinarum epistemon,* 1559; Theodor Zwinger's gigantic *Theatrum humanae vitae* of 1565; and several others. Each author chose a different method of arranging and presenting his facts. Zwinger tried his hand, unsuccessfully, at a complicated systematic order in which subjects are taken up under categories tagged *"avaritia," "memoria,"* and so on. Polydore Vergil found a unifying scheme for imparting encyclopedic knowledge in his *De inventoribus rerum libri VIII* by tracing the first invention or discovery of things. Volaterranus used a complex, but rational and efficient scheme proceeding from geography to history and anthropology, to philology, philosophy, politics, and natural science and mathematics, the items arranged in alphabetical order within each category. Others tried to find a workable scheme in chronology, calendar days, the alphabet, or in idiosyncratic methods like that of the physician and dramatist Tobias Kober, whose description of diseases, injuries, and epidemics proceeds in an order determined by the native countries of his patients.[15] At the very least, these arrangements encouraged consecutive reading, an impossibility where the order was rigorously alphabetical. Provided there is a good index, such as that in Polydore Vergil's *De inventoribus rerum* and in Volaterranus' *Commentaries,* the book could be easily used for reference and thus made to serve the function of a modern encyclopedia without destroying its character as a work of literature.

As a matter of fact, the indices to the editions of Münster's *Cosmography* give a rather clear indication of the use to which these volumes must have been put. The *Cosmography* was, I think, an encyclopedia in the sixteenth-century sense: universal in scope, touching on nearly all subjects, incorporating, or making use of, all pertinent sources of information as they were or became available, and aiming at completeness: *all* the emperors of Rome with dates and brief biographies, *all* the Turkish sultans, lists of *all* the islands off the Greek mainland and of *all* the cities and towns in Tuscany, and so on. Though the manner in which such knowledge was conveyed to the reader was informal, often anecdotal, the amount of solid learning packed into the text makes perusal a formidable task. To be sure, the appearance of the books was inviting and designed specifically to counteract the massive text: each page diversified with chapter headings, marginal summaries, and—above all—splendid illustrations. But the writing itself is utilitarian and does not ring with the sonority usually associated with historiography in humanist circles.[16] It was not for style or moral uplift that the *Cosmography* was read, but for the concrete facts contained on its crowded pages.

To these facts the Index, or *Register* as it is called in the German versions, is a key. As the later editions swelled the pages of the work to more than twice their original number, the text became gradually less manageable without a guide of some sort, and in response to this need the index was made ever more elaborate and effective. The first edition of 1544 had no index at all, the second edition, published a year later, came supplied with a *Register* covering fourteen and a half pages, a fact announced to readers on the title page: "This *Cosmography* has been greatly augmented and improved by the author himself, and a Register has been added to make it much more useful than before." The indices of the later German editions are longer, more detailed, and technically superior. Instead of merely giving place and proper names, the later registers analyze the contents: "CHILDREN, how they are to be brought up"; "METALS, how they are extracted, why some are preferred to others, their mixture and utility . . ."; "TURKS, invade Italy, what laws they keep, how they treat Christian prisoners, why they may not drink wine . . ."; "JEWS, when expelled from Spain, expelled from France, murder a child in Trent, massacred in Nördlingen . . . ." Since the indices had to be redone in any case each time a new edition was being prepared, there were many opportunities to improve them in amplitude and clarity. The 1628 edition, the last one published, is equipped with an admirable working index indispensable to the modern student of the *Cosmography*. Every battle taken up in the text is listed in the index under BATTLES, every river under RIVERS, every island, monastery, bishop. There is a long list of entries under the name of each country. Exotic information, which a chairbound traveler might well turn to first, is carefully analyzed: BRASILIANS, with wife and child [illustration]; how they go to war; how they kill and slaughter a prisoner [illustration]; how their wives welcome guests; terrible drinking; how they eat; how they mourn their dead. . . ."

The clearest evidence of the importance attached to the index by both readers and publisher is given by the Latin versions which tended to enlist the collaboration of the professionally most competent editors. The first Latin edition of 1550 had an index of only 12 pages; in the edition of 1572 the index extended over 176 pages. In 1550 the index had been rudimentary, only general references being made: ALEXANDER MAGNUS, CUBA INSULA, GLADIATORA ARS, and so on. In 1572 the editors provided a properly analytical instrument for surveying the entire contents of the *Cosmography* and locating each item on its page. The forty-two separate entries under ALEXANDER MAGNUS constitute in themselves a thumbnail history of Alexander's conquests. The entries under ANIMALS refer to fauna in all countries taken up; ROME and ROMANS cover nearly five columns of analyzed entries. There are references under HOMICIDE, PEPPER, SULTAN, and a thousand more. The date and the full story of the Turkish siege of Vienna, the parts of Hungary under occupation—such information can be looked up in a moment. There is an analyzed index entry for every city described and depicted, as there is for every individual whose name figures in the text.[17] To make the work still more useful, editors often inserted cross references linking information presented in different parts of the volumes. For example, a note attached to the description of Waldshut: "For the battles fought in or near this town, see above in the description of Switzerland." Or a marginal note: "For more information on this, see above, page 238." These cross references are carefully altered in later editions to take account of changes in pagination.

In general, the tendency of the editions is to become not only bigger and richer, and more profusely illustrated, but also increasingly practical as works of reference. Even visually this is true. In the earlier editions, the lists and inventories which, in accord with the taste of the time for such things, make up much of the bulk of the book, are always written out as lines of text, indistinguishable by the eye from the narrative and, of course, difficult and wearisome to read. In the later editions, these catalogues of islands and bishops and delegates to the Council of Constance[18] are usually arranged in columns down the page according to some rational order, alphabetical, chronological, geographical, hierarchical. Order and arrangement were evidently major concerns with the editors of the later versions. Münster himself had not worried much about methodology. His organization, as he explained in 1545, was that of the ancient periegesis:

> I shall take you on a tour from country to country and across the oceans, and I shall point out cities, mountains, rivers, deserts, and other things diverting and pleasant to know about, such as the customs and ways and activities of strange peoples, also what the soil of their country produces. . . .[19]

Thirty years later, Belleforest not only vastly expanded the range of subjects, but brought method to its organization. In addition to everything that previous editions had offered, he writes, his two big volumes contain

> catalogues of law makers, philosophers, poets, orators, historians, nymphs, muses, sybils; also myths, oracles, rites, idols, marvels and other prodigies surpassing nature; also the names of the inventors of many arts, of the founders of religious orders. . . ; also the names of mountains, promontories, mines, quarries, fountains, rivers, lakes, oceans, gulfs, whirlpools, and deeps—all this well and clearly arranged and disposed according to the principles of chronology, topography, and prosopography.[20]

Clarity and logic of organization, the disposition of matter on the printed page, became, in fact, a preoccupation of editors, almost an end in itself. It is a phenomenon familiar to a student of encyclopedic books of the late sixteenth century, related to the increased fascination with the technical possibilities of typesetting and to the great influence exerted by the methodology of Peter Ramus on the accumulation and distribution of knowledge. The Ramist doctrine that every subject could be treated topically, that the best kind of exposition was that which proceeded by analysis, by breaking everything down into its constituent parts, was enthusiastically adopted by publishers and editors, including Münster's. The years of Ramus' greatest impact on German thought coincided precisely with the publication of the later editions of the *Cosmography*.[21] While the dispositions and layouts of the *Cosmography* do not attain (or, if one is to follow Walter Ong, descend to) the extremes of the manifold divisions and endlessly dichotomized tables of Johannes Piscator and Bartholomäus Keckermann,[22] the method of Ramism is clearly discernible in the editions from 1578 to 1628. The entire geography of Italy faces us on eleven large pages of carefully associated and bracketed names of regions, cities, and other settlements, down to hamlets, rivers, islands, mountains, thermal baths, bridges, fortified towers, and ancient monuments.[23] The territorial and political organization of Sicily is set out on three and a half pages of differentiated type showing feudal relationships and political jurisdictions.[24] A complete list of popes provides each pontiff with his dates and gives the duration of his pontificate in years, months, and days.[25] An elaborate bracketed table indicates the places of hundreds of German localities in the Imperial Circles.[26] Delegates to the Council of Constance are tabulated by rank, title, origin, and size of retinue.[27] Genealogical tables illustrate nearly every line of descent. In aspect alone, these devices render the later editions of the *Cosmography* very different from the volume that had appeared in 1544, more useful as reference books, as repositories of rationally organized items of related knowledge, but also far less readable. Readers could, and—as marginal remarks in many surviving copies seem to indicate—often did, follow the narrative through the 1544 or 1550 versions from cover to cover. By 1580 the bulk had become so great and the massed material so oppressive that it is not possible to imagine a reader so keen as to take in the entire volume. Readers of the later versions probably tended to spot read, to consult, to refer, to check.

The character of the book thus being transformed, it became a matter of urgency that its contents be full, accurate, and up-to-date. Throughout the career of the *Cosmography,* therefore, its editors were busy (though not always very successful) keeping their volumes abreast of new and better sources of knowledge. Münster himself augmented and improved those editions of his work which he lived to oversee. That he worked the text over carefully is evident not only from the addition of specific items, but also from the interpolation of remarks and comments where the text re-engaged his opinions.[28] There is very little rewriting: changes are made by means of insertions between existing sentences or by addenda at the end of a paragraph. But there is a conscientious attempt to correct errors[29] and to fill gaps.[30] Above all, Münster tried to broaden the purview of his work and give its contents a more lucid exposition.

Lengthy addenda take up such matters as mining in the Alsace,[31] business life in Augsburg,[32] the characteristics of Silesians and the scenery of their country, the course of the Nile.[33] In 1544 Münster had had to concede his ignorance of the northern countries: "I went to great pains," he noted, "writing to Denmark and to the Archbishop of Upsala in Rome, but I was not able to obtain the information I lacked on the kings of Denmark." But soon after seeing the first version through the press, he must have succeeded, for the second edition adds nineteen pages on Denmark, Norway, and Sweden, bringing the history of Scandinavia up to the year 1543.[34] The changes respond to the interest of Münster's time in such topical questions as the Turkish wars (there are eight new pages on Turkish government and customs in the 1545 version), the Mediterranean naval campaign of Charles V against Barbarossa (a good account of the attack on Fez and the siege of Algiers[35]), and the news coming in from the East Indies and the New World (there are additional pages on Sumatra, China, and on the later voyages of Columbus[36]). Throughout, Münster tried to improve the arrangement of his facts. Several scattered chapters on Swiss history were gathered into a connected account in 1545. Kings and bishops and abbots are, sometimes, arranged in catalogues with running numbers in the left-hand margin and vital dates on the right. Münster seemed to be aware that his big book, if it were to hold its readers, would have to be not only diverting and interesting, but also efficient.

The editors of the later versions carried on with Münster's procedures for keeping the work up to date.[37] Wars, even such local conflicts as the protracted feud between the Margrave Albrecht of Brandenburg and the city of Nuremberg[38] are reported as soon as they occur. Death dates of rulers who died shortly after one edition went to press are given in the next, though frequently the changes reflect national limitations of interest.[39] The editors must have kept close track of the careers of even minor European, particularly German, princes; deceased rulers are rarely listed among the living.[40] The 1559 Latin edition inserts an account of the civil war in Germany,[41] and the articles on important or notorious persons increase in length from edition to edition as their impacts on European history are appreciated.[42] There is a tendency to incorporate information of a statistical character: a list of knights and princes fallen in the Swiss wars, a list of abbots of every monastery mentioned, a monster catalogue of all tournaments ever held in Germany, with a complete roster of all participants by rank,[43] and so on. A great deal of local history provides much of the bulk of the later editions;[44] in this, too, the updating is conscientious. Another welcome change was the replacement, in the later editions, of stereotyped faces by proper portraits. In the early versions illustrations of rulers, heretics, philosophers have only symbolic and decorative value. In the editions of the 1580s and after, true-to-life likenesses of famous men add a great deal of topical interest to the volumes. Maximilian, Charles V, Frederick the Wise, Franz von Sickingen, Luther, Oecolampadius are familiar faces on the pages.[45] The same is true of the city profiles which, from 1550 on, form one of the main attractions of the *Cosmography*. In the 1544–1545 editions, there had been little attempt at verisimilitude. Stock woodcuts are used over and over to illustrate different towns. Beginning in 1550, however, the stereotype outline of moat, walls, church towers, and tile roofs disappears, and proper city portraits, drawn at the scene, usually by local artists, make their appearance.

One of the flaws in Münster's original work was its abrupt decline, quantitatively as well as qualitatively, as the author strays from Western and Central Europe into the East.[46] This imbalance is corrected to some extent by the editors of later versions, depending on their independence from the original work and on the quality of the sources available to them.

François de Belleforest, of all the editors, did most to improve the Eastern sections of the *Cosmography*. In the chapters on Greece, for example, he was entirely on his own, merely retaining Münster's general scheme of history and politics on a geographical basis, with stress on institutions and customs. Belleforest, despite the disdain in which he was held by many of his contemporaries and successors,[47] made an able and ingenious adapter of a work of this sort. He increased the emphasis on political and administrative matters, taking his facts from good classical and modern sources, which he cites conscientiously, by book and often by chapter, in the margins of his text. This competent interest in practical politics, amounting, in the aggregate, to a comparative description of government, is the main intellectual contribution Belleforest makes to Münster's original work. "Münster is very weak on the government of this city," he notes occasionally, then sets out to describe in detail the political structure of, for example, Genoa and the operation of her government.[48] His most notable achievement is the long section on France which replaces Münster's meager chapter: 627 pages of geography, history, chronology, genealogy, flora and fauna, folklore, government, and municipal histories and descriptions. In the narration of these matters, Belleforest was in full stride, writing confidently from the fullness of his erudition, the extent of which he was to show soon in his lavish *Grandes Annales et histoire générale de France,* published in two huge volumes in 1579. Especially interesting is the long account of French government, with descriptions of the Court, the role of the aristocracy, the *parlements,* and the organs of municipal government.[49] There is an interesting, detailed chapter on the University and its colleges,[50] described with enormous pride as the greatest institution of learning in Christendom, also a great many plans and illustrations of cities, each punctuated with numbers indicating and identifying landmarks and noteworthy buildings.

But elsewhere, too, Belleforest improved the proportions of Münster's badly balanced work, adding paragraphs or whole sections,[51] cutting and trimming where Münster was verbose.[52] The entire work reveals, in its organization, its style, and in its usefulness as a repository of concrete knowledge, Belleforest's superior critical acumen. He made a show of scrutinizing the works of others, and he regularly dissected the books on which he based his own account.[53] On the other hand, he served the less scientific prepossessions of his age by retaining Münster's fanciful genealogies and the ubiquitous references to natural portents and to freaks and monsters.[54] Where it counts, however, Belleforest is precise and objective. In the chapters on the New World, the whole tone is different. To Münster, the reality of these exotic countries and their strange creatures and vegetation was still nearly incredible. His words are full of wonder and his account underlines the extraordinary and the fabulous. Belleforest, on the other hand, is businesslike. The New World exists, it is part of our extended experience, it needs to be described. In his handling, Brazil and Peru emerged from the mists of fantasy into the light of the empirical world.

The adequate description of "The Islands Newly Discovered" constituted one of the thorniest tasks for the later editors of the *Cosmography*. Despite his professional interests in geography, Münster had, in his own editions, furnished little of value on the New World, probably because, when he wrote the pages on America at the end of his fifth book, and with the description of Africa in the sixth still to be undertaken, his energies had flagged and the size of the work had begun to frighten him. In any case, his main purpose had been to explain the European world, especially Germany. The chapters on the New World were chiefly intended to titillate his readers' taste for the outlandish.

Although the subsequent descriptions of America never attained the amplitude proper to the subject, editors made a valiant effort to improve on Münster in scope and quality. The description became realistic where it had been fanciful—though favorite tales of bestial cruelty and cannibalism persisted—and illustrations and maps became informative where they had been merely quaint. The 1572 Latin edition, for example, inserts a *Novi orbis succincta descriptio*[55] summarizing all the voyages and incorporating some new information procured since 1550. It adds a fine two-page drawing of Cuzco, the famous Inca city,[56] a map of Cuba, and various other items. But it is only in the last edition, of 1628, that the new material takes on significance. Here the narrative for the first time is ample. It opens with a few questions: Did the ancients have knowledge of America? (The answer is in the negative.) How did the present inhabitants reach the New World? (Various possibilities, including migration from Russia and Lapland, are considered.) The Columbus voyages are described, then come illustrations and descriptions of animals and plants, the histories of the settlement of Virginia and Florida, quite competently told, the exploration and conquest of Central America, a long description of Mexico, then of Guatemala, Venezuela, Brazil, Argentina, Patagonia, Chile, Peru, and the Caribbean Islands. The stories of the circumnavigations of the world bring the account to a close. The narrative returns again and again to details of customs, dress, agricultural procedures, methods of warfare, religion, funeral practices. There is no attempt to conceal the cruelty of the conquests, but the Spanish excesses are more than matched by Indian barbarism, illustrated in much descriptive and pictorial detail. The sources for all this are cited in the margins and, sometimes, in the text. They corroborate the impression conveyed by other parts of this edition, that the editors made an informed effort to procure pertinent books as they appeared and to incorporate them in their expanding text.

Given the size which the *Cosmography* had now attained, keeping it current was a considerable task. It is perhaps not surprising, then, that the great enterprise came to an end in the second quarter of the seventeenth century. The book had become too big and too amorphous to serve a clear purpose. It was, in structure, a narrative work, telling a story in books and chapters, but the story had become too prolix and too disjointed to be readable. Its pictures and maps and portraits were to have illustrated the world, but the woodcuts in the later editions are noticeably inferior to the ones in 1550; even the magnificent double-page city illustrations of the edition of 1550 were later reduced in size, and show up blurred and cramped. For all practical purposes the book had turned into an encyclopedia, but it could not change its format to dispose its contents accordingly. By 1600, furthermore, there existed competitors for each of the several purposes served by the *Cosmography:* Johann Rauw's *Cosmographia* of 1597; the splendid regional topographies of Johann Stumpf, Peter Albinus, Cuspinian, Guler von Weineck, and many others; Braun and Hogenberg's *Civitates orbis terrarum* of 1572 to 1618; and, from 1642 on, Merian-Zeiller's visually superb *Topographia Germaniae.* As an encyclopedic repository of universal learning, Münster could hardly match Johann Heinrich Alsted's *Scientiarum omnium encyclopedia* which was first published in 1630,[57] two years after the printing of what turned out to be the last edition of Münster's work.

Münster's *Cosmography* thus vanished from the shelf of the great books of general knowledge, books to be consulted and used, and took its place among the stacks of tomes which, when exhumed by an occasional scholar, serve merely to illustrate the intellectual predilections of their time. It was one of the last attempts to contain between the covers of a single narrative volume all that was useful and interesting to know. When it disappeared in the early seventeenth century, it made way for works of specialized erudition to whose authors Münster's procedures were to seem amateurish and a little foolish. But in the more than eighty years of its publishing life, the *Cosmography* had taught nearly three generations of laymen most of what they knew about the world beyond their native places. Today it serves as a reminder that sixteenth-century readers were not so parochial in their interests as they are often made out to be, that there were sources of information available to all who could and would read, and that the knowledge purveyed in them was not only broad, but by and large also sound.

NOTES

1. Viktor Hantzsch, "Sebastian Münster: Leben, Werk, wissenschaftliche Bedeutung," *Abhandl.d.philol.-hist.Cl.d.kgl.sächsischen Ges. d.Wiss.*, XVIII, no. 3 (Leipzig, 1898). Herbert Hunger *et al.*, *Geschichte der Textüberlieferung der antiken und mittelalterlichen Literatur* (Zurich, 1961), p. 202. Hantzsch's treatise, until now the only biographical-critical study of Münster's life and work, has been superseded by Karl Heinz Burmeister, *Sebastian Münster: Versuch eines biographischen Gesamtbildes* (Basler Beiträge zur Geschichtswissenschaft, Vol. 91; Basel and Stuttgart, 1963).

2. Several of the editions listed by Viktor Hantzsch, *op. cit.*, note 77, are declared non-existent by Werner Horn, "Sebastian Münster's Map of Prussia and the Variants of it," *Imago Mundi*, VII (1950), pp. 67–73, notes 29 to 33. See also Harold L. Ruland, "A Survey of Double-Page Maps in thirty-five Editions of the *Cosmographia Universalis* 1544–1628 of Sebastian Münster and in his Editions of Ptolemy's *Geographia* 1540–1552," *Imago Mundi*, XVI (1962), pp. 84–97.

3. For titles, see *British Museum General Catalogue of Printed Books* vol. 166 (London, 1963), column 413.

4. The full title, in the first edition of 1544, reads: *Cosmographia, Beschreibung aller Lender* . . . , *in welcher begriffen aller völcker herrschafften, stetten, und namhafftiger flecken, herkommen, sitten,*

gebreuch, ordnung, glauben, secten, und hantierung, durch die gantze welt, und fürnemlich teutscher nation. Was auch besunders in jedem landt gefunden unnd darin beschehen sey. . . .

5. The paging of all the volumes is confused and replete with errors. My figures are approximate, but tend to low estimates. The last page of the 1628 edition is numbered 1,752; that of Vol. One of the 1575 Paris edition is numbered 1,873, of Vol. Two 2,235.

6. For example, the fine description of Rouen missing in earlier editions; also illustrations and plans of Poitiers, Tours, Bourges, Bordeaux, Montpellier, Lyon.

7. 1628 German edition, p. 1,752. Cf. Münster's address to the reader on the last page of the 1545 edition.

7a. Burmeister, *op cit.*, p. 160, refers to the "encyclopedic character" of the *Cosmography* but does not explore it. The present essay was finished and in the editor's hands when a copy of Burmeister's excellent book reached me. Burmeister's work will be, from now on, the starting point of every serious study of Münster.

8. *E.g.*, 1578 edition, leaf a iii recto ff. Münster's preface is maintained unchanged in the various editions.

9. *Ibid.*

10. For a detailed description of how a compilation like Münster's was put together, and for some additional information about the publication history of the *Cosmography*, see Gerald Strauss, "The Production of Johann Stumpf's 'Description of the Swiss Confederation,' " *Medievalia et Humanistica*, XII (1958), pp. 104–122. Burmeister, *op cit.*, pp. 133–51, deals at length with the collaboration and the collaborators that produced the *Cosmography*.

11. Last page of Preface, any edition.

12. The absence of conceptual unity is best exemplified by the half-hearted attempts to make the 1568 French edition, published by Petri in Basel with a privilege from King Henry II (cf. verso of title page), acceptable to Catholic readers. Some offensive passages, references, illustrations were taken out, many others left untouched.

13. For the following paragraph, see Gert A. Zischka, *Index Lexicorum: Bibliographie der lexikalischen Nachschlagewerke* (Vienna, 1959), Introduction. Also, the article "Encyclopaedia," *Encyclopaedia Britannica*, eleventh edition (1910), Vol. 9, pp. 369–382; Bernhard Wendt, *Idee und Entwicklungsgeschichte der enzyklopädischen*

Literatur (Würzburg, 1941), 13 ff.; Ernst Herbert Lehmann, *Geschichte des Konversationslexikons* (Leipzig, 1934).

14. Zischka, *op cit.*, xv; "Encyclopaedia," *loc. cit.*, p. 370.

15. *Decades tres observationum medicarum castrensium Hungaricarum* (Frankfurt, 1606).

16. Münster himself echoes the humanist exaltation of history. But it is a perfunctory exhortation, quite unrelated to the body of his work. See Address to Charles V in the 1550 Latin edition, p. 2 recto.

17. The Czech edition (Prague, 1554) has an index of twenty-seven pages; the French edition of 1575 expanded by Belleforest has the most detailed index of all the editions: eighty-seven pages in Vol. I, 174 pages in Vol. II.

18. *E.g.*, 1598 German edition, pp. 584 ff.; 1588 German edition, p. 1,023; 1572 Latin edition, p. 854. These are random examples.

19. 1545 German edition, a iiii verso.

20. 1575 French edition (Belleforest), verso of title page.

21. See Walter Ong, *Ramus, Method and the Decay of Dialogue* (Cambridge, Mass., 1958), esp. pp. 298–301, and the same author's *Ramus and Talon Inventory* (Cambridge, Mass., 1958), pp. 407–14, for titles and descriptions of "methodized" compendia published in Germany between 1582 and 1663. Ong states that the peak of Ramist influence in Germany falls between 1580 and 1620 and that it was most intense in the upper Rhineland, where Ramus himself had visited earlier, while in exile from France. "In Germany," Father Ong continues, "[Ramism's] diagrammatic approach to knowledge fires the imagination of polyhistors and of codifiers of all the sciences, so that Ramist method moves into the uppermost branches of the curriculum with a drive which cannot be matched in any other country." (*Ramus, Method and the Decay of Dialogue*, p. 298.)

22. Cf. Ong, *Ramus, Method. . .* , pp. 299–300.

23. 1598 German edition, 218–28.

24. *Ibid.*, 379–82.

25. *Ibid.*, pp. 244–45.

26. *Ibid.*, pp. 479–80

27. *Ibid.*, pp. 584–92.

28. For Example: 1545 edition, p. 426: an anticlerical comment added to the account of an altercation between the Bishop of Cologne and the city. Or the comment on the hardships of the German peasant, added to the chapter on customs in Book three. Or the outburst on slave trade: 1545 edition, p. 672.

29. For example: an error in numbering Byzantine emperors in 1544 is rectified in 1545: 1544 edition, p. 620; 1545 edition, p. 676.

30. For example: The 1545 edition gives the pre-Roman rulers of Spain, describes the emancipation of Geneva from Savoy, gives a sketch of the contemporary politics of the Italian states, explains the government of Genoa, devotes five pages to the Swiss-Austrian wars and a paragraph to the great flood of the Rhine in 1480.

31. As a result of a letter from Johann Hubinsack, a judge, who wrote to Münster regretting the absence of references to mining in the 1544 edition. Münster immediately indicated his interest, whereupon "a huge letter arrived, crammed with facts on mining and similar wonderworks of God." Cf. chapter "Von Berkwercken," 1545 edition, Book three.

32. 1545 edition, pp. 491–92.

33. *Ibid.*, pp. 797 ff.

34. *Ibid.*, pp. 511, 595–613.

35. *Ibid.*, pp. 781–82.

36. *Ibid.*, pp. 767–70.

37. One example for many to illustrate updating: The German editions of 1578, 1592, and 1598 bring the list of Spanish kings up to date: 1578, p. 82; 1592, p. 80; 1598, p. 88.

38. Cf. 1568 French edition, p. 786; 1572 Latin edition, p. 789; 1575 Italian edition, p. 721.

39. For example: In the 1550 Latin edition, Henry II is given as the reigning King of France. The 1568 French edition extends the line of French kings to Francis II, while the 1575 Italian edition retains the genealogy as it was in 1550. The same is true of the Dukes of Lorraine and many other lines.

40. For example: The 1559 Latin edition records the death in 1552 of Margrave Ernst of Baden who had been given as the reigning prince in the 1552 edition. (1552, p. 556; 1559, p. 556 also.)

41. 1559 Latin edition, p. 725.

42. Cf. the article on Charles V in 1628 (p. 650), five or six times as long as the one in 1559.

43. 1628 German edition, pp. 1204–1248.

44. For example: Worms, in 1559, merits two pages of description; in 1628 seven pages.

45. 1598 German edition, pp. 456, 457 (Maximilian and Charles V), p. 458 (Luther), p. 886 (Oecolampadius).

46. On the paucity and unreliability of sources for Eastern Europe and Asia, see Gerald Strauss, *Sixteenth-Century Germany: its Topography and Topographers* (Madison, Wisconsin, 1959), p. 126.

47. See the article on Belleforest in Pierre Bayle's *Dictionaire historique et critique* (fourth edition, Amsterdam, 1730), I, pp. 510–11.

48. 1575 French edition, I, p. 637.

49. *Ibid.*, I, pp. 181–87.

50. *Ibid.*, I, pp. 187–202.

51. *E.g., ibid.*, I, pp. 150–55: long addition on the provinces and bishoprics of the Iberian kingdoms.

52. Belleforest does a good deal of judicious cutting in Münster's book on Germany, which is, however, left substantially intact.

53. For example: he discovers that Franz Irenicus, the author of *Germaniae exegeseos volumina duodecim* (Hagenau, 1518), in his attempt to ascribe all existing virtues to the ancient Germans, quotes not only the complimentary comments of Tacitus, but appropriates also a nice passage from the Greek medical writer Athenaeus, who had written about the Celts, not the Germans. 1575 French edition, I, p. 909.

54. See especially *ibid.*, II, p. 161, where specific arguments for the existence of monsters are presented. Also I, pp. 1,720 ff.

55. 1572 Latin edition, pp. 1,273–74.

56. *Ibid.*, pp. 1,276–77.

57. Gert A. Zischka, *Index Lexicorum*, pp. xxxvi–xxxvii.

WILLIAM ALLEN'S
USE OF PROTESTANT
POLITICAL ARGUMENT*

ROBERT   M.   KINGDON

State University of Iowa

One of the main themes distinguishing Garrett Mattingly's work
was an abiding appreciation of the fundamental unity of
Western civilization. He emphasized it in his teaching and
he illustrated it in his work. To his students he often made the point
that the American historian, detached as he can be from the bitter
national tensions which so often distract the European historian,
should employ his vantage point to call attention to those international and supranational forces that have created Western unity. To
his readers he pointed out many ways in which the diplomats active
in the Europe of the Renaissance worked to maintain this unity,
often against bitter odds. This same theme can also be illustrated
by studies in the history of ideas, since ideas are particularly fluid,

* This essay is a by-product of an edition I am preparing, at the suggestion of Garrett Mattingly, for the *Folger Documents of Tudor and
Stuart Civilization,* of William Cecil, Lord Burghley, *The Execution of
Justice in England* (1583), and William Allen, *A True, Sincere, and
Modest Defense of English Catholics that suffer for their faith* (1584),
hereafter cited as Allen, *Defense.* I have used the Folger Shakespeare Library
copies of both of these books. [Punctuation has been slightly modernized
in some places where clarity was at stake, and the ambiguous contemporary
spelling "then" has been modernized to "than"; otherwise, quotations are
reproduced here as in the editions cited.—Ed.]

hence particularly likely to seep through or wash over the dikes of nation or confession which have so often been erected to segment the West. An illustration of this theme emerges, surprisingly, from a study of English Catholic use of Protestant political argument in the late sixteenth and early seventeenth centuries. Polemicists like Father Robert Parsons and Dr. William Allen deliberately crossed lines of confession and nationality in a search for ideas that would advance their cause. Perhaps the most striking example can be found in a book the importance of which Mattingly himself pointed out, Allen's *A True, Sincere, and Modest Defense of English Catholics that suffer for their faith* (1584).[1]

Allen's *Defense* was designed most obviously to counter William Cecil's *The Execution of Justice in England* (1583), a semiofficial pamphlet developing the claim that the Elizabethan government was putting to death Jesuits and other Catholic missionaries in England, solely on charges of treason, never because of their religious beliefs. Allen, as the acknowledged leader and principal spokesman for a militant new party of English Catholics in exile, felt obliged to answer Cecil's claim, potentially so damaging to the English Catholic cause in the eyes of the Continental princes upon whose support it depended. It seems quite clear, however, that Allen also had a second, less obvious purpose in drafting his *Defense*. He had been engaged in a series of secret plots to mount an invasion of England by Continental Catholic armies in order to depose Elizabeth I and re-establish the Roman Catholic faith.[2] For such an invasion to succeed, however, the plotters felt it would have to be supported by a simultaneous rising of those Englishmen within the realm who remained loyal to Rome. Allen apparently hoped, with his writings, to prepare these Englishmen, living "under the cross," for the great revolt to come.

Both purposes led Allen to devote much of his *Defense* to a justification of the papal right to depose heretic rulers. Cecil had argued that *Regnans in Excelsis,* the bull by which Pope Pius V in 1570 had excommunicated Elizabeth and absolved her subjects of obedience, revealed the Roman Catholic Church to be an international political conspiracy, determined to destroy all governments which would not bend to its will. Allen argued that the bull was an occasionally necessary standard method of implementing the pope's spiritual duty to guide all Christian souls, that right then it was not binding upon English Catholics, but that it could be put into effect whenever the pope decided that circumstances made enforcement appropriate.

In developing his justification of this papal right, Allen appealed to standard Catholic authorities, of course.[3] He quoted St. Thomas Aquinas and such an authoritative contemporary commentator on his work as Francisco Toledo. He referred to canon law, particularly to a decree drafted by the Fourth Lateran Council in 1215. But this part of his argument was relatively perfunctory, since, as he himself acknowledged, it would carry relatively little weight with his adversaries. Most of his argument was based on extended exegesis of key passages in Holy Scriptures, in the writings of early Church Fathers, and in the standard histories of the early church.[4] In this, Allen was employing a technique typical of many Jesuits and other intellectual leaders of the Catholic Reformation. He was debating Protestants on their own grounds, arguing from the authorities they valued most. Much of his exegesis would seem forced or fanciful to modern Biblical scholars. But so would much of that advanced by his opponents. Generally speaking, this Catholic technique seems to have been quite effective in reversing, among intellectuals at least, the great tide toward Protestantism.

Allen, however, carried his polemical counteroffensive one step further. He not only cited the Protestants' favorite authorities. He also cited the Protestants themselves. In a few brief pages of his book, he inserts a set of quotations and paraphrases taken from the works of such great intellectual leaders of the Protestant Reformation as Luther, Zwingli, and Calvin, and from the writings of certain of their respected followers. The Protestant arguments were not, of course, for any papal right to license revolt. But they were for a general right of revolt quite analogous in certain ways to the kind Allen favored. It is upon Allen's use of these arguments that this article will focus. The particular arguments he cites reveal something about the general knowledge then current in informed circles of what early Protestant thinking on politics was. His use of them helps establish with increased precision the ways in which Protestant resistance theories which developed from 1520 until the 1570s can be linked to Catholic resistance theories which developed in the succeeding decades of the late sixteenth and early seventeenth centuries.

Allen established a background, although he introduced it only part way through this section of his argument, with a number of statements from Lutheran writers in justification of political revolt for religious reasons. He realized that they would not carry the same authority among Englishmen as certain other Protestant writers. But he knew that the Lutherans had established the foundation upon which all other Protestants had built, and, in addition, the Lutherans had drawn the main lines of controversy which continued to govern debate between Protestants and Catholics. Allen's examples of Lutheran political thought do not come from the actual writings of the men who stated them. They come rather from Sleidan's *De statu religionis et reipublicae, Carolo quinto, Caesare, Commentarii*.[5] This precise and detailed history of the course of religious politics, primarily in Germany, during the reign of Emperor Charles V, was thoroughly Protestant in its sympathies. It had been widely circulated throughout Europe and was even available in English translation. In the fashion of many histories of that day, it contained entire texts of certain key public statements and manifestoes, and paraphrases or detailed summaries of others. Altogether it served Allen's polemical purposes admirably.

In Sleidan Allen discovered that Luther himself, at the time of the formation of the Schmalkaldic League, had stated that "indeed he was in doubt for a time, whether they might take armes against their Supreme Magistrate or no; but afterward seing the extremitie of thinges, and that Religion could not otherwise be defended, nor themselves, he made no conscience of the matter, but ether Caesar, or anie, waging warres in his name, might be resisted."[6] This particular sentiment had been stated by Luther in 1530, at a conference in Torgau with certain lawyers and other advisers of the Protestant princes who were trying to devise ways to ward off what seemed to be an impending attempt by the emperor to suppress their faith through military action. It marks a critical point in the development of Luther's political thought, since heretofore he had repeatedly and expressly denied any religious right to political resistance. His denials had been particularly sharp after he had seen the bloody results of the use of mad violence by certain Anabaptists in the

Peasants' Revolt and other uprisings. Even at Torgau, however, Luther did not grant the existence of any religious right to revolt. He merely acknowledged the weight of certain legal and constitutional arguments for revolt, and conceded that the Christian tradition had nothing to say either for or against such arguments. The concession was fateful, nevertheless. It was put into writing in a terse note generally called the Torgau memorandum.[7] The memorandum was widely circulated and proved to be of substantial use to the princes organizing the newly militant kind of Lutheranism which supported the Schmalkaldic League.

These new militants among the Lutherans did not find it necessary to resort to war immediately, however. The imperial threat to suppress Lutheranism by force waned. It was not until 1546, as Luther was dying, that the militancy of his followers was put to an armed test, in the Schmalkaldic war. But this time new spokesmen had to be found to announce the Lutheran position. The first of these of whom Allen took note were two of the leading Lutheran princes—the Landgrave of Hesse and the Elector of Saxony. They were now the leaders of the Schmalkaldic League, they rallied some of its forces for military action, and its manifestoes were issued in their name. A manifesto to which Allen paid particular attention was issued on September 2, 1546. It was issued in response to the Emperor's announcement proscribing Hesse and Saxony as rebels and placing them under the imperial ban. The imperial announcement declared that they were being proscribed only for political rebellion, not for their religious views. Consequently they found themselves in a situation analogous to that of Allen and his English missionaries in the 1580s, and their reaction was similarly bellicose. The heart of their argument was that they had been forced to raise armies to defend what they believed to be the only true religion. In the passage quoted by Allen, they concluded: "Forasmuch as Caesar intendeth to destroy the true religion and our ancient libertie, he giveth us cause inough why we may with good conscience resist him, as both by prophane and sacred histories may be prooved."[8] Thus they extended the Protestant grounds upon which revolt may be supported. Now the argument to justify revolt for religion no longer was merely legal and constitutional. It had also become explicitly religious.

A yet more extreme Lutheran justification of revolt was still to come. The early result of Charles V's attempt to crush Lutheran power was smashing victory. Hesse and Saxony were imprisoned and a temporary compromise settlement, the Augsburg Interim of 1548, was imposed upon the entire empire. Most Lutherans, including Luther's close colleague Philip Melanchthon, saw no alternative open to them but acceptance either of this settlement or of some modified version of it. A few resolutely orthodox Lutherans refused to accept the Interim, however, even though it meant defying the assembled might of the entire Holy Roman Empire. The most vocal of these more orthodox Lutherans were gathered in the city of Magdeburg. There both city magistrates and city ministers resolved to defy local promulgation of the Interim, no matter what the cost. They explained and defended their defiance in a series of impassioned printed treatises and manifestoes. Perhaps the most famous of these was the Magdeburg *Bekenntnis* of April, 1550. Allen summarized the contents of this confession, again drawing his information from Sleidan, in these words: "The same writer [Sleidan] reporteth the like of the Ministers of Magdeburge; declaring how the inferiour may defend him self against the superior, compelling him to doe against the truth and rule of Christes lawes."[9] Allen left one really crucial word out of this paraphrase of Sleidan, however, and thus gave a somewhat misleading impression of the Magdeburgers' position. That word was "magistrate." While the ministers of Magdeburg, led by Luther's own disciple Nicolaus von Amsdorf, had advanced beyond Luther's position to one of justifying on religious grounds the right of political revolt, they were not prepared to vest this right in the entire population or in any random fragment thereof. It was to be vested only in "inferior magistrates," regularly constituted agents of government such as princes or city councillors, agents who could lay equal claim with the emperor to having been "ordained of God," and hence were equally charged with the responsibility of protecting the true worship of Him. Here we have come to a more sophisticated statement of Protestant resistance theory. For the Magdeburg *Bekenntnis* specifies not only the causes that justify revolt but also the institutions which may rightfully license it. This Magdeburg position was to be restated in significant and influential ways by later Protestant thinkers, most of them in the Calvinist rather than the Lutheran camp.

Before the Calvinist position jelled, however, even before the Lutherans had reluctantly decided to claim a religious right of resistance, another Protestant position had been stated—that of Zwingli. The general Zwinglian position, as Allen noted several times in his book, had won great favor in England. In fact Allen believed that the entire religious settlement developed by the government of Edward VI, the first really Protestant government of England, was basically Zwinglian. Zwingli's position on the problem of political resistance was much more bellicose than that of Luther, and it was stated at a much earlier point in his career. Zwingli had launched his campaign to reform the city of Zurich by triumphantly winning a public debate on sixty-seven articles of Christian doctrine. Among these articles was a group of ten on the role of government in religion. One of them, article forty-two, flatly justifies a right of resistance. It reads, in Allen's quite accurate translation: "When kinges rule unfaithfullie, and otherwise than the rule of the Gospel prescribeth, they may, with God, be deposed." Furthermore, within a few months after his defense of these articles, Zwingli had published a lengthy defense of each and every one of them. His defense of article forty-two, a part of which Allen also quotes, specifies that kings may be deposed "when they punish not wicked persons, but speciallie when they advaunce the ungodlie, as idle Priests, &c. such may be deprived of their dignitie, as Saul was."[10] While this gloss does mention agents or institutions who may rightfully depose a ruler, it remains rather vague as to who they are.

Zwingli did not abandon this strong view in his later career, even when the excesses of the Peasants' Revolt, which shocked him as they did Luther, must have tempted him to soften its bluntness. Shortly before his untimely death, he repeated the view in a letter to Konrad Sam and Simpert Schenk, ministers of the free German cities of Ulm and Memmingen. The letter was drafted in August of 1530, a few months before Luther was persuaded to sign the Torgau memorandum. It consequently represents a parallel reaction to the same Protestant fear of suppression by imperial arms. But Zwingli's reaction was predictably stronger and less ambiguous than

Luther's. He openly endorsed resistance, and on religious rather than merely constitutional grounds, and he justified his endorsement with yet another appeal to Scripture. His words, again in Allen's translation: "If the Empire of Rome, or what other Soveraigne so ever, should oppresse the sincere religion, and we necligentlie suffer the same, we shalbe charged with contempt, no lesse than the oppressors thereof themselves: wherof we have an example in the fiftenth of Jeremie, wher the destruction of the people is prophecied; for that they suffred their K. Manasses, being impious and ungodly, to be unpunished."[11] This particular letter of Zwingli's was soon published, in a collection of letters written by him and his fellow Reformer Oecolampadius,[12] and so it also became widely known and generally available.

In Allen's eyes the most important of the Continental Protestant positions he cited was the Calvinist one. He frequently argued that the Elizabethan settlement was basically Calvinist, that it had received its theology from the Reformer of Geneva, and that even the precise wording of one of the parliamentary statutes which had created the Elizabethan church had been influenced by Calvin's opinions.[13] In his summary of Protestant resistance theories, consequently, he gives pride of place to Calvin's. The entire summary begins, "And first their grand-maister, Jo. Calvin putteth doune his oracle, as a conclusion approved of their whole sect and confraternitie in thes wordes. . . . 'Earthlie Princes doe bereave themselves of al authoritie when they doe erect them selves against God, yea they are unworthie to be accompted in the number of men: and therfore we must rather spit upon their heades than obey them when they become so proude, or perverse, that they wil spoile God of his right.' "[14] The quotation is from Calvin's commentary on Daniel. It was published in 1561, as tempers in France were rising toward the fever pitch that within a few months was to plunge the nation into nearly forty years of bloody religious war. The commentary on Daniel is preceded by a dedicatory letter to Calvin's followers in France.[15] This letter reminded the faithful that Calvin had repeatedly urged them to avoid any resort to violence. But it also warned the authorities that further persecution of the atrocious sort his followers had had to endure might easily drive them to desperation and revolt. Calvin clearly recognized in the story of Daniel a parable of peculiar relevance to the contemporary situation. The courage and resolution of Daniel and his friends in the face of persecution should provide an encouraging example to his own followers. The dreadful fate of the kings of Babylon who persecuted these servants of God should provide a usefully stern warning to the rulers of France. The particular passage from Calvin's Daniel commentary which Allen chose to cite is remarkable for the vehemence with which it criticizes established authority. It is a peculiarly sharp example of the picturesque language which resulted when Calvin lost his celebrated temper. But it did not justify armed revolt, unless spitting be regarded as a form of revolt. It really justified only passive disobedience of laws which prohibit the exercise of "true religion," a position which Calvin had held consistently for years, and which he developed at length in this particular commentary.

These are nuances which are lost to Allen, however. He hastened on to advance his argument by quoting Calvin's principal lieutenant and successor, Theodore Beza, and he tied this opinion directly to England, to the Queen herself, in fact. He noted with horror, in the 1565 version of Beza's great New Testament, an epistle dedicatory to the Queen of England, proudly dated on an anniversary of the day "that the nobilitie of France (under the noble Prince of Condey) laid the first foundation of restoring true Christian religion in France, by consecrating most happilie their blood to God in the batail of Druze [Dreux]."[16] Clearly Beza was here glorifying a revolt against the laws and lawful king of one of the greatest kingdoms in Christendom. Obviously he thus approved of revolt to advance religion. Elsewhere Allen also noted that Beza accompanied the Huguenot armies through much of this campaign.[17]

Allen concluded his analysis of the Calvinist position by quotation from a yet more definitive authority, the Confession of Faith adopted by the national synod of the French Reformed Church. This statement had a far greater binding force upon the Calvinist movement than any particular commentary or letter drafted by its leaders, since its exact wording had been the result of lengthy deliberation and had been ratified by official representatives of the entire church, several times. Unfortunately for Allen's argument, it does not appear to give him very powerful support. The exact wording of the article he quotes: "We affirme that subjects must obey the lawes, pay tribute, beare al burthens imposed, and susteine the yoke even of infidel Magistrates; so for al that, that the supreme dominion and due of God be not violated."[18] Allen did not explain his construction of this article. Apparently he felt the final clause created a loophole which could be used to justify disobedience of laws, refusal to pay taxes, avoidance of other governmental responsibilities, and revolt.

Finally Allen connected these assorted justifications of resistance directly to England, by quoting two English proto-Puritans, Christopher Goodman and John Knox. And in their writings he found statements which substantiated his case more fully than any he could find among Continental writers. Goodman, in his inflammatory tract, *How Superior Powers Ought to be Obeyed* (Geneva, 1558), published while he was a refugee from Marian persecution in Calvinist Geneva, had called for revolt, preferably revolt led by nobles and others charged with governmental responsibility in the realm, but if necessary revolt led by anyone in the population. He had, in providing an example, praised the abortive revolt of 1554 against Mary's regime led by Sir Thomas Wyatt, in these words quoted by Allen: "Wyat did but his dutie, and it was the dutie of al others that professe the Gospel, to have risen with him, for maintenance of the same. His cause was just, and they al were traitors that tooke not part with him."[19] Knox, in a variety of tracts, developed an argument quite similar to Goodman's. The parallel is particularly striking in the book which contains Knox's most complete argument for resistance, the *Appellation . . . to the Nobility and Estates of Scotland* (Geneva, 1558). From this work, Allen quoted a statement which summarizes neatly the position of these firebrands: "If the people have either rashelie promoted anie manifest wicked person, or els ignorantlie chosen such an one, as after declareth himself unworthie of regiment above the people of God (and such be al Idolators and cruel persecutors) most justlie may the same men depose and punish him."[20] Here the justification for revolt is really constitutional, based on a rough notion of social contract. But the tests of incompetence which justify revocation of the contract remain religious. They are idolatry and religious persecution, two prime characteristics, for Knox, of Roman Catholicism.

These are the specific Protestant political arguments to which Allen alluded in this section of his treatise. Together with the few traditional Catholic arguments he quoted, they led him to this conclusion: "Thus both Schooles and Lawes speake and resolve for the matter in hand: both Catholiques and Protestants agreing, that Princes may for some causes, and especiallie for their defection in Faith and Religion, be resisted and forsaken: though in the maner of executing the sentence and other needful circumstances, Protestants folowe faction and populer mutinie; we reduce al, to lawe, order, and judgement."[21]

The last clause of Allen's conclusion, of course, is hardly fair. It is in fact a caricature of the position held by the most responsible Protestant thinkers. This was quickly pointed out by the polemicist assigned by the English government to prepare a careful refutation of Allen's book. Thomas Bilson, an Anglican divine, had begun working on a refutation of one of Allen's earlier works even before the publication of the *Defense*. He enlarged it to include a partial refutation of the *Defense,* and then, for good measure, added a refutation of much of the gloss on the Reims New Testament which had been recently published by a committee of scholars organized by Allen. The total result was a hefty tome which attacked the Catholic polemicists on several different fronts. Its title reveals its emphasis: *The True Difference between Christian Subjection and UnChristian Rebellion* (Oxford, 1585).[22] In keeping with this emphasis, the very part of Allen's *Defense* upon which it concentrated attention is his defense of the papal power to depose. Most of Bilson's counterattack, of course, was a refutation of Allen's Biblical and patristic exegesis. But he included within it a critique of the very passage which we have been considering, the passage which summarizes Protestant arguments for armed resistance.[23] He pointed out that some of the arguments quoted, *e.g.,* the one from Calvin, really justify only passive disobedience, not armed revolt. He noted that others, *e.g.,* the ones from Luther and Beza, accept armed revolt, but only when it is led by inferior magistrates, such as the princes of the blood royal in France or the hereditary princes of the empire in Germany, men who had a defined legal position within the government of their countries which limited in significant ways the power of the superior authority. Generally his case is plausible and would be accepted by most modern scholars. He had some trouble with Zwingli, whom he made a German, loyal to the imperial tradition of vesting certain powers in inferior magistrates. But the opinions which gave him most difficulty were those of Goodman and Knox. Goodman's opinion, he suggested, was a personal one, later repudiated by its author, not really typical of his party. Knox's opinion he rather rashly suggested might be justified if the Scottish kings were elected, like the German emperors, but he was inclined to reject Knox too, as atypical.

The debate did not end with Bilson. Later references to Protestant political argument figure in later quarrels between Protestant polemicists and Father Robert Parsons, Allen's chief collaborator in the Catholic polemical war on the English establishment.[24] Particularly in Parsons' *A Treatise Tending to Mitigation . . .* of 1607, can one find quotations from Protestant writers supporting a right of religious resistance.[25] But by this time Parsons and his party had become less sanguine. Their hope now was more for toleration of Catholics within England than for any reconquest of their native country for their faith. The particular examples of Protestant political argument used by Parsons are, most of them, quite different from those cited by Allen. Few of them, however, are used with more care.

Even if Allen did not analyze Protestant political ideas with due attention to the differences among them and the nuances in their statement, however, there remains a kernel of truth in his conclusion. Protestants and Catholics did generally agree that governments may be overthrown, sometimes must be overthrown, for religious reasons. Those among them who were most responsible, furthermore, generally also vested the right to license or lead the overthrow in specific established institutions: Catholics in the papacy, Protestants in "inferior magistrates" with constitutional positions within existing governments. Only rarely did either side seek to throw the gates open to popular rebellion. Those on both sides who were most militant stimulated a bloody fanaticism which plunged the West into some of the most appalling wars it has ever seen. But they also encouraged,

9. Allen, *Defense*, p. 80; from Sleidan, *Commentarii*, lib. 22, fol. 359. For an abridged text of the *Bekenntnis*, in English translation, see Roland H. Bainton, *The Age of the Reformation* (Princeton, N.J.: Van Nostrand, Anvil Original, 1956), pp. 172–73. For comment on it and its influence, see Robert M. Kingdon, "The First Expression of Theodore Beza's Political Ideas," *Archiv für Reformationsgeschichte*, XLVI (1955), pp. 93–94; Irmgard Höss, "Zur Genesis der Widerstandslehre Bezas," *ibid.*, LIV (1963), pp. 198–214.

10. Allen, *Defense*, pp. 78–79. For text of article and gloss, see *Huldreich Zwinglis Sämtliche Werke* (*Corpus Reformatorum* ed., 1905—), II, pp. 342–46. For comment on this text, see Alfred Farner, *Die Lehre von Kirche und Staat bei Zwingli* (Tübingen: Mohr, 1930), pp. 65–66.

11. Allen, *Defense*, p. 78; original in *Zwinglis Werke, op. cit.*, XI, pp. 68–70. This text was not mentioned by Farner, *op. cit.*, and it suggests a modification of his conclusion, p. 67, that Zwingli's resistance argument was purely theoretical.

12. *DD. J. Oecolampadii et H. Zvinglii Epistolarum, libri quatuor* (Basel, 1536), listed in British Museum Catalogue.

13. Allen, *Defense*, p. 7.

14. *Ibid.*, pp. 77–78; original text in *Ioannis Calvini Opera* (*Corpus Reformatorum* ed., 1863–1900), XLI, pp. 25–26. For comment on this text, see Émile Doumergue, *Jean Calvin, les hommes et les choses de son temps* (Lausanne: Bridel, 1899–1927), V, pp. 497–98; Josef Bohatec, *Calvin und das Recht* (Feudingen in Westfalen: Buchdruckerei & Verlagsanstalt, 1934), pp. 137–38; J. W. Allen, *A History of Political Thought in the Sixteenth Century* (London: Methuen, 1951), p. 57.

15. Text in *Calvini Opera, op. cit.*, XVIII, pp. 614–24, "Calvinus Piis Gallis," *n.b.* pp. 619–20.

16. Allen, *Defense*, p. 78. The letter is dated 1564, but printed in the Geneva, Estienne ed. of 1565. I have used the Folger Library copy.

17. *Ibid.*, p. 80.

18. *Ibid.*, p. 78. See the edited copy in John Quick, *Synodicon in Gallia Reformata* (London, 1692), I, xv, article 40. There are many variant copies of these synodical decisions. M. Michel Reulos of Paris is preparing a critical edition of them.

19. *Ibid.*, p. 79. For full text, see facsimile edition introduced by Charles H. McIlwain (New York: Columbia University Press, 1931), p. 204. For comment on the entire work, see Charles Martin, *Les Protestants Anglais réfugiés à Genève au temps de Calvin*, *1555–1560* (Geneva: Jullien, 1915), pp. 177–92; J. W. Allen, *op. cit.*, pp. 116–18.

20. Allen, *Defense*, p. 79. For full text see edited copy in David Laing, ed., *The Works of John Knox* (Edinburgh: Thin, 1895), IV, p. 540. For comment on the entire work, see J. W. Allen, *op. cit.*, pp. 110–13.

21. Allen, *Defense*, p. 88.

22. I have used a Folger Library copy.

23. Bilson, *op. cit.*, pp. 509–19.

24. Several examples are cited by Thomas H. Clancy, *Papist Pamphleteers: The Allen-Persons party and the political thought of the Counter-Reformation in England, 1572–1615* (Chicago: Loyola, 1964), especially pp. 65 and n.44. One can also find examples in works which precede Allen's *Defense*, e.g., in Thomas Stapleton's *Counterblast* of 1567. See Marvin R. O'Connell, *Thomas Stapleton and the Counter Reformation* (New Haven: Yale, 1964), pp. 201 ff., particularly p. 207.

25. Parsons, *A Treatise Tending to Mitigation*, pp. 38–51, 113–19. I have used the State University of Iowa Library copy.

26. The phrase is used by Clancy, *op. cit.*, p. 192.

LINGARD AND
THE ST. BARTHOLOMEW

MGR. PHILIP HUGHES
University of Notre Dame

E veryone knows, at least since Professor Butterfield revived the memory of it,[1] how John Lingard was the first English historian to publish the view that the massacre of St. Bartholomew was not the outcome of long premeditation, and how his account was the occasion of a controversy with the *Edinburgh Review*. Since the controverted account has never been reprinted, it ought here to be set before the reader. I propose, besides, to say something of the inner history of the controversy, and to add some original papers about it.

Here, then, is Lingard's account, which appeared in his *History of England* as a long note (for reasons which he explains) with its own nine reference notes.[2]

I had originally inserted in the text a narrative of this bloody transaction: but as it is not immediately connected with the history of England, I have since preferred to give it a place among the notes. The reader will observe that I have not adopted the usual hypothesis, that the massacre was the result of a premeditated plot, concealed, with infinite cunning, for the space of several months: but he may be assured, that my opinion was not formed till after a diligent perusal and comparison of the most authentic documents on the subject.

From the fall of the prince of Condé, the admiral Coligni had been acknowledged leader of the French huguenots. He maintained accredited agents in most of the foreign courts, that had abandoned the ancient faith, and he ruled among his partisans at home with the authority of a sovereign prince. Monthly contributions for the support of "the cause" were poured into his treasury: officers, whose duty was to execute his orders, were stationed in every province, and thousands of soldiers were always ready to hasten into the field at his call.[3] So powerful a nobleman, who had twice led his army against that of the crown, was naturally an object of jealousy to the administration: but he had of late obtained a considerable ascendency over the mind of the young king, by hinting suspicions of the designs of the queen mother, by exhorting Charles to take a more decided part in the government of the kingdom, and by proposing to him the conquest of the Netherlands, during the contest between the king of Spain and the insurgents. This project gratified the ambition of the young monarch: he allowed the admiral to furnish count Lewis of Nassau with five thousand Gascons to invade the county of Hainault;[4] was perpetually in his company, when he was at court; and if he were absent, maintained an active correspondence with him by letter. The queen mother began to tremble for her own power: she resolved, with the duke of Anjou, to dissuade her son from taking any part in the war in Flanders, and undertook to detach him from all connexion with the leader of the huguenots.

Since the assassination of the duke of Guise, Coligni had ventured but once to enter the city of Paris. He was at last drawn to that capital, by the invitation of Charles, who wished him to be present at the marriage of his sister Margaret with the king of Navarre; by the solicitation of Elizabeth, who requested him to aid and instruct her ambassador; and chiefly, perhaps, by his own anxiety to promote his favourite project of a war against the duke

---

[3] "Par les quels (his papers) il a apparu au roi, que ledit amiral avoit etabli es seize provinces de son royaume, des gouverneurs, des chefs de guerre, avec certain nombre de conseillers, qui avoient charge de tenir le peuple armé, le mettre ensemble et en armes aux premiers mandemens de sa part, auxquelles etoit donné pouvoir de lever annuellment sur les sujets de sa majesté notable somme de deniers." Bellièvre, apud Caveirac. [Notes 3–11 are Lingard's; Monsignor Hughes's own notes continue in sequence at the end of this chapter.—Ed.]

[4] Digges, 204.

of Alva. The ardour, with which it had originally been received by the king, had been lately cooled by the defeat of Genlis, one of the commanders of the insurgents, and by the warm remonstrances of Catharine. The admiral repeated his former arguments; offered the king an army of ten thousand huguenots; declared that if he refused to aid the protestants in Flanders, those in France would again be compelled to take up arms for their own safety:[5] and exhorted him to throw off the tutelage of an ambitious mother, who kept the sovereign in the background, that she might bring forward a favourite son, and perpetuate her own authority. These insinuations made a deep impression on the mind of Charles: his words and behaviour warned Catharine and the duke of their danger; and it was determined to remove the admiral, their most formidable enemy, by assassination. As he returned through the city from the council, an arquebuss was discharged at him from an upper window. One ball shattered his hand, a second lodged in the shoulder. The wounds were not dangerous: but his partisans hastened in crowds to his house, and offered to spend their lives in his quarrel.

At the first news Charles burst into lamentations, which were succeeded by threats of vengeance. He proceeded to visit the admiral; and Catharine thought it prudent to accompany him with her two sons, and the chief officers of the court. They found the wounded man in bed: he requested to speak with the king in private, and Charles commanded his mother and his brothers to remain at a distance. The queen afterwards acknowledged that these were the most painful moments that she ever experienced. Her consciousness of guilt, the interest with which her son listened to the admiral, the crowds of armed men, in constant motion through the house, their looks, and whispers, and gestures, all conspired to fill her with terror. Unable to remain any longer in such a situation, she interrupted the conference, by pretending

---

[5] This, though asserted by several French writers, appeared to me too insolent to deserve credit. I find it, however, confirmed by one of Walsingham's despatches. "The gentlemen of the religion here have made demonstration to the king, that the enterprise of the prince of Orange lacking good success, it shall not lie in his power to maintain his edict. They therefore desire him to weigh, *whether it were better to have foreign war with advantage, or inward war to the ruin of himself and his estate.*" Digges, 226.

that silence and repose were necessary for the recovery of the admiral. During her return in the same carriage with the king, she employed every artifice to draw from him the particulars of the conversation. He disclosed sufficient to add to her alarm.

After a restless night, Catharine spent the morning in anxious deliberation with the duke and her confidants: in the afternoon they communicated their determination to Charles. They reminded him of the two rebellions of the huguenots, and of the formidable power of the admiral: they observed that the man, who could offer a force of ten thousand armed men against the king of Spain, might at his pleasure employ the same number against the king of France: they informed him that the chiefs of the party were at the moment plotting the destruction of their adversaries; and that if he were to wait till the next morning, his mother, brothers, and most faithful officers, perhaps he himself, would be sacrificed to their vengeance: they implored his permission to anticipate the cruelty of their enemies, and to wreak on Coligni, and his friends, that destruction which *they* had prepared for others. The young king was subdued by the ascendency, and entreaties of his mother: he struggled for some hours in favour of the admiral: and, at ten in the evening, retired in considerable agitation, exclaiming, as he left the room, that he hoped no one would be left alive to reproach him afterwards with so foul a deed. Four hours had elapsed before the plan was arranged, and the necessary orders had been given: it wanted two more to the appointed time. To sleep in such circumstances was impossible: and the king, his mother and brothers, repaired to an open balcony, where they stood gazing at the stars, and waiting the result. A little before the time, the silence of the night was broken by the report of a pistol. They shuddered with horror: their resolution forsook them: and a messenger was despatched with contrary orders. But the bell of St. Germain l'Auxerois tolled: the duke of Guise with three hundred men burst into the admiral's house; and the dead body of that unfortunate chieftain was thrown from a window into the court:[6] the tocsin

[6] These particulars are taken from the narrative of the duke of Anjou, with a few additional circumstances from the Memoirs of queen Margaret, and those of Tavannes. All three were in the Louvre at the time: and two of them were among the devisers of the massacre. Those who believe that this

immediately rung from the parliament house: the duke of Nevers and the marshal de Tavannes, at the head of a troop of guards, rode through the streets crying "treason": companies of armed citizens, under their respective leaders, hastened to the work of blood: and the populace, whose passions were excited by the example of their superiors, and the circulation of the most alarming reports, imitated and surpassed the cruelty of the original assassins.

Of the objects of their fury those who slept in the fauxbourg St. Germain, had sufficient time to escape: others, in different parts of the city, found an asylum with their friends and relatives: but numbers of both sexes of every rank, not only those proscribed by the court, but many in the lowest situations in life, and in several instances catholics as well as protestants, were immolated to the undistinguishing vengeance of the mob. It was not till the afternoon, that Charles by sound of trumpet ordered every man to return to his home, and to abstain from deeds of violence, under penalty of death.[7] The massacre had been infinitely more extensive than had been foreseen: even its original projectors stood aghast at the multitude of the slain.

The same day dispatches were forwarded to the governors of the provinces, ordering them to prevent the repetition of such horrors, and to forbid all persons, under the peril of capital punishment, to take up arms and insult others.[8] Subsequent events,

---

bloody event had been planned six months before (an hypothesis unsupported by contemporary authority, and almost irreconcileable with the intermediate events) will say that the duke had an interest in diminishing the odium of the transaction. But a perusal of the document will shew, that it has all the appearance of truth, that it is the work, not of one who seeks to excuse, but who fairly accuses himself. It was written by Miron, his physician, to whom the duke, during a restless night, when his conscience was harassed by the recollection of the massacre, unbosomed himself. See Caveirac, xvi–xxi. I may add, that Mathieu asserts the same, concluding with these words: "J'ai ecrit plus au long, et je crois plus veritablement que nul autre ce qui s'est passé en cette journée, parceque je l'ai appris de ceux mêmes qui furent au conseil, et a l'execution." Hist. de Charles IX, Tom. i, p. 347, fol. Paris 1631.

[7] "A diverses fois le Roi itera vers le soir les premieres defences à tout homme sous peine de vie, etc." La Popelinière, ii. 67.

[8] See those to Chabot and Montpezat in Memoirs de l'etat sous Charles IX. Tom. iii. p. 214, 215, 12mo. Meidlebourg, 1578: and that to Joyeuse in Caveirac, Dissertation sur la S. Barthelmi, xxxii.

however, gave rise to a suspicion that these orders were but a feint. The bloody scenes at Paris were repeated at Orleans, Lyons, Rouen, Toulouse, and Bourdeaux: and the sufferers believed that as they were not protected, they were persecuted by the commands of the court. But the memory of Charles needs not to be loaded with additional infamy. There is no evidence that the other massacres had his sanction or permission: and when we consider that they happened at very different periods,[9] and were confined to the places in which the blood of catholics had been wantonly spilt during the preceding insurrections,[10] we shall attribute them rather to sudden ebullitions of popular vengeance than to any previously concerted and general plan. Of the number of the victims in all these towns it is impossible to speak with certainty. Among the huguenot writers, Perefix reckons 100,000, Sully 70,000, Thuanus 30,000, La Popeliniere 20,000, the reformed martyrologist 15,000, and Masson 10,000. But the martyrologist adopted a measure, which may enable us to form a probable conjecture. He procured from the ministers in the different towns, where massacres had taken place, lists of the names of the persons, who had suffered, or were supposed to have suffered. He published the result in 1582; and the reader will be surprised to learn that in all France he could discover the names of no more than 786 persons. Perhaps, if we double that number, we shall not be far from the real amount.[11]

The volume of Lingard's *History* in which this note appeared was published in May, 1823. It was not until June, 1826, that John Allen's[12] sixty-two-page review was published.[13] To appreciate Lingard's feelings as he read it we need to remember that this article was the latest shot in a duel that went back to the year 1815, when Allen had reviewed—also in the *Edinburgh*—the new edition (1810) of Lingard's *Antiquities of the Anglo-Saxon Church.*[14]

[9] The dates are as follows: Paris, Aug. 24. Maux, 25. La Charité, 26. Orleans, 27. Saumur and Angers, 29. Lyons, 30. Troyes, Sep. 2. Bourges, 11. Rouen, 17. Romans, 20. Toulouse, 23. Bourdeaux, Oct. 3.

[10] Nismes was an exception. Though the catholics of that city had been twice massacred in cold blood, as lately as the years 1567 and 1569, they remained quiet on this occasion. Menard, Histoire de Nismes, v.9.50.iv. Paris. 1750.

[11] Caveirac, Dissertation xxxviii.

The opening words of this review set the tone, and they do much to explain the rest of the story: "Of all the virtues of an historian, impartiality is the most rare. . . . National partiality . . . the deep-rooted prejudices communicated by sect or party" are passions against which "even the candid temper and philosophic mind of Hume are not proof." Hence, "It would be unreasonable . . . to expect that a Catholic clergyman, zealously attached to his communion, should be able to write, with impartiality, the history of a period . . . perplexed by the controversies of Catholic and Protestant."

One hundred and fifty years ago the critic was rare in England who could write dispassionately about the Dark Ages and their monks. Allen was one of the rarities. "To the clergy of the dark ages, Europe owes much of her civilisation, her learning, and her liberty." His complaint about Lingard had nothing to do with any one of Lingard's particular religious beliefs, but related to "the artifices" which he employed in the *Antiquities* "to palliate the faults, or throw a veil over the crimes" of these clergy. "Where it serves his purposes . . . we find him suppressing or perverting the evidence. . . ." This, although the book as a whole was "learned and liberal," excluded it from "a place . . . otherwise . . . justly merited . . . among the most valuable of our modern histories."

And to show what he meant Allen criticized in great detail[15] Lingard's account of the intervention of St. Dunstan of Canterbury in the affairs of the Anglo-Saxon King Edwy (955–9) and the Lady Elgiva. It is a powerfully written analysis, supported by a wealth of citations from sources. "What does Mr. Lingard oppose to this evidence," Allen asks at one point. "He takes no notice of it at all; he keeps it entirely out of sight. . . ." The review concludes with compliments about the interesting matter of the work and the author's "agreeable style." But "Candour and impartiality are least of all to be expected from ecclesiastical historians," and the reviewer ends with one of those outbursts against theologians and their writings which Charles Greville, who knew him very well, describes.[16]

A century and a half ago, authors who felt that reviewers had misrepresented them had only one recourse—to print their grievance at their own expense. Allen's attack must (accidentally) have coincided in time with Lingard's resolve to write, not a student's abridgement of English history—his first intention—but a full-scale work. The first volumes of this appeared in May, 1819; he seized the opportunity in a lengthy, well-documented note[17] to answer "a writer in the *Edinburgh Review* for October 1815." It was now for Allen to bide his time. His moment came in April, 1825, when the *Edinburgh* commissioned him to review all that had so far appeared of Lingard's *History of England,* the whole story down to the death of Elizabeth I.

Lingard was no longer a learned nobody. He might consider that by now he had made the grade. Not only had the five volumes of the original quarto edition sold well, but since 1823 there had simultaneously been on sale two cheaper, octavo editions. Translations of the work into German, Italian, and French were in preparation. Allen, after some compliments to Lingard on his style—"periods poised and musical in their cadence . . . the perspicuity of Robertson, with more freedom and fancy . . . the ornament of Gibbon without his affectation and obscurity"—gives generous praise for "the rare merit of having collected his materials from original historians and records." This has enabled Lingard "to explain many transactions that were before obscure . . . and to make many silent corrections . . . not ostentatiously obtruded on our notice. . . . We know no general history of England we should sooner recommend."

However, since "Dr. Lingard has honoured us with a note in reply [to his 1815 critique]," the *Edinburgh* reviewer proceeded[17a] "To try the degree of confidence that may safely be placed in Dr. Lingard's History." Lingard himself later described[18] how Allen

purpose selects the hacknied story of Edwy and Elgiva, (a selection which to the initiated reader must appear to savour of art and mystery); and having given the substance of the narrative, which is inserted in the first volume, pretends to admire the dexterity with which the objections to it have been omitted, the difficulties with which it is attended, have been concealed, and the facts at variance with it, have been suppressed.

It is painful to be obliged to notice such a statement. Whoever will turn to the pages referred to by the reviewer (History of England, 1, 511–518) instead of condemning the author of conceal-

ment and misrepresentation, must award him the praise of candour
and impartiality. Those very pages offer the proof of his claim.
They contain a selection of the most material passages bearing on
the subject, which could be found among ancient documents; and
this selection was made indifferently from writers favourable or
unfavourable to the author's opinion, and expressly for the purpose of enabling the reader to exercise his own judgment. . . .

But is it not the writer's practice to represent persons in an
odious light, because they had the good fortune to be praised by
Hume?[19] He may confidently answer that it is not. With the
exception of a few particular passages, to which his attention has
been directed by his friends, he has not read a hundred pages in
Hume's history during the last eight years. If the reason be asked,
it was because he wished to preclude the possibility of imitation,
and to stamp on his own work the features of originality.

Almost the whole of Allen's critique of April, 1825, is directed
to Anglo-Saxon history. As to the account of the sixteenth century,
so far no more than glanced at, "We have no reason to think it entitled to more implicit credit" than the portion already examined:
Dr. Lingard "will require to be watched as closely in his account of
our free constitution as of our Protestant church."[20]

"The result of our scrutiny," so Allen reminiscently summed up
this review fourteen months later, "was unfavourable to [Dr. Lingard's] reputation as a candid and faithful historian."[21] Allen now
chose, as a means to finish Lingard once and for all, the historian's
note on the Massacre of St. Bartholomew, because, said Allen, he
"had little doubt that [in] a more trying period, where the credit
and interests of [Lingard's] church were more directly concerned,
[he] would see displayed in a stronger light the passions and prejudices of the author. . . . We were prepared for many errors and misrepresentations. The harvest has been infinitely more abundant than
we had expected."[22] Lingard, in that Note A now under review,[23]
had written that he had formed his opinion about the massacre "after
a diligent perusal and comparison of the most authentic documents
on the subject"—a crucial sentence, in the coming controversy.
Allen flatly declared he did not believe this. Of some of the authors

Lingard refers to, "he has not seen even the title page."[24] "Careless-ness . . . haste, borrowed learning . . . indifference to historical accuracy" mark his account. All he knows about the massacre is what he read in the Abbé de Caveirac's dissertation annexed to an account of the revocation of the Edict of Nantes.[25]

The spirit of these introductory remarks is that of the whole long review, where in 62 pages 266 references to 50 writers, mostly con-temporary, [26a] are pressed into service to prove Allen's case against Lingard's integrity. "If the instances of carelessness and bad faith . . . collected from so small a portion of his book are insufficient to convince [readers] that prejudice and partiality usurp the place of truth, we despair of producing conviction. There is no fact to be credited . . . on the mere authority of Dr. Lingard's statements."[26]

Lingard, pastor of a handful of Catholics in the village of Hornby, ten miles northwest of Lancaster, two hundred fifty miles from London, suffered one notable disadvantage as he faced his ad-versary. The nearest libraries of any size were a day's journey away from him, at Manchester and Liverpool. He had comparatively few books of his own, and had always relied for what he needed—and never in vain—on loans from those Catholic gentry who were bibliophiles. By now the tomes lent for the work on his Elizabethan volume, four and five years ago, had long been returned. In conflict with the *Edinburgh Review's* heavily documented attack he needed more than his own phenomenal memory and the extracts he had made when preparing his own summary account of the massacre. So, once more, he must write around. Time, again, was an enemy. The *Review* had been on sale for two months already by the time it came to Lingard's notice.[27]

Lingard's reply to Allen's review was a pamphlet that ran to four editions in a few weeks.[28] It can hardly be summarized here, any more than Allen's rejoinder of three months later.[29] Both ran to nearly a hundred pages. But for Lingard's confident, scornful, and indignant tone as, with a master hand, he exposed his adversary, one could not find a more curious metaphor than that "Lingard in turn received his scourging from John Allen."[30] "It is not my disposi-tion," Lingard wrote haughtily, opening his *Vindication,* "to affect an apathy which I do not feel, or to sit down tamely under reproach which I do not deserve." There are, of course, in such encounters, more important elements than tone and literary skill. And as to the vital substance, the interested reader must judge for himself. Lingard's reply keeps to the line hinted at in his first letter of August, 1, 1826: there does not exist any real evidence that the massacre had been long-prepared; that it was premeditated is no more than hypothesis; and the detail of the undoubted facts makes any such hypothesis ridiculous. He distinguishes carefully between the different kinds of sources which the comment of contemporaries provides, insisting that what may be called "the party pamphlet" must give way to the record left by those who actually had a share in determining the massacre. His final shot—considered at the time as fatal to Allen—was his citing from Chateaubriand, who had seen the actual papers, the testimony of the Papal Nuncio at Paris A. M. Salviati, present at the massacre.

The *Vindication* reveals two not unimportant facts about the genesis of that Note A that was the center of the storm. Firstly, the "memoir"—Lingard's name for it—did not appear in its original shape. Volume V of the *History* was already overgrown and so the original St. Bartholomew note was cut by half. "Minor, though corroborative, circumstances were omitted; many of the particular authorities were suppressed. . . . On this account it was that . . . I requested the reader to believe that my opinion . . . was not formed without a diligent perusal and comparison of the most authentic documents. . . ."[31] Secondly, "When I sat down to compose the memoir, I entertained no doubt of the received opinion, that the massacre was the effect of a preconceived plot."[32] The critical argumentation now put forward by Lingard is, then, not something "thought up" to defend a challenged preconception. It is the reasoning which has converted him to the view he now holds, from a theory "replete with improbabilities."

And then the *Edinburgh* itself made an *amende*.

"I have just read the critique in the *Edinburgh*," Lingard wrote[31a] to another historian, Dr. George Oliver, April 30, 1831, "and considering the offensive tone of the former critiques, think I have good reason to be satisfied with it. I was told beforehand that I should be so: that it was to be so written as to make me some amends without at the same time compromising the infallibility of the reviewers."

] II [

The selection of letters which follows tells something of the activities of Lingard and of the friends and admirers who helped him in the months between his first knowledge of Allen's article and the appearance of his *Vindication*.[33]

The Allen attack, it will be recalled, was in the June, 1826, issue of the *Edinburgh*. On the first of August, Lingard wrote to Joseph Mawman, his publisher and a close friend:[34]

I have just perused the article concerning myself in the *Edinburgh Review*, the fruit, I conceive of Dr. Allen's visit to Paris. I must own that at the first view I could not contemplate such an array of authorities and citations without feeling some alarm: but that alarm began to subside when I saw him at the conclusion toiling and writhing under the attempt to reconcile his theory with an undisputed fact; and it existed no longer when I had compared my own statement with the critique.

I was fully aware that the perpetration of the massacre provoked a belief that it had been long before determined and planned, and that this belief was admitted not only by all the Calvinist, but by many Catholic writers: but when I considered that none of them had adduced any convincing proof, and that it was impossible to reconcile the supposition with the facts preceding the massacre, I felt no hesitation in stating my opinion that the latter was not premeditated. I cannot find that the critic has disproved any part of my statement. He quibbles, indeed, about the hours of the night, and the assertion that the king etc. could not sleep. But these are immaterial circumstances, and I do not see that in them I am incorrect. That the king, as I state it, did forbid any more violence in the evening, and sent orders to the governors in provinces to prevent violence within their jurisdictions is admitted by himself. He, indeed, produces many writers who say that other and contrary orders were secretly sent at the same time. Of these assertions I was aware: but I know that they had no other authority than mere report: and it appears that all the orders which have hitherto been discovered among the papers of these governors, are of a prohibitory tendency. Not one commanding violence can be found. . . .

The only advantage which he has against me is, I think, my blunder of calling all the writers, whom I have mentioned as enumerated by Caveirac, not as consulted by me, Huguenots, though two of them, Perefix and Masson, were Catholics. How this escaped me I know not: probably I supposed there might be Protestant writers of the same name, and meant to examine, but forgot it. However the mistake regards not the substance of my statement, though the critic, to make the most of it, transposes it from the conclusion of my note to the very front of his article. But of this enough. Shall I have the pleasure of seeing you this month, as you stated? I flatter myself with the hope. . . .

On the 18th Lingard wrote to Mawman:

It seems to me that I ought to answer the *Edinburgh*. This I intend to do without delay, and in the mean time what think you of advertising my vindication without delay? It would prevent the readers of the critique from taking it into their heads that it is unanswerable. . . .[35]

On September 2 he wrote to the Rev. M. A. Tierney,[36] chaplain and librarian to the Duke of Norfolk:

Your kind letter dated the 8th of May, with the accompanying documents has just reached me, and I lose not a moment in writing to return you my best thanks. . . .

I am now busy in preparing my answer to the savage attack made upon me by Dr. Allen in the *Edinburgh Review*. Have you access to the Duke of Norfolk's library? If you have, does it contain any of the following books: Capilupi, *Lo Stragemma; Mémoires de l'état sous Charles IX; Mémoires de Tavannes;* Adriani, *Storia;* Castelnau; Matthieu, *Histoire de France;* Popeliniere, *Historie.* I have no doubt of procuring the most of them, but if his grace have any which I cannot procure, I have no doubt you would have the kindness to consult them for me. Should therefore any of the books aforementioned be in the library, have the goodness to inform me. If I hear not from you I shall understand they are

not there. I have written the above in the greatest haste, for I have
more upon my hands than I well know how to execute. You will
therefore excuse me, and believe that I feel most grateful for the
service you have rendered me, with the hope that you may prove
of still greater service on some future occasion.

To the Rev. M. A. Tierney

September 20

Not to lose a post, I return an answer to your kind letter[37]
immediately; and as I know not what room I may have left after
I have exposed to you my several wants, I thank you now, and
most sincerely.

. . . Does Le Laboureur in this part, or in any other, give any
account of the letters sent after the massacre to put to death the
Huguenots in every part of the kingdom? I am much inclined to
deny the existence of such letters. My argument is this. We do not
find that a single governor of a province put to death any
Huguenots at that time; we do not find that, out of all the cities
and towns in the kingdom, more than seven were disgraced by
massacres at that time, and these were places where the Huguenots
had furiously massacred the Catholics. Is it possible to believe that
if the king had ordered massacres everywhere, he would have been
obeyed only in these seven instances? My argument must fall, if
there be any instances of massacres by order of the governor, or in
other towns than the seven, between the 24th of August and the
2 or 3 of September. If therefore you should observe in Le
Laboureur, or in any other work, instances of such massacres,
have the goodness to let me know.

Perhaps you may have the *Wars of Flanders* by Fabianus Strada.
If so, I will trouble you to look into b.IV, anno 1565. There you
will find the abstract of a letter from Philip of Spain, to Margaret,
Duchess of Parma, detailing the particulars of the meeting at
Bayonne. Afterwards Strada says, that many persons supposed
that at these conferences the massacre at Paris was concluded:
id quod mihi neque abnuere neque affirmare promptum fuerit.
Now I am convinced that the reviewer in quoting this has been
guilty of a most glaring falsification: for he immediately adds
potius inclinat animus ut credam. Thus giving us to understand

that Strada is inclined to believe that it was so. But if I can believe my edition—it is but a common one for schoolboys—these words have nothing to do with what goes before, but are the beginning of a sentence, in which Strada says that he is inclined to believe that the mutual succours furnished by the two crowns, and a marriage, were the real effects of the interview. The reviewer quotes the Roman edition of 1632. It is possible that such edition may be in the library. If not, perhaps you may find some other edition in folio, or worth quoting; and if so, I wish you would give me the very words with the exact punctuation as far as the end of the sentence. Also the sentence before the letter in which Strada says, that many historians have filled up from their imagination, the vacancy, which their ignorance had caused. . . .

From the Rev. M. A. Tierney

Arundel, September 27

. . . On the subject of the letters sent into the provinces ordering the general massacre of the Huguenots I must confess that I have never been able to bring myself to agree with you. Indeed the testimony of all the historians is so unanimous on this point, and the names of the different places in which the orders were disobeyed, with the reasons which encouraged that disobedience, are so particularly specified, that I think it difficult to refuse one's assent. The following instance—it is the only one I have been able to meet with—has confirmed my opinion, and goes, I think, to overthrow your argument. The Comte de Tende, Governor of Provence, is always numbered among those who refused to obey the injunctions of the court in this instance; and Davila, you know, says that he was poisoned for his pains. Brantôme speaks of him in this manner, "Après le massacre de la St. Barthélemy, qu'il luy fust mandé, *comme aux autres,* de mener les mains basses envers les huguenots, et en faire la mesure en son gouvernement comme à Paris, il n'en voulut jamais rien faire, disant que l'acte en seroit trop vilain, et que le Roy l'avoit pu bien faire, et s'en laver quand il luy plairoit, estant Roy; mais pour luy, à jamais il en sortiroit son âme chargée, et son honneur souillé. . . ."

The paper runs on through another folio page, in which we are informed only that Vauclause, after the departure of the Sieur de

la Molle, obtains an interview with the king, and having satisfied
Charles [IX] of his fidelity is sent back to countermand the former
orders, and prevent the massacre if possible. The reason given for
this resolution is, "qu'il avoit résolu de faire une entreprise de
grande importance, et que si on faisoit la tuerie en Provence, cela
pourroit détourner la sienne." *Ibid*. This account, so circumstantial
in all its parts must, I think, convince you that such letters were
in this instance certainly written, though the orders which they
contained were never executed: and it is scarcely too much to
suppose that, in the other provinces, the vacillating conduct of
Charles, which is here displayed, and which could not be altogether
unknown to the different governors, would tend greatly to
encourage a neglect of his orders, wherever either the situation
of the parties was likely to promise them indemnity, or the
passions of the people were not so roused by the remembrance
of former outrages as to prevent their rulers casting the sanguinary
edicts aside. Do you not think too, that, in the conduct of Charles
as here portrayed there is something to warrant the idea that his
endeavours to stop the progress of the massacre in the provinces
were insincere, and that his despatches to that purpose were but a
feint? Was there no *Apostille,* no secret and contradictory
instructions? . . .

From Charles Butler[38]

Lincoln's Inn, September 27
    Yesterday, from a gentleman, upon whom I think I can depend,
I learned the following circumstances. Mr. Wilkes and his son,
the member elect for Sudbury, have long been agents to the
Dissenters. They profess themselves warm friends to civil and
religious liberty; and, on some occasions, have rendered some
services to the Catholics. They are great Biblemongers, and the
younger brother of the elder Wilkes was sent to France to
superintend the distribution of Bibles in that country. Through
him all the narratives respecting Nismes have been transmitted to
England. Doctor Allen is very intimate with the elder Wilkes. I
met him at that gentleman's house. Mr. Silvertop was much taken
with them; but for this last twelve months has been suspicious of

them. I can say the same of myself. The Wilkeses are much patronised by Lord Holland, who, you know, is the patron both of Dr. Allen and Blanco White. By the Wilkeses Dr. Allen became intimate with the French Huguenots, most of whom are of the party called Constitutionelle, and these have supplied Dr. Allen with all his information respecting the massacre upon St. Bartholomew's day. This was mentioned to me months ago, but I did not then attend to it. I was surprised by the various and curious information displayed by Dr. Allen: but it now appears how he obtained it. . . .

From the Rev. M. A. Tierney
Arundel, October 2

Since I wrote you my last letter the Review has fallen into my hands. Much stress, I perceive, is laid (139 et seq.) on the letters which were written on the evening of the Massacres to exculpate Charles, and throw the blame on the house of Guise; and the Reviewer seems to consider the contradictory accounts which were put forth as conclusive evidence of the Massacre having been preconcerted. I know not whether the following passage from Le Laboureur will be of any use to you; but as I have the opportunity of a frank there can be no harm in my sending it to you. . . . The letters, it appears then, were never sent: but does not this passage account for all the contradictions which have been objected to Charles, without necessarily charging him with having premeditated all the horrors of the St. Bartholomew?

I told you in my last that I had been unable to obtain a good edition of Strada; the passage however which you want you will probably have received by the time this reaches you. I wrote on Friday to Dr. Poynter[39] for it, and he tells me that Mr. Butler will this day go to the Museum, and transcribe it for you. . . .

From Charles Butler
October 9

I have read the passages in the *Edinburgh Review* and Cardinal d'Ossat's Letters which you have pointed out to me. I think it impossible to contend with success that the conversation between Charles IX and Cardinal Alessandrino referred to the Massacre of St. Bartholomew's day. As to the expression, "le Roy m'a tenu promesse," Sir Thomas Smith called the Cardinal a fool and he seems to have been one. Is it possible the king would have confided the promise to him? It is of so little consequence whether your Defence appears or not in the form of a dialogue, that it cannot be worth your while to take any trouble to put it into that form. . . .

From Charles Butler

Brighthelmstone, October 27

I have been in this very wholesome and gay place during the last ten days. The first person whom I met was Dr. Allen. He mentioned of his own accord his critique in the *Edinburgh Review,* and said he had been provoked to it by a letter in one of the newspapers, which he knew to be yours, in consequence of a conversation which he had at Paris with a gentleman, who said that letter mentioned a circumstance known only to himself and you. I recollect the letter; if it be not yours, I think you should disavow it. I took care to inform him that the delay of the publication of your answer was owing to Mackintosh's detention of Caveirac.[40] He instantly said with fervour, "I hope it has now reached Dr. Lingard." This confirms the suspicion of their co-operation which I have hinted at before.

I send you a letter which I have just received from Paris. It contains some observations which will please you: and the writer will, I am sure, exert himself to execute any commissions with which you may think proper to charge him. . . .

I am impatient to see your answer; but I see no reason why the publication of it should not be delayed till the meeting of Parliament after the holidays. . . .

Butler had reference to his correspondence with Charles Browne-Mostyn,[41] who had written on the 20th and again on the 23rd:

Since receipt of your last of the 4th inst. I have been in close correspondence with several in Paris, and have also spent much time in our valuable public library here. I have before me a note from Monsieur Picot on the subject. . . . I expect others daily and if I receive any worth sending I shall forward them. . . .

If I can be of any use or assistance whatever to Mr. Lingard, I beg he will freely address himself to me. . . .

I put a long letter to the post for you, or rather for Mr. Lingard, on Saturday 21st—which I hope will arrive safe. The enclosed should have gone with it, had it come to hand sooner. I feel pleasure in being able to send you the inclosed as it appears to me to be a most useful and important document for Mr. Lingard. Whatever opinion the public may have of Monsieur Chateaubriand as a politician and statesman, his literary pretensions are denied by none. They that are inclined, as I feel, to give him credit for what he asserts here to have come to his knowledge must, I think, consider the question between Mr. Lingard and the reviewer, as completely decided, in respect at least to the premeditation of the St. Batholomew, as well as for the respectability and correctness of Caveirac's report. Monsieur Claussel de Coussergue who sends it is one of the ablest and best informed men in France. You may assure Mr. Lingard, in case he has no opportunity of comparing the extract I send him, with the original in *Chateaubriand's new Edition* (by l'Avocat, 1826) that I have this day compared them, and will assure him the inclosed extract is verbally exact. . . .[42]

Along with this "Extrait des *Mélanges Littéraires* de M. le vicomte de Chateaubriand," Browne-Mostyn had enclosed two brief notes relative to the affair. In one (of October 20) J. F. Tilt, conservator at the Bibliothèque du Roi, declared that *"Pour une si bonne cause on ne peut trop faire."* In his covering note with the extract, Claussel de Coussergue asserted that *"Le docteur Lingard ne peut trouver une meilleure réponse à la* Révue d' Edimbourg." The most useful part of the extract read:

Lorsque la Bibliothèque du Vatican était à Paris (trésor inappréciable auquel presque personne ne songeait) j'ai fait faire des recherches: j'ai trouvé sur la journée de la Saint Barthélemy les documens les plus précieux. Si la vérité doit se recontrer quelque part, c'est sans doute dans les lettres écrites en chiffres aux Souverains Pontifes, et qui étaient condamnées à un secret éternel. Il résulte positivement de ces lettres que la Saint Barthélemy ne fut point préméditée; qu'elle ne fut que la conséquence soudaine de la blessure de l'amiral: et qu'elle n'enveloppa qu'un nombre de victimes,

toujours beaucoup trop grand sans doute, mais au dessous des sup-
putations de quelques historiens.[43]

Probably before Butler's letter and these enclosures had reached
him, Lingard was able to write Mawman of the draft he was preparing of the *Vindication:*[44]

. . . It is finished: and I am looking over it a second time. You may
have it next week if you please. But, if there be not any particular
time for its appearance, I would keep it by me, as long as I could, as
there is no day, in which something or other that is new, may not
suggest itself. I think you will find from it, that Mr. Todd is a complete old woman, and the *Quarterly* reviewer not much better (he is
said to be Milman, but, whoever he was, it is plain to me he was
aided by Mr. Turner),[45] and as for Dr. Allen, if I mistake not, he
will regret that he attacked me. I think there is no need of advert-
ing to the article in the *Morning Chronicle;* I have enough against
him—mistakes, and downright misrepresentations. I have always
thought that he is but a very indifferent Latin scholar. I am now
sure of it: for he could not intentionally have laid himself so open to
reproach, as he has done in a quotation from Strada. But of this
afterwards.

I had yesterday a letter from Dr. Gradwell. He tells me, what you
undoubtedly know, that that pirate Galignani, at Paris, has published an English edition of the history which he sells for £3,3.0—
or 75 francs. The rascal! Roujoux, the translator, informs me that
the whole is published in French. . . .

To Joseph Mawman

October

I send you almost one half of the *Vindication*. The tract will be
shorter than you suppose. It will not, I hope, exceed 100 pages. The
subject is not inviting, and I should fear that, if the book were long,
it would find few readers. I have therefore confined myself to as
narrow a space as I could consistently with justice to myself.

For the same reason, that is that it may not tire the readers, I
have divided it into four chapters, of which two are devoted to
Dr. Allen. . . .

Can you discover the fate of my ticket? The number is 11,115.
They do not publish these things in the papers, and I have no means

of learning in the country that it has drawn a prize of £ 80,000.

As Mr. Butler has been useful to me, I shall feel obliged, if you send him the sheets, or a copy, as soon as any may be ready.

To Dr. John Kirk[46]

October

. . . I am busy in getting my *Vindication* ready. Indeed the greater part of it is gone to the press. I flatter myself that Dr. Allen will repent the attack which he has made on me, and of which I know that many of his friends speak in terms of reprobation. They, though they suppose him correct in his view of the Parisian massacre, think that he has used me ungenerously and unfairly, in taking a note on a subject not properly English as a specimen of the whole work. I shall however prove, if I am not much deceived, that I have represented the matter in its true light, and that he has been guilty of artifice and misrepresentation. Be not, however, afraid that I shall lose my temper. I shall do the business gently, but, I hope, effectually. . . .

To Joseph Mawman

November 5

I send the rest of the MS with the revise. When you send me more copy to revise you will perhaps let me have also another revise of the first part. I have often known new errors to creep in by the correction of the old.

The extract from Chateaubriand is most valuable.

Dr. Allen met Mr. Butler at Brighton, and without any introduction told him that he should never have written the article, had it not been to revenge himself on me for the letter published in the newspaper last year, at the end of which was something that highly offended him. He therefore inquired in Paris of Mr. Buchon, who it was that had examined the MS, and found by that that I was the author. I recollect that there was something rather sharp added to what I wrote, but the exact particulars I know not now. I have therefore desired Mr. Butler to say that I was not privy to the offensive passage, and should probably have informed him so through you or Mr. Butler, if he had been in England. This I have added that he might not suspect your having any hand in the letter. I conceived it best for your interests and mine to say so much: for though

I may be able to defend myself against his attacks, yet he has an overwhelming advantage in the *Review*. What he writes is read by
thousands: what I may reply, will not be seen by as many hundreds.
If therefore the disavowal keep him quiet for the future, I conceive
a great point will be gained. . . .

Lingard had asked that Charles Butler be sent sheets of the *Vindication*. On November 11 Butler wrote to Lingard from Lincoln's Inn
that

> By the favour of Mr. Mawman, I have perused the whole of the
> printed part of your reply, with great delight: you have beaten off
> your adversaries on all your points: the quotation from Chateau-
> briand is very apposite and must produce a great effect on your
> readers. You don't give me my full age, as I am in my 77th year.
> Mr. Mawman and I think you should mention, in some convenient
> place, that with the exception of your present defence and the few
> lines in your *Preface,* you never directly or indirectly published a
> line in vindication of your history, or respecting any critique upon it,
> or any writer of any such critique; and that, if any such have ap-
> peared, it has been without your knowledge and against your will.
> I will take care to inform Dr. Allen that you had no concern in the
> letter in the newspaper. Mawman thinks you should begin with
> Allen, and proceed from him to the others. . . .

To Joseph Mawman

November 16

. . . I have adopted the order you suggest. My object in placing
Todd etc. first, was that the reader seeing how easily I overcame
them, might anticipate my success in the third encounter.

I have twice or thrice mentioned Dr. Allen's revengeful motive.
Perhaps I have not been so severe as you would wish. But I think I
hurt his feelings more by treating his abuse with a tone of contempt. It will appear more dignified; and he will not have the pleasure of asserting that he has vexed me. . . .

To the same

[no date]

Never was man so puzzled as I have been by Mr. Butler. He has
begged me to omit the commencement of the first chapter. Why?

He does not say, but I suspect that he was not authorised by Dr. Allen to mention the cause of Allen's writing against me. I have therefore sent for the printer a passage, as nearly as I can judge of the same length, to be inserted in its place. Still I have so contrived it, as to hint pretty plainly, that revenge was the real cause of his abusive language: but in such manner that he can have no reason to charge Mr. Butler with having betrayed his secret, if it be a secret, to me. . . .

To the same

December 4

On my return from the country to Durham, I found the parcel with the *Vindication* waiting for me. The addition, which you introduced, was very proper, and the whole appears to be got up in good style. The sale on the first day is very flattering: but I can suggest no improvement for a second edition, for I have been so busy, that I have had no time to read it over, and yet I write, that you may not delay under the expectation of hearing from me. . . .

It has not, of course, been any part of my purpose to decide the issue between Lingard and his reviewer. The space required would alone have forbidden it. For those interested there are, besides the excerpts and correspondence presented here, Allen's review, Lingard's answer, Allen's rejoinder, and Lingard's comment on this.

N O T E S

1. *Man on his Past* (Cambridge, England, 1955), p. 175.
2. Vol. V, Note A (pp. 646–50) of the 1st ed. of the *History of England* (1823), and vol. VIII, Note T (pp. 353 ff) of the 2nd ed. (now much rarer than the 1st ed.). [Lingard's nine reference notes, superscript numbers 3–11, appear with his text; Monsignor Hughes's own notes continue in sequence herebelow.—Ed.]

12. For John Allen (1771–1843), an intimate of the Whig Maecenas, Lord Holland, and warden of Dulwich College, see *Dictionary of National Biography*.

13. *Edinburgh Review*, June, 1826, pp. 94–155.

14. *Ibid.*, October, 1815, pp. 348–54.

15. Allen, pp. 347–54.

16. "*September 19* [1834] . . . After dinner we had much talk about religion, when Allen got into a fury; he thundered out his invectives against the *charlatanerie* of the early Christian converts. . . ." Henry Reeve, Greville's friend and editor, records "John Allen was himself so fierce an unbeliever, and so bitter an enemy to the Christian religion, that he was very fond of asserting that other men believed as little as himself. It was almost always Allen who gave an irreligious turn to the conversation at Holland House when these subjects were discussed of there." This a propos Allen's talking of the infidelity of Sir James Mackintosh and Lord Melbourne. *The Greville Memoirs*, III [1820–37], pp. 135, 324.

17. *A History of England from the First Invasion of the Romans . . .* [1819] Vol. I, pp. 543–48.

17a. *Edinburgh Review*, April, 1825, p. 9.

18. Advertisement, July 4, 1825, prefixed to Vol. 6 [1603–49] of the first edition of the *History of England*, pp. vi–viii; also to Vol. 9 of the second edition.

19. "If a person of note is praised by Hume, he has a good chance of being represented in an odious light by Dr. Lingard; and, if censured by Hume, Dr. Lingard generally contrives to say a word in his commendation." *Edinburgh Review*, April, 1825, p. 27.

20. *Edinburgh Review*, as before, pp. 30–31.

21. *Edinburgh Review*, June, 1826, p. 94.

22. *Ibid.*

23. For the text cf. *supra.*

24. *Edinburgh Review*, as before, p. 95.

25. *Ibid.*

26. *Ibid.*, p. 125.

26a. That is, with the massacre.

27. How remote, before the railway, the daily postal delivery and daily newspapers—there were none outside London until thirty years later than this—was English rural life! Tierney, at Arundel, sixty miles only from London, did not see a copy of the review until October, librarian though he was to a duke.

28. *A Vindication of Certain Passages in the fourth and fifth volumes of the History of England* (London, J. Mawman, 1826). The fourth edition (1827) has a postscript commenting on Allen's reply.

29. *Reply to Dr. Lingard's Vindication in a letter to Francis Jeffrey Esq.* [editor of the *Edinburgh Review*] London, 1827 (March).

30. Butterfield, *op. cit.*, p. 175.

31. *Vindication*, p. 7.

31ª. Of the magazine's review of the final volume.

32. *Ibid.*, p. 17.

33. The letters are from the manuscripts and transcripts at Ushaw College, Durham, England, now being prepared for publication by the author of this paper.

34. Lingard to Mawman, August 1 [1826].

35. Lingard to Mawman, August 18 [1826].

36. 1795–1862, editor of the well-known edition (1839–43) of Dodd's three-volume *Church History of England*.

37. This letter is lost.

38. 1749–1832. A leading lawyer on the Chancery side, and a noted scholarly writer, as well as a society figure. Lingard's lifelong friend.

39. 1762–1827. The Catholic bishop in London, 1812–27, who made much use of Lingard's cool judgment and literary gifts in the campaign for Catholic Emancipation.

40. Sir James Mackintosh had earlier written Mawman "Cadogan Place, Friday: . . . I was surprised to hear of a rumour that I had a share in the *Edinburgh Review* on Dr. Lingard. Nothing is more groundless. The particulars of it were unknown to me till I read it in print. Mere accident indeed prevented me from going out of my way to Hornby when in the north last autumn to present myself to Dr. Lingard."

41. A descendant of the Mostyns of Talacre and the Brownes of Kiddington, Oxon.; elder brother of the Francis Mostyn who was (1840–47) Lingard's Bishop.

42. Browne-Mostyn to Butler, Versailles, October 20 and 23, 1826.

43. Extracted from *Oeuvres Complètes de M. le vicomte de Chateaubriand* (Paris, chez l'Avocat, 1826), T.XXI, p. 352.

44. Lingard to Mawman, October 28 [?].

45. John Henry Todd, D. D., Lambeth librarian, had attacked Lingard's account of Cranmer. Milman is the future author of the *History of Latin Christianity*. Turner is Sharon Turner, the historian of Anglo-Saxon England. The last third of the *Vindication* dealth with Todd and the anonymous *Quarterly* reviewer.

46. 1761–1851. The scholarly priest at Lichfield, Staffordshire, whose life was given to collecting materials for a history of the English Catholics in the eighteenth century.

FRANCO-SPANISH
DIPLOMACY
AND THE ARMADA*

D E   L A M A R   J E N S E N

Brigham Young University

I n spite of the chronic civil wars and political chaos in late-six-
teenth-century France, that unfortunate country still occupied
a vital position and played a key role in the international affairs
of Europe. Its size, population, location, and resources all contributed to making it potentially a useful ally or a dangerous foe.
For centuries France had been the traditional rival and threat to
England, and the dynastic entanglements of the Renaissance guaranteed a continuation of that enmity. But many new factors had also
arisen in the sixteenth century to complicate and obscure the lines
of affiliation and competition. In 1559 the Treaty of Cateau-Cam-
brésis formally ended a half century of dynastic wars which had
intermittently pitted England and Hapsburg Spain against France.
The treaty set the tone for a hopeful period of peace in Europe, but
its realization was thwarted by the increasing bitterness of religious
extremism. The growth of Calvinism in France tended to complicate

---

* The question of French diplomatic involvement in the Spanish Armada
is one that interested Professor Mattingly a great deal, and which he
frequently encouraged me to investigate. This essay is in part an outgrowth
of many pleasant and stimulating discussions with him on the subject.

French diplomatic relations with both England and Spain. Although she was far from being a Calvinist herself, Elizabeth of England was sympathetic to the Huguenots because their activities in France reduced the likelihood and effectiveness of French assistance to her archenemy Scotland. By 1572 Anglo-French relations had improved to the point that a defensive alliance was negotiated and signed at Blois. This treaty constituted the formal diplomatic framework of Anglo-French association for the remainder of the century.[1]

During the same period, relations between France and Spain deteriorated noticeably, especially after the death in 1568 of Elizabeth of Valois, Philip II's wife. The religious wars in France caused both satisfaction and apprehension in Spain. On the one hand the wars guaranteed the virtual neutralization of a potential rival, but on the other they threatened to capture for Protestantism the largest political prize of Europe. After the ascension of Henry III in 1574, the position of France became an increasing enigma. Henry of Valois vacillated not only in relation to the shifting international balance but also in response to the violent fluctuations of power within France. By the mid-1580s several points of friction irritated the already strained relations between France and Spain. Catherine de' Medici, still smarting from Philip's rebuff of her claim to the Portuguese throne, reacted by throwing her support and influence to the pretender Don Antonio de Crato, whose bothersome escapades gave Philip many anxious moments for the next ten years. The Marquis d'Ayamonte's occupation of Saluzzo, adjacent to Spanish possessions in northern Italy, caused further apprehensions in Madrid, as did the Duc d'Anjou's capture of Cambrai in 1581.[2] When Anjou suddenly died in June, 1584, Cambrai was passed on to his mother, Catherine de' Medici, and it became a festering sore in all subsequent Franco-Spanish negotiations.

Anjou's death had an even greater impact on the diplomatic balance of Europe. With him died also the Valois succession in France and with it the hope of a forseeable end to the civil wars. Henry of Navarre, leader of the Huguenots, was next in line to the French throne. If the Huguenots were not destroyed before Henry III died France would become Protestant by dynastic default. This realization precipitated the founding of the Catholic League, led by the ambitious Henry, Duc de Guise, and its conclusion of a formal treaty with the King of Spain.[3] For the next five years the complexities of diplomatic negotiation were thus compounded by the existence of three separate and institutionalized powers in France: Crown, Huguenots, and League.

Recognizing the precariousness of their position, the Dutch estates began looking to both England and France for protection. Frightened by the implications of the Spanish-League alliance, Henry III refused the enticing Dutch offer of sovereignty over the Netherlands. But Elizabeth, reluctant to turn down a promising opportunity, just as she was to accept its responsibilities, decided finally to cast her lot with the Dutch revolutionaries and at the same time give open aid to the French Huguenots.[4] Elizabeth had hoped to keep the Dutch rebellion alive without a victory so clear-cut that France would reap the benefits, but now it seemed that the rebellion would founder if it were not supported.

These and other events prompted Philip II, the "Prudent King," to make the fateful but still wavering decision to invade England. Such a strike could at once put an end to English support of the Dutch revolt and also, by deposing the heretical Queen, bring the wayward nation back to the Catholic fold. Projects for sending an "armada" against England were not new, but not until Philip's acquisition of Portugal and the Portuguese fleet in 1580 did he possess more than a fraction of the seapower necessary to carry it out. Plans and activities were still erratic and vague, but by early 1586 precise preparations for a massive sea-borne invasion of England were well under way.[5]

] II [

In the summer of 1585, Don Bernardino de Mendoza, Philip's enterprising ambassador in Paris, and his official liaison with the Catholic League, was instructed to determine the attitude in France toward such an operation.[6] These initial probings revealed not only Guise's willingness but an eagerness on the part of Henry III and Catherine de' Medici to participate with Philip in a joint Franco-Spanish attack on England.[7] The ambassador, however, took the

French offers with a healthy skepticism, for he knew the comparable eagerness with which Henry had accepted Elizabeth's proposals for a joint Anglo-French operation against the Spanish Netherlands less than a year before.[8]

Henry seems to have been motivated as much by fear as by reasoned planning, yet his readiness to cooperate with Spain in deposing Elizabeth is not surprising. Mary, Queen of Scots, was the logical successor to the English Throne, and Mary was not only French by training and by blood, she was Queen Dowager of France and cousin to the Duc de Guise. Henry's submission to the League in July (Treaty of Nemours) was probably based on objectives more clear-sighted than at first appears. In August he further emphasized the new direction of French policy by replacing his pro-English ambassador in London, Michel de Castelnau, Sieur de Mauvissière, with a known Guise partisan, Guillaume de l'Aubespine, Baron de Châteauneuf, and in October sent two openly anti-English representatives to Scotland.

For many months the air was full of rumors, counter-rumors, "confidential" reports, and official declarations regarding alignments and realignments of the major powers. Elizabeth was warned in December that Spain and France had reached a formal agreement and that she was destined to follow the footsteps of William of Orange.[9] Scores of similarly foreboding advises reached the English Queen from French, German, and Italian sources. Elizabeth's ambassador in France, however, Sir Edward Stafford, thought these were only Spanish rumors to frighten the English into granting some unmerited concessions to Spain. "I do not think," he confided to Secretary Walsingham, "that there is such strict intelligence between these two Kings, though I watch for it as much as I can," adding wisely, "howbeit, 'to provide for the worst is the best course, and to suspect all naughtiness of them is a thing their former actions commandeth us to do.' "[10] In France the chief concern was that a treaty would be reached between England and Spain, while in the latter country rumors held that Elizabeth was negotiating a military alliance with Henry III for an invasion of the Spanish Netherlands.

More correct than any of these reports was the news that Elizabeth had submitted to Navarre's persistent requests for aid and that she also intended to support and help finance a levy of German mercenaries to assist the Huguenots in an all-out attack against the League and its current ally, the King of France. The Duke of Parma's letter of February 28, 1586, reminding Philip of the imminent danger of the League's being forced into a peace with the Huguenots and the two remaining parties (Navarre's and the King's) then striking Parma in the back, underscores the fear that plagued Spanish policy-makers for the next two and a half years. Parma expressed gravest concern for the protection of the Flanders frontier adjoining France. To insure the safety and success of the Armada, he insisted, France must be neutralized by maintaining the unsettled conditions which already existed (no peace to be reached between either the League, the Crown, or the Huguenots); and the Armada would have to be gathered and launched in complete secrecy.[11] Two months later, Parma summarized Spanish policy by declaring that, "Three points are most vital to the invasion of England: secrecy, the continuance of the civil war in France, and a wise settlement of arrangements in the provinces adjoining France."[12]

Philip hardly needed to be reminded of the crucial position occupied by France, but by mid-1586 Henry III and his mother had cooled in their attitude toward Spain and the Armada. Convinced by Catherine de' Medici's confidence in the imminence of a general peace in France, Henry listened to the new Spanish offers with less enthusiasm than he had a year before. When Mendoza assured the King that Spain had no territorial ambitions and invited him to associate himself with the "Enterprise," Henry declared that the cause of Christendom would be better served by peace than by warlike preparations against England. In reply to the ambassador's query about the availability of French ports to ships of the Armada, the King announced firmly that no French facilities could be used.[13] Reassured by dispatches from his ambassador in Madrid that the sailing of a Spanish fleet in the near future was highly unlikely, Henry not only rebuffed Philip's offers but also tried, through his diplomatic connections in Rome, to persuade the pope to discourage the venture.[14]

Throughout 1586 the international cat-and-mouse game continued with its complexity mounting and its volatility increasing with each new rumor and report. Sixtus V, the politically prudent Roman pontiff, was not overly enthusiastic about the Armada at any time, but became obdurate and even cantankerous when Philip began negotiations with him for financial and diplomatic assistance.[15] Furthermore, the frustrations arising from the three-way civil war in France tended to make even the most formal alliances and agreements uncertain. Catholic opinion in Europe generally favored some sort of military operation against the English "Jezebel" and the liberation of the Queen of Scots, but beyond that point there was very little agreement as to motives, objectives, or method. And among the Spanish planners themselves there could hardly have been less unity of opinion. Between January, 1586, and July, 1588, there were no fewer than fifteen "enterprises" planned (and several attempted) in Spain, France, Italy, the Netherlands, and England. Some called for a joint Franco-Spanish attack on the rebellious Netherlands, others for a direct cross-Channel invasion of England assisted by naval power from Venice and Genoa. Scottish Catholic nobles, led by the Earls of Huntley, Morton, Crawford, and Montrose, proposed an uprising in Scotland which, if given sufficient help, might carry over into England.[16] Some conspirators planned for an uprising in England, and others thought the Irish rebellion could be strengthened and used to overthrow the Queen.[17] Of all these, the Babington Plot is the best known because its miscarriage irrefutably implicated the Queen of Scots and brought her to the executioner's block.

Mary's death in February, 1587, revealed a new complication which, although anticipated before, had never really been faced: the problem of succession to the English Throne. No relationship was more intimately affected by the English succession than that between Spain and France. Although his sympathies had been with Mary, her death raised Philip's hopes for a more favorable solution to the English problem. At least it reduced the likelihood of a predominantly French victory from the Spanish Armada, through Mary's accession to the English Throne. But for the same reasons it further dampened French enthusiasm for the venture. Whereas Philip now stood to gain more from a resettlement in England than he had before, Henry III—and even more directly the Duc de Guise—were more apt to lose. French interests now favored non-intervention, since a peaceful succession would bring their kinsman, James VI, Mary's son, to the English Throne; while a Spanish invasion would just as surely favor Spain. Guise's dilemma was more perplexing. His interests were neither those of France nor entirely those of Catholic Christendom; but his eventual decision to support the latter (for it is unlikely that he favored the Armada in order to advance Spanish political interests), instead of championing his family fortunes through James VI, is highly significant.

Philip II followed several lines of action as he attempted to bypass young James while simultaneously preserving his alliance with Guise and avoiding a rupture with France. At Paris, the Spanish ambassador compared James's position in relation to the English Crown with that of Henry of Navarre to the Crown of France. Both were heretical pretenders whose succession would be serious defeats to Catholicism and to the French nation. Henry was urged to support the Spanish suit at Rome for the exclusion of James's claim to the Throne. Mendoza's appeal to Guise followed a different tack. Ignoring as far as possible the whole Scottish matter, he emphasized the immediate threat from the Huguenots in France and the ominous gathering of German mercenaries in the Rhineland. With enticing offers of additional funds and even armed forces, Guise was entreated to maintain and expand the war against heresy.

Another approach, pressed eagerly by Mendoza during 1587 and early 1588, was the promotion of Philip's own claim to the English Throne. Eight months before Mary's execution, Mendoza had received a letter from the Queen of Scots promising that she would cede to Philip, by will, her right to the English Throne, provided her son still refused to become a Catholic by the time of her death.[18] A similar letter, threatening to disinherit James, was sent to the Pope through Mary's representative in France, the Archbishop of Glasgow.[19] It is still questionable whether or not that will was ever made,[20] but many people believed it existed and acted on the assumption that it did. The evidence of Mendoza's correspondence strongly suggests that he thought the will was drawn up by the Queen of Scots just before her death, and that Philip too was convinced of its existence and validity.[21] Nevertheless, without the will in his possession, Philip was legally handicapped in asserting his claims through that authority. That is why Mendoza began popularizing the notion that even without it, and without the conversion of James VI, Philip's personal claim to the Throne, through the house of Lancaster, was stronger than anyone else's.[22]

Philip II, however, was reluctant to make such claims openly. He cautioned his ambassador on several occasions to speak of his "blood rights" in strictest confidence and only to certain people. On occasion Philip proposed the succession of some prominent nobleman of England, whose claim to the Throne was without serious legal question, with the precisely attached condition that he marry Philip's daughter, the Infanta of Spain. But most frequently the Spanish King preferred silence and non-commitment on the subject of succession until after the Armada had been launched and Elizabeth deposed.[23] During the final year of preparation he feared that either France or the papacy (or both) might frustrate the whole Armada project out of jealousy and apprehension of his dynastic ambitions. Philip's anxiety was not unfounded, for by late spring of 1587 anti-Spanish feeling was running high in both Rome and Paris.[24] In May, Mendoza reported ominous negotiations under way between the French and English for joint opposition to Philip's claims to the English throne.[25] Equally disturbing, from the Spanish point of view, was the information that Catherine de' Medici was trying to wean the Duc de Guise away from Spain by offering him support in a Franco-Scottish enterprise to place James VI on the English Throne.[26]

But the French diplomatic project least likely to succeed in 1587 was Henry's attempt to reach a general peace settlement with both the League and the Huguenots. To do this, the King sought the mediation of Sixtus V and also the aid of Philip II in ending the Huguenot menace and in pacifying the League. He also hoped to capitalize on the forthcoming German invasion of France to prove his own military prowess and win back the allegiance of his subjects. Thus French policy was directed simultaneously toward improving relations with Spain for the purpose of reducing tensions and warfare inside France, and toward tightening the ties of friendship with both Scotland and England. Fear of Spain pushed Catherine de' Medici and her son into the arms of Elizabeth, but their resentment over her execution of the Queen of Scots drove them toward collusion with Philip. The French dilemma is revealed in the following interview between the French ambassador in Constantinople and the Grand Vizir, as reported by the Venetian resident.

> The Capadun Pasha asked him if his master favoured the Spanish attack on England. The Ambassador answered that Spain would be favoured if in nothing else, at least in being allowed to use French ports; for the Queen of England had deeply injured the King of France by killing her sister-in-law, the Queen of Scotland. "Oh!" said the Capadun, "then your master will allow Spain to take England, and to become so much more powerful." "No," replied the Ambassador, "he will not consent to that, but England will be conquered to the King of Scotland."[27]

Philip's dilemma was equally perplexing. He was fully aware of his need for French cooperation in the "Enterprise," if not actively, at least by refraining from helping England or molesting the Netherlands. But he distrusted the French whole-heartedly. In response to Henry III's overtures to the Pope, Philip instructed his ambassador in Rome to

> Keep his Holiness well posted in this project for peace, so that he shall not think that the desired result can ever be expected from Frenchmen, whose only aim is to make public any secret that may be entrusted to them, and countermine the intentions of his Holiness and myself; whilst under the pretence of going to England they may patch up a peace prejudicial to our holy Catholic faith in France.[28].

Could Philip trust the Duc de Guise any more than he could the King of France? This was another question which, in the autumn of 1587, could not yet be answered with assurance. If he could not, chances for the Armada's success would be greatly reduced. Parma insisted that the fleet must sail before October, but Drake's audacious raid on Cadiz in the spring and his costly plundering off Cape Saint Vincent forced that deadline to be abandoned.[29] Then came the long-threatened Huguenot-German invasion of France, and Philip could hardly risk pulling Parma out of the Netherlands until this latest crisis was resolved. The simultaneous defeat of the German mercenaries by the Duc de Guise and Navarre's victory over the royalist army sent against him increased the strength of both

Huguenots and League at the expense of the Crown, and convinced Philip that thenceforth his principal reliance in France must be on Guise and his followers rather than on the King. Consequently, the crucial negotiations in the early months of 1588 were primarily between Spain and the French Catholic League and not, as the attempted alliances of 1586 and 1587 had been, with the government of France.

] III [

In the early weeks of 1588, Henry III's anxieties were renewed and intensified. His two immediate enemies inside France had both been strengthened, and he was continually haunted by the fear that Philip's demands for the use of French ports on the Channel coast might be intended as preparation for an attack on France. This apprehension was increased when news spread of the reopening of Anglo-Spanish negotiations between the Duke of Parma and Elizabeth's representatives in the Netherlands.[30] Therefore, with a nervous eye on the meetings in Flanders and on the restless League stirrings in northern France, Henry began a counter move.

Encouraged by his favorite, the Duc d'Épernon, Henry hoped to persuade Navarre to abandon the heretical faith and come to terms with the French Crown. This of course was not a radically new policy, especially for the Queen Mother who still clung to the hope that her son-in-law could be reconciled to the church.[31] But previous attempts to effect such a reconciliation had failed. Now Henry turned to Queen Elizabeth to solicit her aid in a plan of mutual defense. Knowing that the English Queen was hard-pressed in face of the threatened Spanish attack, Henry offered her a new and active alliance, promising to assist with twice the number of troops that had been agreed upon in the Treaty of Blois. Henry reminded her of the precarious position she was in and asked her to break off negotiations with Parma. In return for his sage advice and his promised support, Henry asked that Elizabeth intercede with Navarre and use her influence to attract him away from the Huguenots and back to the Catholic Church.[32]

Elizabeth's reply to Henry was typically Elizabethan. Pleased with his offer of assistance and by his desire for peace with Navarre, she encouraged him to continue in such a noble pursuit, but suggested that a better basis for peace would be his concession of religious tolerance to Navarre.[33] After all, she reminded the King, if Navarre became a Catholic, Henry would still have the Huguenots to fight, albeit without their illustrious leader, but if the French Crown granted amity to them a lasting settlement could be reached. The idea was intoxicating but enough different from Henry's own proposal to make immediate agreement impossible. Thus, through the first four months of 1588, Anglo-French talks continued without any arrangement being reached. Negotiations also continued between Spain and England and between Spain and France, as the Armada completed its final preparations.

Mendoza soon learned of the Anglo-French discussions from a well-informed secret agent, and quickly relayed the news to the Spanish King.[34] As might be expected, Philip was as apprehensive about this turn of events as Henry was about the Anglo-Spanish talks.[35] His alarm was amplified in the Duke of Parma, whose concern over secrecy, a French attack against his flank, and control of at least one good port, was even more vital than it had been a year before. In a sharply worded note of January 31, 1588, Parma reprimanded the King for not guarding the secrecy of the Armada, and for not guaranteeing against the threat from France.[36] Although his negotiation with Elizabeth was largely a ruse to gain time and disarm the Queen, no one knew better than Parma himself that a diplomatic settlement with England might become a necessity to Spain if their policy in France should fail.

After the death of the Marquis de Santa Cruz in early February, many voices were heard around the courts of Europe suggesting that Philip was unable or unwilling to send the Armada, and that the whole affair was a grandiose deception to keep the Pope off Philip's back and to prevent England or France from taking over the Netherlands.[37] Most of the information received by the French King regarding the Armada's preparations and plans came from the official French representative in Madrid, Pierre de Ségusson, Sieur de Longlée-Renault. Well-meaning and hard-working, but poorly informed and supported, Longlée could never quite decide what the Armada was intended to do, though he was fairly certain it was not going to make a direct attack on England—that was too obvious and too risky. The opinions expressed in his dispatches vacillated between the notion that the Armada was intended to protect the plate fleets, attack the Netherlands or France, land in Ireland, or remain near Spain as defense against a suspected English attack.[38] Much of the French fear that Philip intended to use the Armada directly against France to recover Cambrai can be attributed to Longlée's repeated warnings. Paramount in his reasoning was the belief that Philip would not risk an invasion of England without the guarantee of Henry's neutrality, especially since Philip was so worried about the possibility of a Turkish attack from the Mediterranean.[39]

In spite of his misleading reports, Longlée was the most persistent advocate of peace and alliance between France and Spain. Almost two years earlier he had proposed a formal treaty and ever since had encouraged the peace parties in both countries.[40] In February, 1588, hoping to capitalize on the prevailing uncertainties, Longlée advised his government that the Spanish were very anxious to recover Cambrai and that it might be profitably used as a means for arriving at a general peace. Specifically, he advocated going along with the Spanish Armada plans—whatever they were—and, while showing every sign of submission to Spain, keeping a sharp eye open for the opportune moment to propose general peace talks through the exchange of specially accredited ambassadors.[41] At any rate, Longlée cautioned, negotiations would have to be proffered carefully and astutely because "the normal thing for this nation [Spain] is to negotiate more with those who do not seek it than with those who do."[42]

Under other conditions Longlée's peace plans might have been followed, but by early 1588 Philip was slowly coming to rely more on the French League and less on the French Crown. Moved by Spanish insistence, League forces under command of the Duc d'Aumale made a sudden show of force in Picardy, hoping to gain by direct assault what they had been unable to assure by treaty. The prime target of this League attack was Boulogne-sur-Mer, guarding, from the mouth of the Liane river, the Strait of Dover. Aumale's siege was massive and closely coordinated, but the city, fortified and defended by its indomitable governor, Raymond Roger de Bernet, held out for five months before it was forced, by the treacherous Edict of Union, to capitulate.[43] According to the League plan, Calais was to have followed Boulogne, but the latter's tenacious resistance delayed Aumale too long and forced him to postpone the Calais attack. This setback later proved costly to the Armada.

While Aumale campaigned in Picardy, Philip carefully considered more drastic steps to neutralize France, should Henry III decide to oppose the Armada. Mendoza's first orders were to keep the civil war in France going, not only by preventing a truce among any of the Three Henrys, but also by not allowing one of the parties to become powerful enough that either of the others might be eliminated.[44] A decisive defeat of the Huguenots at this point could easily become as troublesome to Philip as a Huguenot victory. The Duc d'Épernon's sardonic remark, "It is not heresy which causes the greatest woe in France, but the ambitions of those who, in showing themselves most against the Huguenots, would be very distressed if they saw them overthrown and annihilated,"[45] proved to be more perceptive than poetic.

It is generally recognized that Philip II was closely involved in the rebellious events in Paris associated with the "Day of the Barricades," but many questions remain unanswered as to the exact nature of this involvement and the relationship between the various events. Reliable sources seem to support the conclusion that Philip did intend some show of force that would occupy the King of France, or at least distract him, during the crucial weeks of the Armada's sailing. Furthermore, the evidence also suggests that Philip was willing to give his blessing to an eventual League overthrow of Henry III, even though Philip had as strong an aversion to rebellion as did any monarch of the century. Judging from the outcome, however, Philip probably used such extreme promises to Guise as incentives to keep the ambitious duke from being diverted from the Catholic cause at the crucial moment he was needed most.

By March, 1588, Paris was seething. Mass feeling against Henry III had never been more intense than it was in early 1588, while the Duc de Guise had never been more popular. Parisians clamored for Guise to enter Paris; the King ordered him to stay away. Incensed, the Paris League began plotting the King's overthrow, and Guise desperately sought Mendoza's advice.[46] The other Lorraine princes urged Guise to go to Paris and "have it out" with the King, but Mendoza advised the contrary. Fearing that a personal meeting between Henry and Guise might lead to conciliation and peace, the ambassador recommended that the duke remain at Soissons until word was received from Madrid.[47] Philip's answer soon came, and was emphatic: "Those in Paris who advise Guise to go there do not counsel him well [no le aconsejan bien]."[48] Mendoza's orders were to tell Guise to stay away from Paris. On March 31 Guise asked for Spanish troops to intervene in France and assist the League, but Philip again refused. He could not afford a settlement in France at this point, even against the Huguenots. Mendoza assuaged Guise's restlessness by suggesting that he send reinforcements to Aumale in Picardy.[49]

Early in April, however, Philip made his greatest concession and commitment to Guise. Juan de Moreo arrived at Soissons with an offer of 300,000 escudos for the League head and a reminder that the King of France must not be allowed to assist the English when the Armada sailed. Philip also offered military support to the duke and promised to sever diplomatic relations with Henry III and accredit an ambassador to the new government when the Leaguers came into power.[50] Nothing more specific was contained in the agreement, but from these promises Mendoza inferred Philip's acceptance of the League's intention to seize the King and take over the government. By now the ambassador had become convinced that the revolt was necessary and the time was right. Besides, Mendoza's League friends in Paris would see to it that Guise's move to the capital would not result in submission to the King.[51]

By April 24 the League was ready to make its bid for power, but Henry, uneasy over the restlessness in Paris, moved four-thousand veteran Swiss infantry from Lagny to Saint-Denis as a precautionary measure.[52] The maneuver was effective. Mendoza immediately ordered Guise to stay at Soissons until the situation looked better in Paris. From Philip's notes of the same date to Parma and to Mendoza it is apparent that the Catholic King was not fully aware of the extent or even the exact nature of the League intentions against Henry III, but he did know that some sort of "demonstration was planned against Henry III to persuade him not to interfere in the operation against England."[53] Philip ordered that the demonstration be undertaken as soon as it was ready. Two weeks later, Henry Duc de Guise entered the capital. The fanatical revolt which ensued was ill-coordinated and chaotic, but at least to Mendoza's experienced eye the Day of the Barricades guaranteed that "the French King will be unable to assist the English in any way."[54]

] IV [

As on other occasions, Mendoza was overly optimistic. The Armada sailed in late May, and shortly thereafter Épernon was withdrawn from Normandy, but Henry III was still dangerous. By his flight from Paris he had lost even more of his diminutive prestige. But what had it cost him in actual strength? This depended largely upon Henry himself and upon the success of his diplomacy during the next two months—while the Armada was hauled up at Coruña after being scattered by a treacherous Atlantic gale. Did the Day of the Barricades signify Henry's complete submission to the League and to Spain, or did it rather mark the beginning of his carefully planned recovery of power? Did Henry believe in the invincibility of the Armada, and thus in his own dependence upon Spain, or was he merely biding his time in the belief that the Armada would soon be defeated? Answers to these questions must remain tentative, but the evidence is more available and more instructive than is usually assumed.

The ignominy of Henry's retreat caused Elizabeth to reconsider her relations with the French King. Just as six months earlier Philip had turned from Henry to Guise, so now did Elizabeth shift the weight of her French alliance from the Valois government to Henry of Navarre. By summer it was only too apparent that Elizabeth needed an ally on the Continent more reliable than Henry III.[55] This English *démarche* with Navarre forced Henry to abandon any hope for an anti-Spanish alliance and left him with only one alternative—a rapprochement with Spain. Hopefully, Henry tried once more to reach a favorable agreement only to be rebuffed by Philip and insulted by his ambassador. More in despair and fear than in cunning, Henry turned to the League and eventually submitted to all of its demands. It has been suggested that Henry hoped by this move to drive a wedge between Philip and his French allies through separate negotiations with Guise.[56] But if he really entertained such a notion he must have refused to believe what he already knew about the Spanish-League connection. Guise had now submitted completely to Spanish orders and to the idea that his personal fortunes were tied to the cause of Catholicism as interpreted by Philip II.[57] After the Day of the Barricades, Philip no longer feared a separate peace in France.

Still there remained some apprehension in Madrid over the status of the French Channel ports and some occasional reminders that any Guise treachery at this point could be costly to the Armada. On May 23, Mendoza met with the Queen Mother and asked for the guarantee of free entry and exit for Armada ships in French ports. Catherine replied that she understood this had already been taken care of before the flight of her son.[58] Cautiously accepting her assurance that she would communicate with the King on the matter, Mendoza took the further step of riding to Chartres and there demanding point-blank Henry's intentions in regard to the Armada. Henry's allusive reply was not completely satisfying, but it did give Spain the formal assurances Philip had sought.[59] Beyond that, only power could tell.

Meanwhile, Longlée convinced himself, and his master, that the opportune time had arrived for formal peace talks with Spain. From Chartres on May 20, Henry sent Longlée a letter of credence authorizing him to propose the opening of alliance negotiations. Enclosed in the pouch was also a note to Philip asking him to remove his bothersome ambassador in Paris, to sever relations with the French Leaguers and unite with France in a "Christian union" for the maintenance of peace and the extirpation of heresy [?].[60] After repeated delays and harassments in transit these letters were finally delivered to Longlée on July 6. Immediately the French ambassador went into action. He arranged an audience with Philip for July 10 and at that time presented his peace proposal in brief outline.[61] Philip listened with interest and invited Longlée to prepare a more detailed proposal for submission to the Council of State. This he did and on July 28 it was considered by the whole council. As Philip and the council studied the French appeal, news arrived from Paris of Henry's complete capitulation to the League and his signing the Edict of Union.[62]

By the terms of the Edict of Union, Henry agreed to all of the League demands, including the turning over of Normandy and Picardy to the League. Bernet was removed as governor of Boulogne, and Henry agreed to renounce his alliance with England.[63] Before the Armada came into sight of the Eddystone the last French impediments to its success had been removed. At this critical moment, observed the late Conyers Read, "when the Spanish Armada was already on the way to England, her neighbour across the Channel was delivered over into the hands of her determined enemies."[64] If Henry's submission to the League was intended to disturb Spain it missed its mark. Not only did the edict obviate the Spanish necessity for peace with France, it guaranteed the success, through the Duc de Guise (now declared Lieutenant-General of France), of three and a half years of Spanish diplomacy. Parma's relief is revealed in his July 21 note to Philip: "I have received news from Don Bernardino de Mendoza of the peace concluded in France, to the great advantage of the Catholic cause. Your Majesty's thanks are due to the League. There will be much less danger now of interference with the principal business we have in hand, which was to have been feared if the dissensions had continued."[65] Had the Armada itself been as successful as Spanish diplomacy, the year 1588 might have held a very different kind of significance in Western history.

N O T E S

1. Bibliothèque Nationale, fonds français, 5140, fol. 74–104; also Conyers Read, *Mr. Secretary Walsingham and the Policy of Queen Elizabeth* (Oxford: Clarendon Press, 1925), I, pp. 190–97.

2. See Albert Mousset, *Un résident de France en Espagne au temps de la Ligue (1583–1590): Pierre de Ségusson* (Paris: Champion, 1908), pp. 51–52; Inocencio Vallina, *Relaciones políticas entre*

España y Francia durante el reinado de Felipe II (Oviedo: Vicente Brid, 1893), pp. 97–106.

3. De Lamar Jensen, *Diplomacy and Dogmatism: Bernardino de Mendoza and the French Catholic League* (Cambridge, Mass.: Harvard University Press, 1964), pp. 41–55.

4. *Calendar of State Papers, Foreign Series, of the Reign of Elizabeth, Preserved in the Public Record Office*, Sophie Lomas, ed. (London: H. M. S. O., 1927), XIX, pp. 49–50, 119–20, 222–24, 233–34, 284–85, 295–97, 315–19. [Hereafter cited *C.S.P., For.*]. Also see Read, *Walsingham*, III, pp. 72–98; John L. Motley, *History of the United Netherlands* (New York: Harper, 1876), I, pp. 70–81, 105–9, 119–23, 388–415; and Léon Van der Essen, *Alexandre Farnèse, prince de Parme, gouverneur générale des Pay-Bas* (Brussels: Librairie Nationale d'Art et d'Histoire, 1937), V, pp. 6, 85.

5. Cesáreo Fernández Duro, *La Armada Invencible* (Madrid: Rivademeyra, 1884), I, pp. 250 ff.; Roger B. Merriman, *The Rise of the Spanish Empire* (New York: Macmillan, 1934), IV, pp. 517–19.

6. Philip to Mendoza, July 23, 1585, Archivo General de Simancas, Legajos de Estado, K. 1448, fol. 26; and August 17, fol. 29. Henri Forneron, *Histoire de Philippe II* (Paris: E. Plon, 1887), III, p. 234.

7. Mendoza to Philip, Simancas, K. 1563, fol. 78, 79; Philip to Mendoza, August 17, K. 1448, fols. 28, 29. Cf. Motley, *United Netherlands*, I, pp. 135, 156–57. Catherine's letter of January 13 to Longlée, French ambassador in Spain, suggests her earlier willingness to participate, *Lettres de Catherine de Médicis*, G. Baguenault de Puchesse, ed. (Paris: Imprimerie Nationale, 1901), VIII, pp. 232–33.

8. *C.S.P., For.*, XIX, 49–50, 119–20, 222–24. Read, *Walsingham*, III, pp. 75–78. In summer and autumn of 1585 Elizabeth again offered Henry III a closer military alliance, *C.S.P., For.*, XIX, 675, *passim;* Lawrence Stone, *An Elizabethan: Sir Horatio Palavicino* (Oxford: Clarendon Press, 1956), pp. 106–8.

9. M. de Combes to Walsingham, December 14, 1585, *C.S.P., For.*, XX, 196. William had been assassinated in June, 1584.

10. Stafford to Walsingham, February 17, 1586 (O.S.), *C.S.P., For.*, XX, 382.

11. Parma to Philip, February 28, 1586, Archives Générales du Royaume en Belgique, cited in Van der Essen, *op. cit.*, V, pp. 165–68, 173.

12. Quoted by Motley in *The United Netherlands*, II, pp. 208–9.

13. Giovanni Dolfin to the Doge and Senate, Paris, July 4, 1586, *Calendar of State Papers and Manuscripts, Relating to English Affairs, Existing in the Archives and Collections of Venice, and in other Libraries of Northern Italy*, H. F. Brown, ed. (London: H. M. S. O., 1894), VIII, pp. 176–77 [hereafter cited *C.S.P., Ven.*]; *Lippomano* to the same, July 26, *ibid.*, p. 185; Jules Martin, "La préparation de l'Armada," *Revue d'Histoire Diplomatique*, XXIV (1910), 573.

14. Longlée to Henry III, February 15, 1586, *Dépêches diplomatiques de M. de Longlée, résident de France en Espagne*, Albert Mousset, ed. (Paris: Plon, 1912), p. 228; March 6, p. 234; March 25, pp. 241–43; April 3, pp. 243–44; April 13, p. 249. Girolamo Lippomano, also reporting from Madrid, reminded the Venetian government that "it is impossible to be sure of his Most Christian Majesty's intentions; from informations forwarded by Don Bernardino de Mendoza, however, it is certain that France will allow Frenchmen to help England, all the more so as the King of France is absolutely convinced that the King of Spain has done all he could to set France in a blaze and to feed the flame when once alight." Lippomano to the Doge and Senate, August 24, 1586, *C.S.P., Ven.*, VIII, 201.

15. Giovanni Gritti to the Doge and Senate, Rome, June 14, 1586, *ibid.*, 169–79; and Gradenigo and Lippomano to the same, Madrid, June 25, 1586, *ibid.*, 173. See John Lynch, "Philip II and the Papacy," *Transactions of the Royal Historical Society*, fifth series, Vol. XI (1961), pp. 23–42.

16. Mendoza argued for a Scottish operation instead of the direct attack on England. Fewer ships would be required, he maintained, and because of the earlier sailing there would be much less risk of discovery. "The French are so involved with the queen that, even though they cannot send forces from here, they can and will do their utmost to obstruct Your Majesty and prevent you from punishing your enemies. . . . These difficulties will all be avoided if you anticipate the Englishwoman by assisting the Scots." Mendoza to Philip, December 24, 1586, Simancas, K. 1564, fol. 247. Also cf. Mendoza to Parma, October 14, 1586, K. 1564, fol. 201.

17. See, for example, *C.S.P., Ven.*, VIII, 223–25, 241, 263, 269, 313, 331; Van der Essen, *op. cit.*, V, 176–77; *Correspondence du cardinal de Granvelle*, Charles Piot, ed. (Brussels: Hayez, 1896), XII, p. 487.

18. Mary Stuart to Mendoza, Charley, May 20, 1586, Simancas, K. 1564, fol. 72. Cf. *Calendar of Letters and State Papers Relating to English affairs, of the Reign of Elizabeth, Preserved Principally in the Archives of Simancas*, Martin A. S. Hume, ed. (London, 1895), III, pp. 581–82 [hereafter cited *C.S.P., Span.*].

19. Mendoza to Philip, December 22, 1587, Simancas, K. 1565, fol. 149; also Alexandre Teulet, ed., *Relations politiques de la France et de l'Espagne avec l'Ecosse au XVI*ᵉ *siècle* (Paris: Renouard, 1862), II, pp. 514–15; and *C.S.P., Span.*, IV, 177–91. Martin, "La préparation de l'Armada," *R. d'H. D.*, XXIV (1910), pp. 596–97.

20. See John D. Mackie, "The Will of Mary Stuart," *Scottish Historical Review*, XI (1914), pp. 338–44, and "Scotland and the Spanish Armada," *ibid.*, XII (1914), esp. pp. 12–13.

21. Mendoza to Philip, October 24, 1587, Simancas, K. 1565, fol. 85; December 22, 1587, K. 1565, fol. 149; Philip to Mendoza, January 28, 1587, K. 1448, fol. 99; November 27, 1587, fol. 151. Also Lippomano to the Doge and Senate, August 18, 1587, *C.S.P., Ven.*, VIII, 306.

22. Mendoza to Philip, May 3, 1587, Simancas, K. 1566, fol. 124. The ambassador went so far as to have a book written by an English exile, Robert Heighinton, which demonstrated the legal claims of Philip. Mendoza to Philip, November 28, 1587, K. 1565, fol. 120. Olivares to Philip, *C.S.P., Span.*, IV, 233, 253.

23. Philip to Mendoza, April 11, 1587, Simancas, K. 1448. fol. 114. Philip told Mendoza that he could advise "well disposed Englishmen" about his rights of succession, but ordered him not to tell the French. Philip to Mendoza, May 13, 1597, K. 1448, fol. 119. *C.S.P., Span.*, IV, 54–56.

24. See Olivares to Philip, March 30, 1587, *C.S.P., Span.*, IV, 54–5; Sixtus V to Philip, August 7, *ibid.*, 132–3; Guise to Mendoza, June 12, 1587, Simancas, K. 1566, fol. 152; and Cavriana to Belisario Vinta, Paris, May 18, 1587, *Négociations diplomatiques de la France avec la Toscane*, Abel Desjardins, ed. (Paris, 1872), IV, pp. 687–90, June 7, pp. 691–93.

25. Mendoza to Philip, May 3, 1587, Simancas, K. 1566, fol. 124; May 20, fol. 134; and Philip to Mendoza, June 20, K. 1448, fol. 122.

26. Mendoza to Philip, May 20, 1587, K. 1566, fol. 132. For Mendoza's actions against Catherine's policy, see fol. 136.

27. Lorenzo Bernardo to the Doge and Senate, June 17, 1587, *C. S. P., Ven.,* VIII, 286–87. Cf. Bibl. Nat., fonds fr., 16144, fol. 182.

28. Philip to Olivares, 24 June 1587, *C. S. P., Span.,* IV, 113. Cf. Philip to Mendoza, July 6, Simancas, K. 1448, fol. 124.

29. See Garrett Mattingly, *The Armada* (Boston: Houghton Mifflin, 1959), pp. 93–128.

30. Henri de l'Épinois, "La politique de Sixte-Quint: Négociations diplomatiques avec la France pendant les premiers mois de 1588, d'après des documents inédits conservés aux archives du Vatican," *Revue des Questions Historiques,* XIV (1874), p. 393.

31. See Villeroy to de Maisse, January 4, 1586, Bibl. Nat., fonds fr., 16093, fol. 5. Also *Recueil des lettres missives de Henri IV,* Berger de Xivrey, ed. (Paris: Imprimerie Royale, 1843), II, pp. 228–29; and Jensen, *Diplomacy and Dogmatism,* pp. 76–79.

32. Stafford to Elizabeth, February 25, 1588 (O.S.), *C. S. P., Span.,* IV, 198; and Froude, *Hist. of England,* XII, pp. 410–13. Cf. Read, *Walsingham,* III, pp. 211–13; Motley, *United Netherlands,* III, 270; and Mendoza to Philip, February 28, 1588, Simancas, K. 1567, fol. 31.

33. Stafford to Elizabeth, March 30, 1588 (O.S.), *Calendar of the Manuscripts of the Most Hon. the Marquis of Salisbury, K. G., preserved at Hatfield House* (London: H. M. S. O., 1889), III, pp. 314–17; Read, *Walsingham,* III, pp. 213–14. Giovanni Mocenigo to the Doge and Senate, Paris, March 11, 1588, *C. S. P., Ven.,* VIII, 343, and *ibid.,* May 6, pp. 353–54; Mendoza to Philip, April 5, 1588, Simancas, K. 1567, fol. 53.

34. On the possible collusion of Sir Edward Stafford with Mendoza in these negotiations, see Hume's footnotes in *C. S. P., Span.,* IV, and especially Read, "The Fame of Sir Edward Stafford," *American Historical Review,* XX (1915), pp. 292–313, XXXV (1939), pp. 560–66. This interpretation is seriously challenged by Sir John E. Neale in *The English Historical Review,* XLIV (1929), pp. 203–20. From Mendoza's papers it does seem difficult to equate Stafford with both "Julio" and Mendoza's "New Confident" as Hume and Read have done.

35. Philip to Mendoza, March 6, 1588, Simancas, K. 1448, fol. 168.

36. Parma to Philip, January 31, 1588, *C. S. P., Span.,* IV, 199–201.

37. Abstract of Letters sent by Duke Casimir to Elizabeth, *C. S. P., For.*, XXI, part 1, 561–63; Olivares to Philip, March 2, 1588, *C. S. P., Span.*, IV, 226; Mocenigo to the Doge and Senate, April 8, 1588, *C. S. P., Ven.*, VIII, 349, *passim*.

38. Longlée to Henry III, February 6, 1588, *Dépêches diplomatiques de M. de Longlée*, p. 343; March 5, pp. 352–53; March 25, p. 359; April 2, p. 363; and April 30, p. 368; also see Stafford to Walsingham, April 24, 1588, *C. S. P., For.*, XXI, part 1, 599.

39. "One cannot understand that the said king was resolved to send his forces to England without being assured first that Your Majesty would not stop these plans," Longlée confided. Believing that Philip would not dare risk invading England without the active support and cooperation of France, Longlée suggested that the Armada's real purpose was to cut off Dutch supplies from England then subdue the rebellious provinces and recover any territories, such as Cambrai, which had been lost. Longlée to Henry, May 6, 1588, *Dépêches diplomatiques*, p. 370; also May 13, p. 372. On May 22, Longlée reported the departure of a Turkish fleet from Constantinople which gave Philip great concern. Longlée to Henry, *ibid.*, p. 373.

40. Longlée to Villeroy, October 11, 1586, *ibid.*, pp. 316–18, *passim*. Mousset, *Un résident de France*, pp. 80–81.

41. Longlée to Henry, February 20, 1588, *Dépêches diplomatiques*, pp. 349–51. Longlée was particularly anxious to have an exchange of ambassadors for, even though it would mean his own withdrawal, it would also force Mendoza's removal, and the Spanish ambassador was Longlée's bitterest enemy. This jealousy can perhaps be traced in part to the greater support and trust from his government enjoyed by Mendoza than by Longlée, and to Mendoza's more favorable financial condition. In February, for example, Longlée complained pathetically that he had not been paid for two years. "All I do is borrow from one source to pay another, and the interest which I must pay will be as much at the end, if there is not soon a remedy, as the principal which I am to receive." Longlée to Henry, February 6, 1588, *ibid.*, p. 346. Furthermore, although he performed the same functions, Longlée had never been given full accreditation as ambassador. See Mousset, *Un résident de France*, pp. 20, 31, 39.

42. Longlée to Henry, March 5, 1588, *Dépêches diplomatiques*, pp. 353–54.

43. Thomas Jefferey to Lord Admiral Howard, May 11, 1588, *C. S. P.,
For.,* XXI, part 1, 607–18. John K. Laughton, ed., *State Papers
Relating to the Defeat of the Spanish Armada* (London: Navy
Records Society, 1894), I, pp. 177–78. Jean H. Mariéjol, *La
Réforme et la Ligue* [Ernest Lavisse, ed., *Histoire de France,* Vol.
VI, part 1] (Paris: Hachette, 1911), pp. 268–69.

44. See Mendoza to Philip, March 26, 1587, Simancas, K. 1586, fol.
80; Olivares to Philip, June 30, 1587, *C. S. P., Span.,* IV, 114–15;
Lippomano to the Doge and Senate, *C. S. P., Ven.,* VIII, 212, 264.

45. Quoted by l'Épinois in "La politique de Sixte-Quint," *R. Q. H.,*
XIV (1874), p. 398.

46. Guise to Mendoza, March 9, 1588, Simancas, K. 1568, fol. 15,
and Joseph de Croze, ed., *Les Guises, les Valois et Philippe II*
(Paris: Amyot, 1866), II, pp. 318–20.

47. L'Épinois, "La politique de Sixte-Quint," p. 403. See A. Viñas,
"Felipe II y la Jornada de las Barricadas," in *Hommage à Ernest
Martinenche: Études hispaniques et américaines* (Paris: Editions
d'Artrey, 1939), pp. 524–25.

48. Philip to Mendoza, April 5, 1588, Simancas, K. 1448, fol. 172. Also
see *ibid.,* May 13, fol. 186.

49. Philip to Mendoza, April 5, 1588, K. 1567, fol. 51. Cf. Croze, *Les
Guises,* II, pp. 324–26, and l'Épinois, "La politique de Sixte-Quint,"
pp. 414, 417.

50. Guise to Parma, May 21, 1588, Simancas, K. 1568, fol. 42; Philip to
Parma, April 24, 1588, *Correspondance de Philippe II sur les
affaires des Pays-Bas* (2e *Partie, 1577–1591*), Joseph Lefèvre, ed.
(Brussels: Palais des Académies, 1956), III, p. 295; Motley, *United
Netherlands,* III, pp. 268–69; l'Épinois, "La politique de Sixte-
Quint," pp. 404–5.

51. "If the project in question is carried out as planned," Mendoza
assured Philip, "the king will have his hands so full that he will
be unable even by words, and much less by deeds, to give aid to
the English Queen," Mendoza to Philip, April 14, Simancas, K.
1567, fol. 61. Cf. L'Épinois, "La politique de Sixte-Quint," p.
416; Viñas, "Felipe II y la Jornada de las Barricadas," pp. 525–27;
and Bibl. Nat., coll. Dupuy, 47.

52. Pierre de l'Estoile, *Mémoires-Journaux de Pierre de l'Estoile,* MM
Brunet, Chapollion, Halphen, *et al.,* eds., Vol. III, *Journal de*

Henri III, 1587–1589 (Paris: Alphonse Lemerre, 1888), p. 133. Nicolas Poulain, "Le procez verbal," *ibid.* pp. 364–66.

53. Philip to Parma, April 24, 1588, *Correspondance de Philippe II,* III, p. 295. Bibl. Nat., fonds fr., 5045, fol. 136.

54. Mendoza to Philip, May 15, 1588, Simancas, K. 1568, fol. 33; cf. Croze, *Les Guises,* II, p. 337; Forneron, *Philippe II,* III, pp. 247–48; and Gustave Baguenault de Puchesse, "La politique de Philippe II dans les affaires de France," *Revue des Questions Historiques,* XXV (1879), p. 38.

55. See *Lettres missives de Henri IV,* II, p. 383; *C. S. P., For.,* XXII, pp. 53–54; and Stone, *An Elizabethan,* p. 154.

56. For example, Jean Héretier, *Catherine de Médicis* (Paris: Arthème Fayard, 1959), pp. 594–95. But Henry did not begin to move against the League until *after* he learned the fate of the Armada.

57. Simancas, K. 1568, fols. 42–43, 45, 62, *passim;* Croze, *Les Guises,* pp. 339–48; Lefèvre, *Correspondance de Philippe II,* III, 415; Edouard Frémy, *Essai sur les diplomates du temps de la Ligue* (Paris: E. Dantu, 1873), p. 146.

58. Mendoza to Philip, May 30, 1588, Simancas, K. 1568, fol. 48.

59. Jensen, *Diplomacy and Dogmatism,* pp. 154–55. See Bernardino de Mendoza *La harangue au Roi Très-Chrétien faite à Chartres par monseigneur l'ambassadeur pour le Roi d'Espagne vers sa Majesté* (Paris and Lyon, 1588); and Baguenault de Puchesse, "La politique de Philippe II," pp. 38–39.

60. Simancas, K. 1586, fol. 80. Longlée to Henry III, Madrid, July 6, 1588, *Dépêches diplomatiques, pp.* 366–87.

61. *Ibid.,* pp. 387–88. Mousset, *Un résident,* pp. 82–83. Resumé of Longlée's note to Philip in Simancas, K. 1568, fol. 71.

62. Simancas, K. 1568, fol. 81bis; Philip to Mendoza, July 31, 1588, K. 1568, fol. 83. Bibl. Nat., fonds fr., 3958, fol. 308.

63. Mendoza to Philip, July 24, 1588, fol. 77. On the negotiations leading to the Edict of Union see especially Henri de l'Épinois, "La reconciliation de Henri III et du duc de Guise, d'après les documents des Archives du Vatican, mai-juillet, 1588," *Revue des Questions Historiques,* XXXIX (1886), pp. 52–84, and on the edict itself, pp. 84–91; also cf. Edouard Frémy, "La médiation de l'Abbé de Feuillants entre la Ligue et Henri III, 1588–1589," *Revue d'Histoire Diplomatique,* VI (1892), esp. pp. 449–59.

64. Read, *Walsingham*, III, p. 215.

65. Parma to Philip, July 21, 1588, *C. S. P., Span.*, IV, 351. Also see Archivo Histórico Español, *La Armada Invencible*, Enrique Herrera Oria, ed., *Colección de documentos inéditos para la historia de España y de sus Indias* (Valladolid: Casa Social Católica, 1929), II, p. 211.

AN INTERPRETATION OF
VRANCKEN'S *DEDUCTION* OF 1587
ON THE NATURE OF THE STATES
OF HOLLAND'S POWER

P I E T E R   G E Y L

University of Utrecht

(*Emeritus*)

In 1587 the Netherlands revolt against Philip II of Spain was faced with the possibility of complete defeat. The Duke of Parma had already reduced to obedience the majority of the sixteen provinces[1] that in 1576 at Ghent had concluded an alliance to drive out the Spanish troops. The assassination of William the Silent in 1584 had seemed to deprive them of the respected leadership they needed more urgently than ever. When Antwerp had to capitulate in 1585 after a siege of more than a twelvemonth, only Holland and Zeeland, Utrecht, part of Gelderland, protected by the rivers crossing the Netherlands from east to west and by the river IJssel, and Friesland, behind its lakes and marshes, were holding out. These were the circumstances in which Queen Elizabeth consented to a treaty of assistance and sent a small auxiliary army across, commanded by the Earl of Leicester; and although the Queen, careful not to provoke Spain to an open rupture, had refused to establish him in an avowed political position, the States-General themselves almost immediately conferred upon him the title of Governor-General with powers enabling him to play a leading part in the conduct of political as well as military affairs.

But the province of Holland (to which I shall confine my argument) was the mainstay of what remained of the independent union, and from 1572 on, the highest authority in Holland had rested with the States of that province, composed of the Committee of Noblemen, regarded as the First Member and casting one vote, and the eighteen Voting Towns, each, large or small, also casting one vote, making nineteen in all. The Advocate of the States (it was only later that the term Grand Pensionary came into use), an official supposed to regard the States as his "masters," was Oldenbarnevelt, a man of high ability and strong character who actually became the director not only of the policy of Holland but, through Holland's preponderant power, of the Union itself as well, hardly less so than William the Silent before him.

Before long the views of Leicester and those of the States of Holland and Oldenbarnevelt came to diverge and clash. It was the Governor-General's wish to have trade with the Spanish lands strictly prohibited, and this especially aroused the States of Holland to stubborn opposition. In 1587, while Leicester was spending some months in England, the treason of some of his officers stationed in key positions on the river IJssel shocked opinion so much as to embolden Oldenbarnevelt and the States of Holland to disregard the English claim to supervisory powers and to demand of the military a new oath to the province.

Thomas Wilkes, the English member of the Union of Utrecht's Council of State, and who represented Leicester in his absence, issued a strong protest. The States of Holland, as the States of the other provinces, had always to reckon with opposition on the part of the commonalty, especially as voiced by the preachers of the new religion and the more extreme of the Calvinist minority to whom they ministered. In the eyes of these men the burgher regents were too much moved by materialistic considerations and too much inclined to extend toleration to Catholics and dissenters. In Utrecht these tendencies had actually come into power, and under the leadership of some Brabant refugees a regime had there been established in which the captains of the civic guard played a leading part and which looked to the English to put an end to the overbearing influence of the Holland "libertarians." It was from these ideas now prevalent at Utrecht that Wilkes took his cue when he bluntly told the States of Holland: "The sovereignty or supreme authority in the absence of a lawful monarch belongs to the commonalty, gentlemen, not to you."

To this denial of the lawfulness of their position the States of Holland replied with a set justification of it, drawn up by François Vrancken, Pensionary of Gouda. This *Deduction* (often called the *Brief Demonstration,* though it would cover some twenty pages of this book) was presented to the public and was accepted not only by contemporaries but by later generations down to the revolution of 1795,[2] and indeed by historians of the nineteenth and twentieth centuries, as an authoritative exposition of the constitutional ideas prevailing in Holland during the two centuries of the Republic of the Seven United Netherlands. I shall try to show that the interpretation of one essential aspect, current among historians after the dissolution of that Republic, was erroneous.[3]

The *Deduction* was intended to disabuse Mr. Wilkes of his misconception of the constitution of Holland and Zeeland (these two provinces were sufficiently closely connected for the Hollanders to speak for Zeeland as well) and to instruct him as to the true state of affairs. Let me first turn to Vrancken's exposition, bringing out the point at issue in my dissent from earlier authors.

For a period of 800 years [so he affirmed] these provinces had been ruled by Counts, to whom the nobility and towns had entrusted the government. Until at last the King of Spain, in spite of the wise councils given him by his father Charles V, had tried to coërce the States with violence of arms. Mr. Wilkes was entirely wrong in thinking that the States after having freed themselves from this despotic rule were now acting on their own unfettered authority. The authority of the States is not vested in the thirty or forty persons attending their assembly. As during the entire period of the above-mentioned 800 years, the authority of the States, from which the Counts had derived their power, was itself rooted in the inhabitants of the land, divided as these were into two estates, the nobility and the towns. These towns are governed by corporations of from 24 to 40 persons, who sit for life and fill vacancies by co-optation. They annually appoint burgomasters and aldermen. These bodies have exclusive power to decide about matters regarding their particular town. This in accordance with centuries-old privileges, and there has never been any contravention or opposition on the part of the citizens. The corporations and magistracies, with the nobility, undoubtedly represent the entire body of the inhabitants and no form of government can be devised which could resolve with more certain knowledge of the interests of the country and execute its resolutions with greater concord, authority or effect. The deputies composing the States are appointed, partly by the nobility in its entirety, for the rest by the magistracies and corporatios of the various towns, with strict injunction to see that the privileges and liberties of the country shall be maintained. So far from having the powers of sovereignty in their own hands, they are obliged to act in harmony with their principals, with whom they must remain in close correspondence.

Mr. Wilkes and whoever labours under similar misapprehensions will now understand that when our deputies assert that the sovereignty rests with the States, they are not referring to themselves but to their principals, whom they represent by virtue of their commissions.

Only enemies of our Republic can attempt to discredit the States. It would amount to undermining the foundations of the building so that it might collapse, and this to the detriment of the prince [here Leicester is alluded to in his capacity of Governor-General] as well as of the commonalty. For what will be the power of a prince (unless he be a violent despot) without good relations with his subjects? And how can he have good relations with them if he allows himself to be goaded into enmity against the States who represent the commonalty or, rather, against his people itself? Also, how can the country's well-being exist if the commonalty were to be brought to practise enmity against the States, that is against the nobility and the corporations and magistracies of the towns, who are their advocates and lawful rulers, who in fact must often bear the ill-will of Princes and Governors.

Mr. Wilkes, in saying that the sovereignty is with the people, not with the States, cannot have meant this. Otherwise he would be asserting that the nobility, magistracies and corporations have not now the same powers they have had for so long (as has been said), have exercised during the fifteen years of the revolt, and had at the time, two years ago, when the treaty with Her Majesty was concluded.

Let us now see what the great nineteenth-century historian, Professor of National History in the University of Leyden, Robert Fruin (1823–99), had to say about this *Deduction* of 1587. In a study on the Leicester episode, written after the publication of Motley's *United Netherlands* (1862), his verdict was that this *Brief Demonstration* "was to become, so to speak, the basis of the oligarchic constitution of the Republic." He further remarked that "Vrancken's argumentation went wrong in that he did not confine himself to the years immediately behind him, the period of the revolt, but wanted to prove that the sovereignty had rested with the States of Holland for the last seven or eight hundred years, having been delegated by them to the Counts merely to carry it out in practice. An astonishing heresy, which seems to us incomprehensible. Nevertheless this view was accepted for generations. Soon indeed Hugo Grotius was to confirm and elaborate it." (As a matter of fact Grotius went still further back into the past and boldly affirmed that the States of Holland were already in existence at the time of the Batavians!)

In his *Staatsinstellingen van de Republiek,* edited after his death by his pupil and successor Colenbrander, and to this day the only comprehensive account of the institutions of the Republic, Fruin writes to the same effect. The old rulers of the country had, according to Vrancken, derived their power from the commission given them by the States (that is, by the knighthood and towns representing the States of said country) and had never carried out any act of authority except with their consent. Since the deposition of the ruler in 1581, consequently, full sovereignty rested with the States, that is, with the nobles and towns convened.

Vrancken's history, even though repeated in a more extreme form by Grotius and generally accepted until late-eighteenth-century scholars (Kluit and Pestel) began to question it, does indeed show how little the Renaissance knew of the Middle Ages—that, of course, is undeniable. But what seems to me unsatisfactory in both these passages quoted from Fruin is that he gives no attention to Vrancken's stressing the representative character of the States. Fruin's interpretation nevertheless was followed unquestioningly by writers of the next generation. Dr. Japikse, in his authoritative textbook of Dutch history (second impression 1927), wrote that according to Vrancken the sovereignty over Holland belonged to the States and already had so belonged in the times of the Counts. The strongest party accepted this theory and so it became the constitutional doctrine of the Netherlands for two centuries.

I fell into the same error myself—for to leave out so important an aspect as that of Vrancken's insistence on the representative character of the States must be called an error—when, in vol. I of the first edition of my *Geschiedenis van de Nederlandse Stam* (1930), I wrote that the States, over against the theory of Wilkes or of the Utrecht citizen party, placed the theory that they were since immemorable times the lawful possessors of absolute sovereignty; and left it at that.

In 1953 the fifth volume of the large-scale co-operative (Dutch-Flemish) *Algemene Geschiedenis der Nederlanden* came out with a chapter by Dr. De Pater in which the author says, quite correctly, that Vrancken tried to prove that the States, as representatives of the knighthood and the towns, were sovereign. But he concludes his paragraph with the identical words used by Fruin nearly a hundred years earlier: "The *Deduction* was to become the basis of the oligarchic constitution of the Republic."

What all the passages quoted have in common is that they overlook the repeated asseverations contained in the *Brief Demonstration* to the effect that the States were not sovereign in their own right, that they represented the sovereignty of the people, which was delegated to them for practical purposes. Now it may be argued that Vrancken's exposition was no more than make-believe. Certainly the "thirty or forty persons" composing the assembly did not dispose of sovereign power after their pleasure, but were bound to follow the instructions of their principals (the knighthood and, especially, the corporations of the eighteen "voting towns"), and the fact deserves attention in this connection. But when in the

Deduction of 1587 the assembly is claimed to be representative of "the entire body of the citizens," one comes up against another fact: these corporations which commissioned and instructed a town's delegates on the provincial assembly were not elected by the citizens, but perpetuated themselves by a system of co-optation. Is there, then, any sense in ascribing to them, or to the provincial assembly of their delegates, a representative character? Indeed it cannot be denied that the "regents" did form an oligarchy and it is even true that in the course of time this oligarchy, as is inherent in the system, became more strictly closed and more subject to the abuses typical of the system. And yet I believe that Vrancken's insistence on the representative character of the regime had a profound significance.

Our first reaction to his making light of the absence of election at the bottom of the regime is one of surprise. But then we remember that in medieval and early modern thinking *representative* and *elective* were by no means necessarily linked. It was possible for Vrancken to use the term *representative* and to identify the States with the people in all sincerity, and, as regards the theory of popular sovereignty, not so much to contest as to annex it. And, indeed, these features of his demonstration can be seen to have had a part in shaping political thought and public life in those two hundred years for which Fruin and his disciples recognized nothing but doctrinaire oligarchism as its fruit.

I admitted already that the regent oligarchy came to indulge in absolutizing the system to its own advantage. The period of DeWitt's Grand-Pensionaryship, 1653–1672 (almost coinciding with the "First Stadholderless Period," 1650–1872), was complacently called by his supporters the period of True Liberty. It was, in fact, liberty for the States to rule in unfettered sovereignty. It meant, in the first place, maintaining the republican regime against the monarchical ambitions of a Prince of Orange, Stadholder of Holland, Captain-General of the Union. The latest of the line, William II, who in 1650 had attempted to occupy Amsterdam with the army of the States-General, had died young later that same year, and the States of Holland were determined to bar the offices of his forefathers to young William III. Often the Stadholders and the classes below the regent class had found each other in order to put pressure on the States. Now absolutist theories of the exclusive sovereignty of the States, as against monarchical or quasi-monarchical power, as well as against interference of the lower orders or of the Reformed Church, were worked out, sometimes with the help of the doctrine of Hobbes. I am thinking here especially of the works published by the two brothers De la Court, and by Graswinckel. The representative character of the constitution seemed forgotten.

True, even these self-confident and overbearing regents were frequently upheld by the conviction that they knew better what was good for the people than did the rabble clamoring outside or the preachers thundering from the pulpit. That the aim of government should not be to serve the interests of the governing class, but that its members were called to represent the interests of the community, was a doctrine, not always scrupulously observed, but frequently and sincerely asserted. In these assertions by the best of the True Liberty regents an undertone of paternalism can generally be detected which is far removed from the theories set forth in the *Brief Demonstration.*

Nevertheless, that Vrancken's laying stress on the representative character of the government, and representative of the entire body of the citizens, had more than incidental interest, that it was more than special pleading in the awkward case presented by Mr. Wilkes's searching question, appears from the vigor with which these conceptions continued to live among broad classes of the population.

There was in the Dutch Republic a rich pamphlet literature, token of the keen interest with which political questions were debated in a much wider circle than that of the governing class (hardly more than four-hundred men in the eighteen voting towns). I shall quote some passages from pamphlets that appeared in the year 1672. It was a year of shocking events. The very existence of the Republic seemed in jeopardy. Louis XIV and Charles II jointly declared war. The French army invaded the country from the east, seizing with startling ease the Dutch outposts on German territory, crossing the river IJssel where the army of the States-General was stationed but from where it had hurriedly to retreat. The invaders were stopped only—for how long?—by the inundation line protecting the province of Holland. The Hollanders and Zeelanders were thrown into a panic which found an outlet in bitter charges against the States and their Grand Pensionary. The young Prince was, under menacing popular pressure, raised to the Stadholdership. Later, De Witt and his brother were murdered by a mob at The Hague. Behind this there was the widespread suspicion that De Witt and his partisans (for the patriciate itself was divided) were supinely or even treasonably accommodating to the French; a groundless suspicion—De Witt had stood for a manly policy of resistance.

At the numerous tumultuous gatherings in the various towns and in the pamphlets, the oligarchic system as such came in for criticism. Even the idea that the corporations should in future be elected by the citizens was occasionally mooted—in marked contrast to the more common statement, of which I shall give some instances in a moment, that they *were* elected, a statement that seems patently divorced from reality. As a rule, indeed, the people gave no attention to the actual workings of the constitution; they only looked to the Prince to remedy their grievances for them. When the States of Holland had, reluctantly, authorized the new Stadholder to "change" the town governments (a measure sometimes resorted to in a crisis, "without prejudice to the privileges," as the States were always careful to add), leaders of the popular movement at Amsterdam presented him with a list of names to guide him in his choice (perfectly realistic, this time!). William III took no notice of their suggestions. He was prepared to act as a bridler of the oligarchy and he used the people's enthusiastic support for his own political program, but he had no use for democratic aspirations such as were stirring blindly in the streets and only a little more purposefully in the pamphlets. One idea, nevertheless, namely that the town or the state did not belong to the regents only, that the commonalty were also concerned, was voiced with striking and articulate insistence, and it was exactly this that lay at the basis of Vrancken's argument.

Many of the pamphlets express disgust at the violent scenes that accompanied the movement and call for the "obedience due to the authorities in accordance with God's word." But even a writer of that persuasion interrupts himself to assure his readers: "Not that I want to assert that the authorities in the lawful succession cannot err: that would be popish, and I know well enough that it is the people that makes the King, not the King—that is, the supreme sovereign government—the people."

I detect here a double allusion to sixteenth-century declarations. First to the Act of Deposition of 1581, which in its famous preamble affirmed that the people were not created for the King, but the King for the people, to govern them wisely and in accordance with the privileges; the King, so it was said later in that same preamble, had been received on the basis of a contract, on certain conditions. But there is an allusion also to the *Deduction* of 1587, which, as we saw, did not scruple to assert that not only did the corporations, and consequently the States, *represent* the people, but that they were *elected* ("made") by the people. The people? Our writer is careful to exclude from it "what we call the rabble, all sorts of rogues who are out all the time for change and disruption in order to be able to plunder and rob, murder and burn. The contract was made between the Government and the good, the decent citizens." (A distinction often made, then and later, even in the third quarter of the nineteenth century, by self-styled democrats.)

In 1672 another writer repeats even more complacently that curious misrepresentation of the regents being elected, and deduces from the Act of Deposition of 1581 ("from the example of what happened to the King of Spain") that the authorities of today also are, in accordance with their oath, obliged to maintain the people in the possession of their privileges, the privileges guaranteeing the people's freedom.

"A free people," a people that has "fought itself free"—this is a notion at the back of these theorizings which one will frequently come across in the pamphlets of 1672. One of them (in three parts) stands out from the rest by its strikingly vivid style of writing. It uses the old metaphor of the ship, the ship *Hollandia*, and shows the crew interfering when "the unfaithful steersman [De Witt, of course, sadly misrepresented] sets the course for France." The steersman begins by resisting and exclaims: "You are mutineers rising against your superior. I have nothing to do with you, I *know* no sailors in this matter." They, on their part: "If you know no sailors, we know no steersman. You are there for us, not we for you. [Allusion to the Act of Deposition again.] You cannot sail without the crew."

The principle could not be enunciated more clearly. The practice remained less impressive. All that the indignant sailors wanted was that young William Williamson, who was on board, should be put in charge. "A boy!" the steersman said contemptuously: "How shall a boy teach me how to sail and turn!" But the sailors cried: "He has learned better than you, who knew nothing of the art when you hired yourself out for steersman!" And, indeed, when young William took the steersman's place, "It was a wonder how well he managed. The oldest sailors said, with tears in their eyes: 'Look now, that is the way as of old, so the ship used to be handled in a storm!' "

It is worth noting how these spokesmen for the people still swore by the hereditary principle. They had no further ambition than that the Prince should step in and put matters right. Nevertheless, that the people had a part to play was stated clearly enough, and it was emphasized even more strikingly in the sequel.

In his second pamphlet the writer shows us the sailors ashore, afraid that they may still be punished for their high-handed action. On the way home in the canal boat one of them gets into conversation with a fellow traveler. According to this "gentleman," a regent who turns out to be an extreme adherent of the absolutist Hobbesian views that were now only too common among his class, the matter is simple enough: "He and his equals were entitled to rule the country as they saw fit and to surrender it to whom they pleased."

"Excuse me, sir," said the sailor, "where did they get that power? Let them surrender what is theirs, what they have bought and paid for or gained by marriage, but that they might sell and abandon to a murderous people like the French my box, my mattress, nay my wife and children, that I cannot believe."

The gentleman sticks to his opinion and reminds the sailor of God, who has given this power to the men in authority. The sailor, as he tells his opponent, has also read his Bible, but this law he cannot find in it. And, in any case, these provinces are free and any ruler transgressing his oath will *ipso facto* have lost his right and his sway over the country. The conversation has been growing more heated all along, and the gentleman threatens the sailor with God's judgment over his rebellious conduct.

"No," says the other man. "We do not come aboard to keep as

quiet all the time as if a mouse were lying-in, but to look out alertly for what may serve for the preservation of the ship. . . . What you call mutiny, we regard as honour and faithfulness and as a much needed warning which everyone, yea even the kitchen boy, is not only permitted to, but must, give."

What makes these ideas even more remarkable is that this writer, too, is by no means an extremist. In his third pamphlet, written after the murder of the De Witt brothers, he unreservedly repudiated the crime.

The crisis of 1672 blew over without the existing system having been democratized. William III had introduced numbers of new men into the corporations so that the membership of the States, too, had undergone a drastic change. But the criterion that had governed his choice was that his appointees (taken from the same class as the men they replaced) should be likely to be docile supporters of his foreign policy. The tension between the oligarchy and the commonalty was eased for the moment, but it could not but revive, and indeed it was to be a marked feature of the Republic's political life in the eighteenth century. A great outburst took place in 1748, under circumstances somewhat reminiscent of those of 1672: a French invasion threatening, the States of Holland and of Zeeland compelled by riotous popular demonstrations to appoint William IV to the Stadholdership. (William IV until then had been Stadholder only in Friesland and two more northern provinces, so that in Holland the period from William III's death on is known as "the Second Stadholderless Period.")

I spoke of "unskilled democracy" a moment ago. In 1748 a determined attempt was made at Amsterdam to establish regular citizen influence upon the town government. But even now the idea of direct popular election did not come within the range of practical politics. A proposal adopted at more or less revolutionary citizen meetings aimed at no more than that the officers of the civic guard should be freed from regent control and thus constitute a "free military council" representative of the rank and file, a council which would have some standing to impress the wishes and views of the citizenry upon the town corporation and burgomasters. In the end even this plan came to nothing as after fine words and empty promises William IV, on whose support the citizens had counted, came down on the side of the oligarchy.

One lesson was now at least learned. The movement for restraining the power of the oligarchy got lost in a long period of confusion, but when it revived, in the seventies, it looked no longer for help to the Prince of Orange (William V now). The "Patriots' Movement," which began about that time, was in the first instance directed against what was felt to be the exorbitant power of the Stadholder. Regents and democratic citizens worked together, until the more conservative regents, alarmed by the rising importance of the latter element, sought shelter with the Prince of Orange. As a result the Patriots' Movement, encouraged by the spectacle of the American Revolution, took on a more and more radical character. Intellectuals, often close to the patriciate, helped to direct the development of the movement's philosophy and program, and in the end it could fuse quite naturally with the great European renovation of the ideas and the practice of government activated by the French Revolution.

Now the point I want to make is that in essence these developments proceeded from, or at least were promoted by, deep-seated traditions of Dutch history. This is in fact the leading idea of the whole of this little essay. And the fact to which I will now draw attention, that the Patriots themselves quoted the *Brief Demonstration* of 1587 (and, of course, the Act of Deposition of 1581) to strengthen their case, seems to me to clinch the argument.

In 1775 Pieter Paulus published the first volume of his *Explanatory Comment on the Union of Utrecht* (of 1579). He was only twenty-one years old at the time and was to die little more than twenty years later, a short while after having been chosen to be the first president of the revolutionary National Assembly that was to devise a constitution for the Batavian Republic which was to leave precious little of the Union of 1579. It is not without irony, therefore, to find Paulus writing in the introduction to his youthful work that he "could never contemplate that ancient constitution without emotion, nor read it without feeling myself elated in wonderment at the transparent wisdom and perspicacity of its composers." He had already written a eulogy of the Stadholdership as well. In spite

of this, the Patriot or Batavian of later years can be seen stirring
beneath the veneer of acceptance he wore in his youth.

In 1776, discussing the leading Patriot Van der Capellen's translation of Dr. Price's *Observations on Liberty,* Paulus was of the
opinion that Price had gone too far in many respects, but that in the
main he had drawn into light an old truth, illustrated by abuses:
"The authorities are, when viewed without prejudice, nothing but
the servants of the people, *administratores publici.*"

In the introduction to his great work itself he had expressed his
satisfaction that in the blessed Republic of the United Netherlands
the study of the Republic's constitutional law is open to anyone.

"Have not the States of Holland, in the famous *Deduction* of
1587, concerning the antiquity of the Batavian Commonwealth,
expounded the governing system of their country, the right of
noblemen and the urban corporations and magistracies and of the
States composed of the foregoing, so clearly and unmistakably as
to make it plain that they will in no wise exclude their citizens from
a sound knowledge of these matters? Such may be the policy of
rulers whose interest requires that their subjects should have no
exact knowledge of the country's rights—governments that apply
a lawful rule over free men will follow a different line of conduct."

A popular publication of 1783, *Pocketbook of the Netherlands
People, for Patriots and Anti-Patriots,* provides another example.
The writer, Demofilus as he calls himself, quotes the *Brief Demonstration* to prove that the States are not sovereign in their own right,
but *represent* the entire body of the inhabitants.

Then take the two-volume *Constitutional Restoration,* a book
originated in the circle of Van der Capellen (who had died when it
appeared) and in which, in 1784 and 1786, the political program
of the Patriots was developed. These writers state plainly that they
were out to bring the constitution into harmony with the principle
of the sovereign power being vested in the people. And they find
that principle already laid down in the Act of Deposition of 1581
and, more explicitly, in the *Brief Demonstration* of 1587. After
quoting the unqualified praise with which Vrancken concluded his
description of "the entire system of urban government"—"No form
of government can be devised which would result in resolutions
being passed with more certain knowledge of the conditions pre-

vailing in the country or in those resolutions being executed with greater unanimity, authority or effect," the *Constitutional Restoration* comments: "It cannot be denied that the foundations of this form of government are very wisely arranged." But it continues: "How is it, then, that from the beginnings of the Republic until today an unquenchable fire of jealousy, hatred and disunity has been smouldering between these two members [the government and the people], the outbursts of which have more than once threatened the state with ruin?" It is due to the fact (so the argument concludes) that the wholesome principle has been in several ways defectively or injudiciously worked out in practice. Hence the need for "a restauration of the constitution," not, mark well, of a subversion or total rejection.

The basic principle of the sovereignty belonging to the people is driven in all through the work. In one passage the authors remark that the contemporary conservatives, ranged behind the Stadholder, argue that the people, after having been for a moment, upon the collapse of the monarchy, the depository of sovereign power, had divested themselves of it completely and transfered it unreservedly to the States, so that ever since, no particle of the sovereignty over the country is to be found anywhere but in the hands of the States. Let them prove, so the argument continues, this contention. Lack of evidence is sufficient to prove the contrary. But in fact the States themselves, as soon as they began to exercise the sovereign power in its various parts, expressly pronounced themselves upon this point: "In the famous *Deduction* of 1587 they themselves declared to be no more than representatives of the commonalty."

So we see that the democrats appealed to the *Deduction* against "the oligarchic constitutional law," for which Fruin taught us it had laid the foundation.

I shall not deny that the adherents of a more purely "oligarchic constitutional law" could also find encouragement in the *Deduction*. Even in this same period of the Patriots' Movement, the man in command of the threatened stronghold of conservatism, the Grand Pensionary Van de Spiegel, writing to the Princess of Orange at the end of September, 1787 (that is to say shortly after the Stadholder had been restored to his position in The Hague by the troops of her brother, the King of Prussia), suggested that the fortunate turn of events might be consolidated "by an authoritative exposition of the true foundations of our Constitution, Government and Liberty, in the way it was done by the States of Holland in 1587, in order to contest and eliminate the monstrous conceptions of our Government and the nature of Civic Liberty which have now again been revived."

Not that he resorted therefore to "absolutist-oligarchic" speculations as had in De Witt's time the De la Courts and Graswinckel. But it is certain that *their* conception of constitutional law had been formed in contravention to the *Deduction.*

Two ways of thinking can be distinguished in the Patriots' Movement: the abstract-theoretical, basing itself on natural law, and the historical. Most writers employed both simultaneously, albeit with unequal emphasis. In the historical way of thinking it came naturally to refer to the *Act of Deposition* and to Vrancken's *Deduction.* There can be no doubt that the conceptions of the original sovereignty of the people and of the representative nature of the power wielded by the town governments and by the States composed of their delegates, formulated as they were especially in the latter declaration, continued to be regulative forces in the public life of the Republic. They contributed to the self-confidence with which men from outside the circle of the oligarchy took part in the discussion of public affairs, and in the end they facilitated the transition to more modern institutions which at the same time made a breach with the old Republic's self-contradictory past.

NOTES

1. That is, the "seventeen provinces" minus Luxembourg, which had stood apart from the rebellious movement all along.

2. Jan Wagenaar, the author of the great *Vaderlandsche Historie* in twenty-one volumes (1752–59), says with characteristic caution

RESILIENCY OF ENTERPRISE:
ECONOMIC CRISES
AND RECOVERY IN THE
SPANISH NETHERLANDS
IN THE EARLY
SEVENTEENTH CENTURY

F R A N K   J .   S M O L A R ,   J R .

Western Reserve University

Before civil war disrupted and then divided the Netherlands, those seventeen provinces and an ever-widening peripheral area had the most highly developed and active economy outside Italy.[1] The center was Antwerp; in the completeness of its economic services, in the complexity and volume of the business transacted there, it was a true economic capital.[2] By the beginning of the sixteenth century Antwerp had taken this leadership from Bruges[3] and become the unrivaled center of organization, not only for regional but for European and even world-wide trade.[4] Her docks and shops and warehouses were filled with goods in greater variety and larger quantities than had ever been seen. Her exchange, as well as her town hall and cathedral, inspired awe and imitation. She was envied by princes and eulogized by poets until the middle of the seventeenth century, when other cities divided her hegemony.

Since Guicciardini's memorable description of 1567, few have captured the greatness of Antwerp in prose. Henri Pirenne showed that he understood the exceptional character of the place in his authoritative national history.[5] In analyzing the elements that determined the city's ascendancy, Pirenne stressed the role of what he called the *banlieue economique,* the "economic suburb" surrounding Antwerp. This area, which progressively expanded beyond Amsterdam in the north and nearly to Paris in the south, became increasingly dependent upon Antwerp as a center of international exchange of money and goods and as a source of finance capital and new business techniques borrowed from the Italians. Antwerp served not only as *entrepôt* for the export of the region's products and the import of all classes of foreign goods for local consumption and for sale in adjacent areas, but also as the main center for redistribution of regional commodities within the region itself. Merchants from distant commercial centers and nearby market towns came to the city for anything they could not find at home.[6]

Surpassing Italy, Antwerp and its interdependent region constituted the most important area of international business activity in Europe—and the world—around the middle of the sixteenth century. But in the same epoch city and countryside began to suffer the troubles that were to bring about a radical transformation of political and economic organization in the Low Countries. In Pirenne's view, the structure was first disturbed at the time of the iconoclastic riots of 1566, foreshadowing the effects of more serious crises for Antwerp and its territory beginning with the capture of Flushing (1572) and rebel control of the Scheldt.[7] But the death blow, according to Pirenne, came only after Parma's reconquest of Antwerp from the Protestants in 1585.[8]

From that year Pirenne portrays the once proud city fallen.[9] The quays were quiet and the galleries of the exchange had emptied. The city lost much of its population after the successive Protestant and Catholic persecutions and because of the fear of military and legal reprisals. Though Pirenne cautions that the effects of these emigrations, even those to the north, should not be exaggerated, he reports many vacancies in the business of the city and claims these places were no longer tempting. This was due largely to the persistence with which the United Provinces denied their southern neighbors the outlet to the sea which had made their geographic position an ideal link between maritime shipping and a great inland market.[10]

However, Pirenne maintains, the population of the southern provinces in the period of the Archdukes (1598–1633) showed a vitality to resist such handicaps, if not entirely to overcome them. Avoiding the Scheldt, they found new routes for the conduct of international trade. Without developing this observation, Pirenne maintains that much was made possible through the energies of government and populace alike, marshaled to mend dikes, drain flooded fields, and repair roads and canals that could lead to new opportunities for commerce and industry. The twelve years of the Truce were those that gave the greatest impetus to this activity.[11]

Like so many of Pirenne's accounts, this broad picture has evoked debate, reinterpretation, and often fresh research. Among many to whom the same facts have had far different meaning is Pieter Geyl. The national history of this distinguished Dutch historian differs not only about the nature of the rebellion against Spain but also about conditions in the loyal provinces after the rupture.[12] For Pirenne the separation of the two cultures, urban south and rural north, is the logical fulfillment of a long evolution.[13] But to Professor Geyl it was a betrayal of the "Netherlands' race"— an arbitrary sundering of a linguistic tribe that had composed a homogeneous nation.[14] Inasmuch as the split released the north from Spanish domination, it was, though hard-won, a blessing, at least for the seven rebel provinces. The loyalty of the southern provinces to their legitimate prince meant only humiliating subservience to a foreign power and separation from their northern brethren. According to Geyl's thesis these injustices sapped the spirit of the southern populace.[15] Its servitude to Spanish rule, and not to the hardships caused by Dutch obstructiveness (as Pirenne would have it), led to a decadence of cultural, political, and economic life throughout the south.[16] Holland became the heir to its civilization just as Amsterdam inherited economic leadership from Antwerp.[17] With few exceptions,[18] Geyl's somber picture of chaos and decline is painted far darker than Pirenne's and admits none of Pirenne's occasionally bright, optimistic detail.

These two classic interpretations differ sufficiently to suggest that much work remains to be done. Both historians present their theses in works of broad scope, and inevitably neither narrative draws heavily upon unpublished sources. Recent scholarship, continuing the quest for historical reality, has made greater use of such materials in articles and monographs on particular aspects of life in and around Antwerp. Economic subjects have included various "nations" or merchant communities;[19] commodities, prices, and wages;[20] public institutions and fiscal policies;[21] industries and agriculture;[22] as well as demographic trends[23] and localized conditions.[24] When the best of these analyses come to deal with the turbulent years of the late sixteenth century they give full credit to the number and variety of disasters which befell the metropolis and its dependencies. Thus, most of them reject the single "turning point," even important years like 1566[25] and 1585,[26] in favor of various combinations of circumstance that culminated in various kinds of unfavorable economic conditions at various times. Yet this abandonment of the determinism of the solitary, dramatic event for a more realistically complex series of conjunctures in the sixteenth century[27] has seldom helped to change the widely held preconceptions about the state of the economy in the *next* century.[28]

The years of pronounced economic expansion or those of repeated recession still preoccupy researchers at the expense of a later epoch that poses problems which are considerable in value, complex to investigate, and revealing of long-term institutional development and of secular business trends. Work on topics restricted to the fifteenth and sixteenth centuries suggests that the components of the Antwerp-oriented economy were too stable and diverse to be imperiled everywhere at the same time and in the same degree. After all, they had suffered often before. Yet in many histories this most elaborate and evolved of the European sub-economies tumbles down—if not at one moment, then during several decades before 1600—to crumble to pieces unworthy of inspection.[29]

These presumed ruins do not attract historians transfixed by "rise" and economists hypnotized by "growth." Their efforts turn toward the United Provinces, to sturdy Dutch merchants and their aggressive companies in distant lands.[30] Antwerp and the Spanish Netherlands lurk in footnotes and parenthetical remarks, languishing in pathetic contrast to the painstaking consideration given to giant strides made toward modern capitalism at Amsterdam.[31] Drawn to the shores of the Zuider Zee, brainpower, manpower, and capital have deserted the banks of the Scheldt. The provinces loyal to the Spanish King, according to this persuasion, may be written off with perhaps some sober moralizing about the inevitability of the disaster and the absoluteness of the decline.

It is as if the baroque laments of the chroniclers have been swallowed whole.[32] Or worse, that the standard complaints of merchants, dutifully registered and sometimes sent to higher authorities, have been used as conclusive evidence.[33] As Pirenne remarks, men remembered the astonishing prosperity of the past and were often then blinded to the accomplishments of the present.[34] Less charitably, one might emphasize that merchants, inveterate complainers in good times and bad, reveal more about their kind than about the economy.[35] Most of the plaintive petitions in question here, in fact, involve particular impositions and restrictions, providing little or no concrete, specific information about the general economic climate.[36]

Relatively undisturbed continuity in certain activities and aspects of economic life escaped or did not interest petitioners with axes to grind. Not all merchants, for example, left Antwerp, and of those who did, not a few returned to their homes and work.[37] The city still attracted men drawn by its financial resources and by opportunities assured by the large-scale borrowing and spending of the governments at Brussels and Madrid.[39] Seville continued to supply silver for the military and administrative expenses of Spain in Northern Europe,[40] most of which was sent to Antwerp. The funds for the Army of Flanders, for example, were deposited and dispersed there; army contracts helped prime the pump for recovery.[41] And, in addition to normal investments of private capital from the city in rural property, the need for renewal provided fresh demands and opportunities for capital investment: reclaiming lands flooded near Lille, or ravaged by brigands in the Campine to the east of Antwerp.[42]

In spite of the modest progress that has been made toward an understanding of these questions of continuity and integral transformation, the beginnings of prolonged depression continue to be attributed almost solely to control of the Scheldt estuary by the admiralties of Holland and Zeeland. Though a detailed examination of the blockade—the consistency, extent, and effectiveness of its application—has yet to appear,[43] plenty of evidence suggests that, except for goods classified as war matériel, most commodities were able to pass through upon payment of tolls that were gradually being reduced.[44] The revenues collected were, in fact, indispensable to the rebels' war chest,[45] while to pay these charges in addition to the import duties levied by the Archducal government was commercially worthwhile whenever demand for specific merchandise raised prices enough to cover these added costs. Examples abound.[46] They demonstrate clearly that shipping patterns were not radically changed by the Eighty Years' War; Antwerp and other southern ports had previously depended upon vessels from the north, and continued to do so.[47] These bottoms carried cargoes between rebel north and loyal south during war as well as peace.[48] Goods of Netherlandish origin in fact were entirely freed from frontier tariffs during the Truce (1609–21).[49]

Substitutes for routing via the Scheldt were fully exploited by business in the southern provinces. Calais and the Flemish ports along the North Sea littoral became foreports for Antwerp, in the same way as in the past they had served the textile industries of west Flanders.[50] River, canal, and overland transportation connected coast and countryside and linked the Spanish Netherlands with sources and markets in Southern and Eastern Europe.[51]

Besides all of this, Antwerp merchants contrived to expand their activities in other cities, substantially offsetting contraction in some areas of opportunity at home. Earlier, prior to the Troubles, Antwerp's commercial firms had frequently dispatched or contacted correspondents to represent them in the principal European business centers. During and after the Troubles, these individual, occasional contacts evolved into large colonies of merchants in the Italian and Iberian peninsulas, in France, the Germanies and England, closely aligned with commercial interests at Antwerp. Emigrants, forced to flee Antwerp for safety or to preserve their convictions, not only swelled these groups in foreign cities but served to closen ties with those who remained behind.[52] The latter, for their part, were ever more ready to deal at a distance as opportunities became less attractive at home. By the time the Scheldt came under Dutch control,

Antwerpers could, for example, use this network to buy olive oil in Seville for sale at Bremen, then turn the proceeds into a cargo of wheat destined for Portugal. The commission agents who made these purchases would arrange for shipment and be paid a small percentage-based fee for their services. These men might themselves employ agents to trade in their behalf at other commercial centers, even at Antwerp, where a firm might be serving as agent for one of its own agents abroad.

These repeated transactions in various locales in the interest of one Antwerp firm were individually subject to the fortunes of the trade, but the general pattern was one of success, with capital being augmented by profits as they accrued, and reinvested in a continuing series of commercial exchanges. Capital and profits might continue to migrate and grow around Europe for years, but eventually—in the form of credits, cash, or imported goods—would return home to Antwerp as solid capital gain.

Indications of inherent economic strength and potential for extensive recovery are strong; the evidence for it is large, and largely unexploited. Though some use has been made of public papers containing statistics and qualitative information about industrial and agrarian enterprise,[53] more extensive documentation in private papers bearing on mercantile and financial affairs remains largely unread and often unorganized.[54] Strange that these sources should be neglected, when the economic achievements of the sixteenth century are generally associated with credit and commerce much more than with farm and factory productivity.

It is, in fact, only private papers—journals, letters, and books of account—that record sufficient detail about investment and interest or profits from sale and resale; only they can reveal the total activity of firms and trades and areas—not just the fractional quantities that passed through a particular market or a particular customs house. And, perhaps most important, only they reveal individual decisions and actions, the day-to-day human responses in the Spanish Netherlands to the conditions created by the policies of Madrid and Brussels, Amsterdam and The Hague, Paris and London.

The few heavily documented biographical studies which have been made of figures in business pursuits are generally convincing in detail, suggestive of common thought and behavior, but are often suspect as samplings because not sufficiently typical to characterize total activity in markets of capital and goods. The recent study of the family firm Della Faille,[55] a model of the rigorously systematic analysis that can be made of family business papers, is instructive of the power and practices of one of the large firms that enjoyed its greatest prosperity at Antwerp in the very years that brought repeated crises to the city. But Dr. Brulez does not deal in depth with the mass of small and middling business houses which were much more sensitive to adverse conditions than the great firms usually were and which provide better economic bellwethers than do giants capable of riding out storms with little damage. Nor does his subject allow the exhaustiveness with which he treats the sixteenth century to be continued in his discussion of the early years of the seventeenth —the very years in which the economy's resilience was significantly tested, as much by peace as by war.

Though the Della Faille had begun to withdraw from the international business world shortly after the close of the sixteenth century, other long-established houses continued to participate and prosper in this trade, while new firms were organized that helped to compensate for those which had disappeared. Much of this new energy, indicative of the continuing vitality of enterprise in the Spanish Netherlands, was infused by newcomers who initiated their commercial transactions with the rest of Europe in the years of crisis, and sustained their interest and their commercial commitments well into the seventeenth century. If fame and fortune were more modest and short-lived for them than for the illustrious concerns like that of the Della Faille, the most creditable explanations for the differences arise from close examination of individual cases rather than from generalizing about the condition of the economy as a whole. The histories of three business houses will help to illustrate this point.[56]

Of these, the establishment of Pierre de Moucheron and his descendants in many ways best exemplifies the sort of firm that managed to weather the crises of the 1500s.[57] This might be expected, since it was the oldest of the three, having its origins early in that century. By mid-century it was one of the foremost commercial houses in Antwerp and one must give ample credit for the firm's continued survival to the time it had had to gain maturity, reputation, and substance before the crises began. On the other hand, it was both large enough to be heavily and extensively involved in the disordered economy and small enough to be buffeted severely in its storms.

As of 1574, for example, this relative size is reflected in the amount Pierre de Moucheron was assessed for his share of a forced loan imposed upon Antwerp's four hundred wealthiest merchants—such levies being a rough but useful indication of what various houses were considered able to pay. De Moucheron had the twenty-second highest assessment, at 1,200 guilders. Below his level the amounts dropped sharply: only five places further down the list the assessment was 400 guilders, less than the average for the entire four hundred merchants. Above de Moucheron's level the amounts climbed just as sharply. Of the twenty-one higher assessments, five were at least two thirds higher, and another ten ranged from more than double to more than triple; François van de Cruyce & Co. was assessed more than four times as much, the giant Vincent de Smidt & Co. more than seven times as much as the house of de Moucheron. As for the previously mentioned Della Faille, that firm had recently been split between two quarrelling brothers—yet there were still only five assessed higher than Jan alone, and nine higher than Jacob. De Moucheron was clearly one of a small group quite different in kind, both from the giants above and small fry below—a middling order of magnitude.[58]

Comparison with the Della Faille family is instructive in another way as well, for it had gained much of its strength, and during the crises preserved it, largely through close association with other prominent families, especially by intermarriage, and this was true also of Pierre de Moucheron and his successors.

Pierre de Moucheron, born in 1508, the youngest of twelve children of a poor noble family of Normandy, went to Middleburg in 1530 where he entered the service of the merchant Antoine de Gerbier and soon married the boss's daughter Isabella, and moved on to improve his fortunes among the greater opportunities of Antwerp early in the 1540s. Before he died (a Calvinist) in 1566, he was well established in the city's commercial aristocracy, conducting business with the great houses of Antwerp and other leading centers. That he furnished the court of Henri III testifies to the nature and scope of his trade; that he was a friend of William the Silent testifies to the kind of connections he had. But perhaps most important of all, as a symbol of his bootstrap rise in the world, is the fact that Louis de Gerbier, son of de Moucheron's former employer, ended up as one of de Moucheron's factors.

Pierre's eldest son Baltazar[59] traded actively for the firm, especially at Amsterdam and the Zeeland ports, but after his dashing exploits as colonel of militia for the "Christian Republic" during the siege of Antwerp he was, when the town surrendered in 1585, among the Protestant exiles fleeing northward. He was later to make a name for himself as a pioneer of Dutch imperialism, but, of more importance here, was effectively lost as his father's successor to the firm in Antwerp. For this reason it was especially propitious that in 1577 Isabeau, one of Baltazar's sisters, married a man capable of heading the firm, Jerome Andrea, a native of Seville who traded between Spain and Antwerp. Settled with Isabeau on Venusstraat in Antwerp, Jerome Andrea directed the family's affairs and left a son—Baltazar Andrea de Moucheron—to succeed him and to see the family through the early seventeenth century.[60]

The expansion of ties through Baltazar Andrea's own marriage in 1598 provided considerable strength for the difficult years ahead. His wife, Elizabeth Perez de Barron, came from an Antwerp family of Spanish origin and considerable wealth. It was merchant money, accumulated through commercial activities earlier in the century, but long since invested in real estate in Antwerp and its countryside, and in rents and loans. The fortune of Perez de Barron had already proven large enough, and its investment sufficiently judicious and widely dispersed, to withstand such blows as the radical fall in urban property values during the late 1580s, the kind of financial strength and stability that would be invaluable to any commercial enterprise in the years ahead; conversely, the Perez family welcomed a match with a house of the widespread business activities and growing reputation that Andrea de Moucheron could provide.

Baltazar Andrea had, of course, more to gain than just a wife with property. Such a good match was itself a measure of good credit, and it opened up entirely new connections.

Confidence in the firm was enhanced by the prestige of his wife's relations—Nicolas Rockox, for example, the illustrious burgomaster of Antwerp and one of Rubens' patrons, was her uncle by marriage. Such high-level contacts provided Baltazar with an entrée to opportunity, which was especially valuable for one too young to have made much headway as yet in that important regard, being only twenty-one when he married (and his wife nineteen).

Elizabeth's older brother, Louis Barron, was for many years close to the court at Madrid; Marco Antonio Perez, her mother's cousin, was an important figure in Antwerp politics, later a favored gentleman in the entourage of the Elector of Cologne; numerous members of the family had similar connections. It is not surprising that Andrea's contact with these highly placed relatives and those around them colored his own activities and ambitions. He was in a position to familiarize himself with the needs and tastes of these classes, and he profited from the opportunity in a variety of ways. He contracted loans, for example, to the Duke of Mantua and to Hurtuño de Ugarte, the Spanish Paymaster at Antwerp, and provided the wealthy with precious gems from Lisbon and Seville, gold thread from Milan, and silks from Naples.

Most of his activities, however, were typical of any merchant. Foremost were profitable transactions in change, especially with the great Italian houses and their branches in London. Dangerous seas made insurance desirable for every ship and offered a man like Andrea, with money and courage to risk it, a chance for high returns; he invested heavily in marine policies, calculated correctly and lost little in claims. Through his agents in other ports he dabbled in any products which had good prospects of profit. Upon news of bad harvests in Iberia from his correspondent at Madrid, he would instruct an agent working on commission in Bremen or Amsterdam to buy wheat and send it on the earliest ship departing for Bilbao. Good prices for Merino wool in Venice would cause him to order the forwarding of a shipment from Barcelona by his representative there, a fellow merchant. The products of America and the Orient —such as cochineal, spices, or hides—were ordered from his agent at Seville when prices for those things held high at Rouen, Lille, or some other center of industrial and urban consumption in Northern Europe.

But the capitalization, received from many sources, that allowed Andrea to engage in finance through insurance and loans, and to speculate in commodities also enabled him to aspire to distinctions beyond the rank of an ordinary merchant. He not only paid to secure the letters patent that ennobled his name but "in keeping" with his new role, spent vast sums on such things as country house and livery and personal finery for himself and his wife. This investment in title and display—not unnatural for any European in Andrea's time and circumstance—reduced the amount of capital that might have been allotted to remunerative ends. His expenses continued to mount along with his splendor and self-esteem. Then his world collapsed around him, as though he were a mercantile version of a tragic hero cursed with Hubris.

Among his debtors was the influential Count of Algiere; when Andrea sought payment—perhaps too aggressively—his action provoked the Count to bring suit against him. Though details of the proceedings are not clear, their apparent injustice is not astonishing in a time when powerful aristocrats, and especially those who resented intrusions into their class, could still exert their influence to stop their opponents. Costs of the trial were most excessive, and so were the demands on his time, which Baltazar Andrea could ill afford, for he had no son, nor even a daughter, to protect his wife and property and to sustain his business interests. With no one to collect outstanding debts, much of the credit he had extended was sure to be lost. Debtors became more reluctant to pay as the trial dragged on, then refused when the verdict was in, pronounced against Andrea. In 1622 he was imprisoned in Antwerp's *Steen* —a disgrace that meant ridicule, then shame. By the time Elizabeth, his wife, had done everything needed to obtain his release, his reputation was already ruined. He died the next year, 1623; his widow, who lived on in poverty for another thirty-two years, bore the brunt of the bankruptcy.

But not every Antwerp firm that had survived the Troubles was dissolved in this way—barren of issue and wasteful of its own resources. After their own initial success, others were similarly eliminated by external pressures: not by war, blockade, or a lack of trade on the local scene, but by the peculiarities of the social, legal, and business infrastructure everywhere in Europe, as well as by the forces of Euro-Atlantic conjuncture. The cases of two other families may briefly illustrate this.

Founded before the time of the Troubles, the Flemish firm of the Van Immerseel[61] eventually had been fashioned by William Van Immerseel into a concern of moderate dimensions specializing in the sale and distribution of madder to Antwerp and the other nearby textile processing centers which used this dyestuff. William's son Jan inherited the business shortly before Parma's seige, during which he was forced to flee and join his wife in temporary refuge north of the rivers in the rebel provinces. It was there that she died; like the alliances of de Moucheron and his successors, the marriage with Susanna Boutry had introduced Jan to a series of correspondents who were to form the nucleus for his network of business agents abroad. While he was still in the northern provinces, Jan remarried, choosing a bride—Agnes Fasse—who not only was to provide the key to many new contacts but was to make considerable capital available for the expansion of her husband's business activities. She also raised Jan's fifteen children (thirteen of them her own)—an ample assortment from which to select a successor to the father.

The boy picked was Chrysostomo, the eldest after Jan, Jr., who had suffered a fatal fall from his horse. Born in the year of the Armada, Chrysostomo apprenticed at the firm's local *comptoir* before being sent to Seville in 1606, where he was to represent his father, as well as to work for his own account and on commission for others. He returned to Antwerp in 1612 to take over direction of the firm's headquarters from Jan the Elder. The reputation Chrysostomo had earned in Spain was enhanced at Antwerp, where he was counted among the most respected and successful merchants of his day. There was no doubt about his suitability as a mate for Marie de Fourmestraux, related to a rich mercantile family at Lille. From the marriage in 1613, Chrysostomo's range of clients and correspondents reached its greatest dimensions, numbering hundreds; his capital assets, already made large by inheritance from his father and brother, Jan, Jr., were greatly enhanced, in money, merchandise, rents, and real estate from his wife's dowry.

With these resources, Chrysostomo continued to develop and expand the international trade whose outlines had been set by his father. The variety and bulk of its cargoes were more like those of the Della Faille than of Andrea: Spanish wool and Spanish wine from Bruges via Calais or Ostend; tapestries, a carved table and wax tapers from Antwerp overland to the cathedral chapter at Rouen; casks of Bordeaux smuggled from Middleburg, delivered to Brussels; wax and grain from Lübeck, bound for Lisbon; Rouen linens outbound from Cadiz to Cuba, where tobacco is on order. From Italy and France close friends correspond about these matters once each week or two; from Iberia and the German ports relatives may write daily when the fleets are in.

From 1612, for example, William Van Immerseel, Chrysostomo's younger brother, represented the firm at Seville. Every month he would send copious reports on business conditions and his activities. Though his first responsibility was to work for Chrysostomo, William also conducted his own separate affairs. In doing so he proved less able than his brother, for in 1619 he found himself bankrupt and imprisoned. This disaster was partly due to his heady speculation in goods from America and the late arrival of the fleet that brought them. Beyond that was William's imperfect use of the letter of change as an instrument of credit. The bankruptcy laws of Seville were, furthermore, badly drawn and poorly understood. Chrysostomo, however, having long disapproved of his brother's practices, gave no succor, though the value of his own credit was rendered momentarily suspect at Antwerp because of his brother's troubles.

Though Chrysostomo's own affairs had suffered little from events at Seville, he had already longed for years to return to Spain, which in his youth had impressed him deeply. He had, in fact, purchased Spanish nobility in 1615; in 1621 he removed his home to Spain, where his wife joined him two years later; by 1631 he had become naturalized a Spaniard. In the first decade after the move, Chrysostomo returned several times to Antwerp, largely to fight legal battles with his brothers and more distant relatives, and to inspect his properties, which were no better for his absence. Back in Spain, his chosen retirement, Chrysostomo was gradually drawn into lending money to Philip IV and he finally lost his credit standing when it became evident that no repayment would be made. He died a poor man in 1652.

The promise and prosperity of Chrysostomo's early years became as grim as Andrea's tale. At the center of the Van Immerseel failure was a crisis of association of the kind that had resulted in the division of the firm Della Faille between Jan and Jacob. The first Jan Della Faille, like the founding Jan Van Immerseel, had unified family control. But their patriarchal organization was impossible for second-generation rivals like Chrysostomo and William, who were unable to resolve their squabbles in the interests of a unity essential to promoting and perpetuating the importance of their firm. Instead, first William, then Chrysostomo elected self-imposed exile; both bought patents of Spanish nobility; and both ended by serving the Spanish state, the former as King's Rentmaster General at Madrid till 1631, the latter through his loans to the court.

Like the Van Immerseels, the family of Clarisse was native to the neighborhood of Antwerp, though it probably originated in northern France. From the area near Lille and Roubaix, Walraven Clarisse, who managed the firm through the time of Troubles, did a growing business in lengths of borats, or mixed cloths, for sale in Antwerp and her markets. By 1600 Walraven's son Louis was directing the family business and had extended its activities in trade, credit, and exchange as far as the Iberian Peninsula, where in 1605 he dispatched his brother Pieter to represent the firm at Lisbon. Together with Louis' brother-in-law, Jan Very, Pieter sold mixed fabrics and linens from looms in the Spanish Netherlands and northern France for profits that were plowed back into sugar from Brazil and the Canary Islands; both the refined and unrefined product were shipped to Antwerp for distribution in the surrounding area, or to French, German, and Scandinavian ports. In 1627 Louis sent his son Jan-Baptista to join Pieter in these activities.

In the correspondence of these men there is little altercation of the kind that is frequent in the letters of the Van Immerseel brothers. Thus, besides being smaller and more specialized in its activities, the Clarisse firm was better unified than any of the foregoing family establishments. Perhaps this was, in part, because its immediate members seem to have had none of the others' aspirations to social roles outside their class. They made no effort to be Hispanicized or ennobled. On the other hand, Louis Clarisse's uncle, also named Louis, and his son Rogier, both of whom, though nobles, engaged in the importation of Italian silks and in the export of tapestries from the Spanish Netherlands, did so completely apart from the more varied and commonplace trade of their relatives. The fact that the two branches of the Clarisse family never merged their efforts suggests that once again independence of economic spirit precluded greater growth.

While all of the forementioned firms attempted to exploit the commodities and channels of traditional trades which had been left relatively undisturbed, each also sought to employ extraordinary and often extra-legal means to profit from normal or novel commercial opportunities which had become indirectly accessible. In seeking maximal rewards with minimal risks, they also sufficiently divided their investments to avoid damaging losses caused by singular disasters, not alone by trading in several commodities, but also by investment in services and property both at home and abroad.

If these means did not prevent such houses from finally disappearing, under constraint or voluntarily, it was the weaknesses of certain commercial laws and business techniques that were to blame, along with social aspirations and psychological attitudes that deflected talent and energy away from economic objectives. Unfavorable trends in Continental and Euro-Atlantic conjuncture may have also played a part, for during certain years an increase in business failures at Antwerp coincided with an increase in the number of bankruptcies throughout Europe. When compared to these factors, the role of particular disadvantageous political and economic constraints in the Spanish Netherlands begins to seem less deterministic.

NOTES

1. This writer's belief that one must say "outside Italy" until the mid-sixteenth century supposes a later decline in Italy than is usually maintained, but involves a separate subject too vast to treat here and, being relative, does not affect the present concern with absolute conditions, but one may cite two provocative works on the matter: F. Braudel, J. Meuvret, R. Romano, and P. Jeannin, *Le déclin de Venise au XVIIe siècle* (Venice, 1957), and C. M.

Cipolla, "The decline of Italy: the case of a fully matured economy," *Economic History Review*, second ser., V (1952), pp. 178–87.

2. The two best introductions to the subject are E. Sabbe, *Anvers, métropole de l'Occident (1492–1566)* (Brussels, 1952), and J. A. Van Houtte, "Anvers aux XVe et XVIe siècles. Expansion et apogée," *Annales, Economies, Sociétés Civilisations*, XVI (1961), pp. 248–78.

3. On this shift, see Van Houtte, "Bruges et Anvers, marchés nationaux ou internationaux au XVIe siècle," *Revue du Nord*, XXXIV (1952), pp. 89–108; H. Van Werveke, *Brugge en Antwerpen. Act eeuwen vlaamsche handel* (Ghent, 1941); and M. K. E. Gottschalk, "Het verval van Brugge als wereldmarkt," *Tijdschrift voor Geschiedenis*, LXVI (1953), pp. 1–26.

4. See, *e.g.*, Van Houtte, "La genèse du grand marché international d'Anvers à la fin du Moyen-âge," *Revue belge de philologie et d'histoire*, XIX (1940), pp. 87–126; H. Van der Wee, *The growth of the Antwerp market and the European economy (14th–16th centuries)* (3 vols. The Hague, 1963).

5. H. Pirenne, *Histoire de Belgique* (7 vols, Brussels, 1922–29).

6. *Ibid.*, III, pp. 268 ff.

7. *Supra*, note 1.

8. *Belgique*, IV, p. 194.

9. *Ibid.*, pp. 415–16.

10. *Ibid.*, p. 417.

11. *Ibid.*, p. 415.

12. While Pirenne's national history remains untranslated and thus inaccessible to many, three parts of Pieter Geyl's *Geschiedenis van de Nederlandse stam* (3 vols, Amsterdam, 1930–37) are available in good recent English versions: *The Revolt of the Netherlands* (London, 1958), and *The Netherlands in the Seventeenth Century* (2 vols, London, 1961–63).

13. Geyl, *Revolt*, pp. 256, 259.

14. *Ibid.*, p. 275.

15. *Seventeenth Century*, I, pp. 17, 22, 29, etc.

16. *Revolt*, pp. 256–57.

17. *Ibid.*, pp. 274–75.

18. Professor Geyl does state that Antwerp remained "a large town with a great deal of old-fashioned wealth," that there was some migration toward the south (*ibid.*, pp. 276–77), and that "Economic recovery. . . , save where religion or foreign policy intervened, was intelligently promoted [in the southern provinces]" (*Seventeenth Century*, II, p. 26).

19. *E.g.*, J. A. Goris, *Étude sur les colonies marchandes méridionales à Anvers (1477–1567)* (Louvain, 1925); O. De Smedt, *De Engelse nati te Antwerpen in de XVIe eeuw (1496–1582)* (2 vols, Antwerp, 1950–54); E. Coornaert, *Les Français et le commerce international à Anvers (fin XVme et XVIme siècles)* (2 vols, Paris, 1961). For German and Scandinavian merchants, see P. Jeannin, "Anvers et la Baltique au XVIme siècle," *Revue du Nord*, XXXVII (1955), pp. 93–114, and H. Kellenbenz, *Unternehmerkräfte im Hamburger Portugal- und Spanienhandel, 1590–1625* (Hamburg, 1954).

20. Much of the most significant study of these subjects is produced by Professor Charles Verlinden and his circle at the University of Ghent, *e.g.*, J. Craeybeckx, *Un grand commerce d'importation: les vins de France aux anciens Pays-Bas (XIIIme-XVIme siècle)* (Paris, 1958), and "Brood en Levensstandaard. Kritische nota betreffende de Kprijs van het brood te Antwerpen en te Brussel in de 17e en de 18e eeuw," *Cahiers d'Histoire des Prix*, III (1958), pp. 133–62; E. Scholliers, *Loonarbeid en honger. De levensstandaard in de XVe en XVIe eeuw te Antwerpen* (Antwerp, 1960); C. Verlinden, *et al.*, "Mouvements des prix et des salaires en Belgique au XVIme siècle," *Annales, E. S. C.*, X (1955), pp. 173–98— all of which extensively employ the *Dokumenten voor de geschiedenis van prijzen en lonen in Vlaanderen en Brabant (XVe-XVIIIe eeuw)* (C. Verlinden, *et al.*, eds., Bruges, 1959).

21. Such publications of the Royal Historical Commission as *Prijzen-en lonenpolitiek in de Nederlanden in 1561 en 1588–1589. Onuitgegeven adviezen, ontwerpen en ordonnanties*, Verlinden and Craeybeckx, eds. (Brussels, 1962), and the large collections of official documents bearing on governmental policies and institutions that body has long published with the Royal Commission for the Publication of Ancient Laws and Ordinances of Belgium, have been essential for such studies as M. Hoc and H. A. Enno Van Gelder, *Les monnaies des Pays-Bas bourguignons et espagnols,*

1434–1713 (Amsterdam, 1960), or J. Craeybeckx, "Aperçu sur l'histoire des impôts en Flandre et au Brabant au cours du XVIe siècle," *Revue du Nord,* XXIX (1947), pp. 87–108.

22. *E.g.,* E. Coornaert, *La draperie-sayetterie d'Hondschoote* (*XIVe– XVIIIe siècle*) (Paris, 1931); E. Sabbe, *De Belgische Vlasnijverheid. I: De Zuidnederlandsche Vlasnijverheid tot het verdag van Utrecht* (*1713*) (Bruges, 1943); P. Lindemans, *Geschiedenis van de landbouw in België* (2 vols., Antwerp, 1952); B. H. Slicher van Bath, "The rise of intensive husbandry in the Low Countries," *Britain and the Netherlands. Papers delivered to the Oxford Netherlands Historical Conference of 1959,* J. S. Bromley and E. S. Kossmann, eds. (London, 1960), pp. 130–53.

23. R. Boumans, "Le dépeuplement d'Anvers dans le dernier quart du XVIme siècle," *Revue du Nord,* XXIX (1947), pp. 181–94, indicates depopulation over the short term selected, but shows, in the long run, significant repopulation traced in his "L'évolution démographique d'Anvers (XVme–XVme siècle)," *Bulletin de statistique,* XXXIV (1948), pp. 1,683–1,691, that is further substantiated for a wider area by H. Van Werveke, "Demografische Problemen in de Zuidelijke Nederlanden (XVIIe en XVIIIe eeuw)," *Mededelingen van de Koninklijke Vlaamse Academie van België, Klasse der Letteren,* XVII (1955), no. 1.

24. The entire locale, as in K. Maddens, "De krisis op het einde van de XVIe eeuw in de kasselrij Kortrijk," *Verslagen en mededelingen van de Leiegouw,* I (1959), pp. 75–94, and "Geluwe op het einde van de XVIe en het begin van de XVIIe eeuw," *ibid.,* pp. 187–213, may be discussed or only some of its characteristics, as in H. G. Koenigsberger, "Property and the price revolution (Hainault, 1474–1573), *Economic History Review,* second series, XI (1956), pp. 1–15.

25. Elected by Goris, *op. cit.,* Floris Prims, *Het Wonderjaar* (*1566– 1567*) (second edition, Wetteren, 1940), and others.

26. A date championed by the late F. Blockmans: " 'Het Wonderjaar' en het afsluiten van Antwerpen's 'Gouden Eeuw,' " *Lode Baekelmans ter eere* (Antwerp, 1946), pp. 7–24, and now accepted by many.

27. Well illustrated by P. Chaunu, "Séville et la Belgique, 1555–1648," *Revue du Nord,* XLII (1960), pp. 259–303.

28. That these presuppositions should be questioned is made clear by Van Houtte, *Onze zeventiende eeuw, "ongelukseeuw"?* (Brussels, 1953).

29. Typical of the genre is J. Wegg, *The decline of Antwerp under Philip of Spain* (London, 1924).

30. G. Masselman: *The Cradle of Colonialism* (New Haven, 1963).

31. V. Barbour, *Capitalism in Amsterdam in the 17th Century* (Baltimore, 1950).

32. As examples: C. Scribanius, S. J., *Origines Antverpiensium* (Antwerp, 1610), and E. Van Meteren, *Histoire der Nederlandscher ende haerder nabueren oorlogen tot den jare M; VIC; XII* (The Hague, 1614).

33. *Stadsarchief, Antwerp: Privilegekamer,* Pk 1012, 1013, 1014.

34. H. Pirenne, *op. cit.,* IV, p. 415.

35. Interesting in this respect is C. Verlinden, "La 'lamentation' de Zegher van Maele sur la situation de Bruges de 1565 à 1592 et l'histoire des prix," *Revue du Nord,* XLII (1960).

36. *Supra,* note 33.

37. *Supra,* note 23.

38. Public finance as a catalyst in Antwerp's revival is treated in J. Gentil Da Silva, *Stratégie des affaires à Lisbon entre 1595 et 1607* (Paris, 1956).

39. H. Lapeyre, *Simon Ruiz et les asientos de Philippe II* (Paris, 1953), pp. 59–60, 90.

40. P. Chaunu, "Séville et la Belgique, 1555–1648," *Revue du Nord,* XLII (1960), pp. 259–303.

41. V. Vazquez de Prada, *Lettres marchandes d'Anvers* (4 vols, Paris, 1960), I, p. 144.

42. H. Van der Wee, *op. cit.,* II, pp. 269–72.

43. The author intends publication of an article on the feasibility of this project in the light of resources available at Antwerp, Middleburg, and The Hague.

44. J. H. Kernkamp, *De handel op den vijand, 1572–1609* (2 vols, Utrecht, 1931–34), II, p. 344.

45. *Ibid.,* pp. 348–49.

46. In the collections of *licences* and *sauf-conduits, Chambre des Comptes, Archives générales du Royaume* (Brussels).

47. P. Voeten, "Antwerpse reactie's op het Twaalfjarig Bestand," *Bijdragen tot de geschiedenis inzonderheid van oud hertogdom Brabant,* X (1958), pp. 209–10.

48. J. H. Kernkamp, *op. cit.*

49. P. Voeten: " Antwerpse handel over Duinkerken tijdens het Twaalf-jarig Bestand," *Bijdragen tot de Geschiedenis van Brabant,* XXXIX (1956), p. 68.

50. *Supra,* notes 47 and 49.

51. W. Brulez, "L'exportation des Pays-Bas vers l'Italie par voie de terre au milieu du XVIme siècle," *Annales, E. S. C.,* XIV (1959), pp. 461–91; J. Gentil Da Silva, "Trafics du Nord, marchés du 'Mezzogiorno', finances génoises: recherches et documents sur la conjoncture à la fin du XVIme siècle," *Revue du Nord,* XLI (1959), pp. 129–52.

52. W. Brulez, "De diaspora der antwerpse kooplui op het einde van de 16e eeuw," *Bijdragen voor de Geschiedenis der Nederlanden,* XV (1960), pp. 279–306.

53. *Supra,* note 22.

54. See, *e.g.,* F. Smolar, "Materials relevant to European trade with Spanish America," *Archives, Bibliothèques et Musées de Belgique,* XXXIV (1963), pp. 1–10.

55. W. Brulez, *De Firma Della Faille en de internationale handel van vlaamse firma's in de 16e eeuw* (Brussels, 1959).

56. The bulk of the documentation for these case histories is in the *Insolvente Boedelskamer, Stadsarchief,* Antwerp, for which see *supra,* note 54.

57. The best published account of Moucheron is E. Coornaert, *op. cit.,* I, pp. 349–50, II *passim.*

58. W. Brulez, *Della Faille,* pp. 222–23.

59. The descriptions in E. Coornaert, *op. cit.,* and G. Masselman, *op. cit.,* are based on J. H. de Stoppelaar, *Balthasar de Moucheron, Een bladzijde uit de nederlandsche handelsgeschiedenis tijdens den tachtigjarigen oorlog* (The Hague, 1901).

60. A small fraction of the documentation on Andrea is published in

J. Denucé, *Koopmansleerboeken van de XVI* en *XVII* eeuwen* (Brussels, 1941).

61. A few of the documents concerning this firm appear in J. Denucé, *"Spaansch en Mechelisch goudleder te Antwerpen in de XVII* eeuw,"* *Antwerpsch Archievenblad*, second series, IX (1934), pp. 161–85; the family is summarily discussed in Brulez, *della Faille*, pp. 356–58 and 366–68.

THE AMBASSADORS
OF EARLY MODERN EUROPE:
PATTERNS OF
DIPLOMATIC REPRESENTATION
IN THE EARLY
SEVENTEENTH CENTURY

CHARLES H. CARTER
Tulane University

G arrett Mattingly carried his examination of *Renaissance Diplomacy* well into the seventeenth century, by which time the concepts and practices involved had become recognizably similar to "modern" diplomacy. In a contribution to a volume in his honor it seems appropriate to continue the analysis of that subject, approaching it here from a different angle. It is thus the purpose of this essay to examine the general pattern of diplomatic representation in Counter-Reformation Europe, with special attention to the individual variations of the more important autonomous states, the main participants in the development of the machinery for handling the international affairs of the "modern state."*

---

* Because of space considerations I have eliminated most of the footnotes from this article, especially the many which must be either general or random citations. When possible I have cited places where I have dealt with some aspect of the subject and where fuller reference may be seen.

Emphasis on this particular kind of polity necessarily involves an emphasis on a particular kind of representation, the resident embassy—agent and symbol of permanent liaison for the conduct of normal affairs, the most significant mark of modern diplomacy. Because permanent representation is incomplete in wartime and abnormal even among allies, it is more useful to focus for detail upon the generation or so from about 1598 to the 1620s, the only substantial period of general peace in the whole century from the 1550s to 1648 during which international affairs were characterized by Counter-Reformation issues; but if one makes the obvious adjustments for changes in possibility and circumstance, the generalizations made are applicable also to the troubled times preceding 1598 and the more "normal" times after 1648.

Some aspects of diplomatic representation, especially matters of formal usage, followed a generally consistent pattern throughout most of early-seventeenth-century Europe. Others, more pragmatic and more important, varied widely, but with fairly consistent patterns for individual powers. A good many of these did not participate directly in the development of the forms of modern diplomacy for the simple reason that they were not, or not yet, or not importantly, involved in the growing system of sovereign states and, so had little to do with the shaping of its diplomatic handmaiden. Before going on to those that did, it is necessary to give a moment's attention to those that did not.

One can define three general types of such cases: *1.* those political entities with no diplomacy of their own, because they were subject to outside rule or so minor that technical independence did not entail diplomatic activity of any importance; *2.* those occasionally active diplomatically, but with no resident diplomacy; and *3.* those which did not fit into an *inter*national system because they were themselves *supra*national.

It is ironic that the most conspicuous examples of the first type comprised most of Italy, the cradle of modern diplomacy. Naples, once an important independent kingdom, and Milan, one of the chief innovators of the balance-of-power device, were both totally subject to Spain. Genoa, independent but a close satellite of Spain, was little better off. Tuscany was diplomatically independent, but of interest mainly as a source of dowries. Such lesser fragments as Mantua existed only to be used and fought over. Aside from the papacy, a special case, only Venice and Savoy intruded themselves from Italy into the larger affairs of Europe.

The second type consisted mainly of the German states and free cities, and groupings thereof.[1] The individual units conducted relations with the Emperor mainly through the Empire's internal machinery; with each other in no uniform manner; and with non-German states on an *ad hoc* basis, in frequent but irregular anticipation of the diplomatic autonomy formally recognized later in the Peace of Westphalia. Each of the opposing confessional alliances of German princes—the Evangelical Union founded in 1608 and the Catholic "League" in 1609—conducted an independent diplomacy, normally through embassies sent specially on particular matters, as did the Hanseatic cities.

The third type involves a difference in kind, for both the Empire and the papacy fall outside the focus of this essay not because they were *unimportant* as "states," but because they were entirely incompatible with that pluralistic political form. Schematically at the top of the medieval hierarchy and together rulers of the ideal Christian unity, these two were least fitted of all for playing well-integrated roles in the "new diplomacy" among sovereign states, and were unavoidably anomalous in an increasingly standardized system of multilateral liaison.

For the papacy, so active in the secular affairs of the Italian "Renaissance state," this fact involved a considerable change in the recent nature of the institution, a reversal of a trend toward conformity with evolving secular forms. That this was a Counter-Reformation papacy not only made an increasing difference in its general relations with others, but made its degree of nonconformity specifically with the newly developing system of forms and procedures inevitably great, in practice unbridgeable.

Several broad reasons can be assigned for this. The reformed papacy was concerned more than before with problems and goals that transcended its secular interests and were not so easily handled by the machinery of secular diplomacy. Even had this not been true, Rome was incapable of really being integrated into a Europe-wide system of liaison that functioned actively—often most importantly—across confessional lines, for its permanent diplomacy was woefully incomplete, omitting all the Protestant states. Even where permanent representation was maintained, diplomatic action was restricted by previous agreements and established procedures, as with Spain and France; by old and continuing rivalries and deep-seated conflicts, such as with Venice; and by widespread Gallicanism on the part of rulers and ecclesiastics alike. Where permanent nunciatures were maintained, the nuncio (having many other duties) was only a part-time diplomat, and one whose effectiveness was further impaired by whatever degree of conflict existed between the nunciature and the secular authority. Elsewhere, institutional structure permitted such anomalies as papal representatives who were officers of the local church, and often natives, envoys to their own temporal ruler. Papal diplomacy, in sum, however successful one finds it to have been, had little relation to the standard machinery of international dialogue and settlement.

The Emperor, for his part, was far from being *the* Emperor, of all Europe, but he was still *an* emperor, different in kind from all other princes in Christendom. Though his suzerainty was not recognized outside Germany,[2] his preëminence was. And, since resident ambassadors are normally exchanged, not unilaterally sent, and this between equals in sovereignty, he did not, as a general practice, either send or receive them. There were exceptions, of course, as in the intra-family exchange with Spain, but on the whole the conditions and practices in which the emperorship was involved were quite alien to the increasingly standardized network of international diplomacy.

The general pattern of that network is the pattern of actual diplomacy in the period, not of an ideal schema. The consistent aspects of this pattern are a suggestive partial measure of the degree to which procedures and forms had become standardized; the variations within it and from it reflect rather closely the varying ways individual powers went about their diplomacy. To arrive at an overall picture of this combination of useful standard procedures and meaningful variations, it is necessary to examine the types of envoys sent out or received by the various powers, and to do so under two sets of terms: the formal ones of category and rank, and the more pragmatic ones of the personal qualities of the men themselves.

The most conspicuous distinction in formal rank was that between the ordinary and the extraordinary envoy, but the simplicity of the division is deceptive. There were gradations of rank within each of the two categories, and differences in status between missions of the *same* rank and category sent from *different courts*.

Ordinary representation might be on any of three distinct levels of rank. Two were simple alternatives for the regular head of a permanent embassy, the third an accommodation of irregular circumstance; all conform to modern usage. Of the two regular levels, the resident envoy might carry full rank and be properly referred to as ambassador-in-ordinary, or he might have the lesser status of "agent," equivalent to the present-day "minister."[3]

The reasons for the distinction are embedded in conditions basic to diplomacy, and unsurprisingly resemble modern ones. Residents exchanged by major powers naturally held the higher rank of ambassador: those exchanged among Spain, France, and England did so by obvious right. Envoys sent to those courts by clearly insignificant states were automatically agents. Between these extremes, the rank held by envoys from states that were "lesser" but still significant was at the option of the great power, though it might require concurrence, and tradition played a great part.

Venice's envoys were granted full rank for a combination of reasons: the Venetians were sensitive about precedence and insisted upon all the perquisites they could possibly obtain; they had had ambassadors in ordinary before these great powers had even adopted permanent diplomacy, providing a traditional claim no one seems to have been inclined to challenge; and everyone seems to have been willing to grant them the title on the republic's own merits. Savoy's friendship was valued (largely because of strategic location) and her Throne esteemed; perhaps for these reasons her envoys were generally *called* "ambassadors," though they really were not. But there was a limit to how far even this nominal grace was extended. For example, in spite of repeated insistence by the States General and their residents that the latter be called "ambassador" and be given the perquisites of that status (some of real value), they were mere agents, though local sympathizers generally used the higher title, and it was occasionally used loosely in the generic sense as well.

As the greater powers' option was equally strong regarding envoys they sent, and as they preferred to have the status of their envoys reflect their own status, the exchanges were not necessarily symmetrical: France and England received only agents from The Hague, but they kept ambassadors there. On the other hand, for example, Frederick V was sent only a resident agent from his father-in-law, James I. (James also kept an agent at Rome, but that was an irregular matter.)

A typical contemporary definition of the distinction and its identifying perquisites, in this case speaking specifically of the Spanish court, puts it this way: "Ambassadors properly so called" are limited to "those that are sent by the Highest Pontiff, by the Emperor, or by the crowned kings." The first include a wide variety of specified church officers in addition to the papal nuncio; the third is limited exclusively to the ambassadors from France, England, and Venice (the writer seems unbothered by the contradiction of his first sentence). "The households of such ambassadors are privileged and exempt from all types of justice [if] it is not a case of heresy or the crime of lèse majesté. In all other offenses the offenders merit and enjoy this immunity without any justice [brought against] them in any manner. A house is given free to these ambassadors at the court of Spain without it costing them anything. To these the king takes off his hat and they are covered in his presence, and are given seats in the royal chapel." They are also the king's special guests when he attends an assortment of public functions. "In all the places and kingdoms referred to, the king of Spain keeps ordinary ambassadors, and besides these he keeps them in Flanders and Savoy [and] Genoa."

In addition: "There are others at the court of Spain who, although they are called and call themselves ambassadors, are not, but agents of the governments and potentates such as" Genoa, Lucca, the Duke of Savoy, the Grand Duke of Tuscany, and the Dukes of Parma, Mantua, Urbino, and Modena. "These are not covered [in the king's presence] nor do they have seats in the royal chapel nor places at the public acts where the king appears." They are, however, like the "ambassadors properly so called," supplied a residence free, and they and their households are covered by diplomatic immunity, but here again the distinction is specific: only minor offenses are covered by immunity, though in practice arrests are seldom made even in serious cases.[4]

Sir John Digby's report to James I on a particular question may serve to illustrate some aspects of these matters of precedence:

According to Your Majesty's commandment at my departure from England, I have informed myself the best I can what place or rank was given to the Venetian ambassadors in this court, or what difference was made betwixt them and the Archduke's ambassadors in matters of precedence. But I have not been able to attain to any such perfect information as may serve for a public declaration in that point. Neither (as I conceive) may serve Your Majesty for any precedent to decide the controversy betwixt the said ambassadors in Your Majesty's court. For here is no Master of Ceremonies nor officer of that nature (as in other places). But the only distinction that is made betwixt ambassadors here is by granting some seats in the King's Chapel, which to others is not allowed. I find that to the ambassador of the Commonwealth of Venice there hath not only been granted the liberty of accompanying the king to the chapel and of taking their seats there, but likewise they have also enjoyed all privileges and preëminences which the ambassadors of kings did. But this custom and distinction of Embaxadores de Capilla (as they call them) hath been introduced here in Spain only since the beginning of Charles the fifth his reign, since which time there have been no distinct dukes of Burgundy, but that title hath been confounded with many other, united in the persons of the kings of Spain, so that it will not be possible to find any precedent wherein these two ambassadors have concurred in any solemn or public act. And here some grave men (with whom I have had conference of this business) have alleged that if this king hath been sparing in giving equal honors with the Venetian to any ambassadors of late sent unto him from the Archduke it hath been in regard of the respect and observance which it is fit the Archduke should bear unto him, both for many obligations as likewise for the holding his estate in the manner as he doth. But there is no reason (as they allege) that this should any whit prejudice him in his rank with other princes. Further, whereas the Venetian ambassador seemed to allege in England that it would be without difficulty declared here, he hath questionless therein been misinformed. For I dare confidently say unto Your Majesty that there is not any minister of this king's to whom the question should be propounded which would not absolutely protest against it. Although they can not deny but that next unto the ambassadors of kings, by a long continued practise the ambassadors of Venice have received privileges and particular respect above any other whatsoever.[5]

The third type of "resident," irregular and temporary in nature and different in kind from the former two, was also often called agent, but only in the general sense. Usually an embassy secretary, he was the equivalent of a modern *chargé d'affaires* left to maintain liaison and continue transacting diplomatic business while the regular man went home for consultations or simply on leave, or during a delay in replacing one ambassador with another.

The *chargé's* status was far inferior, of course, to that of a normally accredited envoy. The regular resident would be accredited to a ruler or ruling body by a formal letter of credence from his own; the scope of his powers as set forth in his formal instructions might also be shown in whole or in part. But the *chargé's* "accreditation" was usually only a simple request that representation be accepted from him and that representations normally made to the permanent envoy be made to him. Sometimes he was specifically confined to routine tasks, but even if not his powers were naturally limited compared to those of the regular resident, especially if it was the latter who had made the temporary arrangement, for the powers granted specifically to him in his own instructions were not easily devolved upon another.

Nevertheless, the *chargé's* role was especially important in that age of slow communication, in which the most routine absence was inevitably long, and in a period in which almost universally inadequate financing of the diplomatic establishment caused frequent and substantial delays in replacing one ambassador with another. With his salary and expenses usually far in arrears, the typical resident had to live on his own or on credit, but he could not travel to his post on credit, and it often took a long while to find a qualified man willing and able to pay his own expenses and, if none could be found, perhaps even longer for the government to raise cash of its own. Meanwhile, the *chargé*'s interim as acting head of the embassy might become quite extended.[6]

Like the resident, the extraordinary envoy occurred in two ranks;[7] like the resident, whether he was "ambassador" or "agent" depended on who was sending and receiving. But that pattern, uneven enough in regard to ordinaries, was here more various still, because of an added factor: the reason it was an extraordinary embassy that was sent.

If the sender had no ordinary at the receiving court the embassy was by definition extraordinary, but, especially at an important court, this would be a reflection of the sender's insignificance. "Extraordinary" status in such circumstances would not even imply any particular importance of the individual sent; he would normally be treated as a mere "agent," and his case would not necessarily be accorded any more consideration than that of a minor resident. Nor did the "extraordinary" status of such a mission necessarily imply that its "extraordinary" business was of any great importance, for fairly routine matters had to be handled in this way when there was no resident. This was normally the position of envoys sent by minor rulers such as Frederick V and groups such as the Huguenots and the Princes of the Union.

If the sender already had an ambassador in ordinary it required a special occasion to bring an extraordinary mission. The importance of such an occasion, however, might be only a matter of protocol, typically one of a recurring sort: an occasion for congratulation, such as accession or a royal marriage, or for condolence at a death in the king's family. These required great formality and a person of importance as envoy, but not a numerous party. Another recurrent but much less routine occasion was that of the formal taking of a monarch's oath to a treaty of peace, which involved reciprocal sending of large, distinguished, resplendent embassies, comprising dozens of nobles and droves of retainers, financially ruinous to send and perhaps worse to receive because of the large number of ostentatious gifts expected from the host.[8]

These routine protocol missions did not normally have negotiation as even a secondary purpose or function, except of course as opportunity might haply serve. But the arrival of an extraordinary mission when no formal occasion demanded it could always be understood to involve negotiation, and on matters considered too important for the regular man or regular channels.[9] The ambassador would be a personage of unusual importance[10] (typically, either a high-ranking member of the old nobility or someone personally high in his ruler's confidence), accompanied by three or four dozen persons of quality and a total entourage that might run to two or three hundred—all of which was sure to set diplomatic antennae aquiver.

Those political entities which do not very well fit the pattern that was developing into "modern" diplomacy perhaps need no further word here, but one might examine more closely the activities of those which more truly possessed attributes of the modern state. On the most fundamental level[11] this involved their being sovereign but neither "universal monarchy" nor petty principality—that is, it required the possession of *imperium,* but of a sort also possessed by others (else how could one have a plural system of sovereign states?); plus the capability of preserving that complete autonomy (and keeping the question from becoming academic). With unequal but adequate justice Venice, the United Provinces, England, Spain, and France can be included as examples of various types.

The kinds of residents any of these countries sent followed fairly consistent patterns, sometimes dictated by tradition, but more often by the nature of government, the manner in which it generally handled its foreign affairs, and the sort of business this was apt to entail. Because of the wide implications involved, one must focus briefly upon the variations in the usual sort of ambassador each of these five states used in its permanent diplomacy.

Venice. In spite of her declining importance in the early seventeenth century Venice is an unavoidable example, for she still had the most highly articulated diplomatic service in Europe. Her ambassadors were rotated from post to post, serving a few years—seldom more than three—at one embassy, returning home to report, then going to another. They were members of leading families—indeed, the Foscarini, Contarini, and others furnished ambassadors generation after generation—but the diplomatic corps was not just a training ground for statesmen: the members tended to be career diplomats, spending long years in the service.[12]

Being less of a force in the world than the other four of these examples, Venice had fewer important matters to press, and generally sent extraordinary embassies to handle them; thus her permanent ambassadors were, by comparison, less negotiators, more purely observers. Their most conspicuous function was voluminous diplomatic reporting, in their regular dispatches and the formal *Relazioni* (*Relations*) they delivered to the Doge and Senate on their return for reassignment.

This being so, the quality of Venice's regular diplomacy can perhaps fairly be measured by the quality of these reports, so heavily drawn upon by historians. Since publication began over a century ago—the *Relazioni* printed, the dispatches calendared in large numbers—they have been the best source of contemporary evidence for their period generally available to historians: in the past several generations, almost every relevant work written on political or diplomatic history would have been vastly different without them.

But this is only to say that they have been the best of their kind available in print. Their shortcomings as sources are great; more importantly in the present context, so are their shortcomings as ambassadorial accomplishments in their own time. The reasons are fairly obvious and, given the reasons, it seems rather surprising that they have been valued quite so highly as they have been. In the first place, frequent rotation meant that after a man had been in one country long enough to become familiar with it he was replaced by a stranger to that place, and himself sent to a place strange to him. Even without this handicap, a Venetian ambassador lacked the means of getting very much information of value. He had not enough prestige or precedence to gain personal access to the seats of power and thus to first-hand information at that indispensable level, nor enough importance to have personal contacts highly enough placed to keep him informed about inner affairs, nor enough money to engage in effective espionage. The information he sent home was usually either given to him formally by the host government, or picked up in public, or obtained from other ambassadors.

One need hardly belabor the questionable reliability of information of such interested provenance as government handouts (generally verbal in those days, of course) and messages designed for transmission. Public gossip was then a standard source of general news, but for use as a basis for government decision "control" was the key verb: one had always to check such information against a more reliable source, in which case the latter would have been sufficient by itself, except when the rumor served as first intimation that something was planned or had happened.

But it was the information derived from other ambassadors that provided the greatest opportunity for important error. Hardly any resident of another power was both influential enough to have access to important information *and* likely to pass it on to his Venetian colleague with dependable accuracy. The English were sometimes willing, but often badly informed; the French and Dutch were friendly and perhaps better informed, but normally spoke from policy; the Spanish, better informed than any, could not be counted as friends. Yet Venetians often reported with apparent equanimity information gained even from their Spanish counterparts: every Spanish ambassador whose records I have seen in any quantity made a practice of planting misinformation on his Venetian colleague, and spot checks indicate that it was regularly passed on to Venice, rarely with a caveat.

But perhaps the best indication of the qualitative level of Venetian diplomacy is to be found at home, in the government whose system this was and whose procedures the ambassadors were following. The *Relazioni* conventionally opened with a general description of the country, and regarding England typically began with the fact that Great Britain was an island off the northwest coast of Europe, with Scotland in the north and England in the south, and with another island called Ireland further west. The most significant question to ask, it seems to me, is what sort of diplomacy do we have when its policymakers gather together every two or three years to listen to a returning ambassador tell them once more that Great Britain is an island?

The United Provinces. The Dutch were very active diplomatically and had permanent representatives in most of the important places —France, England, Venice, etc.—but not in Spain, the place that mattered most because vastly predominant in Europe. Neither did they have a resident in the neighboring Spanish Netherlands nor any relations with Rome. They thus resembled the papacy in participating only partially in the overall diplomacy of Europe. But hindsight assures us that the United Provinces were indeed a viable state, for a while a great one; and, in the present context, they provide the best available example of a power the forms of whose diplomacy were in high degree governed by the nature of both its political structure and the diplomatic business to be conducted, in this case heavily commercial.

Two basic facts are fundamental to this. For one, envoys "from the United Provinces" were specifically from the States General (all regular diplomats represented a sovereign person or group; nobody represented a *country* directly, nor for that matter do they today), and that body delegated little final power to its envoys, perhaps partly because of their own responsibility to the provincial States, and certainly because Their High Mightinesses preferred to keep direct control of state affairs in their own hands so far as possible. For another, this nation of fishermen, merchants, and carriers (and interlopers, smugglers, colonial squatters, and pirates) exceeded all others in the extent of their day-to-day contact with foreigners, and thus in the number of opportunities to be involved in the breaking or misapplication of laws and trading agreements or in disputes arising from competition for markets, fishing grounds, and so forth. In one statistic, the number of complaints which arose out of routine economic activity to be settled, usually, by routine diplomacy, only the English rivaled the Dutch, and most of the English disputes were *with* the Dutch.[13]

The combined result of these two basic facts was that a Dutch resident spent much of his time on a great volume of matters more "consular" than "ambassadorial" in nature, and beyond this generally confined himself to transmitting messages, observing, and reporting. Another power desiring action through diplomatic channels was well advised to go though its own ambassador at The Hague, who could present the matter directly to the States General and probably negotiate with greater effect.

When that body, for its part, had to make important representation abroad it sent an extraordinary mission, but, significantly enough, not the usual single appointee with entourage but a deputation of several of its own members—the lowest number that has come to my attention is three, the highest sixteen.[14] Also significantly, when the matter involved the affairs of the Dutch East India Company that organization usually did its own negotiating at home and sent its own deputations abroad, almost as though it were itself a sovereign authority—a symptom of the degree of identification of interests, not of competition for authority, between the two bodies.

In contrast to that of, say, France, Dutch diplomacy was not only unspectacular but almost embarrassingly unimaginative. But if their embassies were unostentatious, they spread money lavishly in bribes and gifts. If their agents and deputies were unskilled in the devious ways of diplomacy, they were devotedly stubborn, and deft in their own peculiar way. They were maddeningly obtuse, seemingly incapable of calculated compromise or traditional *quid pro quo*, unwilling to consider the legitimate needs or interests of others when these did not square with their own, and geniuses at antagonizing those they had to deal with; yet I am unfamiliar with any case in this period in which their diplomacy was not at least partially successful when at least partial success was possible. Nothing even close to this was true of Spain or England or France.

Spain and England. The foreign relations of Spain and England were generally dealt with in opposite fashion: the former abroad, the latter at home. In their relations with each other, their opposite approaches dovetailed very conveniently. Elsewhere, as they were the recognized heads of the two factions of Europe and in this sense the two most important powers, their preferred modes of procedure were fairly readily imposed upon others—even, to a degree, upon a rather disorganized France.

Spain's "land's-end" location had always affected her contact with the rest of Europe, and increasingly so as she became deeply involved in northern affairs. She had a long tradition of employing high-caliber men and of depending heavily upon their service and advice even under the relatively personal rule of Philip II. After his death the formation and conduct of Spanish foreign policy was in the hands of the Council of State, a rather cumbersome operation which made negotiation and discussion with ambassadors in Madrid far less effective than it would have been on a one-to-one basis.[15] Now that remoteness from other capitals and a tradition of strong individual representation abroad[16] were combined with collegial government at home, it was perhaps inevitable that the bulk of Spain's more important affairs with other powers should be handled through her ambassadors at those courts rather than through theirs at the Spanish.

One has only to look at the European diplomatic corps at the time to see that Spain was well equipped for this sort of approach. If one were to ask a contemporary to list the greatest diplomatic figures of the first quarter of the seventeenth century—a period in which ambassadors loom unusually large as makers of history—the first three he named would surely be Gondomar, Oñate, and Baltasar de Zúñiga. The next several names would likely include non-Spaniards such as Jeannin, Digby, and Richardot, but would also include numerous Spaniards such as Villamediana and Pedro de Zúñiga.[17] It was a common saying in Spain that the first qualification for a great ambassador was that he come from Galicia; on the European scale one might almost say that he should come from Spain. Significantly, the first three named, whose preëminence would be challenged by few, were all permanent ambassadors-in-ordinary.

In contrast to the Spanish approach, James I preferred to hold the threads of his diplomacy more tightly in his own hands. He used his ambassadors, of course, but handled most important matters in converse with the foreign ambassadors resident in London, supplemented by extensive correspondence directly with the other monarchs and governing bodies in question.[18]

Naturally, he had to conduct a fair amount of his diplomatic business abroad, just as Spain did at home, their opposite usual methods yielding as needed to practicability. Thus they, too, were involved in the functional dualism inherent in ambassadorial exchanges, the often redundant use of two states' separate diplomatic channels. But the external symmetry of this apparent duplication of function is deceptive, for the main and often conclusive activity involved in Anglo-Spanish relations—the negotiation, the arguing, the give and take, personal pressure, reassurance, cajoling, begging, wheedling, threat, and bluff—took place mainly in England, not Spain. And the same patterns—Spain working mainly abroad, England mainly at home for their basic diplomacy and the settlement of great matters—generally held true for their relations with other powers as well, a fact somewhat disguised on the English side by the large number of "extraordinary" missions sent that were tentative, preliminary, exploratory in nature or concerned with the execution of decisions already taken (such as the delivery of subsidy money to allies).

James I's personal approach to diplomacy resulted quite naturally in a caliber of English resident abroad very different from the Spanish. Limited in the scope of responsibility assigned them, they were similarly limited in the personal prestige they brought to the job. They were usually knights,[19] but that is minimal in context; James appointed no nobles to permanent embassies. Only when matters of unusual importance had to be negotiated abroad did he send persons closer to him or in whose abilities he had greater confidence, and then it was as ambassadors extraordinary. James Hay was a frequent example of the former, John Digby the most conspicuous example of the latter: after having proved himself thoroughly as permanent ambassador to Spain, Digby was ennobled, given other reward, and thereafter used on extraordinary missions of extraordinary sensitivity.

But Digby, who, as resident, had shown exceptional ability, had been promoted out of that rank for precisely that reason; he was far from typical. Compared to the caliber of men Spain employed—and by any absolute standard that is demanding at all—the ordinaries James maintained tended more toward mediocrity than they did toward greatness. Spain considered it normal to have a Pedro de Zúñiga or a Gondomar on permanent assignment in London, a Baltasar de Zúñiga or an Oñate with the emperor, or a Bedmar at Venice or Brussels—men a cut, if at all, below the caliber one sought for viceregal posts and important governorships (indeed, Baltasar de Zúñiga became chief minister). For England, the typical permanent envoys were such as Cornwallis and Aston at Madrid, Carew and Edmondes at Paris, Winwood and Carleton at The Hague.[20]

They were usually competent, but usually limited in greater ability: of this half dozen, only Aston might be called bumbling; Cornwallis and Edmondes performed reliably; Carew was a perceptive observer; Winwood and Carleton did journeyman service and became secretaries of state. But none were real movers and shakers. The replacement of Baltasar de Zúñiga by the Count of Oñate with the Emperor, of Alonso de Velasco by Gondomar in England, of Guadaleste by Bedmar at Brussels, profoundly affected the course of events; I do not know of a single change of English residents that made very much difference. J. R. Seeley describes a whole decade of British history as "the period of Gondomar";[21] can one imagine, for example, an "age of Winwood"?

France. France's residents generally fell between England's and Spain's in rank and ability. England's residents were typically gentry of modest descent, Spain's were nobles or members of ancient *hidalgo* families almost certain to earn high noble rank through service; France's were usually nobles, but usually petty ones.[22] Their individual effectiveness can safely be described as generally greater than that of the English residents and less than that of the Spanish, a point I shall return to.

In the terms of here-or-there applied above to Spain and England, France's approach varied, roughly according to the other's power and position vis-à-vis her own. Regular diplomacy with lesser states was normally conducted through their envoys in Paris, as befitted their usual role as supplicants.[23] Given the inconstancy of French aims and fortunes, however, and the importance of strategically located states to the strength of France's position, powers of the middling sort such as Venice were frequent exceptions to this.

As the United Provinces' French policy alternated between obsequious petition and intransigent aloofness, France was sometimes able to play the patron in Paris and sometimes had to deal directly with the States through her ambassador to The Hague. There was one major difference: for more pressing matters of the former category, the Dutch used the special deputations referred to earlier, while the greater powers of a French resident made French use of extraordinary embassies to the States less frequently necessary.

France's handling of her relations with Spain generally conformed to the Spanish practice of conducting most of their regular diplomacy through their own residents, though—given the tenuous and shifting nature of Franco-Spanish relations in the period, compounding the generally erratic nature of French policy under a miscellaneous series of governments—too consistent a picture would be misleading. There was not the same amount of day-to-day contact, the sort that brings up frequent incidents that need settlement, between France and Spain that there was between, say, the United Provinces and England, so that the practical context for "regular" diplomacy was rather more limited. Important matters which France could not handle satisfactorily through regular channels were of course handled by extraordinary embassy. It is symptomatic, or at least symbolic, of France's uncertain position during much of this period that such an embassy rather naturally went from Paris to Madrid, not the reverse.[24]

To say that France's diplomatic position vis-à-vis England was weaker than that with the United Provinces and stronger than that with Spain is to define the obvious: in the long run the Dutch could not do without France's support, Spain was in essence an enemy largely immune to the influence of French diplomacy, and England was in neither of these polar positions. There was relatively little day-to-day contact between the two nations to raise minor disputes, and matters of great importance, such as their individual policies toward third parties, were often governed by common interests; as already described, James I was disinclined to delegate much responsibility to residents, and a series of weak governments in France after 1610 were unable to delegate much telling power to theirs. Thus few great matters were settled between them through the ordinaries of either; both parties resorted to extraordinary missions with unusual readiness.[25]

A cross-section of diplomatic representation at almost any time in this period—showing who was at the head of the various permanent legations, what sort of business they were handling and how, and what extraordinary embassies were abroad at the moment—would illustrate the general pattern described: the distribution of individual talent, prestige, and responsibility, the customary practices and preferences of the various states, and so on.[26] But there remains the question: Which of these variations was the best? The answer, I think, is all of them, or any.

Perhaps it is typical of diplomatic method, which tends to adjust itself to opportunities and limitations, individual strengths and other such practical considerations, that no real pattern of success or failure emerges in this period which can be related directly to the manner in which affairs were handled. This is not to say, however, that such a pattern does not *seem* to emerge at times. For example, as Spain maintained ordinaries of markedly higher caliber than France did, and had more diplomatic successes and fewer failures in this period, it would seem obvious that better men get better results.

As a case in point, Gondomar was originally sent to England to try to prevent an Anglo-French marriage alliance. It was a difficult task, but he was able to stall the negotiations until they were finally abandoned; viewed as a test of two men's abilities—those of Gondomar and the French resident Buisseaux—it was no contest at all.[27] This seems undeniable if one tries to imagine them in opposite roles, Buisseaux as Spanish ambassador trying to foil Gondomar's negotiations (as French ambassador) for an Anglo-French marriage: Buisseaux could no more have wrecked French policy against Gondomar's defense than he could, in the real event, defend it against Gondomar's attack. The conclusion to be drawn from such a hypothetical test of comparative ability is obvious: Spain gained immensely by maintaining strong residents, and France should have followed suit.

But this is misleading, for it assumes more flexibility of choice than existed. It assumes in this example that the regency government of Marie de' Medici and the Maréchal d'Ancre, under constant attack by its opponents, could be expected to send out representatives as strong and independent as the solid, secure Council of State in Madrid was willing and able to send. On the other hand, while there is a marked difference in these two states' representation abroad, there is an even more important similarity: the pattern of representation of each was the best suited for its own case. Stated differently, the general approach to diplomacy of these two states and of the others mentioned, including the caliber of men they sent and the channels through which they normally conducted their affairs, was not chosen from among options equally available and equally desirable to all. The problem was not that of discovering an absolute best way of functioning in the diplomatic world, but of perceiving and employing, or merely gravitating toward, the method best suited to the governing system, the available talent, the diplomatic goals, the position in the world, of the particular state in question.

If one measures the effectiveness of these states' diplomatic efforts in the period as a whole according to the possibilities that existed and the goals actually found desirable, not according to "possibilities" too readily assumed by historians and goals unjustifiably imposed on the dead, it becomes apparent that, in spite of occasional failures and of the frequently modest scale of success, these states got about as much out of their diplomacy as possible. Generally, they were individually as successful as their own positions and aims and external circumstances allowed, and this, if nothing else, suggests that the particular diplomatic service of each, and the respective approach to diplomacy that underlay it, was indeed the one best designed for its own needs.

This is not to pretend that perfection existed, for of course it did not. But it does seem valid to suggest that historians' explanations of the course of international events ought to be concerned with such specific matters as individual action and judgment and such fundamental ones as the actual range and limit, positive and negative, of possibility, of the choices available, the decisions feasible, much more than with the "appropriateness" of a state's diplomacy in general, a middle-sized matter that provides a temptingly easy but wholly inadequate explanation of why things turned out as they did. One of the more conspicuous examples may illustrate the matter: James I did not succeed in imposing his solutions on Europe (increasingly troubled during the latter half of his reign), which has traditionally been given the omnibus explanation of an irresolute approach to diplomacy, but if one gives proper credit to his specific mistakes in specific cases, recognizes the extent of what he did do successfully, and measures the rest within the context of what England at that specific time was capable of doing in the situation at hand, not nearly so much remains to be disposed of by that facile catch-all.

But it has not been my purpose to describe patterns which were irrelevant to events or are irrelevant to the writing of history: a good deal can be learned from them about what guided events. Little, however, can be learned from measuring their appropriateness by an absolute standard, by a single ideal pattern. The most fundamental matter was the individual state's need, while not violating the general European pattern, to follow a variation within it that would most satisfactorily serve that particular sort of government, with its particular resources, problems, and goals. The appropriateness of the way in which it handled its diplomacy should be measured against an individual ideal way, not a general one. And if, as argued here, the various states' individual patterns were organic adjustments to unique combinations of positive and negative circumstance, then a state's *ideal* pattern was its *usual* pattern.

This, I think, has a double relevance. On the one hand, aberrations and lapses from normal procedures offer possible explanations of diplomatic successes and failures of a sort not to be had by assuming that diplomatic defeat is *prima facie* evidence of inadequate diplomacy, for this latter, in granting at least momentary single-cause status to diplomatic effectiveness, not only assumes that bad diplomacy explains defeat but implies that good diplomacy explains victory, which in turn robs historical analysis of the numerous other multiple causes, and indeed distorts the relevance of diplomatic effectiveness itself. On the other hand, failure of "proven" methods in a situation in which they had been successful before might suggest inquiry into the possibility that unnoticed changes have occurred in the government or its position, changes to which its diplomacy has not yet adjusted, or that undetected elements in the situation make it in fact substantially different from what one had supposed.

In addition to being a significant part of the European context, these patterns can thus sometimes be useful to historians both in those cases in which the approach to diplomacy was well adapted to conditions and those in which it was not. The argument of this essay, however, has been that the former was generally true. But if the diplomatic machinery of the nascent modern state was this good (one has not of course said perfect), one may very well ask why, by the beginning of the 1620s, diplomacy became so completely ineffective as a means of settling international disputes, and continued so for decades.

The answer, I think, is a double one, and doubly tragic. The deeper divisions of Europe had only been papered over, had not really been settled by earlier diplomatic "solutions." Definitive settlement of the fundamental issues would have required a sacrifice of principle by at least one side, and this was considered unacceptable; there was a limit to how long their resolution could be delayed, and they ultimately proved non-negotiable. Practical issues could be settled by compromise and concession, but for ideological ones men were willing, even eager, to die, and of course to kill; only after a generation of bloodshed did Europe decide that such things were irrelevant to international affairs.

The second part of the answer is just as ironic: the diplomatic machinery may actually have been too good. Or at least too convenient and attractive a recourse for a world that had not yet learned from experience that when diplomatic activity and agreement are proliferated beyond a certain point for too long, diplomacy loses its currency and sworn settlement its sanctity. The machinery was good, the issues many, and diplomacy was resorted to with increasing frequency from the end of the sixteenth century through the long period of armed peace to the generalization of disputes into the Thirty Years' War. The machinery for permanent settlement of profound differences was increasingly used to achieve temporary, even momentary, gains: perpetual treaties that no one expected to last more than a few weeks or months; delays by negotiating treaties with no intention of concluding them; unenforceable agreements that depended upon enforcement; agreements so contrary to one's own interests that they must be dishonored later. Such reckless use of the apparatus of peace could not do otherwise than undermine its effectiveness and eventually rob the guilty states themselves, in times of crisis, of the last alternative to war save surrender.

It would be unfair, of course, to say that the greatest flaw of diplomacy in the period was that it was too well devised. But one can say without question that it ultimately failed because there was simply too much of it.

NOTES

1. The Baltic states, arbitrarily omitted from this treatment, might arbitrarily be classed under this heading. It may suffice here to say that their diplomatic activity expanded and contracted as their individual importance increased and waned.

2. The question of exceptions to this is rather academic, as most of the apparent ones were in the Habsburgs' own patrimony.

3. Both terms were also used in the generic sense. "Nuncio" could mean *1.* a papal envoy, *2.* any envoy, or *3.* any agent; see, *e.g.*, *Archivo General de Simancas, Sección de Estado*, 7031/119 (hereafter cited as Est.). The term "agent leiger" was used colloquially for "resident."

4. Headed "Los embajadores que residen de ordinario en la corte del Rey de España, y las partes fuera della donde el Rey los tiene y quales se llaman embajadores, y quales agentes," British Museum, Additional Manuscripts 10236/445–6 (hereafter cited as Add.). The Spanish also apparently considered their envoy to Tuscany to be permanent and of full rank (British Museum, Harleian Manuscripts, 3569/165v.). *Biblioteca Nacional de Madrid, Sección de Manuscritos,* 2353/216 is an interesting eighty-one-page Italian pamphlet on why the Grisons accepted no residents at all.

5. Sir John Digby (amb. ord. to Spain 1611–16) to James I, Madrid, February 12, 1614, Public Record Office, SP 94/21/40–41 (English spelling modernized).

6. Legation secretaries could also attain the permanent post. *E.g.*, William Trumbull (d. 1635) succeeded Sir Thomas Edmondes (see note 20) as English resident in Brussels, 1609–25. For the converse case of Jean-Baptiste Van Male, see my *Secret Diplomacy of the*

Habsburgs, 1598–1625 (New York: Columbia University Press; 1964), chaps. 11, 13 ff.

7. Though a special mission had no occasion for a *chargé,* there is a seeming analogue in the resident left after successful peace negotiations at one of the combatants' court. But it was the monarch's oath that cued the re-establishment of a permanent legation, necessarily delayed at the other capitals involved.

8. Perhaps the most conspicuous was the English mission to take Philip III's oath to the Treaty of London, of which countless descriptions exist. The taking of oaths to treaties of alliance was more simply done. The actual negotiation of a peace treaty was done by several commissioners accredited for each party, and often met on neutral ground—substantially different from the more usual extraordinary embassies.

9. Two examples of early 1621 are not uncommon: The Maréchal de Cadenet (brother of the Duc de Luynes), as extraordinary ambassador to James I, refused to allow the French resident Tillières any part in his negotiations or even to know the purpose of his mission; Fernand de Boisschot did the same to the Archduke's resident de Vicq in Paris. Such cases caused much ill feeling and needlessly undermined the resident's prestige and effectiveness. *E.g.,* Van Male to the Archduke Albert, London, January 15, 1621, *Archives Générales du Royaume de Belgique, Manuscrits de Vienne, Répertoire P, Section C,* 57/26–29v. (hereafter cited as MV); Gondomar to Philip III, London, January 16, 1621, Est. 7031/23; de Vicq to Charles della Faille, Paris, May 28, 1621, in MV 29. Tanneguy Leveneur (d. 1652), Seigneur de Carouges, Comte de Tillières, was later chamberlain to Queen Henriette Marie; Add. 20762/56. Boisschot (d. 1648), Seigneur (baron 1622) de Savanthan, Comte d'Erps (1645), had himself been resident in London 1610–15 and Paris 1617–20. Henri de Vicq, Sire de Meulevelt, was Brussels' resident in Paris 1620–30.

10. For example John Digby reports on Spain's appointment for a sensitive mission in 1612: "Don Pedro de Zúñiga (who I doubt not is well known to Your Lordship) is elected ambassador extraordinary into England. . . . The king, to qualify him the better for this employment, hath very lately made him Marquis de Floresdávila, and hath bestowed upon him 2,000 crowns a year rent for three lives and sixteen thousand crowns ayuda de costa for the defraying of his journey. The causes (as I understand) which hath

moved them to make election of Don Pedro for this employment have been principally these two. First, for that in regard of the favors which Their Majesties in England were pleased to do him and the testimonies which they gave him at his return of their extraordinary approbation of his courses and carriage, they are of opinion that he will be a man very welcome and well seen in England. The second reason of his sending is, for that the chief reason for his employment being to give an account unto His Majesty of the marriages betwixt France and this crown, they hope with this color the more to justify their own proceedings. . . ." Digby to Salisbury, Madrid, March 28, 1621 OS, SP 94/19/52–56 (spelling modernized).

11. And, one hopes, the least equivocal, not wanting to engage here in a debate on the proper use of the term "modern state."

12. For tenures see, *e.g.*, Add. 20760.

13. See, *e.g.*, G. N. Clark and W. J. M. van Eysinga, *Colonial conferences between England and The Netherlands, 1613 and 1615,* (2 vols, Leyden, 1940–51), and (for December, 1620–September, 1622) Add. 30,069.

14. When seeking French support as the expiration of the Truce of Antwerp (April 10, 1621) neared; see, *e.g.*, William Sterrell to [Charles della Faille], [London], February 24, 1621, MV 57/97. If for no other reason than numbers, *all* members were not necessarily deputies to the States General; others were typically holders of other high political positions, and of the same general class.

15. In "The nature of Spanish government after Philip II," *The Historian,* Vol. 1, no. 1 (November, 1963), I have attempted to show that effective government power lay not only in the conciliar bodies but specifically in the Council of State, and that this was, in fact, quite a well-conceived system.

16. Spanish ambassadors to the Archdukes Albert and Isabella were a major exception; see Joseph Lefèvre, "Les ambassadeurs d'Espagne à Bruxelles sous le règne de l'archiduc Albert (1598–1621)," *Revue belge de philologie at d'histoire,* II (1923), pp. 61–80 (which has an error of detail: Felipe Cordona, Marqués de Guadaleste, did not serve 1606–19; he died 1616, and the post was vacant for three years); I have described the alternative channels of liaison in "Belgian 'autonomy' under the Archdukes, 1598–1621," *The Journal of Modern History,* Vol. 37, no. 1 (September, 1964).

17. For Diego Sarmiento de Acuña, Conde de Gondomar, see my "Gondomar: Ambassador to James I," *The Historical Journal* (Fall, 1964), and references there. Iñigo Vélez de Guevara, Conde de Oñate, and Baltasar de Zúñiga are discussed in Garrett Mattingly's *Renaissance Diplomacy* (Boston and London, 1955) and Bohdan Chudoba's *Spain and the Empire, 1519–1543* (Chicago, 1952). Pierre Jeannin, president of the Parlement de Dijon, and Jean Richardot, Sire de Barley, *chef-président* of the Privy Council (Brussels), were prime movers in the almost continuous series of peace conferences from the later 1590s to 1609. Juan Bautista de Tassis, Conde de Villamediana, among many diplomatic services, headed the mission sent to negotiate the Treaty of London (the higher ranking Constable of Castile arrived later), after which Pedro de Zúñiga, Marqués de Floresdávila, became the first Spanish resident in England in more than two decades.

18. See, *e.g.*, the records of his French and Latin secretaries in Add. 12,485 and 38,597. Discussions with ambassadors were often delegated to the Privy Council or commissions drawn from it.

19. But not always: Trumbull (see note 7), for example, was not.

20. Their residencies: Charles Cornwallis, Spain 1605–09; Walter Aston, Spain 1620–25, 1635–38; George Carew, France 1605–09; Thomas Edmondes, Brussels 1604–09, France 1610–17 (with two long absences); Ralph Winwood, France 1601–02 (as sec. had been frequently *chargé* 1599–1601), The Hague 1603–14; Dudley Carleton, Venice 1610–15, The Hague 1616–25. Fairly typically, most were knighted not more than two years before becoming residents, and Winwood not until 1607. Aston became a baron in the Scottish peerage 1627, Carleton a baron 1626 and Viscount Dorchester 1628—*i.e.*, both in Charles I's reign; by contrast, Digby became a baron 1618 and a bit later Earl of Bristol. Digby was also used frequently by James I as ambassador extraordinary after having been a resident; of the others, only those surviving the reign were so used to any extent. Of these, Carleton's extraordinary embassies to France 1625–26 and The Hague 1626–28 illustrate how extended such missions could be.

21. John Robert Seeley, *The growth of British policy*, (2 vols, Cambridge, 1897), I, pp. 263–4, 280.

22. See, *e.g.*, Add. 20761–2, 20764.

23. *E.g.*, Frederick V, at the time of his defeat in the Bohemian War, was represented in Paris by the Sieur de Borstel.

24. Even when the Spanish government itself was disordered; see, *e.g.*, François de Bassompierre, *Ambassade du maréchal de Bassompierre en Espagne l'an 1621* (Cologne, 1668).

25. See, *e.g.*, the high number of extraordinary missions in Add. 20761-2 and 20764-5.

26. There is unfortunately not room for such a comprehensive illustration in so brief an essay. A partial one is implicit in the book cited in note 7 above.

27. The most convenient documentation for this duel between Gondomar and Samuel de Spifame, Sieur de Buisseaux, is in *Correspondencia oficial de Don Diego Sarmiento de Acuña, Conde de Gondomar*, Antonio Ballesteros Beretta, ed. Vols I–IV of *Documentos inéditos para la historia de España*, new series (Madrid, 1936–45), Vols III–IV.

THE MANY-HEADED MONSTER
IN LATE TUDOR AND
EARLY STUART
POLITICAL THINKING

CHRISTOPHER

HILL

Master of Balliol College,

Oxford

M ost writers about politics during the century before 1640 agreed that democracy was a bad thing: from Sir Philip Sidney and Sir Thomas Smith to a conservative Parliamentarian like Richard Baxter, a defender of the Good Old Cause like Henry Stubbe, or a detached observer like Francis Osborn.[1] "The people" were fickle, unstable, incapable of rational thought: the headless multitude, the many-headed monster. The educated could find confirmation of this prejudice in classical Greek or Latin literature; they could also find it in current theology, Protestant and Catholic alike, which assumed the natural wickedness of the mass of the population. Government was a consequence of the Fall: democracy, by handing power to the sinful majority, would defeat the objects of government.

But of course the men of property did not need to go to church or university to learn class hostility: it was a simple fact of the world in which they lived, so obvious that it was rarely discussed. 1549 had shown their dependence on the central power of the monarchy.[2] "So hated at this time was the name of worship or gentleman that the basest of the people, burning with more than hostile hatred, desired to extinguish and utterly cut off" the gentry. In Norfolk, where "all have conceived a wonderful hate against gentlemen and taketh them all as their enemies," they were driven out of the county, and had to wait till the government sent foreign mercenaries to restore them. Meanwhile men were saying "there are too many gentlemen in England by 500"; "gentlemen have ruled aforetime, and they [*i.e.,* the commons] will rule now."[3] Norwich, second city of the kingdom, had been at the mercy of the peasantry too; in Cambridge the non-freemen seized the opportunity to assert their rights against the citizen oligarchy. Hence the class solidarity, among gentlemen and merchants alike, which bridged the religious differences of the later sixteenth and seventeenth centuries.[4] In all countries of Western Europe the period of peasant revolts was the period of the formation of absolute monarchies.

In the famine year of 1596 there were anti-enclosure riots in Derbyshire, rumblings in Northants and Somerset, where men "stick not to say boldly, They must not starve, they will not starve." There was a minor rising in Oxfordshire, whose aim was "to knock down the gentlemen and rich men"; the rebels hoped that they would be joined by the London apprentices, who had themselves been rioting. If "the ruder sort" were "privy to their own strength and liberty allowed them by the law," a Member of Parliament observed in 1597, they "would be as unbridled and untamed beasts."[5] In 1607, another year of bad harvests and high prices, men called "Levellers" and "Diggers" rose in Northamptonshire, Warwickshire, and Leicestershire. There was support from craftsmen and the poorer sort of the town of Leicester, who for a time scared the ruling burgesses.[6] Shakespeare's *Coriolanus* first appeared on the stage in 1607.

The lean years 1628–31 again saw much violence. The Crown was forced to give up land which it had tried to claim in the Forest of Dean. The High Sheriff of Gloucestershire was "soon and easily repulsed by . . . base and disorderly people." In Kent and Rutlandshire there was seditious talk and threats of violence. In Wiltshire royal enclosure gave rise to "extreme discontent" which expressed itself in "popular revolts" which "ushered in the Great Rebellion."[7] There were also agrarian disturbances in Dorset, Worcestershire, Shropshire, and riots against the draining of the fens.

The idea that to be many-headed is the same as to be headless is easier to conceive metaphorically than literally. It relates to the theory of degree, to the conception of a graded society in which the feudal household and the family workshop or farm were the basic units. The many-headed monster was composed of masterless men, those for whom nobody responsible answered. Dread and hatred of the masses were often reflected in literature. In Sidney's *Arcadia,* whenever "the many-headed multitude" appears, we are in for naturalistic violence that contrasts as sharply with the artificial scenes of shepherds' life as does the brutality of depopulating enclosure with the splendors of Penshurst which resulted from it. In Laconia there was permanent civil war and bitter hatred between "the base multitude" and the gentry. In Arcadia the violence of "the unruly sort of clowns" was wholly irrational: "like a violent flood," they were "carried, they themselves knew not whither." "Like enraged beasts," they "show the right nature of a villein, never thinking his estate happy but when he is able to do hurt." "The mad multitude" was utterly disorganized; "he only seemed to have most pre-eminence that was most rageful."[8] Once liquor gave them Dutch courage, "public affairs were mingled with private grudges, . . . railing was counted the fruit of freedom; . . . disdainful reproaches to great persons had put a shadow of greatness in their little minds." They declared that "their blood and sweat must maintain all, . . . the country was theirs and the government adherent to the country."[9] "They had the glorious shadow of a commonwealth with them." "So, to their minds (once past the bounds of obedience), more and more wickedness opened itself." "A popular licence is indeed the many-headed tyranny." Naturally, when faced with such a "rascal company," the chivalrous princes used their superior weapons to cut off vulgar arms, legs, and heads in the most amusing manner.[10]

So for the gentle Sidney, who within limits was a liberal constitutionalist in his politics. The sweet Spenser had an equally

virulent hatred and fear of the lower orders. I hasten to quote, to
show that this is not putting it too strongly:

> Then as he spoke, lo! with outrageous cry
> A thousand villeins round about them swarmed
> Out of the rocks and caves adjoining nigh:
> Vile caitiff wretches, ragged, rude, deformed. . . .

In Book V (Of Justice) there is a curious passage on egalitarianism.
It is the Giant speaking:

> For why, he said, they all unequal were,
> And had encroached upon others' share;
> Like as the sea (which plain he shewed there)
> Had worn the earth, so did the fire, the air;
> So all the rest did others' parts impair,
> And so were realms and nations run awry.
> All which he undertook for to repair,
> In sort as they were formed anciently,
> And all things would reduce unto equality.
>
> Therefore the vulgar did about him flock,
> And cluster thick unto his leasings vain,
> Like foolish flies about an honey-crock,
> In hope of him great benefit to gain
> And uncontrolled freedom to obtain.

Artegall, when he saw "how he misled the simple people's train,"
talked Aristotelianism to the Giant. But the latter, reasonably
enough, replied:

> Seest not how badly all things present be,
> And each estate quite out of order go'th? . . .
> Were it not good that wrong were then surceas'd
> And from the most that some were given to the least?
>
> Therefore I will throw down these mountains high,
> And make them level with the lowly plain;
> These tow'ring rocks, which reach unto the sky,
> I will thrust down into the deepest main,
> And, as they were, them equalize again.
> Tyrants, that make men subject to their law,

> I will suppress, that they no more may reign;
> And lordings curb that commons over-awe,
> And all the wealth of rich men to the poor will draw.

Spenser must have heard someone saying that. Artegall's not unfamiliar reply was to introduce the will of the Almighty, in a passage of heartfelt eloquence. Talus then flung the Giant into the sea, and routed with his flail the popular revolt which followed, since Artegall was loth

> his noble hands t' imbrue
> In the base blood of such a rascal crew.[11]

The contempt for the lower orders shown by Shakespeare's Coriolanus, who "stuck not to call" Roman citizens "the many-headed multitude," need not necessarily represent the dramatist's point of view; nor need Sir Humphrey Stafford, who described Jack Cade's followers as "rebellious hinds, the filth and scum of Kent"; "a ragged multitude of hinds and peasants, rude and merciless." What is interesting is the type of argument which Shakespeare puts into the mouths of the rebels: virtue and labor should be more regarded than birth; "it was never merry world since gentlemen came up": "Adam was a gardener." Prices are too high, lawyers and clerks fleece the poor. J.P.s "call poor men before them about matters they were not able to answer." Cade looked upon education as a class privilege, as indeed it often was: "because they could not read, thou hast hanged them." He proposed to burn all legal records, "and henceforward all things shall be in common." His supporters are patriotic, and accuse the aristocracy of treacherous relations with the national enemy—as Roman citizens might have accused Coriolanus—as well as of clothing their horses better than workingmen. Cade's appeal was to the "clouted shoon," as Lilburne's was to be later: "for they are thrifty honest men." In London "the rascal people" joined the rebels, whilst "the citizens fly and forsake their houses"! Cade was eventually overcome, he insisted, "by famine, not by valour."[12]

Shakespeare was clearly a good listener, and his attitude seems to have been relatively detached. More common was Barnabe Googe's contempt for "crabbed clowns," "dunghill dogs," "peasants vile," when they presumed to rise in revolt. Characters in Dekker's plays referred to "that wild beast multitude,"

> this many-headed Cerberus,
> This pied chameleon, this beast multitude, . . .
> This heap of fools.[13]

Sir Thomas Browne despised "that great enemy of reason, virtue and religion, the multitude, that numerous piece of monstrosity which . . . confused together make but one great beast." The mild Thomas Fuller said of "the headless multitude" that the greatest cruelties "might be expected from servile natures when they command." "The people," the Leveller Walwyn remarked ironically, "is a pitiful, mean, helpless thing, as under schoolmasters in danger to be whipped and beaten in case they meddle without leave and license from their master."[14]

] II [

This contemptuous attitude thinly concealed the fears of the propertied class. "In time of peace," asked Sir Richard Morison in the year of the Pilgrimage of Grace, "be not all men almost at war with them that be rich?" Magistrates existed to keep rich and poor from conflict, Francis Thynne believed about the time of the rising of the Northern Earls. Sir Thomas Smith in 1565, Sir Thomas Aston in 1641, and the Duke of Albemarle in 1671 all agreed that "the poorer and meaner people . . . have no interest in the commonweal but the use of breath," and "no account is made of them, but only to be ruled." Parliament, consisting of the nobility and gentry, dispenses "the rules of government; the plebeians submit to and obey them." But, the Duke added with the experience of a revolutionary general, the multitude "are always dangerous to the peace of a kingdom, and having nothing to lose, willingly embrace all means of innovation, in the hope of gaining something by other men's ruin."[15] "The meaner sort of people," Sir John Oglander agreed in 1630, are "always apt to rebel and mutiny . . . on the least occasion." To prevent this the landed class—the armigerous—

carried weapons; "the meaner sort of people and servants" were normally excluded even from the militia.[16]

The state was the main support of the propertied class. "If there were not a king," James I reminded J.P.s in 1616, "they would be less cared for than other men." "The authority of the king," Sir Thomas Wentworth agreed, "is the keystone which closeth up the arch of order and government, which keepeth each part in due relation to the whole." "Without laws," said a pamphlet of 1629, "the beast with many heads will . . . be head of all," and society will be at the mercy of "the rage of the harrowing multitude." But for sovereignty, a preacher at Paul's Cross confirmed in March, 1642, "the honourable would be levelled with the base, . . . and all would be . . . huddled up in an unjust parity." So obvious was the connection between law and property that there were those, from Sir Thomas More onwards, who saw every government as "nothing but a certain conspiracy of rich men procuring their own commodities under the name and title of the commonwealth." But the view that "all orders, policies, kingdoms and dominions" originated from the devil, or from pride and covetousness, and were nothing but "cruel tyranny and oppression of the poor," was normally confined to "the unlearned and ungodly people": we hear of this position only when their betters are refuting it.[17] Class distinctions in the administration of justice were usually taken for granted.[18]

"The poor hate the rich," said Deloney in 1597, "because they will not set them on work; and the rich hate the poor, because they seem burdensome."[19] In the century before 1640 the standard of living of the mass of the population was steadily declining, whilst the wealth of the rich was visibly increasing. In a city like Exeter harsh poverty was the lot of more than half the population, who had no reserves to meet a crisis such as unemployment or famine. "The fourth part of the inhabitants of most of the parishes of England are miserable poor people, and (harvest time excepted) without any subsistence," said a pamphlet of 1641. This helps us to understand the panic fear of disturbance which government and propertied class showed, and the readiness with which the lower orders resorted to violence in famine years. One consequence of the economic and social changes of the period was vagabondage—roving bands of beggars who were past the possibility of working and who terrorized their betters, animating others "to all contempt both of noblemen and gentlemen, continually buzzing into their ears that the rich men have gotten all into their hands and will starve the poor." "A rabble of rogues, cutpurses and the like mischievous men, slaves in nature though not in law," was the description given by Smyth of Nibley, looking back regretfully to the good old days of serfdom.[20]

The number of such "able men that are abroad seeking the spoil and confusion of the land" was kept down by the wholesale massacres of the law courts. Seventy-four persons were sentenced to death in Devon in 1598, a hundred and sixty in Middlesex in fourteen months of 1614–15; fifty-seven of the latter escaped by pleading benefit of clergy, which helps to explain the hatred of education shown by Shakespeare's Jack Cade. Some were hanged for being without visible means of livelihood. But the beneficent efforts of the courts to solve the problem of vagabondage by hanging were hampered by the fact that "most commonly the simple countrymen and women . . . would not procure a man's death for all the goods in the world," and so failed to prosecute. Hanging, however, was not the only solution. Edward Hext, whose report on vagabonds I have quoted, left £1,000 to found an almshouse in Somerton. The switch in charitable giving from ecclesiastical to secular objects, notably to poor relief and education, which Professor Jordan has so fully documented, may testify to the social fears as well as to the generous sentiments of the rich. One of the arguments put forward in propaganda for colonizing Virginia in 1612 (and on many similar occasions) was that "the rank multitude" might be exported.[21]

] III [

It was the duty of the Church to soften the bitterness of class hatred, to keep the lower orders peaceful and subordinate, to stress the religious considerations which united a hierarchical society against the economic facts which so visibly divided it, to console the desperate. The *Homilies* spoke clearly: "It is an intolerable ignorance, madness and wickedness for subjects to make any murmuring, rebellion, resistance or withstanding, commotion or insurrection." Lucifer was the author of rebellion. "What a perilous thing were it to commit unto the subjects the judgment which prince is wise and godly, and his government good, and which is otherwise; as though the foot must judge of the head. . . . Who are most ready to the greatest mischiefs but the worst men?"[22] Sir Thomas Browne was thus thoroughly orthodox in thinking it was "no breach of charity" to call the multitude fools. "It is . . . a point of our faith to believe so."[23] That "the greatest multitude" was "for the most part always wicked" was accepted by all parties in the Church. Archbishop Parker, who in 1549 had been derided by the Norfolk rebels as a hireling, asked ten years later "what Lord of the Council shall ride quietly-minded in the streets among desperate beasts," if it be "referred to the judgment of the subject, of the tenant, and of the servant, to discuss what is tyranny, and to discern whether his prince, his landlord, his master is a tyrant?" Archbishop Whitgift thought that "the people . . . are commonly bent to novelties and to factions, and most ready to receive that doctrine that seemeth to be contrary to the present state, and that inclineth to liberty." Yet Presbyterians were not democrats either: Knox himself had no use for "the rascal multitude," "the godless multitude."[24]

The sects, especially those which their enemies called Anabaptist, tended to express democratic political heresies as well as doctrinal heresies. Anabaptists, said Nashe comprehensively, were "such as thought they knew as much of God's mind as richer men." "Every man is now counted an Anabaptist if he does not maintain monarchy to be *jure divino*," said Francis Cheynell in 1643. "The Anabaptists are men that will not be shuffled out of their birthright as free-born people of England," wrote one of their defenders in 1655.[25] Anabaptists were regularly accused of adovcating communism, and this clearly corresponded to a popular desire. Lever in 1550 thought that the addiction of the lower orders to communism resulted from lack of preaching and the oppression of the rich; forty years later Bishop Cooper was still denouncing Anabaptists who wanted communism and "a general equality, most dangerous to the society of men." The well-known passage in Spenser's *Mother Hubberds Tale,* in which the Fox advocates a division of landlord's land, attributed communism to laziness. But the Fox's rejection of wage-labor is interesting, since the point seems to have been made by some of the Oxfordshire rebels of 1596, and was to reappear in the program of the Diggers in 1649–50. As late as 1631 it was being alleged that Puritanism led to communism.[26]

Presbyterians tried to curb the dangers of Anabaptism by preaching, discipline, Sabbatarianism, and an insistence on the religious duties of heads of households; and by emphasizing that revolt was never justified unless led by magistrates, who would come from the propertied class. Once the Church had lost its magical controls—confession, absolution (by which "the consciences of the people" were "kept in so great awe," Aubrey said), indulgences, the sacraments—preaching seemed to middle-of-the-road men the best way of influencing the sinful multitude, congregational discipline of controlling it. Yet Presbyterians themselves were open to the charge that they were unleashing the many-headed monster. Marprelate's mockery of bishops shocked many conservatives; and no less a person than John Field declared, in despair of Parliament, "it is the multitude and people that must bring the discipline to pass which we desire."[27] This must have seemed little better than Browne's *Reformation without Tarrying for Anie.*

Bishops were held in "loathsome contempt, hatred and disdain" by "the most part of men," a bishop admitted in 1589. So they had reason to point out that "if you had once made an equality . . . among the clergy, it would not be long ere you attempted the same among the laity." The point was taken up by the Earl of Hertford in 1589—in reaction, significantly, to the Marprelate Tracts: "As they shoot at bishops now, so will they do at the nobility also, if they be suffered."[28] On the eve of the civil war, Edmund Waller looked upon episcopacy "as a counter-scarp or outwork," and was especially anxious that it should not "be taken by this assault of the people." For then the "mystery . . . that we must deny them nothing when they ask in troops" would be revealed. "We may in the next place have as hard a task to defend our property. . . . If by multiplying hands and petitions they prevail for an equality in things ecclesiastical, their next demand perhaps may be . . . the like equality in things temporal. . . . You may be presented with a thousand instances of poor men that have received hard measure from their landlords."[29]

The social case for episcopacy was most elaborately stated in a petition from the gentry of Cheshire in December, 1641: Presbyterianism "must necessarily produce an extermination of nobility, gentry and order, if not of religion." Presbyterianism, added Sir Thomas Aston, would be "dangerous doctrine if once grounded in vulgar apprehensions." "The old seditious argument will be obvious to them, that we are all the sons of Adam, born free; some of them say the Gospel hath made them free. And law once subverted, it will appear good equity to such Chancellors to share the earth equally. They will plead Scripture for it, that we should all live by the sweat of our brows. . . . The empty name of liberty, blown into vulgar ears, hath overturned many states." Aston admitted that gentlemen might be able to control presbyterian elections at first, and "keep the vulgar low enough." But annual elections would amount to a civil war in every parish.[30]

] IV [

Conservatives always hated anything like an appeal to opinion outside the ruling class. James Morice, who had attacked the oath *ex officio*, was told in 1593 that "her Majesty would have me to be admonished . . . if aught were amiss in the Church or Commonwealth, I should not straightway make it known to the common sort, but declare it to her Majesty or some of her Privy Council." Burleigh noted with disapproval in 1595 that "some . . . do secretly entice the vulgar sort to be vehement in desiring" Puritan reforms. "Nowadays there is no vulgar, but all statesmen," commented Bacon wryly, who did not love "the word 'people.' "[31]

In 1629 the Commons really did begin to appeal to the people, in the three resolutions against Popery, Arminianism, and tonnage and poundage. In 1640, even worse, the lower orders were encouraged to sign the Root and Branch Petition, and it was supported by popular demonstrations. In May, 1641, the Protestation was issued to be taken by people all over the country, with the object of rallying support for Parliament. When, in November, Hampden proposed printing the Grand Remonstrance, he was told "You want to raise the people and get rid of the Lords." During the debates Sir Edward Dering had protested against "this descension from a Parliament to the people." "I did not dream that we should remonstrate downward, tell stories to the people, and talk of the King as of a third person." "I neither look for cure of our complaints from the common people, nor do desire to be cured by them." "Considering the necessity of a multitude," it was not good to wake a sleepy lion, Holles told the House of Lords early in February, 1642, a few days after a petition had been presented by fifteen thousand laborers and men of "the meanest rank and quality."[32] Within four years the lion began to roar.

] V [

Historians, I believe, have consistently underestimated the significance of popular tumults in the immediate origins of civil war.[33] As early as February, 1641, Lord Digby was warning that it was unfit "for a Parliament under a monarchy to give countenance to irregular and tumultuous assemblies of people, be it for never so good an end." He foresaw untold dangers "when either true or pretended stimulation of conscience hath once given a multitude agitation." Fiennes replied by asking "whether an act of will in us may not produce an act of will in the people?" A gentleman of Kent said at about the same time "it is thought that things are already gone so far," and the poor driven to such necessity, that outrages could not be prevented. "We must take care," an M.P. warned in October, "that the common people may not carve themselves out justice by their multitudes. Of this we have too frequent experience," he added, referring to anti-enclosure and other riots. In January, 1642, Pym drew attention to the risk of "tumults and insurrections of the meaner sort of people. . . . Nothing is more sharp and pressing than necessity and want; what they cannot buy they will take." There might be general insurrection by "the multitude."[34]

Already Archbishop Williams had warned the Parliamentarians that "you will make so many masters to yourselves that we shall all be slaves." "When the beast did imagine it was loose from the chain of monarchy and laws, who could tie it up again?" Williams' biographer asked. James Howell in 1642 foresaw "anarchical confusions and fearful calamities . . . unless with the pious care which is already taken to hinder the great Beast to break into the vineyard there be also a speedy course taken to fence her from other vermin and lesser animals (the *belluam multorum capitum*)."[35]

In London there were demonstrations and riots at every major political crisis from May, 1640, onwards. In *Eikon Basilike* Charles I was made to emphasize the influence of such popular tumults on Parliament, "like an earthquake, shaking the very foundations of all." They were reinforced by "the multitude, who from all the counties come daily in thousands with petitions to the Houses" and created panic among the "popish and malignant" gentry. One of Fairfax's correspondents in January, 1642, reflected that "the insurrections of the apprentices (as all ungoverned multitudes) are of very dangerous consequence." He consoled himself by the thought that "God, who works miracles, can out of such violent actions bring comfortable effects."[36] But would God always work a miracle? This was the vital question: men's answers to it might determine the side they took in the civil war.

In Gloucestershire, God seemed to be on Parliament's side. For there the royal commission of array was "crushed by the rude hand of the multitude before it saw the light, . . . by the meanest of the people." "That fury that took hold of the ignoble multitude" led them on to sack the house of the leading local royalist. "Their insolency becomes intolerable," said the Parliamentarian historian of the siege of Gloucester. "Nevertheless, they have produced good effects, and oft times a more undiscerned guidance of superior agents turns them to the terror of the enemy, and inexplicable self-engagement upon the common people, which prudent men promote and maintain, yet no further than themselves can over-rule and moderate." Thus, in Gloucestershire, God helped those who helped themselves, just as there were those who alleged that Pym and Pennington called up mobs in London when they needed them. But this was a dangerous game, especially as the economic situation deteriorated. There were riots against enclosure in Durham, Yorkshire, Huntingdonshire, Lincolnshire, Cambridgeshire, Norfolk, Hertfordshire, Middlesex, Somerset, Dorset, Wiltshire, and Cornwall; forest riots in Northamptonshire, Essex, Surrey, Hampshire, Berkshire. In May, 1642, the House of Commons heard with disapproval of rioters against enclosure in the fens who had also said that "the King should shortly be no longer King there." Even in Gloucestershire it was found that "the needy multitude, besides their natural hatred of good order, were at the devotion of rich men," who might not be Parliamentarians.[37]

"The rude multitude in divers counties took advantage of those civil and intestine broils to plunder and pillage the houses of the nobility, gentry and others." Any rich man was liable to be labeled a malignant. In August, 1642, "the King having left the Parliament, and thereby a loose rein being put into the mouth of the unruly multitude," "many thousands" turned out to sack the Countess of Rivers' house in Essex. At Milford "no man appeared like a gentleman, but was made a prey to that ravenous crew. . . . So monstrous is the beast when it holds the bridle in its teeth." "The rude people are come to such a head," said Major Thomas Wade of Colchester, also in August, "that we know not how to quiet them." "The gentry . . . have been our masters a long time," "vulgar hearts" were saying in Oxfordshire; "and now we may chance to master them." Now the lower classes have learnt their strength, Sir Thomas Gardiner reflected, "it shall go hard but they will use it."[38]

"If we take not advantage of this time," said an opponent of enclosure in Essex in April, 1643, "we shall never have the opportunity again." In July a rioter in Northamptonshire hoped "within this year to see never a gentleman in England." In Chelmsford the common people were said to have determined that they would no longer be "kept under blindness and ignorance," or yield themselves "servants, nay slaves to the nobility and gentry." A royalist in the Isle of Wight thought that in 1642–43 the gentry "lived in slavery and submission to the unruly base multitude"; it was in the power of the commonalty "not only to abuse but plunder any gentleman" —a state of affairs which he rightly said had never before been seen in England. Charles I in his Declaration of October 23, 1642 played on social anxieties by speaking of "endeavours . . . to raise an implacable malice and hatred between the gentry and commonalty of the kingdom, . . . insomuch as the highways and villages have not been safe for gentlemen to pass through without violence or affront." By January, 1643, petitioners from Hertfordshire described how "the greatest number of people now (breaking the bonds of law) submit not themselves to government but threaten and commit outrages." They begged the House of Lords to protect them from "the violence and fury of all unruly and dissolute multitudes."[39]

It was "under pretence of religion" that "the lower sort of citizens . . . do challenge" liberty to themselves, Hobbes observed in 1641. The Parliamentarians, an enemy alleged, caused "the very dregs and scum of every parish to petition against the orthodox clergy." Again the question of riding the storm arose. Edward Bowles, chaplain successively to Manchester and Fairfax, said in 1643: "I am far from the monster of a democracy: that which I call to the people for is but a quick and regular motion in their own sphere."[40] But would the people remain in what their betters thought their own sphere? In London and many of the Home Counties they were escaping from the control of ministers. James Howell associated "those petty sectaries which swarm so in every corner" with "the many-headed monster" which was laying England open to "waste, spoil and scorn." In April, 1642, preachers were ominously quoting the lines

> When Adam delved and Eve span,
> Who was then the gentleman?

So we can understand why Henry Oxinden, belatedly agreeing with Waller and his friends, declared in November, 1643, that it was "high time for all gentlemen to . . . endeavour rather to maintain episcopal government . . . with some diminution in temporalities . . . than to introduce I know not what presbyterial government, which will . . . equalize men of mean conditions with the gentry." If the reins are let loose upon "the multitude (that senseless and furious beast)," they will "destroy all government, both in church and state," or bring in such a one wherein themselves . . . may be able to tyrannize over their betters, whom naturally they have ever hated and in their hearts despised."[41]

"I would not have the King trample on the Parliament," said Lord Savile in 1643, "nor the Parliament lessen him so much as to make a way for the people to rule us all." The remark goes far to explain Savile's frequent changes of side: and there were many like him. In the elections to the Short Parliament Serjeant Maynard found that "fellows without shirts" challenged "as good a voice as myself." He would "not easily suffer myself hereafter upon the persuasions of others to appear in any popular assemblies." A participant in the Army Plot exposed in May, 1641, explained that the conspirators feared lest "some turbulent spirits, backed by rude and tumultuous mechanic persons . . . would have the total subversion of the government of the state."[42] In Lancashire in November, 1642, the royalist High Sheriff summoned the gentry of the county to appear for the King, "who we know now suffers under the pride and insolency of a discontented people, also for the securing of our own lives and estates, which are now ready to be surprised by a heady multitude." Even the official historian of Parliament admitted that "some who were not bad men" objected to "that extreme license which the common people, almost from the very beginning of the Parliament, took to themselves of reforming without authority, order or decency."[43]

After civil war started, such social anxieties were alleged by many who deserted Parliament. Hotham in January, 1643, thought that if the war continued, "the necessitous people of the whole kingdom will presently rise in mighty numbers" and ultimately "set up for themselves, to the utter ruin of all the nobility and gentry of the kingdom." "If this unruly rout have once cast the rider, it will run like wildfire in the example through all the counties of England." "The nobility cannot fall if the King be victorious," thought the Marquis of Newcastle, Hotham's correspondent, "nor can they keep up their dignities if the King be overcome."[44]

By 1644 Lord Willoughby believed that "nobility and gentry are going down apace." The Earl of Westmorland warned the Parliamentarian Colonel Harley against "that monster parity," which "so much now seeks to domineer." Bulstrode Whitelocke was afraid that the ignoble would come to rule the noble. Even Parliament's general, the Earl of Essex, feared in December, 1644, lest "our posterity will say that to deliver them from the yoke of the King we have subjected them to that of the common people." He announced that henceforth he would "devote his life to redressing the audacity of the common people." Nobody knew where the sectaries would stop, Thomas Edwards observed in 1646, but they threatened all civil government. "The giddy-headed multitude" even called in question "the saving doctrines of eternal truth" on which the Presbyterian clergy based its supremacy.[45] There were social as well as religious reasons for opposing toleration.

] VI [

In January, 1643, Hotham had envisaged the possibility of the many-headed monster setting up against royalists and Parliamentarians alike. Six months later this seemed to be happening in Kent. On July 28 Sir Thomas Walsingham told the Commons that he had recently been captured by "tumultuary people" near Tunbridge, "most of them men of very mean and base condition." These persons "chiefly aimed at enriching themselves by the robbing and spoiling of such as were wealthy, intending to destroy the gentry."[46] In 1645 George Smith thought that the tyranny and unfair taxation of Parliamentary committees "put the people upon resolutions of setting up a third party." In that year the Clubmen of Somerset formed just such a third party, and were asking "whether the able and rich who will not join with us be not only counted ill-affected but liable to pay for the poor who do their county service?" The main center of the Clubmen was Somerset, Dorset, and Wiltshire; but there were similar movements in Devon, Hampshire, Sussex, Gloucestershire, Herefordshire, Shropshire, Worcestershire, and Glamorganshire.[47] Discontent with the taxation, plunder, and indiscipline which accompanied a prolonged war—the motives for the Clubman movement—forced upon Parliament the military and financial reorganization that produced the New Model Army, with its regular pay and strict discipline. The Clubmen were routed and dispersed.

But the hydra-headed monster was no sooner suppressed here than it reappeared in the rank and file of the Army itself, and in the Leveller party in London. If no agreement could be reached with the Army, an M.P. said in July, 1647, "clubs and clouted shoes will in the end be too hard for both." Lilburne boasted that his support came from "the hobnails, clouted shoes, the private soldiers, the leather and woollen aprons." At Putney in October, 1647, Sexby protested that "the poor and meaner of this kingdom" had won the war for Parliament, and Rainborough ominously added that the common soldier seemed to have "fought to enslave himself, to give power to men of riches, men of estates, to make him a perpetual slave." "Is not all the controversy whose slaves the poor shall be: whether they shall be the King's vassals or the Presbyterians' or the

Independent faction's?" asked a pamphleteer in January, 1648. In May, 1647, Overton had published *An Appeale From the degenerate Representative Body the Commons of England assembled at Westminster: To the Body Represented, the free people of England.* "This way of petitioning by multitude of hands to the Parliament, which was formerly promoted by some of both Houses as a means to carry on their designs at that time," Whitelocke observed dryly, "began now [1647] to be made use of and returned upon them, to their great trouble and danger."[48]

The Independents repressed the Levellers forcibly; but the subtle distinction between the two groups was too much for men like Denzil Holles and Clement Walker. The former wrote from his exile in 1649: "The wisest of men saw it to be a great evil that servants should ride on horses: an evil now both seen and felt in this unhappy kingdom. The meanest of men, the basest and vilest of the nation, the lowest of the people, have got the power into their hands; trampled upon the crown, baffled and ruined the Parliament, violated the laws; destroyed or suppressed the nobility and gentry of the kingdom; and now lord it over the persons and estates of all sorts and ranks of men." The object of the Rump, Walker thought, was "to raise the rascal multitude and schismatical rabble against all men of best quality in the kingdom." Thus some supporters of Parliament now thought (perhaps always had thought) that monarchy and property were indissolubly connected: the stage was set for Charles I's magnificent performance at his trial, and for the legend sedulously built up in *Eikon Basilike,* offering monarchy as the alternative to "the insolencies of popular dictates and tumultuary impressions," and calling on Parliament to shake off "this yoke of vulgar encroachment." For long after the crushing of the Levellers, Oliver Cromwell was able to make the flesh of his Parliaments creep by recalling how Levellers had proposed "to make the tenant as liberal a fortune as the landlord."[49]

Oliver spoke to men easily convinced. "There is no jewel which swine delight more to wear in their snouts than this of liberty," wrote John Gauden elegantly; though he had supported Parliament, he was to win a bishopric at the Restoration. "In these degenerating times," said two royalists in 1657, "the gentry had need to close nearer together, and make a bank and bulwark against that sea of democracy which is overrunning them." In 1659–60 panic increased. "We lay at the mercy and impulse of a giddy, hot-headed, bloody multitude," a Presbyterian believed. "The rabble hate both magistrates and ministers," wrote Richard Baxter, and if they were not bridled "they would presently have the blood of the godly," and also of "the more wealthy and industrious," whom Baxter perhaps identified with the godly. No tyrant was "so cruel as the many-headed tyrant; . . . it being the surest way to be always miserable, to be governed by them that are always naught, that is the multitude."[50]

So Charles II came home again, and with him "elective Parliaments, the bulwark of property." The Army was disbanded, sectaries persecuted, the jewel of liberty torn from the snouts of the swinish multitude. "It is certain that the greater number of men are bad," said the royalist Earl of Derby, explaining to his son why the people should be fooled for their own good; "reason will never persuade a senseless multitude."[51]

] VII [

I have established, I hope, the importance of the many-headed monster in the minds of contemporaries. One problem remains to be discussed: Why did that solidarity, which in the sixteenth century the monster helped to create among the propertied, break down after 1640? Similar arguments were used in 1640–41 to those used against Browne, Field, Marprelate, and Hacket, and they helped greatly in the formation of a royalist party: but in 1641, unlike the 1590s, a significant section of those whom Parliament represented, especially in the south and east of England, and in towns, remained unmoved by those arguments. What had changed?

I can offer only a few suggestions here. First, those whom contemporaries describe as the many-headed monster were politically outside the pale, could affect politics only by revolt or through religious organization. At the Reformation, for the first time since the rise of Christianity, a popular belief had broken through to secure political power. In the long-continuing economic, social, and psychological crisis of the sixteenth and early seventeenth centuries, religious organization offered a means of controlling and directing upheavals of the masses. Calvinism is the most familiar form in which this discipline and direction was exercised for political purposes.[52] By 1640 Calvinism was strongly entrenched in England, though on the defensive. The possibility now existed that popular revolt could occur without escaping from the control of the lesser magistrates. There is no proof that men ever consciously calculated along these lines: but this was the world in which they lived.

Secondly, economics reinforced religion. This century of crisis for the lower orders in England had brought prosperity to the middle classes[53] who were the backbone of Puritanism—the merchants whose charitable legacies Professor Jordan has analyzed, the yeomen whose rising expenditure on household goods Dr. Hoskins has demonstrated. In 1604 William Stoughton had to argue very carefully that there would be enough "men of occupations" to act as elders of presbyterian churches: by 1640 this was no longer felt to be a problem. The century also saw the extension of the economic and intellectual hegemony of London. Sidney in 1580 had shrewdly observed (of Arcadia, but he must have learnt the lesson in England), "the peasants would have the gentlemen destroyed; the citizens . . . would but have them reformed." By 1640 many yeomen, the leading figures in the villages, had more in common with "the citizens" than with "the peasants," including an interest in the preservation of private property. The economic and social advance of the industrial areas reduced the fear of lower-class revolt that had held the rich united in the sixteenth century. At the same time two generations of Puritan preaching, under the patronage of gentlemen especially in the southeast and the Midlands, had built up something of the nature of a political party.[54]

Thirdly, as the risks of loosing the many-headed monster lessened, so the provocation to do so increased. By 1640 Charles I's government had so alienated many members of the landed class that they were prepared for desperate measures. It may even be suggested that Laud *forced* an appeal to the people on the Puritans and their allies if they were not to surrender or emigrate. Official encouragement of the traditional rural sports, and Laud's ostentatious opposition to enclosure, could be interpreted as an attempt to rally the multitude to the defense of a static hierarchical society, just as Laud's attack on Puritan preaching, repetition of sermons, discipline and

Sabbatarianism threatened the preachers' control over the monster. Whatever the reasons, men of property were now more prepared than at any time since 1536 to connive at, if not positively to foster, a popular revolt. There had been allegations of Puritan support for the rising in the west of 1628–31; in the Forest of Dean the Rev. Peter Simon, nominee of the Haberdashers' Company of London, was preaching the equality of all mankind; in the fens Oliver Cromwell put himself at the head of the rioting fenmen; in 1640–41 Pym in London, and "prudent men" in Gloucestershire, promoted and maintained popular tumults.[55] A middle-class intellectual like Milton felt in 1641 that human dignity was in far less danger from the sects than from the Laudians. I am not suggesting that London demonstrations, or riots against enclosures, were created by the Parliamentarians; but some of them at least were no longer afraid to take advantage of popular initiative. The counties in which there is clearest evidence that the "rabble" was royalist—Worcestershire and Gloucestershire—were on the fringes of the area of London's hegemony, and were to produce Clubmen in 1645.[56]

If any of the Parliamentarian leaders did consciously gamble on letting loose the many-headed monster, relying on the ability of parsons, landlords and J.P.s to bring it back under control, the evidence suggests that they calculated rightly. Milton's growing disillusionment with the people, his sense that they were unfit for liberty, suggests that they were more responsive to conservative than to radical influences. Unless and until the Army could be used "to teach peasants to understand liberty," as Hugh Peter wished,[57] manhood suffrage would probably have brought back the King. The real danger of the Levellers lay in the possibility that they might capture the Army.

Yet even the Levellers had a limited conception of who "the people" were. They wished to extend the franchise from Ireton's men of property to all the freeborn, the heads of households. Only perhaps the Diggers would have given the vote to the really propertyless—servants and paupers. It is hardly surprising that the unfree were fickle allies for their betters. The common people were "foolish and ignorant," often illiterate—in consequence, William Stoughton and John Milton agreed, of the failure of the bishops to educate them.[58] They were susceptible to irrational influences—magic, prophecies, anti-papist panics and witch panics, the appeal of divine kingship (remember the long-standing peasant tradition of appealing to the King against local oppressors, which goes back to Wat Tyler and Ket). Yet even on rational grounds it was not self-evident that it was to their interest to support Parliament. What after all did the multitude get from the Revolution? Excise, free-quarter, pillage, conscription: not stable copyholds, abolition of tithes, or protection of industrial craftsmen against their employers. "For the millions it did nothing," said a Chartist in 1837, looking back to the seventeenth-century English Revolution.[59]

The discipline which Puritans inculcated had long-term social and economic effects, as well as short-term political effects. It contributed to the establishment of labor discipline, of individualist habits suited to an industrial society, the antithesis of the communism which its opponents identified with idleness. There was perhaps a real consistency in the attitude of the many-headed monster which, from Spenser's Fox to Winstanley's utopia, rejected not only the gentry-controlled state and its law but also the wage-labor system; and opposed to them a backward-looking and idealized communism.

NOTES

1. For Stubbe, see his *Essay in Defence of the Good Old Cause* (London, 1659) and *A Letter to an Officer of the Army* (London, 1659). For Osborn, see his *Miscellaneous Works* (London, eleventh edition, 1722), I, pp. 182–83.

2. In 1536 the gentry of Cumberland had put themselves at the head of a similar popular revolt, whose original intention was "to destroy the gentry," as the generals were to put themselves at the head of the mutinous New Model Army in 1647 (R. H. Tawney, *The Agrarian Problem in the Sixteenth Century*, London, 1912, pp. 318–19).

3. A. Neville, *De Furoribus Norfolciensium* (1575), quoted by R. Groves, *Rebels' Oak* (London, n.d.), p. 50; Protector Somerset, quoted by G. Burnet, *History of the Reformation* (London, 1825), IV, p. 202; R. H. Tawney and E. Power, eds., *Tudor Economic Documents* (London, 1924), I, p. 47; T. Cranmer, *Miscellaneous Writings and Letters*, (J. E. Cox, ed., Parker Soc., Cambridge, 1846), p. 190.

4. *V. C. H., Cambridge* (London, 1959), pp. 14–15, 67; cf. W. T. McCaffrey, *Exeter, 1540–1640* (Harvard University Press, 1958), p. 190.

5. F. Aydelotte, *Elizabethan Rogues and Vagabonds* (Oxford University Press, 1913), p. 169; Tawney, *Agrarian Problem*, p. 320; *C. S. P. D. 1595–7*, pp. 316–19, 343–44; J. Nalson, *An Impartial Collection* (London, 1683), II, p. 166; A. E. Bland, P. A. Brown, and R. H. Tawney, eds., *English Economic History: Select Documents* (London, 1914), p. 271. Fulke Greville had made a similar point in the preceding Parliament (*Parliamentary History of England*, London, 1806, I, p. 822).

6. Tawney, *Agrarian Problem*, pp. 338–39; E. F. Gay, "The Midland Revolt and the Inquisitions of Depopulation of 1607," *Trans. Royal Hist. Soc.*, New Series, XVIII (1904), p. 214; *V. C. H., Leicestershire*, IV (London, 1958), p. 108; cf. L. A. Parker, "The Agrarian Revolution at Cotesbach," in *Studies in Leicestershire Agrarian History* (W. G. Hoskins, ed., Leicestershire Archaeological Society, 1949), p. 73.

7. D. G. C. Allan, "The Rising in the West, 1628–31," *Econ. Hist. Rev.*, second series, V, pp. 83–85; Bland, Brown, and Tawney, *op. cit.*, pp. 390–91; *C. S. P. D., 1629–31*, p. 387; E. Kerridge, "The Revolts in Wiltshire and Charles I," *Wiltshire Archaeological and Natural History Magazine*, LVII (1958–60), pp. 66–72.

8. A. Feuillerat, ed., *The Complete Works of Sir Philip Sidney*, I (Cambridge University Press, 1922), pp. 318–19, 30, 34, 311; IV (1962), pp. 118–19, 125. For enclosure at Penshurst, see Tawney, *Agrarian Problem*, p. 194.

9. Cf. Shakespeare, *Coriolanus*, III,i: TRIBUNE SOCINIUS: What is the city but the people?

10. Sidney, *Works*, I, pp. 322–24, 201, 312–13, IV, pp. 120–22, 286–88. An almost identical attitude is shown in Sackville's *Ferrax and Porrex* (*Gorboduc*, 1565), where again the inconstancy of the

rebellious people and their violence and desperation are stressed, as well as the ruthless suppression by sword and noose.

11. Spenser, *The Faerie Queene*, book II, canto 9, stanza 13, book V, canto 2, stanzas 32–52, cf. book IV, canto i, stanza 28. In one of the most openly political passages in the whole poem, Artegall was called upon for help by Burbon, "Against these peasants which have me oppress'd." Talus and the knight of justice "made cruel havoc of the baser crew. . . . The rascal many soon they overthrew" (book V, canto 11, stanzas 57–59).

12. Shakespeare, *Coriolanus*, II, iii; *Henry VI, Part Two*, IV, *passim*. Cf. the very similar "causes of sedition" which Robert Crowley had seen in 1549 (*Select Works*, Early English Text Soc., London, 1872, pp. 132–33, 141–43, 164).

13. B. Googe, "An Epitaph on the Lord Sheffield's Death," *Eglogs, Epytaphs and Sonettes* (E. Arber, ed., London, 1871), pp. 69–70, first published in 1563; T. Dekker, Dramatic Works (F. Bowers, ed., Cambridge University Press, 1953–61), I, p. 119, IV, pp. 177–78. Both plays probably date from 1599–1600. Cf. the clowns who revolt in *The Sun's Darling* (?1623–24), *ibid.*, IV, pp. 57–59.

14. Browne, *Religio Medici* (1642), in *Works* (Bohn ed., London, 1852), II, pp. 415–16; T. Fuller, *The Holy Warre* (fourth edition, London, 1651), p. 113; W. Walwyn, *The Fountain of Slaunder* (London, 1649), p. 19.

15. Quoted by W. G. Zeeveld, *Foundations of Tudor Policy* (Harvard University Press, 1948), p. 216; F. Thynne, *The Debate between Pride and Lowliness* (J. P. Collier, ed., London, 1841), p. 14; Sir T. Smith, *The Commonwealth of England* (L. Alston, ed., Cambridge University Press, 1906), Book I, chapter 24; Sir T. Aston, *A Remonstrance against Presbytery* (London, 1641), Sig. B 4; G. Monck, Duke of Albemarle, *Observations Upon Military and Political Affairs* (London, 1671), p. 146.

16. F. Bamford, ed., *A Royalist's Notebook* (London, 1936), p. 61; Sir C. Petrie, ed., *Letters of King Charles I* (London, 1935), p. 84.

17. J. R. Tanner, ed., *Constitutional Documents of the Reign of James I* (Cambridge University Press, 1930), p. 21; C. V. Wedgwood, *Thomas Wentworth, First Earl of Strafford* (London, 1961), p. 74; [Anon.], *Leather* (1629), in *An English Garner* (E. Arber, ed., London, 1895–97), VI, p. 211; Richard Gardiner quoted by M. Maclure, *The Paul's Cross Sermons* (Toronto University Press,

1958), p. 115; Sir Thomas More, *Utopia* (Everyman edition, London), p. 112; Bishop Hooper, *Later Writings* (C. Nevinson, ed., Parker Soc., Cambridge University Press, 1852), p. 78.

18. I have given some illustrations of this point in my *Society and Puritanism in pre-revolutionary England* (London, 1964), pp. 385–87.

19. T. Deloney, *Jack of Newberrie*, in *Shorter Novels: Elizabethan and Jacobean* (London, Everyman ed.), p. 50. Deloney ostensibly referred to clothiers in Henry VIII's reign; but the reference to the year in which he published is obvious.

20. McCaffrey, *Exeter*, pp. 116–17, 247–49; [Anon.], *Considerations Touching Trade, with the Advance of the Kings Revenues* (1641), p. 15; Aydelotte, *op. cit.*, p. 171; J. Smyth, *A Description of the Hundred of Berkeley* (Gloucester, 1885), p. 43.

21. Aydelotte, *op. cit.*, pp. 169, 171; L. Radzinowicz, *A History of English Criminal Law . . . from 1750* (London, 1948), I, pp. 140–41; B. Osborne, *Justices of the Peace, 1361–1848* (Shaftesbury, Dorset, 1960), pp. 83, 24; W. K. Jordan, *The Forming of the Charitable Institutions of the West of England* (Trans. American Philosophical Soc., New Series, L, Part 8, 1960), p. 56; E. G. R. Taylor, *Late Tudor and Early Stuart Geography* (London, 1934), p. 163.

22. *Sermons or Homilies* (Oxford University Press, 1802), pp. 93, 469, 473.

23. Browne, *op. cit.*, II, pp. 415–16. Browne was careful to add that he referred not exclusively to "the base and minor sort of people"; there was also a rabble amongst the gentry.

24. T. Becon, *Prayers and other pieces* (J. Ayre, ed., Parker Soc., Cambridge University Press, 1844), p. 243; M. Parker, *Correspondence* (J. Bruce, ed., Parker Soc., 1853), p. 61, cf. p. 437; J. Whitgift, *Works* (J. Ayre, ed., Parker Soc., 1851), I, p. 466; J. Knox, *The History of the Reformation in Scotland* (Glasgow, 1832), pp. 115, 131, 237, 225.

25. T. Nashe, *The Unfortunate Traveller* (1594), in *Shorter Novels: Elizabethan and Jacobean*, p. 275; F. Cheynell, *The Rise, Growth and Danger of Socinianisme* (London, 1643), p. 57; [J. Sturgion], *Queries for His Highness to Answer* (1655), quoted by D. B. Heriot, "Anabaptism in England during the 17th Century," *Trans. Congregational Hist. Soc.* (London), XIII, 1937–39, p. 29.

The Many-Headed Monster / 321

26. T. Lever, *Sermons* (Arber, ed., Westminster, 1901), pp. 28–29; T. Cooper, *An Admonition to the People of England* (Arber, ed., Westminster, 1895), p. 148; Spenser, *op. cit.*, p. 514; cf. my *Puritanism and Revolution* (London, 1958), p. 52; *C. S. P. D., 1595–7*, p. 344; P. A. Kennedy, ed., "Verses on the Puritan Settlement in North America, 1631," in *A Nottinghamshire Miscellany*, Thoroton Soc., Record Series, XXI, 1961, pp. 38–39.

27. See my *Society and Puritanism*, chapters 2, 5–6, 13, and pp. 240–41; J. Aubrey, *Miscellanies* (fifth edition, London, 1890), p. 213 (written in 1670); T. Becon, *The Catechism* (J. Ayre, ed., Parker Soc., 1844), pp. 595–98; H. C. White, *Social Criticism in Popular Religious Literature of the Sixteenth Century* (New York, 1944), chapter III *passim;* A. F. Scott Pearson, *Thomas Cartwright and Elizabethan Puritanism* (Cambridge, 1925), pp. 252–53.

28. Cooper, *Admonition*, p. 9; cf. pp. 102–3, 118–19, 139, 168–69; Whitgift, *Works*, II, p. 398; cf. Sir J. E. Neale, *Elizabeth I and her Parliaments, 1584–1601* (London, 1957), p. 274; W. Pierce, *An Historical Introduction to the Marprelate Tracts* (London, 1908), p. 182.

29. W. Notestein, ed., *Journal of Sir Simonds D'Ewes* (Yale University Press, 1923), pp. 339–40; *Old Parliamentary History* (London, 1763), IX, pp. 388–89; cf. Clarendon, *History of the Rebellion* (1888), II, p. 512; *Life* (1759), I, pp. 81, 96–97.

30. Aston, *op. cit.*, Sigs b 4, I 4v-K, M 4. Both friends and foes of presbyterianism pointed out that "the people" who were to elect elders and ministers were not the rabble but heads of households, men of some small substance (see my *Society and Puritanism*, chapter 13).

31. C. Read, *Lord Burghley and Queen Elizabeth* (London, 1960), pp. 470, 509; C. D. Bowen, *Francis Bacon* (London, 1963), pp. 142, 21.

32. F. Guizot, *History of the English Revolution* (London, 1884), p. 120; Sir E. Dering, *A Collection of Speeches* (London, 1642), pp. 109, 118; V. Pearl, *London and the Outbreak of the Puritan Revolution* (Oxford University Press, 1961), pp. 226–27; cf. [B. Ryves], *Angliae Ruina* (n. p., 1647), p. 176: the Grand Remonstrance, "that appeal to the people."

33. With the important exception of Mr. Brian Manning's article, "The Nobles, the People and the Constitution," *Past and Present*, IX, 1956, pp. 42–64.

34. Nalson, *op. cit.*, I, pp. 749, 753; D. Gardiner, ed., *The Oxinden Letters*, 1607–1642 (London, 1933), p. 286; "An honourable and worthy speech . . . by Mr. Smith," *Harleian Miscellany* (London, 1744–56), V, p. 251; Rushworth, *Historical Collections* (London, 1659–1701), IV, p. 509.

35. J. Hacket, *Scrinia Reserata* (London, 1693), II, pp. 165, 198; J. Howell, *Instructions for Forreine Travell* (Arber, ed., London, 1869), p. 78 (first published in 1642).

36. *Eikon Basilike*, chapter IV *passim;* W. K. Jordan, *The Development of Religious Toleration in England* (London, 1932–40), III, pp. 39–40; G. W. Johnson, ed., *Fairfax Correspondence* (London, 1848), II, p. 295.

37. J. Corbet, *An Historicall Relation of the Military Government of Gloucester* (London, 1645), in *Bibliotheca Gloucestrensis* (Gloucester and London, 1823), I, pp. 8, 14; S. I. Arkhangelsky, *Peasant Movements in England in the 1640s and 1650s* (Moscow, 1960, in Russian), *passim.* Sir S. D'Ewes, *Diary*, Harleian ms. 163 f. 135 v. I owe this reference to the kindness of Mr. Robert Clifton.

38. D'Ewes, quoted by A. Kingston, *Hertfordshire during the Great Civil War* (London, 1894), p. 36; "The Life of Mr. Arthur Wilson," in F. Peck, *Desiderata Curiosa* (London, 1779), pp. 474–75; Kingston, *East Anglia and the Great Civil War* (London, 1897), p. 64; F. P. Verney, *Memoirs of the Verney Family* (London, 1892), II, p. 69.

39. *Lord's Journals*, V, p. 42; [Ryves], *Angliae Ruina*, pp. 96, 26–27; Bamford, *A Royalist's Notebook*, pp. 104–6; Rushworth, *op. cit.*, V, p. 41: see p. 48 for Parliament's indignant reply; Kingston, *Hertfordshire*, p. 30.

40. T. Hobbes, *English Works* (Sir. W. Molesworth, ed., London, 1839–45), II, p. 79; "A Letter from Mercurius Civicus to Mercurius Rusticus" (1643), *Somers Tracts* (London, 1748–51), V, p. 415; [E. Bowles], *Plaine English* (n. p., 1643), pp. 25–26. I owe this reference, and much other help and advice in the preparation of this paper, to the generosity of Professor C. M. Williams.

41. Howell, *op. cit.*, p. 78; *Portland MSS.* (Historical MSS. Commission), III (London, 1894), p. 86; D. Gardiner, ed., *The Oxinden and Peyton Letters*, 1642–1670 (London, 1937), pp. 36–37.

42. *C. S. P. D., 1641–3*, p. 445; *Historical MSS Commission, Seventh Report* (London, 1879), I, p. 549; *The Examination of Sir John*

Coniers by a Committee of the House of Lords, quoted by Manning, *op. cit.,* p. 61: the explanation may of course not have been the true one; but the speaker clearly expected it to impress his audience.

43. S. M. Ffarrington, ed., *Farrington Papers* (Chetham Soc., 1856), p. 88; T. May, *History of the Parliament* (London, 1647), I, pp. 113–14.

44. *Portland MSS.,* I, p. 87: cf. the similar reasons given by Robert Kirle for his change of side (J. and T. W. Webb, *Memorials of the Civil War in Hertfordshire* [London, 1879], II, pp. 350–53); Margaret, Duchess of Newcastle, *The Life of William Cavendish, Duke of Newcastle* (C. H. Firth, ed., second edition, London, 1907), p. 94.

45. *Historical MSS. Commission, Fourth Report* (Lond, 1874), I, p. 268; T. T. Lewis, ed., *Letters of Lady Brilliana Harley* (Camden Soc., 1854), p. 214; J. H. Hexter, *The Reign of King Pym* (Harvard University Press, 1941), p. 8; *C. S. P. Venetian, 1643–7,* p. 162; T. Edwards, *Gangraena* (London, 1646), Part I, pp. 115–18, Part III, pp. 261–62; [Anon.], *A Modell of the Government of the Church under the Gospell, by Presbyters* (London, 1646), p. 2.

46. Harleian MS. 165, f. 131. I owe this reference to Professor C. M. Williams.

47. G. Smith, *Englands Pressures* (London, 1645), p. 9; A. R. Bayley, *The Great Civil War in Dorset* (Taunton, 1910), pp. 478–79, cf. p. 110; Arkhangelsky, *op. cit., passim.*

48. H. Cary, *Memorials of the Great Civil War* (London, 1842), I, p. 293; J. Lilburne, *The Upright Mans Vindication* (London, 1653), p. 15; A. S. P. Woodhouse, ed., *Puritanism and Liberty* (London, 1938), pp. 70–71; *The Mournfull Cryes of Many thousand Poor Tradesmen,* in *A Declaration of Some Proceedings of Lieut. Colonel John Lilburne* (London, 1648), p. 52; B. Whitelocke, *Memorials of the English Affairs* (Oxford University Press, 1853), II, pp. 128–29.

49. *Memorial of Denzil, Lord Holles,* in *Select Tracts* (F. Maseres, ed., London, 1815), I, p. 191; C. Walker, *The Compleat History of Independencie* (London, 1661), Part II, p. 156, Part I, p. 59, cf. pp. 140–41; Petrie, ed., *Letters of Charles I,* p. 270; W. C. Abbott, ed., *Writings and Speeches of Oliver Cromwell* (Harvard University Press, 1937–47), III, p. 435, cf. p. 584, IV, p. 267.

50. J. Gauden, *Hieraspites* (London, 1653), p. 437; *Verney Memoirs,* III, p. 199; H. Newcome, *Autobiography* (R. Parkinson, ed.,

Chetham Soc., 1852), p. 119; R. Baxter, *The Holy Commonwealth* (London, 1659), pp. 227, 93, 103, 203; *A Christian Directory* (London, 1673), IV, p. 19.

51. T. Birch, ed., *Thurloe State Papers* (London, 1742), I, p. 747; [Anon.], *The History of the House of Stanley* (Liverpool, 1799), pp. 216–17.

52. Cf. H. G. Koenigsberger, "The Organization of Revolutionary Parties in France and the Netherlands during the 16th Century," *Journal of Modern History*, XXVII (1955), pp. 335–51; M. Walzer, "Puritanism as a Revolutionary Ideology," *History and Theory*, III (1963), pp. 59–90.

53. I use the phrase advisedly, *pace* Professor Hexter. I do not know how else briefly to describe those whom I go on to discuss.

54. Jordan, *Philanthropy in England, 1480–1660* (London, 1959), *passim*, and related works; W. G. Hoskins, *Essays in Leicestershire History* (Liverpool University Press, 1950), pp. 123–83; my *Society and Puritanism*, pp. 223–24, 230–31, 236; F. J. Fisher, "The Development of the London Food Market," *Economic History Review*, V (1935); cf. my "Puritans and 'the Dark Corners of the Land,' " *Trans. Royal Hist. Soc.*, Fifth Series, XIII (1963); Sidney, *op. cit.*, I, p. 315; W. Haller, *The Rise of Puritanism* (Columbia University Press, 1938), *passim;* Walzer, *op. cit., passim.*

55. Allan, *op. cit., passim;* cf. my *Economic Problems of the Church* (Oxford University Press, 1956), pp. 61–62.

56. M. Sylvester, ed., *Reliquiae Baxterianae* (London, 1696), p. 89; Corbet, *op. cit.*, I, p. 14.

57. *Mr. Peters Last Report of the English Wars* (London, 1646), p. 6.

58. Woodhouse, *op. cit.*, pp. 53–63; C. B. Macpherson, *The Political Theory of Possessive Individualism* (Oxford University Press, 1962), chapter 3; W. Stoughton, *An Assertion for true and Christian Church-Police* (Middelburg, 1604), pp. 240–47; Milton, *Complete Prose Works* (Yale University Press, 1953), I, pp. 932–33.

59. Bronterre O'Brien, *London Mercury*, May 7, 1837, quoted in Max Morris, *From Cobbett to the Chartists* (London, 1948), p. 161.

A HIGH ROAD
TO CIVIL WAR?

G .   R .   E L T O N

Clare College,
Cambridge

W hy was there a civil war in seventeenth-century England? The question continues to exercise historians, especially as the coherent explanations of S. R. Gardiner, echoing in reality only the partisan account of the Grand Remonstrance of 1641, no longer command easy acceptance. Of late, discussion has mostly concentrated on social analysis, on the supposition that the division which became manifest in 1642 reflected definite and ascertainable groupings within the nation. This paper is not going to treat once more of the much battered problem of the gentry; that controversy has found enough summaries, of varying degrees of sympathy, to deserve the decent rest and respect accorded to old age (if not old hat).[1] Those who took part in the war believed themselves to be defending opposing views on Church and State; they thought—or often said—that religious and political convictions divided them from one another. This interpretation has taken some bad knocks from historians investigating what was actually said and done in the years before 1640. Even the existence of a distinguishably Puritan point of view in the Church of England has been called in doubt,[2] though it should be said that such arguments lead more properly to the conclusion that within the Church there existed both high and

low streams of opinion, and that at least before the age of Laud
these did not represent a conflict between Anglican and Puritan so
much as a struggle for ascendancy between two sections of the
English Church. This is also the interpretation to be placed on Mr.
Haller's and Mr. Hill's demonstrations of the emergence of identi-
fiably Puritan attitudes in religion and society;[3] neither work produces proof that the Puritanism of the prewar period was bound to
lead to an irreconcilable conflict until Laud decided to believe that it
must. As for political thinking, it is only necessary to remember Miss
Judson's revelation that Crown and Parliament agreed far more than
they differed in their views of the constitution.[4] One of her important
suggestions still awaits proper exploration: the idea that in the age of
James I there was some profound conflict between King and common law persists in a shadowy way,[5] even though common law was
King's law, common lawyers composed a main part of the King's
assistants, and James himself expressed pleasure at the advantages
offered to Kings by the law of England. Sir Edward Coke no doubt
identified the common law with himself, but we are possibly ill-
advised to follow him in this and to mistake his personal battles with
James or Bacon for titanic conflicts of principle.

In this welter of negatives there may be some danger of concluding that the civil war cannot be properly explained, though the more
common reaction is to shrug off the criticisms and continue to hold,
in attenuated form, the simpler views of the past. Most historians
remain convinced that social divisions created the parties of the civil
war. Some would follow Mr. Trevor-Roper into his refinement of his
original thesis and divide the political nation before 1640 into
"court" and "country" sections upon which rested the sides of the
civil war, even though the evidence for such identifiable categories
is doubtful enough.[6] Mr. Hill, on the evidence of his latest book,
continues to adhere to a much subtler but essentially unchanged
version of his earlier views concerning the bourgeois and urban
revolutions against the economic and social structure of a gentry-run
rural society.[7] Most historians seem also convinced that there was
something seriously wrong with the system of government inherited
by the Stuarts: it is thought that when James I came to the throne
nothing could have prevented conflicts with Parliament so serious
as to call in doubt the whole survival of the structure. The Tudor

constitution is considered ramshackle. "The problems of James I" remain a favorite topic of undergraduate study, a fact which reflects not only the conservatism of examination papers but also the quite real, if very curious, belief that somehow only James I ever had problems. Even the emphatic demonstration that he either created his own or was responsible for making existing ones insoluble[8] has not disposed of the general notion that in some way the situation was past praying for in 1603. There is a marked reluctance to realize that Sir John Neale's work on the Elizabethan Parliament has made it impossible to see the position in the traditional light. Elizabeth was not dealing with a co-operative, even subservient, Commons, till things changed in the 1590s and an impatient, new generation of "mature" parliamentarians came to make things too difficult for her successor. She faced a troublesome House throughout her reign, and the fact that she had advantages denied to James should not obscure the difficulties she had which he was spared. Thus in the years before 1590 she was confronted by a militant and often revolutionary Puritanism of which there is very little trace in the age of Bancroft and Abbot.

What these views have in common is a sense of inevitability, a feeling that so profound a disturbance as a civil war must have had roots so deep, causes so fundamental, that analysis can be expected to discover them clearly enough. The history of the years 1603–40 remains understandably dominated by what came after; the breakdown in the constitution colors all interpretations of the time when the constitution was either breaking down or failing to adjust itself. But is this readily comprehended approach in fact the right one? No one will deny that in the society, economy, Church and government of England there were strains (as there always are), even real conflicts of interest and opinion which the outbreak of war brought into the open, and which in turn helped to determine the alignments and developments of the years after 1642. The question is whether they had to lead to such results. The mistake is one of logic: to suppose that because the civil war happened therefore it was bound to happen, and that because the war gave arms and voice to rival groupings therefore rival groupings made the war inevitable. Unconsciously ruled by these convictions, historians have run either into an absence of explanation or into explanations somewhat violently fitted to theories not very well borne out by the facts. Such a situation suggests some error in method. Progress would seem to depend on deliberately abandoning the notion that the reigns of the first Stuarts not only led to war but were somehow certain to lead to it. We must stop reading the age back from its drastic end and try to read it forward through vicissitudes which, though serious enough, were not notably different from those that beset any political situation. This involves a better understanding of the true springs of Tudor government and an end to the idea that somehow it was much easier to govern in the sixteenth than the seventeenth century. It is not, of course, suggested that the civil war was just an accident, or that real and serious divisions did not exist which in retrospect may be seen to have made smooth the road to war. The anger of the "country" against the "court," the ambitions of gentry, merchants and what Mr. Hill calls "the industrious sort"; Puritanism of one kind and another, authoritarian government, differing interpretations of prerogative and privilege—all these respectable topics of discussion were real enough. But we shall get nowhere even with them, not to mention the war itself, if we keep studying them so determinedly with the known end in view.

This essay is manifestly not going to attempt anything like a comprehensive attack on all these problems. It will confine itself to some general points which cast doubt on prevalent attitudes, and to one particular event which has been generally read as underlining the inevitability of conflict. Under James I and Charles I, says Mr. Hill, the political nation "was rent by political disagreements which led to civil war."[9] But is this strictly accurate? Assuredly, the nation was rent in those years, but in 1640 the one thing quite out of the question was a civil war. When the Long Parliament met, the gentry—the political nation—were remarkably united, and the King had no party to speak of.[10] Certainly there were strains in the unity, and divisions of opinion and interest, which would show themselves soon enough; but the fact remains that in 1640 the Commons displayed quite unwonted unanimity. The thirty-seven years since Queen Elizabeth's death produced a united political nation, not one lined up in opposing parties and divided for war, and no account of those years can be acceptable which does not remember this.[11] Whatever part larger social movements or bodies of opinion may have played in the ultimate outcome, the fact is that between the supposed growth of a split and that later stage when the nation was unquestionably split there intervened the immediate product of the prewar years: a nation united, a king isolated, no chance whatever of political conflict, let alone civil war.

The importance of looking closely at events is underlined by a curious paradox. In considering the Long Parliament, the only one under the early Stuarts which for a time justified the conventional collective noun of "the Commons," historians are usually concerned to distinguish the parties of the future. When, on the other hand, they look at earlier Parliaments, they are only too ready to suggest a unanimity which never existed by treating "the Commons" as a unit opposed to the government. In no Parliament before 1628 was the King without sizable support, even if his men rarely succeeded in gaining an ascendancy. However, they did so, in a way, in 1624, in one of James's Parliaments (and that the last), when for once government took the sensible step of working with the Commons instead of against them. It is an error to see Buckingham's alliance with the "Puritan" war party of Eliot and Preston as nothing but surrender to popular attitudes; a more fruitful analysis would consider him as for once understanding the essence of the English system of government—the procuring of support in the Commons by adjustments in policy and by the managerial enterprise of creating a strong Crown interest in the Commons. The mixed sovereign of Tudor England required compromise and flexibility on all sides, but above all it required Crown leadership in the Commons, and in the context the fact of Buckingham's haphazard foreign policy is less significant than the fact that a negotiated peace was still possible after over twenty years of quarreling and estrangement. It throws a strange light on the common opinion that the reign of James I, in a series of increasingly clangorous chords, produced of necessity the sound of war trumpets in the offing, as King and Commons drew further and further apart. If in 1624 it was still possible to organize a Crown interest, it should be clear that policy and not inevitable necessity destroyed that interest in 1626–28. Even when this point has been realized, it does not usually seem to have been understood that in consequence any interpretation which sees the situation as so difficult from the start as to be virtually hopeless will not stand up.

Probably no single document had done more to persuade historians of the inevitability of the conflict than the Commons' *Apology and Satisfaction* of 1604, that "lecture to a foreign king on the constitutional customs of the realm which he had come to govern but which he so imperfectly understood."[12] The usual view of it may be summed up in the words of Godfrey Davies:

> It deserves the closest study both because it reveals the position the Commons took up and maintained for the next forty years . . . and because it was an authoritative pronouncement of the reforms and changes deemed necessary at the beginning of the new reign.[13]

The second half of this sentence calls in question the closeness of Davies's study, for the one thing hard to find in the *Apology* is a statement of "reforms and changes": the document is much more noticeably concerned with preventing change. But it is a striking memorial, and close study would certainly seem to be called for. However, such study should surely involve the circumstances as well as the product, and this has not been offered anywhere so far. That the address was composed but never delivered might at once start doubts about the ready way in which the Commons, as a body, are nowadays associated with it. The history of the document is itself curious. Though not unknown in the later seventeenth century,[14] it was effectively discovered by Hallam who was very proud of the fact, noting that Hume and Carte had ignored it and that even Rapin gave it only the briefest mention.[15] Hallam also at once jumped to the conclusion, which has ever since been reiterated, that "it was the voice of the English Commons in 1604, at the commencement of that conflict for their liberties, which is measured by the line of the house of Stuart."[16] Gardiner set his magisterial seal on this view which makes the *Apology* one of the profoundly important constitutional documents in a century full of such things:[17]

> Such was the address, manly and freespoken, but conservative and monarchical to the core, which the House of Commons was prepared to lay before the King. In it they took up the position which they never quitted during eighty-four long and stormy years. To understand the Apology is to understand the causes of the success of the English Revolution. They did not ask for anything which was

not in accordance with justice. They did not demand a single privilege which was not necessary for the good of the nation as well as for their own dignity.

Here is the full mystical concept: an identifiable single body, "the Commons," preserving that unity for eighty-four years on a stand taken from the first. Whether Queen Elizabeth would have called a document conservative and monarchical which preached Peter Wentworth's extreme doctrine of free speech, or whether one may suppose that the Commons "never quitted" the position of 1604 when they passed the Militia Ordinance or the Test Act, may perhaps be doubted. Gardiner's authority is not what it was, but even today criticism concentrates on his politics when it would do well to attend to his scholarship and his predilection for rather flat rhetoric. James I's latest biographers accept the *Apology* in the full sense of Gardiner's dictate, though Mr. Hill, less interested in constitutional issues than social, reverts to pre-Hallam days by ignoring it.[18]

The first session of the first Stuart Parliament was certainly a troubled one. Right at the start there had been a muddle in the Parliament Chamber when the negligence of a gentleman-usher kept "a great part of our House from hearing your Majesty's speech," and soon after some yeoman of the guard distinguished himself by addressing some members in "opprobrious" terms more suitable "to the peasants of France and boors of Germany" than the "whole power and flower" of the kingdom present in the Commons.[19] There followed the more familiar troubles over Shirley's Case, the Buckinghamshire Election Case, James's proposal for a union between England and Scotland, and the Bishop of Bristol's book in favor of the union which the Commons regarded as unwarranted interference. Religion and money also played their part in exciting the Commons, and it had become painfully clear that the government's control was poor. Altogether, a very disturbed session, though not perhaps much more so than a session in many an Elizabethan Parliament. All these troubles were rehearsed in the *Apology*, but the immediate cause of its composition was more specific. This was the bitter dispute over the whole problem of wardship which a Commons' Committee had long and fruitlessly debated with the Lords in April–May, 1604.[20] The Crown, using the Lords in their traditional role as a check on the Commons,[21] had beaten off the attack on prerogative and resources; but in an address to the Commons, summoned to Whitehall, which he delivered on May 28, and "wherein many particular actions and passages of the House were objected unto them with taxation and blame," James had made it very plain how much he resented their attitude to his rights and what he regarded as the general wasting of time. The Commons might well have remembered the much more conciliatory reaction of the late Queen in 1601, to franker attacks on the prerogative of granting monopolies.

On June 1, Sir Edwin Sandys, who had led the Committee that conferred with the Lords, reported on the abortive negotiations and reminded the House of the King's rebuke. "Much dispute followed this report." In the course of the debate, Sir Thomas Ridgeway, one of the knights for Devon, moved "that a Committee might be named to take a Survey of the Proceedings of the House, and to set down something in writing, for his Majesty's Satisfaction; and to exhibit it unto him." The Speaker rephrased the motion to read: "A Petition to be framed, with Reasons of Satisfaction for the Proceeding in Matters of Wardships, &c." It would appear that both motions were voted on and agreed, and the Commons then appointed a Committee

> to take a Survey of all the Acts and Proceedings of the House, which have been excepted unto, or whereof any Misinformation hath been given unto his Majesty, from the beginning of the Session; and to advise of such Form of Satisfaction to be offered to his Majesty, either by writing or otherwise, as may inform him of the Truth and Clearness of their Proceedings; thereby to free them from the Scandal of Levity and Precipitation, so often imputed to them; and particularly to consider of some Satisfaction touching the Proceeding in Matter of Wardship &c. This being done, to make Report to the House, and from thence to receive further Direction.

According to the form of words "conceived by the clerk, being so directed," wardship remained foremost in the Commons' minds, but it was also felt that the business of self-explanation "so advisedly and gravely undertaken . . . might not die or be buried in the Hands of

those that first bred it." There is certainly so far a powerful suggestion that the whole House, or an overwhelming majority of it, felt
strongly about the criticisms they had received and meant to defend
themselves.[22]

The Committee appointed was enormous, consisting of the more
than sixty-six members of the Committee on wardships with six
additions,[23] a body, one would have thought, more likely to founder
than succeed in the task. Not until the 5th did the House receive a
message from the King, softening the blow of May 28 and expressing his willingness to hear their explanations.[24] Barely a fortnight
later—a time, at that, filled with the drafting of another address and
the burdensome business of dealing with the Crown's financial
needs[25]—the Committee reported their document, now for the first
time called *The Form of Apology and Satisfaction, to be presented
to his Majesty.*[26] There is no denying the remarkable quality of the
paper, which runs to over five thousand words. In fact, it is still a
better piece of writing than the familiar version, taken from Petyt's
Jus Parliamentarium, would suggest, for this contains an average of
perhaps twenty-five errors per page of Tanner's printing. Most of
these, though tiresome, are not serious, but the capricious paragraphing and messing about with sentence structure, as well as various omissions and transmutations, do much to impair the grammar,
organization, and effect of the *Apology.* Some of Petyt's coinings
puzzled Tanner who laboriously provided explanations for non-
existent neologisms: "seemingly," glossed as fittingly, is really
seemly (223, 1. 20);[27] "evert," interpreted to mean upset, is reject
(224, 1. 19); "deface," which Tanner took to mean discredit, is
really refute (225, 1. 28); where Tanner, remarking that the text
read "party," emended to "parity," the manuscript has purity, which
makes good sense (226, 1. 26). The picturesque "eye" of the King's
grace and the obscure "affiance" of his dispostion (218, ll. 2, 22)
are more commonplace but more comprehensible as acceptance and
assurance; the "poor united minds and readiness," with which the
Commons credit themselves (219, 1. 3 from foot), were really their
"power, united minds, etc."[28] Sometimes the sense got distorted, as
when the "lawful knight" elected for Buckinghamshire becomes the
Commons' "lawful right" (225, 1. 8). The omission of "just" before
"burdens" (228, 1. 15) makes nonsense of the concessionary addi-

tion, "for so we acknowledge them." Some errors are really serious. When the *Apology* says that in every previous Parliament complaint as well as claim had been made of "your" rights (of purveyance), the transcriber introduced a different basis of discussion by reading "our" (227, l. 6 from foot); and when it is pleaded that a new law concerning purveyance could hardly be agreed to until members had sought their constituents' "counsel," the printed version invented a dangerous constitutional principle by reading "consent" (228, l. 8). And would Godfrey Davies have been so sure that the *Apology* reveals the Commons' attitude "that their privileges were the general liberties of England,"[29] if he had known that in the manuscript the phrase concerning "the right and liberty of the Commons of England" (223, l. 5 from foot) is followed by "in Parliament"? Lastly, we may note that the hitherto rather obscure allusion to the late Queen (222, ¶. 2) was made so only by the omission of a few lines; these also point a contrast with the previous reign which historians have of late tended to ignore:

> For although it may be true that in the latter times of Queen Elizabeth some one privilege now and then were by some particular act attempted against, yet not obscurely injured; yet was not the same ever by as public speech nor by positions in general denounced against our privileges. Besides that in respect. . . .

However, these errors have not prevented the *Apology* from being recognized for what it is: a powerful, formidable justification of parliamentary claims and an equally solid attack on James's handling of the situation. It asserted without reservations some notions on privilege which in the previous reign would have had short shrift not only from the Queen but (if Peter Wentworth's fate is anything to go by) even from a majority of the House, and it offered a definition of constitutional principles which, while never less than respectful, was also firmly directed at all manifestations of autocracy. The logic of its structure—running easily from general propositions to particular discussions and missing never a point—is clearer in the original paragraphing, but can be recovered from Tanner's version. But the important question, of course, is whether all this really represented the Common's views, or only the Committee's—or those of some part of the Committee. For anyone who has ever taken part in the drafting of a paper in committee may well doubt from the first whether any such document could possibly have emerged, in less than two weeks, from the labors of more than seventy men.

On June 20, Ridgeway presented the draft. Gardiner, introducing the *Apology*, said that "the Commons, in whose name it was drawn up, began by explaining. . . ."[30] The *Commons' Journal* says that the draft was "twice read, debated and argued, *pro et contra*, whether the Matter and the Manner fit, or what was fit to be done with it." The clerk noted that seventeen members spoke in the debate; of these no fewer than ten had been on the Committee. We know a little of what was said. Of the Committee, Francis Bacon certainly spoke against the document, and Sir Henry Beaumont and Sir Herbert Crofts as certainly for it; Sir Edward Stafford was probably against, while a member not on the Committee, Dudley Carleton, certainly opposed. Mr. Fuller (of the Committee) either argued that the draft constituted a "Precedent, that the Laity may censure the Clergy," in which case he sounds to have been hostile; or he produced such a precedent from the past, which would probably place him on the side in favor. Mr. Kyrton, who said something about the King's message "within Two Days," would appear to have been warning the House against going too far; Sir William Strode was provoked into inveighing against noisy interrupters of debate. Where the others stood cannot be told, except that the general statement quoted above makes certain that they did not all speak on one side; in any case, the fact that a member of the Committee felt compelled to move that "this Dispute to cease, without further Proceeding, for this Day," indicates that all was far from plain sailing in the House.[31] The clerk began transcribing the *Apology* into the Journal, but, stopping after half a page, left several sheets blank.[32] The reason the task was never completed becomes apparent if, disregarding Gardiner's eclecticism, we read the last *Journal* entry touching the *Apology*. On Friday, June 29, Sir William Strode moved

that the Frame of Satisfaction, touching the Proceedings of the House, penned by the Committee, and by them reported, and read in the House, might be re-committed, and some more Committees [Committee members] added; and such of the first Committee, or others, as found any Cause of Exception, or were not present at the former several Meetings, might be commanded to attend; that they might receive Satisfaction from the rest, or otherwise yield their reasons of Difference; so as, upon Report to the House, some Resolution may be taken for further Proceeding or Surceasing in the said Business.[33]

This was agreed to, and the afforced Committee ordered to meet on Monday (July 2); but on the 7th the Parliament stood prorogued, and no more was heard of the *Apology*.

What happened is therefore plain. The famous form, or draft, which ever since Hallam has been interpreted as a worthy pronouncement from the embattled Commons, seemed less pleasing to the House than it has to historians. It was drawn up in a Committee a number of whose members did not bother to attend; some of these absentees, it appears from Strode's motion, spoke against it on June 20. The debate turned on two fundamental points: was it right to present the King with a document containing so much contentious argument, and even if it was, had the Committee found the right tone? Some, it seems from the clerk's summary of the debate, were at once for dropping it; the mood of the House had changed since, on June 1, it had resolved to put the Commons' side of the story on record. No sort of decision was arrived at on this occasion, and it took nine whole days to revive the discussion. Strode's motion carries a suggestion of annoyance, particularly at members of the Committee who, not having shared in the deliberations, had then attacked the proposal in the House, and it explicitly mentions the possibility of abandoning the whole idea. Though it may be true that the *Apology* received its quietus from the prorogation, this sequence of events strongly suggests that, if not dead before July 7, it was also not very alive. One thing is beyond dispute: the *Apology* was never presented to the King because it was never adopted by the House. All the praise bestowed on its manly language and assertion of profound principle misses the mark. Faced with these excellences, many of the Commons had the gravest doubts, and it was the doubters, not the promoters, who won the day. The Commons not only never got around to endorsing the draft; they may, in all fairness, be said to have deliberately rejected it.

One would naturally like to know whether this difference between the Committee and the House reflected any kind of factional division; was there perhaps a group of opposition men who dominated the Committee but could not carry the House?[34] The answer is complicated by the fact that though we know there were objectors among the Committee men, we know of names only Bacon's and probably Stafford's. However, even the briefest glance at the Committee suggests that it would be dangerous to regard it as either composed of or led by a specifically oppositionist group.[35] True, Sandys was on it, and Sandys had by this time sufficiently demonstrated his views of the government. But over the *Apology* he does not seem to have taken the lead, and it is doubtful whether he contributed to it at all.[36] John Hare was in 1606 described by Speaker Phillips as "an inconsiderate firebrand" whose attacks on purveyance went too far even for the House.[37] Thomas Wentworth (the lawyer, who died in 1628) counted throughout this Parliament as a steadfast opponent of the court. Sir Francis Hastings, the passionate Puritan,[38] Sir Robert Wingfield, who attacked the King over Goodwin's Case,[39] and Sir Nathaniel Bacon, who in 1610 spoke against the Great Contract,[40] may also safely be put on that side. The same is less clearly true but still probable of such men as Sir Robert Wroth, Sir Henry Neville, Sir Edward Montague (who was to speak up for the Commons' privileges in 1610),[41] Sir Jerome Horsey, Sir Peter Manwood the antiquary, Sir John Scott, Sir William Burlacy (foremost against purveyors in 1610),[42] and Sir Thomas Beaumont and Sir Herbert Crofts, prominent in the tussle over the Great Contract.[43] Crofts and Sir Henry Beaumont had spoken for the *Apology* in the debate on June 20.

However, over against a possible opposition group of this kind, the Committee contained a large number of apparent courtiers. The sole two privy councillors in the House, Sir John Herbert and Sir John Stanhope, were, as was customary, members of it; and though, as we know, their influence was "practically at zero,"[44] such as it was it must have worked against getting too tough with the King. In any case they might draw support from other present and future office-holders, like Sir George Moore, chamberlain of the Exchequer and for many years one of the few who seem to have spoken regularly for the court;[45] Sir Thomas Aston and Sir Edward Hoby, gentlemen of the privy chamber; Sir Edward Stafford, career diplomat and from 1603 chancellor of the duchy; Sir Daniel Dunn, the civilian and commissioner for ecclesiastical causes; Sir John Doddridge, appointed solicitor-general a few months after the close of the session; Sir Lawrence Tanfield, elevated to the bench in 1606; Sir Robert Mansell, appointed treasurer of the navy, at the height of the argument between King and Commons; Henry Montague, whom James had in 1603 recommended for the office of recorder of London. Sir Francis Bacon we know was against the *Apology,* and Lord Treasurer Dorset's son, Robert Sackville, may with confidence be placed with the court. Sir Francis Popham, son of the Lord Chief Justice, and Sir Hugh Beeston, who in December, 1604, was given a profitable minor office in North Wales,[46] are probables. Sir John Hollis, who in 1603 disliked Scotsmen, ended up as comptroller to Prince Henry, friend to Robert Carr, and enemy to Sir Edward Coke; his adjournment proposal on June 20 probably makes him a supporter of the *Apology.* Even more problematical was that thoughtful weathervane, Sir Henry Yelverton, in and out of court favor throughout his career; but in 1604 he would seem to have abandoned opposition over Goodwin's Case for support of the court. Though from details such as these it is no doubt not possible to be sure of people's attitude to the *Apology,* the Committee manifestly contained many men far from determined in opposition.

The oddest case is presented by the only two members of the Committee specifically known to be associated with the *Apology.* Sir Thomas Ridgeway, who moved for it and reported it, was in no sense a leader of opposition. A new boy among some very old hands —this was his first Parliament as against Sir George Moore's seventh, Robert Sackville's fifth, Sir Henry Neville's sixth, Sir Nathaniel Bacon's eighth—he was out for a career which in the end, abandoning Parliament, he pursued in Ireland to the consummation of an earldom. What is more, even as he was taking the lead over the *Apology* he was being used to support Robert Cecil's private in-

terests in the House: shortly before the prorogation, Stanhope wrote
to his lordship that a certain private bill would be backed by Ridgeway, "strong with his Devonshire crew," who had given assurance
of "a good party."[47] But his promotion of the *Apology,* as well as his
good standing with the Devon members, suggests that he was willing
to take up causes in order to make a mark: it would be wrong to
infer from his later life that the *Apology* owed its drafting to a
staunch royalist. At the same time, he was no Eliot or Pym.[48] Sir
William Strode, responsible for having the document referred back,
was generally reckoned a courtier;[49] but then it is not clear whether
he made his motion on June 29 in order to kill the *Apology* or revive
it.

The best that can be said after this partial analysis of part of the
Committee is that the *Apology* did not represent a specifically opposition point of view, or (to put it in a more useful way) that the drafting of the *Apology* does not prove the existence in the House of an
organized or systematic opposition to James I as early as 1604. We
ought probably to see the situation in a less clear but more realistic
light. Resentment at the King's ham-handed dealings and peevish
outbursts was not confined to men of fixed opinion: the presence, in
the House and the Committee, of many old parliament men made
certain that attacks on privilege and interference in the Commons'
business would wound feelings in courtier as well as anti-court
breasts. It was this general dismay which the *Apology* was intended
to embody, but it did so in terms so uncompromising and occasionally so intemperate that the House got cold feet. The mood of the
Commons illustrated by the history of the *Apology* is familiar to
any student of the Elizabethan Parliament: touchy, rather pompous,
convinced of their rights, but entirely loyal and notably reluctant to
start serious trouble with the King. High-sounding speeches on
privilege and liberty were one thing; actually presenting a long and
singleminded written defense of them was quite another. As far as
can be judged from this story, there was nothing in the parliamentary situation of 1604 to prevent reasonable co-operation between
King and Parliament, provided that James changed the disastrous
tactics he had hitherto employed.

Indeed, what effect did the *Apology* have on the King? Did he ever see it, as Gardiner claimed, without citing any evidence?[50] Perhaps he was thinking of Hallam's assertion to the same effect.[51] This in turn is based on an alleged letter from James I, "written to one of his ministers about the same time," which, discussing the prospect of a subsidy, mentions the Commons' expectation of an answer "to their petition." It is an odd-sounding letter, and the skeptic is not helped by Hallam's bland reference to an "*MS penes auctorem*," which makes the document untraceable. In any case, the *Apology* was not a petition, had not been presented, and required no answer; if the letter is genuine, the King may well have had in mind the petition concerning religion agreed to by the House on June 13.[52] Or was Gardiner thinking of the fact that a copy of the *Apology* is among the State Papers? He would be extremely daring who would suppose that the presence of a paper in that archive proves that this particular King had seen it. Robert Cecil was informed of the *Apology:* among his papers there is a long report on the whole affair concerning wardships which includes a perfectly accurate account of Ridgeway's motion and the reading of the *Apology,* with a long quotation from it.[53] The surviving copy is much more likely to have been sent to the secretary and read by him than by the King. The evidence of James's extraordinary speech to the Parliament at the end of the session is no less ambiguous.[54] As the King let himself go in a general diatribe of abuse and resentment, many of his listeners must have regretted that they had not after all told him his business in Ridgeway's *Apology*. Those who remembered the "golden speech" of 1601, at the end of an equally troubled session, may well have stood astonished: the legend of Good Queen Bess's glorious days could not help but take wing from this contrast early in the new reign.

In the course of his speech, James did say something that sounds like an allusion to the *Form of Apology:* "The best Apology-maker of you all, for all his eloquence, cannot make all good. Forsooth, a goodly matter, to make Apologies when no man is by to answer." But this proves little enough, and the second sentence would hardly apply to the history of the *Apology*. The King had been aware of Ridgeway's motion and, on June 5, had expressed his interest in a statement from the Commons: the words quoted could easily rest on no more knowledge than that. The rest of the speech makes no attempt to answer the *Apology* or even to refer to it in any particular; the King's complaints of the Commons' doings are not placed in the order of the *Apology* and are confined to the union with Scotland, religion, and purveyance; nothing is said about wardship, the immediate cause of the *Apology,* or parliamentary privilege, its major concern. In all probability, therefore, James knew that an *Apology* had been drafted but not agreed to, and Cecil may have told him something of its tenor. If the King, a man who could never resist displaying both his reading and his cleverness, had read frank remarks about his lack of experience and understanding, it seems very unlikely that he could have refrained from specifically replying to them.

Thus the *Apology* came to nothing at the time. So far from embodying a position taken up in 1604 and firmly maintained thereafter for forty or eighty years, so far from being a constitutional program finally triumphant in 1688, it represented a minority opinion rejected by the House as too extreme. The King almost certainly never saw the "lecture" addressed to his inexperience. The views of the Commons in 1604 cannot be deduced from it. Hale and Petyt, taught by recent history, recognized its importance as a statement of the Commons' claims, but it was virtually forgotten until Hallam raised it on the flagpole of Whig history. So much for the negative side of the story; positively, it may be suggested that, with the *Apology* out of the way, and in view of what by now is known of Tudor Parliaments, it ceases to be necessary to think the Parliament of 1604 any different from its predecessors, or the Tudor constitution already doomed before the Stuarts came to reign. The co-operation, more or less easy, of King, Lords, and Commons on which in the last resort government under Elizabeth had rested, was not shown to be no longer possible by a House of Commons displaying views of its functions and privileges with which no Tudor sovereign would have agreed. The system of parliamentary management perfected by Henry VIII and Thomas Cromwell, and further refined in the more difficult days of Queen Elizabeth, would no doubt have required tactful and sensible adjustment as the seventeenth century developed; but there is nothing in the story of 1604 to suggest that it had already ceased to be practicable.

NOTES

1. The most famous review of the problem is J. H. Hexter's "Storm over the Gentry," *Reappraisals in History* (London, 1961), pp. 117 ff. His convincing reluctance to see much value in the debate is to some degree shared by Willson H. Coates, "An Analysis of Major Conflicts in Seventeenth Century England," *Conflict in Stuart England: Essays in Honour of Wallace Notestein* (London, 1960), pp. 15 ff. C. Hill, "Recent Interpretations of the Civil War," *Puritanism and Revolution* (London, 1958), pp. 3 ff., and P. Zagorin, "The Social Interpretation of the English Revolution," *Journal of Economic History*, 1959, pp. 376 ff., are more inclined to believe in the reality of the discussion, though they disagree with the particular answers offered.

2. C. H. and K. George, *The Protestant Mind of the English Reformation* (Princeton, 1961). Their views receive some support from such studies as R. A. Marchant, *The Puritans and the Church Courts in the Diocese of York* (London, 1960), and I. Morgan, *Prince Charles's Puritan Chaplain* (London, 1957).

3. W. Haller, *The Rise of Puritanism* (New York, 1938); C. Hill, *Society and Puritanism in Pre-Revolutionary England* (London, 1964). However, Michael Walzer has reminded us of the existence of more drastic elements in Puritan thinking than the dominant note of reform within the Church: "Puritanism as a Revolutionary Ideology," *History and Theory*, 1963, pp. 59 ff.

4. Margaret A. Judson, *The Crisis of the Constitution* (New Brunswick, N.J., 1949). And cf. R. W. K. Hinton, "Government and Liberty under James I," *Cambridge Hist. Journal*, XI (1953), pp. 48 ff.

5. Or not so shadowy: Sir Charles Ogilvie, *The King's Government and the Common Law 1471–1641* (Oxford, 1958).

6. Cf. my remarks in *Past and Present*, XX (1961), pp. 79 ff.

7. His *Society and Puritanism* is pervaded by a general and sometimes explicit acceptance of this interpretation.

8. *E.g.* D. H. Willson, *James VI and I* (London, 1956); R. H. Tawney, *Business and Politics under James I* (Cambridge, 1958); R. Ashton, *The Crown and the Money Market 1603–40* (Oxford, 1960),

and "Deficit Finance in the Reign of James I," *Econ. Hist. Review,* second series, X (1957), pp. 15 ff.

9. *Puritanism and Revolution,* p. 14.

10. To my knowledge this point is recognized only by Mr. Coates, *op. cit.,* p. 25; recognition is, however, also implied in B. H. G. Wormald, "How Hyde became a Royalist," *Cambridge Hist. Journal,* VIII (1944–6), pp. 65 ff.

11. It is worth notice that all the true later crises of the century (1673, 1678, 1688) witnessed the same phenomenon. It is this fact and not even the event of civil war which provides the best comment on Stuart political skill.

12. J. R. Tanner, *Constitutional Documents of the Reign of James I* (Cambridge, 1930), p. 202; hereafter cited as Tanner.

13. *The Early Stuarts* (second edition, Oxford, 1959), pp. 6 ff.

14. The bibliography of the *Apology* is difficult and in part remains obscure; this note is based on a comparison of verbal differences which it would be impossibly tedious to detail here. Only one contemporary MS. copy is now known (Public Record Office, State Papers Domestic, James I, Vol. 8, no. 70) which Gardiner appears to have been the last historian to use; however, another copy, vouched for at a later date (cf. note 32 below), may still exist somewhere and may turn out to be contemporary. It was apparently this missing copy, known from the transcript in the MS Commons' Journals, on which the first printed version rested: in Sir Matthew Hale's posthumous *Original Institution, Power and Jurisdiction of Parliaments* (London, Jacob Tonson, 1707), pp. 206–40. William Petyt (1636–1707), keeper of the records in the Tower, had the *Apology* transcribed into his collection of historical materials (London, Inner Temple Library, Petyt MSS., 538, Vol. 19, fols. 91–104v); this was further copied for him in a form apparently edited for printing (Brit. Mus., Lansdowne MS. 512, fols. 119–32), and it was probably this last version which was used when the document was published in his posthumous *Jus Parliamentarium,* 227–43 (London, 1739). Unfortunately it was this printed version, easily the worst available, which was used by both Tanner (pp. 217–30) and G. W. Prothero, *Select Statutes and Other Constitutional Documents Illustrative of the Reigns of Elizabeth and James I* (Oxford, 1894), pp. 286–93. The transmission involved a lot of deterioration. Hale's printed version is slightly better than that of

the Petyt MS.; although Petyt corrected his transcriber's labors, he left many misreadings standing. Both rest on a common ancestor which does not, however, seem to be the surviving State Paper MS., but rather another copy very close to it. The worst damage was done in printing Petyt's book when masses of often confusing errors were introduced. Even the State Paper MS. includes one or two improbable readings, but wherever the versions conflict it seems to me so clearly the best that (quite apart from its contemporaneity) I have decided to accept it as authentic. Quotations here are from it, in modernized spelling.

15. H. Hallam, *Constitutional History of England* (London, 1827), I, p. 329.

16. *Ibid.* p. 331.

17. *History of England* (London, 1883), I, pp. 185 ff.

18. Willson, *James VI and I*, p. 249: "a bold declaration of right, a lecture to a foreign king upon the constitution of his new kingdom"; W. McElwee, *The Wisest Fool in Christendom* (London, 1958), pp. 153 ff. (who even alleges that the Commons presented the document to the King, which no one else has supposed); C. Hill, *The Century of Revolution* (Edinburgh, 1961). The *Apology* is accepted as "great" and truly important in the latest study of James I's first Parliament: Theodore K. Rabb, "Sir Edwin Sandys and the Parliament of 1604," *Amer. Hist. Rev.* LXIX (1964), pp. 646 ff.

19. These parts of the *Apology* are left out in Tanner and Prothero.

20. H. E. Bell, *Introduction to the History and Records of the Court of Wards and Liveries* (Cambridge, 1953), p. 138.

21. Hist. MSS Commission, *Portland MSS.*, IX, pp. 11 ff.

22. For the whole story so far, cf. *Journals of the House of Commons* (hereafter *C. J.*), I, p. 230b.

23. For the wardships Committee see *ibid.*, p. 222. It included "all the serjeants at law," apart from sixty-six named members.

24. *Ibid.* p. 232b.

25. On June 13 the Commons considered a petition for easing the burdens on Puritan ministers, proposed by Sir Francis Hastings' Committee (*ibid.*, p. 238); Hastings was on the *Apology* Committee. On the 14th they passed the bill for tunnage and poundage (*ibid.*,

p. 239a), but they had to deal with Lords' amendments to it after the 18th (*Journals of the House of Lords*, II, pp. 322–23). All this time the negotiations for a subsidy went on, until on the 26th the King made a virtue of necessity by graciously remitting all grants that session (*C. J.* I, p. 246–47).

26. *Ibid.*, p. 243b.

27. References are to page and line in Tanner's printing.

28. Though eighty years earlier, in the early sixteenth century, poor was often spelled power, it is quite clear that power was here intended.

29. *The Early Stuarts*, p. 7.

30. *History of England*, I, p. 180. For the course of events, see *C. J.* I, p. 243b.

31. See the rough diary probably kept by the clerk of the House, printed *C. J.* I, p. 995b. Mr. Rabb, referring to the same passage, claims to identify nine speeches as *pro* and three as *con*, with five unknown (*op. cit.*, pp. 660 and 53 n.). His calculations bewilder me: he seems to identify groups of speakers with the remarks attributed by the diarist to only one of them. Even so I cannot quite see how he arrives at his figures.

32. Or rather, eight pages were blank between fols. 316 and 317 when the editors of the printed *Journals* looked at them, sometime in the eighteenth century. In 1804 these pages were filled with a transcript of the *Apology* from "a MSS. of Speaker Williams communicated by Charles Williams Wynn, Esq., Member of Montgomeryshire, to me, Chas. Abbot, Speaker" (MS. Journal in the Record Office, House of Lords). Speaker Abbot's well-known antiquarian instincts here got the better of him. It is interesting that Sir William Williams, Speaker in the Exclusion Parliaments of 1680 and 1681, should have had a copy of the *Apology*, and that this was apparently available to Hale (cf. note 14 above).

33. *C. J.* I, p. 248b.

34. I may say that I am not convinced by the simple assumption, made by Mr. Rabb in his article (note 18 above) that a true opposition group can be identified in the 1604 Commons. That certain individuals stood out in opposing the court is true enough, but not even they have ever been proved to have adhered consistently to an "opposition" line. Williams M. Mitchell, *The Rise*

of the Revolutionary Party in the English House of Commons (New York, 1957), p. 40, believes that a letter of Bacon's, in 1614, about new attitudes on the part of recent opponents of the court, "lays to rest the question whether there was an opposition party" in the whole Parliament of 1604–10. It is difficult to know what to do with arguments of this order.

35. The Parliament of 1604 awaits its Namier. The following attempt to assess individuals' attitudes, based on *D.N.B.* unless other references are given, does not pretend to be more than a suggestion of probabilities.

36. Mr. Rabb (*op cit.*, pp. 659 and 50 n.) rightly disposes of the suggestion that Sandys was the moving spirit behind the *Apology*. His suggestion that Sandys was responsible for the section dealing with wardship may well be true.

37. *Calendar of State Papers Domestic, James I*, I, pp. 289, 292.

38. Hastings had court contacts but used them, behind a pretence of co-operation, to block such court concerns as the need for a subsidy (Hist. MSS. Commission, *Hatfield MSS.*, XVI, pp. 132 ff.).

39. *Cal. S. P. Dom. James I*, I, p. 90.

40. S. R. Gardiner, ed., *Parliamentary Debates of 1610* (Camden Society, 1862), p. 135.

41. *Ibid.*, p. 51.

42. *Cal. S. P. Dom. James I*, I, p. 593.

43. *Parl. Debates of 1610*, p. 55.

44. D. H. Willson, *The Privy Councillors in the House of Commons 1604–10* (Minneapolis, 1940), p. 56.

45. *Parl. Debates of 1610*, p. 55 (advocated two subsidies and tried to pour oil on troubled waters); S. R. Gardiner, ed., *Debates in the House of Commons in 1625* (Camden Society, 1873), pp. 16, 89, 121.

46. *Cal. S. P. Dom. James I*, I, p. 175.

47. *Hatfield MSS.*, XVI, p. 264.

48. Mr. Rabb thinks that the opposition "cleverly chose an inconspicuous and seemingly impartisan spokesman" in Ridgeway (*op. cit.*, p. 658). He gives no shred of evidence for an argument which associates Ridgeway politically with Sandys solely because his aunt was Sandys's second wife!

49. Willson, *Privy Councillors*, p. 109. Mr. Mitchell (*Revolutionary Party*, p. 40) puts Strode in the opposition. His reason is that he spoke against the government. Of the three speeches in 1604, to which Mr. Mitchell refers (two of his references are to wrong columns in *C. J.*), one shows Strode speaking for the government, one has him join in the almost universal resistance to more taxation at that juncture, and one (a broken half sentence only) cannot be assigned. This example will perhaps act as an apology and satisfaction for my failure to use Mr. Mitchell's book.

50. *History of England*, I, p. 186: "there can be little doubt that a copy of it reached his hands."

51. *Constitutional History*, I, p. 331.

52. *C. J.* I, p. 238.

53. *Hatfield MSS.*, XVI, pp. 142 ff.

54. Public Record Office, State Papers Domestic, James I, Vol. 8, no. 93. Mr. Willson also thought that this speech was meant for an answer to the *Apology* (*James VI and I*, p. 249).

BLACKLO AND THE
COUNTER-REFORMATION:
AN INQUIRY INTO
THE STRANGE DEATH OF
CATHOLIC ENGLAND

ROBERT I. BRADLEY, S. J.

Seattle University

For the contemporary student of English history the collapse of Catholicism as a dominant force in the national life presents a problem which, for all its importance, remains curiously insoluble. The old "Whig interpretation" (on which he still depends more than he may suspect) is hardly a help in the matter, for it seems to postulate two facts that are rather difficult to reconcile. On the one hand, it insists on a kind of *inevitability* in England's becoming Protestant by the mid-sixteenth century; on the other hand, it equally insists on a real *intelligibility* in England's regarding Catholicism even as late as the end of the seventeenth century as a most urgent menace. It is certainly reasonable to suggest that both these postulates are exaggerated, that indeed a reversal of emphasis makes more sense historically. England could have gone either way in the sixteenth century; it could have gone only one way at the end of the seventeenth. Protestantism, in a century and a half, had grown from a vigorous minority to an overwhelming majority. Catholicism, in

348

the same time, had ebbed from a largely complacent consensus to a harmless handful.[1]* This revision of the usual Whig scheme of things does not, of course, end the matter. On the contrary, it reminds us that the matter is anything but ended, that only now has the real problem been identified. How could such a change of fortune have overtaken the mighty, revitalized Catholicism of the late sixteenth and seventeenth centuries? How could the English Catholics have dwindled from a formidable if silent majority in 1550 to a mere object of contemptuous pity in 1700?

In pursuing the problem thus redefined, the student will soon discover that the plight of the English Recusants was a phenomenon neither unique nor again altogether typical. The purely local dimension, the sociological and theological make-up of the English Catholics with their varying domestic connections and conflicts, cannot be made the sole or even the dominant factor. Nor can it be said, on the other hand, that everything in the Europe of the Counter-Reformation was determined by who controlled the state, much less by who controlled the main apparatus—military and diplomatic—of international power. The Recusants were not simply pawns in the *Weltpolitik* played by Madrid and Rome, Paris and Westminster. Rather, the truth lies—much as Garrett Mattingly placed it in the specific situation of the Armada crisis—in a combination of the local and the universal in Church and State, the purely English and the international, the particular church and the Church Catholic.

As with many historical contexts similarly complex, the student is inclined to single out an individual institution or group, or even an individual person, who would provide a kind of focal point for his inquiry. The utility of such a research procedure is considerably augmented if the student finds that his selection was actually anticipated by the contemporaries of the topic he is studying. Such is in fact the case of the present study. Recusant history in the seventeenth century is largely the history of a single institution: the Chapter. And the history of the Chapter is in turn largely the history of a single man: Thomas White, alias Blacklo. Few English Catholics of that

---

* At the editor's request for reasons of space, Father Bradley has drastically reduced the extensive supporting and elaborative footnotes which accompanied this essay; its broad foundation in manuscript and printed sources, however, is indicated in a final, general footnote.—Ed.

century had such an impact on their contemporaries as Blacklo had. That the movement called "Blackloism" is now and has been these past two hundred years quite dead cannot change the fact that at one time it was as important a term in ecclesiastical circles as Jansenism. And the very fact that it is so dead today may help explain why the problem of the Catholic demise in England seems so difficult to resolve. It is just possible that reviving Blacklo might provide a much-needed new approach to an old problem sadly obscured by an outworn Whig account.

When Thomas White alias Blacklo landed in England from Douai, in August, 1623, the natural exuberance of a young man just thirty years old, at last launched on his career as an ordained priest and missioner and returning to the challenge of his native land, must have painted for him a prospect of great success. This optimism, however, was not limited to youthful enthusiasm; that summer older and wiser heads among the Recusants were agreeing that a sixty-year winter of discontent was at last unmistakably thawing. That Roman Catholicism was on its way to resuming, after a tragic hiatus, its immemorial role in the life of England was most evidently signalized by the decision of the Holy See that year to reestablish the hierarchy in the form of a vicar apostolic. It is true, this was not a restoration of the normal regime of bishops that had ended in 1559 (and would not begin again until 1850). The "Bishop" of England was still the Bishop of Rome, ruling through his vicar or delegate. But it was a kind of halfway house: the vicar apostolic, though lacking "ordinary" jurisdiction, had full episcopal orders. As such, it approximated the normal Catholic Church order much more closely than the archpriest regime it was supplanting. William Bishop, the papal appointee, landed in England in July, some weeks before Blacklo, and proceeded to establish that concomitant institution of a normal episcopal rule: a chapter. The fact of its establishment demonstrated once more the growing confidence and sense of maturity of the English Mission—at least on the part of those secular priests who composed it, and of those of their younger recruits from the seminary in Douai, among whom was Thomas White.

To appreciate this renewed optimism of the English Catholics, especially in the wake of their crushing disappointment in James I and the repression following the desperate idiocy of the Gunpowder Plot, it is well to remember that if the Catholics were already a minority in England, their oppressors were even more definitely a minority in Christendom. And a beleaguered minority at that, as the Catholic powers were at last engaged in some semblance of concerted action against the heretics. The Hapsburg victory of the White Mountain in the east was soon to be echoed by the Bourbon victory of La Rochelle in the west. Everywhere, it seemed, the Protestant forces were on the defensive; with their backs to the Baltic and the Bay of Biscay, they faced a concentration of political and military power unlike anything in the previous hundred years. Here at last was the Counter-Reformation in full array, the militant thrust of an aroused Romanism bidding to re-establish once and for all the religious unity of Europe.

This impressive unity of the Tridentine Church, however, was better served by its trumpeting legions of baroque angels than by the mundane legions of the secular states. The Catholic nations were—as they had been, after all, for at least three hundred years—as much "nations" as "Catholic." As long as their national and dynastic interests remained, the very preponderance of their cumulative strength only accelerated their centrifugal intents. The Bourbon had inherited the Valois hatred and fear of the Hapsburg; Philip II's imposed unity of world empire undermined both the Spanish and the Portuguese parts of it; Italy was as ever engrossed in petty anti-Spanish intrigue; the papacy itself seemed less the supranational leader than the parochial partisan—its vendetta against Venice was a costly failure. All this internal tension was necessarily reflected in that part of Catholicism that was still English. For the Recusants had for a generation been forced to base their survival on the Continent. The colleges, convents, and seminaries of the English émigrés were inevitably affected by the politico-religious conditions of their French, Spanish, Italian, and Belgian hosts.

As if this very real political complication were not enough to bedevil it, the Counter-Reformation suffered from another source which, because it was more internal yet, was that much more insidious. It was, quite simply, the confusion latent in the idea itself of "Counter-Reformation." Was it essentially a negative thing, a reaction to the Protestant Reformation? If so, the pre-Lutheran *status quo* would seem logically to have been its goal. Or was it, rather, a positive reformation of its own, competing with Protestantism to achieve a new religious regime? Neither of these views prevailed exclusively; indeed, a certain ambiguity was inevitable. For the Church of Rome was committed to continuity with its immediate past. It could admit no essential break with tradition. Thus the official papal rally, the Council of Trent, recognized the canonical status of the clerical corporations, both regular and secular, that most characterized the medieval Church; yet at the same time it radically altered their training and techniques.

Most typical, perhaps, of this mingling of old and new was the new category of religious order called "clerics regular." Actually antedating Trent but "regularized" by it, these new organizations specifically combined the monastic and clerical ideals. More than the mendicant orders that preceded them, they incorporated the traditional notion of ministerial "caste" with a novel application of ministerial "contact." Diversified and mobile, they appropriately considered their proper work as constituting a "mission." Now, possibly the most notable case of the ambivalence of the Counter-Reformation occurred when the most prestigious of the clerics regular —the Jesuits—became engaged in the most critical mission: England.

The Jesuit mission in England had enjoyed the patronage of the highest ecclesiastical authorities, both Roman and native. Of the latter, William Allen, founder of the English College at Douai and later a cardinal, had closely collaborated with the indefatigable Robert Persons in determining the official policy of the English Mission. This policy was best expressed by the word, "enterprise." To Allen, Persons, and their followers—both Jesuits and "seminary priests," the products of Douai and the other colleges for providing an English secular clergy—the "Enterprise of England" meant a thorough *reformation* of the English Church. Inspired by a profound Hildebrandine view of the Church as the unique City of God, yet splendidly Renaissance in their tactics, they were humanistic, clerical, militant, and internationalist. Primarily spiritual in aim, their means would be primarily spiritual as well. Yet they would not hesitate to use the state—the European states—in a kind of crusade against England, as their answer to that state's capure of the national

Church. Their objective, then, was anything but a restoration of the *status quo ante*. The Church of Morton or Wolsey was every bit as alien and abhorrent a prospect to the Jesuits as was the Church of Whitgift or Laud.

The "enterprise" thus officially and auspiciously launched in the 1570s and '80s for the Roman recovery of England quickly ran, however, into an opposition quite other than the official, anticipated opposition on the part of the English state and Church. There were those Catholics in England for whom the "enterprise" was almost as bad as the evil it was supposed to remedy. For them the true objective of the Catholic effort was less a *reformation* than a *restoration*. So intimate and immemorial were the Catholic associations of the English state that for them it was simply inconceivable that the violent withdrawal of the nation from Catholicism could be permanent. The Elizabethan settlement was for them wholly unnatural, and therefore inevitably short-lived. Instead of an enterprising activism, therefore, they urged a policy of watchful waiting. Conservative in their non-religious attitudes as well—aristocratic, traditional in service to the state, courtly, and legalistic—they were inclined to dismiss the Counter-Reformation as an "un-English" thing. Quite sufficient to their purposes, apparently, were the medieval institutions that had too deeply marked the English landscape not eventually to survive the Tudor storm: the historic episcopate, the monastic foundations, the parishes. If the radical reformers can be epitomized by the term "enterprise," the word that correspondingly best expresses these conservative restorers is "loyalty."

Because of the general disarray of English Catholicism following the swift collapse of the Marian restoration and the equally swift Elizabethan settlement, the fundamental division of opinion among the Catholics regarding the nature of the Counter-Reformation did not become particularly apparent until well past the middle of Elizabeth's reign. With the prolonged crisis, however, of the Spanish war and the consequent pressure of the Tudor state, the Catholic party, already on the defensive, grew more desperate and divided. "Loyalty" could comprehend Recusancy, but could it comprehend the "enterprise" now apparently forcing the issue at the cost of all authentic tradition, both Catholic and English? The "Wisbeach Stirs" of 1595, although explicable largely in terms of personalities, were nevertheless the first real manifestation of this intra-Catholic division. The ideological aspect of the division became unmistakably clear in the decade that followed, when two crises in succession definitively tied in the local problem of Recusancy with the Europe-wide problem of the Counter-Reformation. The first was the Appellant controversy, in which a group of secular priests appealed to Rome against its decision to substitute for a renewed episcopal regime an *ad hoc* administration under an archpriest, on the plea that such an arrangement was contrary to tradition and subservient to Jesuit interests. No sooner was this dispute settled (by a kind of compromise, effected significantly by French mediation) than the second crisis occurred, in the wake of the disastrous Gunpowder Plot. An Oath of Allegiance was skillfully devised by the government to force the Recusants to declare for or against the deposing power still formally maintained by Rome. The Catholics had thus to declare not so much their loyalty to the King as their disloyalty to the Pope. Paul V's condemnation of the Oath in 1606 polarized the English Catholic pattern for the remainder of the century: on the one hand were those who saw a papalist, Jesuitical peril, encroaching on both the episcopal constitution of the Church and the royal constitution of the state; on the other hand were those who saw a secularized undermining of the true reformation by the advocates of divine-right sovereignty for both bishops and kings.

That King James I was having at this very time some ideas of his own on episcopacy and monarchy points to a parallel polarization going on among the Protestants. By the 1620s the Established Church of England was at an impasse regarding those members who would purify her not only in spite of but even from bishops. The inevitable political effects of such a Puritan program were not lost on the court. This, plus the Puritan clamor for a renewal of the war on Spain in the interests of the Continental Protestants, moved James toward the policy that dominated the latter years of his reign and indirectly determined the course of Catholic fortunes through all the subsequent Stuart reigns. His proposed marriage alliance with Spain failed, but it led to a similar alliance with France—the second great Catholic power. These events of the mid-twenties provided that rally in Recusant morale noted earlier in this essay, and obscured for a time the recent divisions. Into this charged context, then, we must place the beginnings of the career of Thomas White alias Blacklo.

The very few details we have of his early life reveal a background rather typical of the "seminary priest" of the early seventeenth century. A grandson of the Elizabethan jurist and Recusant, Edmund Plowden, he seems to have come from substantial stock: Catholic, middle class, and "East Saxon."[2] Shortly after a curiously narrated "imprisonment for the faith" when ten years old (in 1603), he went on to what he would later most certainly have considered a longer imprisonment: a sojourn at the famous Jesuit college at St. Omer in Flanders.[3] Whatever may have been the effect of this early exposure to Puritans and Jesuits, young White by the year 1609 was entered on a formal course of training for the ministry. This took him first to Spain where he spent five years, mainly at the English college in Valladolid, then back to the Spanish Netherlands—the natural center on the Continent for the Recusant émigrés. A short stay at Louvain was followed by his final undergraduate work in theology at the English College in Douai; and there, on March 25, 1617, he was ordained to the priesthood. His talents were already evident, for he was immediately assigned to teach philosophy at the college, which task he fulfilled with distinction until his thirtieth year, in 1623.

Before becoming involved in the deep matters of ecclesiastical polity that were now to involve Thomas White alias Blacklo almost to the end of his days, we must first make some estimate of the intellectual content of the position with which he would be very soon and forever thereafter identified. He was, surely in his own estimation, first a *savant*—a theoretician in theology, philosophy, and mathematics; only then would he have considered himself a technician—a manipulator of persons and policies. Thus the purely speculative was immensely important to Blacklo; and in his speculative world the most important ingredient was undoubtedly his Aristotelianism. At a time when the first great concerted action to depose "the Philosopher" was under way, when the new academies in Italy and France were bringing to full bloom the Platonism of the sixteenth century, it is perhaps surprising to find such uncomplicated commitment to Aristotle as we find in Blacklo. The sensible sureness of the Stagirite must have deeply impressed the young seminarian, for this scholastic loyalty remained with him long after the many concomitant loyalties of those early years had vanished. For Blacklo, *the* enemy, in terms of which all his many enemies would be reductively identified, was skepticism—the sophistical, cynical spirit stemming from that riot of imagination called the Renaissance and threatening all the ancient sanctities.

Blacklo's Aristotelianism did not, however, preclude another element only slightly less conspicuous in his intellectual make-up. He was hardly the austere schoolman absorbed in yet another grand systematization of *Sentences*. Rather, he professed a genuine curiosity (not unlike the original Aristotle's) in contemporary studies that the universities were still largely ignoring. Philology and mathematics had mightily accelerated the tempo of the learned world; there were more things in word and number than were dreamt of in the old trivium and quadrivium of the schools. By a curious convergence of forces, a new textual criticism in theology and a new empirical inquiry in science were threatening the old complacent compendium of philosophy. And just as curiously, we find Blacklo ranged on either side of this confrontation. His Aristotelian sympathies would not preclude his sympathies for such anti-Aristotelians as St-Cyran on the one hand and Mersenne on the other. That he was considerably more than sympathetic toward such a thoroughly Renaissance Man as Kenelm Digby—that very model of the seventeenth-century virtuoso—seems to put Blacklo in that rare intellectual company that lives on Pascalian paradox.

At this point in our inquiry the mention of St-Cyran, Mersenne, and Pascal is no accident, for by the 1620s and '30s France was the magnetic field of first magnitude for any Europe-wide interest. Specifically, the English Catholics were feeling strong French influence —latent in the Appellant and Allegiance affairs, and now quite open in the administration of the first vicar apostolic, William Bishop. Before his appointment in 1623, Bishop was a doctor of the Sorbonne and a long-time resident of the College of Arras, a court-subsidized center for English émigré scholars. The most important accomplishment of his brief term of office was the establishment of the Chapter; and for this act we have his explicit indebtedness to "some wise men of France."[4] Although personally unidentified, these "wise men" must have been his confreres, French and English, at the Sorbonne and Arras. And when he died, in April of 1624, his successor, named some months later, was another Francophile: Richard Smith.

Since Recusant affairs were destined to be centered for nearly thirty years, in one way or another, around the person of this new vicar apostolic of England and Bishop of Chalcedon, the close association he had with Blacklo, especially at the outset of his administration, should be noted. Blacklo left England after only a few months (about the time the Chapter was established), and returned to Douai; but again, on the news of Bishop's death, he got leave to go to Paris. His stated purpose was to study canon law, but in the following year he was sent to Rome as official Agent for the newly installed Smith. It was not long before a bitter quarrel erupted in England, which renewed and complicated all the preceding differences among the Catholics, and neutralized whatever advantages they had gained from the new King's French marriage. At the heart of the quarrel lay Smith's assertion that his right to rule the Church in England was less a matter of papal delegation than a matter of ordinary jurisdiction inherent in his episcopal office. It was a confusing mixture of principles and personalities; for most of the lay Catholic nobility whose "loyalty" would have been expected to rally to him were alienated by what they considered Smith's arrogance, while partisans of the Jesuits whose "enterprise" would have been expected to contemn the sensibilities of the English government protested that Smith's imprudences were sacrificing the good will of Whitehall. A kind of anti-Chalcedon coalition was the result. Smith felt himself more and more isolated; when, finally in 1631, he was informed from Rome that the Holy Office would supplant the Congregation *de Propaganda Fide* in adjudicating the controversy, he requested a leave of absence and returned to France. Thus began the anomaly of a bishop absent from his post in England and under suspicion at Rome, yet refusing to resign and protected from deposition by the favor of France.

Blacklo was involved in this crisis of Chalcedon in a curiously ambivalent way. In 1630, after four years in Rome and at the height of the quarrel in England, he resigned his Agency and became, after another short interval at Douai, president of the recently established English College in Lisbon. He spent three years there, codifying and applying rules for the first English seminary not in any way connected with the Jesuits—and running into trouble with the local Inquisition because of some of his ideas on grace and the sacraments. Whether because of this difficulty or because of his desire to get back into the main stream of things now moving so swiftly, he left Portugal for England, and from there resigned his presidency. He was now forty years old; his ten-year absence from England had endowed him with a varied experience in academics, in diplomacy, in administration, such as could be matched by few if any of his clerical contemporaries. But he had escaped having to make a decision on the spot for or against Chalcedon, and he was something of a stranger in his native country. These ambiguities regarding him perhaps explain the curious fact that he was among the Chapter's nominees for eventual successor to Smith before he was admitted into the membership of the Chapter itself. At any rate, by the mid-thirties Blacklo was an important man in England, one to be reckoned with in any clerical calculation of Catholic fortunes and prospects. And in those years, with the personal "tyranny" of Charles I so strongly influenced by his queen and court, those fortunes and prospects looked propitious indeed.

Sometime toward the end of that decade, when the postponed problems of the King's peace began to consolidate the protests of Puritans and Parliament-men, Blacklo with some others in the Chapter must have become aware of a peculiarly parallel phenomenon in their Recusant world. The Chapter, created and confirmed on the initiative of the vicars apostolic, was never formally recognized by papal authority. Its juridical existence depended, therefore, on Richard Smith. Yet now, who needed whom the more? Who was *de facto* the stronger power among the English Catholics: a vicar apostolic only in name, absent and in quasi-disgrace; or a council of the most influential priests in the country, present individually and corporately at the center of events? The temper of the times was surely running against both King and bishop in England; the civil war in the English state presaged a civil war in what was left of the English Catholic Church.

Despite the meager documentation for these years of Blacklo's life, we can surmise, in the light of later events, something of their crucial import. The Counter-Reformation had clearly arrived at a kind of impasse. The policy of militant state action, so promising a mere fifteen or twenty years earlier, was now at a dead end. The Hapsburg bid for restored imperial and Catholic unity in Central Europe was decisively beaten by an alliance forged by a cardinal of the Holy Roman Church. And in the west, this same Richelieu was leaving as an ultimate bequest not the harrying of the Huguenots but the bullying of Rome. The policy, too, of vigorous, enlightened clerical action had provoked a counter-movement within the Church. The most notable of such "counter-counter-reformations" was, of course, Jansenism—the mention of which immediately involves us in one of the great themes of the remainder of Blacklo's life.

Sometime in 1643, after ten years in England and five years in the Chapter, Blacklo left once more for the Continent. The explicit reason for this move is not clear, but it would seem circumstantially to be due to several converging considerations on Blacklo's part. First, the Chapter had just recommended him for the "vicary" of London, the office requiring the closest Continental connections. Secondly, some notable Catholic émigrés were gathering in Paris around Queen Henrietta Maria and her family. Thirdly, by what must have been a rather pleasant coincidence for Blacklo, Paris was at this very time overtaking the Italian cities as the real center of activity for Europe's greatest savants; thanks largely to the tireless coordinating efforts of Marin Mersenne, an appropriate Parisian platform was made available to Descartes, Gassendi, Hobbes, and the young Pascal. And fourthly, and most hypothetically of all, the enigmatic St-Cyran—the famed "Petrus Aurelius" to whom the Chapter had written thanks for his pro-Chalcedon (and anti-Jesuit) tracts—had just died, following his old enemy Richelieu to the grave and leaving behind his nascent sect of Port-Royal whose devotion to the controversial *Augustinus* would soon make them known across Europe as "Jansenists." Blacklo, in the Paris of the 1640s, has finally reached the crisis of his career—and that of the Counter-Reformation.

As if to highlight this conjunction of crises, in 1645 Blacklo interrupted his French sojourn to accompany his friend Sir Kenelm

Digby on a quasi-ambassadorial mission from Henrietta Maria to the court of Rome. More important, certainly, than the unsuccessful request for papal aid to the beleaguered Charles I (could *any* foreign aid be expected after Naseby!), the renewed experience thus gained of the Roman world apparently sealed all the impressions that for twenty years had been slowly maturing in Blacklo's mind. As he and Digby intimated in subsequent correspondence, Innocent X was the perfect embodiment of this papacy that the times were leaving behind. The papal protest over the Peace of Westphalia was only the most obvious instance of outmoded "enterprise," pathetically unaware of the new secular dominance that, like Leviathan, was subordinating all interests, including religion, to its own survival and aggrandizement. Moreover, Rome's obsolete politics were matched, in Blacklo's eyes, by its obscurantist philosophy: the sophism of a teaching authority that felt it could ignore all reasons other than its own capricious fiat.

Yet, if "enterprise"—that once heroic new idea of a Rome-inspired reformation—was, in Blacklo's mind, something utterly dead by the mid-seventeenth century, so too was "loyalty." Presumably a reliable partisan of that older, Appellant world of fixed allegiances, Blacklo now for the first time clearly shows that for him the idea of an England-inspired restoration is equally out of date. Service in the Stuart cause—such as his and Digby's embassy—was a negotiable affair, certainly not a matter of life or death. By the end of the first Civil War the two men had formed with two others of the Chapter a conspiratorial "committee of correspondence" later to be notorious as "Blacklo's Cabal."[5] The basic proposal of these letters of 1646–1648 was to establish an episcopal regime for England under the direction of the Chapter, in the sense that the bishops selected by them and consecrated in France under their auspices would necessarily be more dependent on them than on Rome. The papacy would necessarily acquiesce in this in order to avoid the greater evil of outright schism; while the civil government would similarly be necessitated by its postwar problems to welcome the proffered cooperation of the Chapter in securing a general domestic peace.

That the Cabal's brave program never got beyond the talking

stage is not particularly surprising. Neither the Chapter nor the civil government was as cooperative as the Paris-based plotters blithely assumed they would be. The victorious Independents were indeed for toleration, but not for Roman Catholics; they could afford to ignore the distinctions among the papists. As for the Chapter, there were still those members for whom Richard Smith, in spite of his nearly two-decade absence from England, was still legitimate superior. By 1649 this group had become a recognizable party under the leadership of George Leyburn. When, in fact, the Chapter met in August of that year, the two factions—Blackloist and anti-Blackloist—faced a stalemate. The Cabal had failed to effect a coup; yet its challenge to Leyburn's caretaker regime was as effectively disruptive of the English Catholic life throughout the 1650s as its proposed secular counterpart, the Independent Army, was of English life in general.

This suggested parallel between the Blackloists and the Army leaders of the Commonwealth was to be recognized by both friends and enemies of Blacklo before the decade was out. Although both he and Leyburn were absent from England through most of this time, their respective factions in the Chapter regularly frustrated its periodic meetings. By 1653 it was as hopeless an organ of government as a Cromwellian Parliament. But Blacklo, the would-be "Lord Protector" of the English Catholic Church, was simply in no position to assert the ascendancy that he was convinced he had. The Chapter's indecision was bad enough; what made it worse was that it was more than matched by Rome's decision. Innocent X had finally condemned the Five Propositions from the *Augustinus,* and thus in effect forced the Jansenists to declare for or against the Roman Church. Here was an echo of the old "enterprise," a seizing of the initiative that would meet the threat of schism head-on. But at the same time, and even more frustrating in its repercussions on Blacklo, there was a counter-revival of "loyalty" implicit in Mazarin's artful rally of the monarchy against the Fronde. On both fronts, then, Blacklo could sense a crisis of constriction. An old man at sixty, he could see his life's work—the true reform of the Catholic Church—in peril. The spate of writing through the next decade would be his last desperate bid to stave off the "restorations" and the "armadas" alike of his benighted co-religionists and countrymen.

Blacklo had, of course, already published several works. By 1654 most of his characteristic attitudes were not only clearly expressed, whether in Latin or English, but more or less permanently fixed. Thus, his simplified Aristotelian thesis on demonstrability appeared in his first book, the *De Mundo* of 1642; and it was followed by the most comprehensive discussion of natural philosophy that he ever wrote, his *Peripatetical Institutions* of 1647. Likewise in polemical theology appeared his *Answer to Falkland* in 1651, in which he lays down for the first time his great thesis on the complete adequacy of the argument from tradition. In speculative theology his *Institutiones Sacrae* of 1652 enunciated a logical application of his previously stated positions: if the divine economy—of creation and sanctification—is based on an intrinsic, demonstrable analysis of essences, and not on an extrinsic, unpredictable intervention of volitions, then there is no room in authoritative Catholic theology for such myths and anthropomorphisms as "souls suffering in purgatory," especially if at the same time there is no clear and consistent witness to such notions in the total tradition of the Church. This instance of purgatory was indeed a kind of touchstone of Blackloism. In the following year he issued his *De Medio Animarum Statu,* the first of several expositions of this spiritualized, detemporalized "middle state" which symbolized most aptly his "school": a severe rationalism equaled only by the severe antiquarianism that accompanied it.[6]

Seeing the accumulating crises of Christendom in the mid-fifties, Blacklo must have felt that the only direct action left to him must no longer be delayed: he must force a showdown by writing a resounding attack on the whole apparatus of Counter-Reformation as devised and maintained these hundred years by the Roman Curia and their Jesuit henchmen. Appropriately entitling this work *Sonus Buccinae,* he would fell the Roman Jericho that was impeding the progress of God's people in both science and faith. Jesuitical word-jugglers were reducing truth to probability, while pompous canonists were inflating opinions into dogmas. The monstrous mechanism of Rome was the main obstacle, to be sure; but there was also the foolish, nostalgic, divisive obstacle of an England that refused to recognize the realities of political power. Accordingly he penned a fateful little commentary on *The Grounds of Obedience and Government:* leaving unnamed both Cromwell and the Stuarts, he urged recognition of the *de facto* regime. He did not have to wait long for answers to his twofold challenge. Rome responded by condemning outright his "trumpet-blast"—it was his first such condemnation; and England, in the person of a cautious Chapter, served notice that it would seek from Rome, quite irrespective of Blacklo, a successor to Richard Smith who at long last had died.

The years that followed these events were almost inevitably anticlimactic, in Blacklo's career as in the general history of the Counter-Reformation. Curiously paralleling the Jansenist Arnauld, who at this time suffered the censure of the Sorbonne, Blacklo maintained his positions while categorically protesting his integral Roman Catholicism. He formally submitted his writings to the Holy See, only to have them condemned again. Throughout the late fifties and early sixties, with all hope gone of ever becoming bishop himself but just strong enough to prevent through his partisans in the Chapter a decision to have any other as bishop, he continued to write—if anything, more voluminously and incisively—on the mathematics, dogmatics, and polemics of his previous works.[7] But by that time they were "thoughts" more than actions; and if this again suggests a parallel with a Jansenist—Pascal—Blacklo himself had anticipated it. Gratified to share the same condemnation of 1657 with the author of the *Provinciales,* he must have perceived that just as the genius of Port-Royal was dead in 1662, so on his return to England in that same year his career was for all practical purposes finished. The Restoration had largely nullified his prestige if not his position, and a Chapter *Manifest* in that year indicated the isolation he had suffered from the impact of the successive Roman condemnations, the fourth and last of which came in 1663. His last published works appeared then, too: his *Exetasis Scientiae,* warning the cardinals of the Holy Office that the Jesuits were as much their enemies as his; and his *Exclusion of Skepticks,* commending his Aristotelian certitudes to the chaos of conjectures he saw ahead.

If Thomas White alias Blacklo, now a septuagenarian and in quasi-retirement in Drury Lane, has almost finished his course, the same cannot be said of Blackloism. It remains to discuss this force that survived its founder by at least a generation until the English Catholic body had almost ceased to exist. Lacking any authoritative self-definition by either master or disciples, we can only speculate on the accuracy of the description that comes most readily to mind: Blackloism is a kind of English Jansenism. If Jansenism is essentially an anti-Jesuitism (as some students, at a loss to find a more positive common denominator for all Jansenists, might contend),[8] then there is some basis for identifying Blacklo with it. For certainly it would be hard to find any feeling or judgment more invariable amid all the varied circumstances of his life than his almost obsessive hatred of the Jesuits. Unlike the papacy, or the English monarchy, or the universities, good things abused by evil men, for Blacklo the Society of Jesus was itself the evil thing abusing what might otherwise have been good men. In this attitude he was as much at one with Jansen and St-Cyran and Arnauld as those three were at one among themselves.

In contrast, however, to this negativeness that seems to designate the Jansenist ensemble, Blackloism implies—as much as Jesuitism itself does—a positive thing: an integral program of reformation in the Catholic Church. The opposition between Blacklo's ideas and Loyola's vis-à-vis Catholicism is thus—as the logicians would say— more one of contraries than one of contradictories. As intimated earlier in this essay, the basic Blackloist ideas can be summarized as a duality: a severe rationalism asserting the *demonstrability* of faith, and an equally severe antiquarianism asserting the inviolability of *tradition*. Blacklo harmonized the apparent dichotomy of these principles by insisting on the one hand that discursive reasoning in theology can produce propositions as clear and cogent as any in geometry, and on the other hand that the data of revelation can be —indeed must be—transmitted from age to age with a quasi-mechanical precision. It all resulted in a system as consistent and complacent as any that that century of mechanistic genius produced.

But the very perfection of the system is its undoing. Taken individually, the rationalism and the traditionalism are both authentically Catholic—and quite Jesuit. But Blacklo tried to identify the two. He took Tradition out of the traditional trusteeship of a living hierarchical authority, and, denying the alternatives of a voice from heaven or an earthly plebiscite (for neither alternative was ever seriously entertained by the non-contemplative, non-democratic Blacklo), he confided it to computers. In revenge this denatured Tradition turned on his Demonstrability and ruined it. For what had set out to be a demonstration of what had been in the Church became instead a declamation on what should be—the Church of antiquity yields to the Church of "the Third Age."[9] And all this theology is geometrically clear because, ultimately, Blacklo wills it so!

Even from this hasty analysis it is evident that we have here a reformer of unusual power and individuality. Yet, unlike Pascal—whose "reasons of the heart" Blacklo could never comprehend—he would not leave behind him simply thoughts in solitude. He was the technician as well as the *savant;* he must have an institution, an apparatus, to implement his reforms. He was less a Jansenist, really, than a Jesuit-*manqué!* For his purpose he found at hand what others took to be merely the fortuitous caretaker government of the Church in England, but what he took to be the providential beachhead for the eventual overhauling of the Church Universal: the Chapter. Here was the most authentic link with the New Testament Church and the most appropriate link with the Church of the future: a presbytery of élite, bound together by a common cause as much as any "Company" or "Covenant" could command. By this means he could effect the *real* Reformation—neither a return to the "loyalty" of the pre-Tridentine particularists, nor a pursuit of the "enterprise" of the post-Tridentine totalitarians. Gothic episcopacy and baroque papacy were both too recent in the Church's past and too irrational for her future. Only a Blackloist Chapter could effect the necessary and definitive "counter-counter-reformation."

No wonder that the first suspicions and the last recriminations came not from the Jesuits or any other clerics regular, but from his own fellows in the secular clergy. Smith and Leyburn voiced the opinion of a probable majority when they saw threatened by Blacklo not only the "enterprise" to which they might be indifferent, but the "loyalty" to which everything English—secular and sacred—committed them. Blackloism appeared to them as both republican and presbyterian; his faction in the Chapter was simply a new ecclesiastical model of the Rump. No wonder, again, that when toward the end of his life Blacklo consorted with the "atheist" Hobbes, the same majority concurred in the cruel verdict: "Thomas White is an evil old man."[10] And as for the verdict from Rome: that too was clear through all those declining years. The censures were never as rigorously logical as the propositions they condemned, but no matter; whatever this man would say could be dangerous. Thus alienated from both Rome and England, yet never having repudiated either, Thomas White alias Blacklo died July 6, 1676; and somewhere near the pulpit of St. Martin's-in-the-Fields he lies buried.

There is no need to dwell on the immediate sequel of Blacklo's death: the Oates Plot of 1678, and all that it meant in terms of the effective demise of English Catholicism as a real factor in the national life.[11] James II, of course, would still become King, but his repeal of Recusancy was stillborn. The decision of 1688 was inevitable in a manner that the decision of 1588 never was. What might have been retrieved even after the Gunpowder Plot became irretrievable even before the Popish Plot. Somewhere in between those dates—in the dark days of the mid-century—the English Catholic body, as a body, died. And on the basis of this preliminary inquiry we have reason to suspect that it was a death not by murder but by suicide.

This hypothesis still leaves problematic the specific role of Blackloism. Was it indeed the true Reformation, purifying the Church of both medievalist reaction and Renaissance radicalism, and for that very reason destroyed by those two unlikely allies? Or was it in turn just strong enough to defeat the last chance of the "loyalty" and the "enterprise" mutually reconciled only in their ruin? Or again, was it its own casualty, self-defeated by the intrinsic tensions of that remarkable spirit, at once so Pascalian and non-Pascalian, so anti-Jesuit and Jesuit-*manqué*? The problems remain largely unsolved —but at least we have moved beyond the old Whig simplicities. And amid the new complexities this much is clear: there was a crisis within the Counter-Reformation in England, and Blacklo was somehow central to it. Indeed, the Roman Catholicism which he tried to reform but never renounced was somehow different—more rigid yet more patient, surer yet wiser—because he had lived.[12]

NOTES

1. There is as yet no adequate study of Recusant statistics in the sixteenth and seventeenth centuries. The best general survey of the numerical decline of Roman Catholicism in England is Brian Magee's *The English Recusants: a study of the post-Reformation Catholic survival and the operation of the Recusancy laws* (London, 1938).

2. His father, Richard White of Hutton, Essex, married Mary Plowden; *Recusant Roll, 1592–93* (Catholic Record Society, Vol. 18, London, 1916), p. 117. From his frequent mention of his native country on the title pages of his works, White must have been proud of "the English Goshen."

3. *Register of the English College at Valladolid* (C. R. S., Vol. 30, London, 1930), p. 100.

4. *The Third Douay Diary, 1598–1637* (C. R. S., Vol. 10, London), p. 224. The writer is William Farrar, Bishop's secretary.

5. The correspondents, besides Blacklo and Digby, were Henry Holden and Peter Fitton. Holden was a doctor of the Sorbonne and was generally considered as Blacklo's "Melancthon." Their letters were collected and published in 1680, in the aftermath of the Popish Plot, by Robert Pugh, entitled by him: *Blacklo's Cabal, discovered in several of their letters clearly expressing designs inhumane against Regulars, unjust against the laity, schismatical against the pope, cruel against orthodox clergymen, and owning the nullity of the Chapter, their opposition of episcopal authority.*

6. An English translation, entitled *The middle state of souls from the hour of death to the day of judgment*, appeared in 1659. Three other, minor works date also from this time: two short polemical pieces on grace, and a collection of devotional meditations.

7. The list is too long to be incorporated here. In all there were twenty-two separate titles: nine in theology, three in mathematics, two in philosophy, one translation of an earlier Latin work, and seven pamphlets of various polemics.

8. Cf. Nigel Abercrombie, *The origins of Jansenism* (Oxford, 1936), p. 174. Blacklo was understandably reticent to talk about his

connections with Jansenists. However, he never disguised his sympathies for them; see, *e.g.*, his *Monumethan Excantatus* (Rouen, 1660), pp. 67–68.

9. The "third age" was that of pure reason, supplanting the first two ages, those of pure faith and of a combination of faith and reason respectively. Although Blacklo denies its caricature by a hostile critic ("S. W.," *Vindication of the doctrine contained in Pope Benedict XII his Bull*, Paris, 1659, pp. 84–92), he defends this scheme of Church history in his *Religion and reason mutually corresponding and assisting each other* (Paris, 1660), p. 115.

10. George Leyburn, "Catalogus spectabiliorum sacerdotum. . . ," written in 1667 or 1668, and inserted in *The Fifth Douay Diary* (C. R. S., Vol. 11, London, 1911), p. 533.

11. There was an ominous connection between the Plot and Blackloism, in the person of John Sergeant. See Malcolm V. Hay's *The Jesuits and the Popish Plot* (London, 1934).

12. *A Bibliographical Note.* Editorial exigencies as well as the general nature of this essay have precluded its full documentation. The few footnotes were confined to citations explicitly occasioned by the text. Of these, it will be noticed, a fair percentage were taken from the series published by the Catholic Record Society (54 vols., London, 1905–), undoubtedly the best edited and most readily available collection of sources in Recusant history. The fragmentary character of this series, moreover, reflects the situation that still obtains in this area of English Catholic studies, especially for the mid-seventeenth century. A brief bibliographical résumé may serve to indicate the direction of further research no less than to substantiate this exposition of what has already been done.

Among manuscript sources, the most pertinent general collections are the Roman Transcripts in the Public Records Office (P. R. O. 31/9, 10) and the twenty-four bound volumes covering the years 1612–1686 in the Archdiocesan Archives of Westminster (Series "A," Vols. XI–XXXIV). These latter are admirably supplemented by the extensive archival materials in the library of the Jesuits' Stonyhurst College (especially A.I.29, A. IV.13, and Anglia A.II–V). A smaller but equally valuable collection, the archives of the Old Brotherhood (the present-day lineal descendent of the seventeenth-century Chapter), is as yet unavailable for general use, as are, of course, the papers of the Holy Office. However, two other important Roman sources, the Propaganda archives and the Barberini papers in the Vatican Library, are doubly available, since they constitute a sizable portion of the P. R. O. transcripts mentioned earlier. Finally, some scattered pieces in the British Museum (Add. and Egerton MSS., mainly) and the Bodleian (Rawlinson and Tanner MSS.), plus, of course, the latter's great Clarendon and Ormonde (Carte) collections, are most helpful, especially for the political side of the study.

For printed sources, the best single repository on this side of the Atlantic is the McAlpin Collection in the library of the Union Theological Seminary in New York. Of the forty-four titles that sum up Blacklo's published work, about half—and by far the more important half—are at Union. There also, in comparable proportion and occasionally in various editions, are the works of practically all the prominent ecclesiastical writers of seventeenth-century England, in particular for this study: Smith, Kellison, Digby, and Sergeant. The McAlpin must yield, of course, to the virtually inexhaustible resources of the British Museum and its close runner-up, the Bodleian. Of unique value, however, are the specialized libraries that share directly the heritage of the émigré colleges. Of these, Ushaw, Oscott (two diocesan seminaries, in the North and in the Midlands respectively), and Stonyhurst come most readily to mind. The indispensable guide for the earlier period, superceding *S. T. C.* which it both supplements and corrects, is A. F. Allison and D. M. Rogers, *A catalogue of Catholic books in English printed abroad or secretly in England, 1558–1640,* which appeared as Numbers three and four of Volume III of *Biographical Studies* (Bagnor Regis, 1956).

Besides the volumes of the Catholic Record Society already mentioned, the more prominent standard collections are the following: Henry Foley, *Records of the English Province of the Society of Jesus* (7 vols., London, 1877–83); Thomas F. Knox, *Records of the English Catholics under the penal laws* (2 vols, London, 1878–82); Auguste Carayon, *Collection de documents inédits concernant la Compagnie de Jésus* (23 vols, Paris, 1863–86); Thomas Law, *Documents relating to the dissentions of the Roman Catholic clergy* (Edinburgh, 1896); and Lucien Ceyssens, *Sources relatives aux débuts du jansénisme et de l'antijansénisme*—Louvain, 1957). After these should be listed the "classical" general histories—all greatly outdated, but still most useful for reference purposes: William M. Brady, *The episcopal succession in England, Scotland, and Ireland* (3 vols, Rome, 1876–77); Charles Butler,

Historical memoirs of the English, Irish, and Scottish Catholics since the Reformation (4 vols, London, 1822); M. A. Tierney's edition of Dodd's *Church history of England from the commencement of the sixteenth century to the revolution of 1688* (5 vols, London, 1839–43); and Joseph Gillow, *A literary and biographical history, or bibliographical dictionary of English Catholics from the breach with Rome in 1534 to the present time* (5 vols, London, 1885–1902).

Rather than trail off with a random list of monographs and articles, I can perhaps better conclude this résumé by listing the contemporary authorities whom I would consider outstanding in Recusant historiography. Although the list is admittedly incomplete, it is fairly representative. It must be headed by the name of J. H. Pollen, who in the first decades of this century pioneered much of this field. He has been ably succeeded by that "historian's historian," Leo Hicks. Basil Fitzgibbon, a third English Jesuit, also deserves special mention. Among the English secular clergy, Gordon Albion and Philip Hughes are perhaps the most illuminating. The present leaders in the field, who have immeasurably accelerated the pace of study especially by their co-editorship of *Recusant History* (the successor to the previously mentioned *Biographical Studies*, Bagnor Regis, 1951–), are Anthony F. Allison of the British Museum and David M. Rogers of the Bodleian, together with their indefatigable collaborator, T. A. Birrell of the University of Nijmegen. Among the new generation of students mention should be made of John A. Bossy of Cambridge, Thomas H. Clancy of Loyola in New Orleans, Albert J. Loomie of Fordham, and Anthony J. Petti of Queen Mary College, London. These are scholars who would have well graced a Mattingly seminar. With them—as with my old master and confreres at Columbia, all of whom shared with me an appreciation of and an encouragement in Recusant studies—I am proud to be associated.

THESE BE BUT WOMEN

SISTER

JOSEPH DAMIEN HANLON

C. S. J.

St. Joseph's College for Women

In a secluded spot on the banks of the Tyne, about three miles below Newcastle, there stood St. Anthony's, the spacious home of a pious and wealthy widow, Dame Dorothy Lawson. Here in the undisturbed serenity of her country home, we have the epitome of the way of life of considerable segments of the Catholic gentry in the middle years of the reign of James I. Diminished and weakened though Catholic tradition might be after several decades of penal laws, Father Pollard in 1610 could still claim:

> The number of Catholics in these parts [Yorkshire] is so great that among my friends and acquaintances, the most of them, if not all, being gentlemen of good account, I can travel from this side Lincoln to York, and so thirty mile farther, which is above eighty mile, and within every six mile come to a Catholic house, and for the most part within three mile, all or the most of them gentlemen's or gentlewomen's houses of good account, and for all this, I will not in all that way, go six mile out of the ready and nighest way.[1]

That this continuance and preservation of the Catholic faith was due chiefly to the Catholic laity of England, especially to the staunch courage of its women, was the opinion of no less a person than the famous Jesuit, Father Robert Persons.[2] Though these lay Catholic men and women were not drawn from any one class of society, almost inevitably one's mind turns first to the integrity and constancy of the great Catholic families of England without whom little or nothing could have been accomplished—to such families as the Talbots, Arundels, Bedingfields, Dormers. Mass centers were necessary to any preservation and no places were more convenient for this than the great houses of Catholic nobility and gentry scattered up and down the country. Often in remote areas, and in some cases immune from search by government emissaries, these houses afforded admirable headquarters for missionary activities.

Though the fame of St. Anthony's as such a center of Catholic continuance and renewal in the north spread widely, Dame Dorothy was but one of a goodly company of "gentlewomen." There were many other Northumberland Recusant[3] families of her rank—the Widdringtons, Fenwicks, Radcliffes, Swinburnes, Collingwoods, Thirlwalls, Selbies, Thorntons, and her close friends and neighbors the Hodgsons of Hebburn, to mention only a few.[4] Among all of these the solidity of a close interrelationship slowly developed as they soberly intermarried their daughters and sons.[5] Nor was Mrs. Dorothy Lawson the only "Pauline widow" in these conservative communities of Catholic gentry to play her part at this time in the expenditure of wealth for the maintenance and expansion of the Faith. There were also, for example, the elderly Lady Magdalen Montague, her daughter Lady Dormer (who was also Dorothy Lawson's aunt), the Dowager Countess of Arundel, Lady Stonor, Lady Lovell, the three Vaux women. The power of wealth was in all these devout households, although wealth was not the only factor in helping their works of piety, and in providing the ladies with protection from the rigor of penal statutes.

Leniency in the observance of the laws owed much as well to the close connection existing between the gentry and civic office in certain towns. This seems especially to have been the case at Newcastle-upon-Tyne, at least as reflected in the roll of mayors and sheriffs in the Carr MS.[6] From the years 1603–34 covered by that list, only one mayor and sheriff seem to have been from outside the families of landed property in that area. Nor do Recusant connections (as opposed to actual Recusancy) appear to have been a bar to election, for names like Sir George Selby, James Clavering, Robert Shafto, Sir Thomas Riddell, and Sir Peter Riddell appear frequently on the lists as sheriffs or mayors. They were of great help in furthering the work of Dorothy Lawson, especially Sir Thomas Riddell, a coal owner, who was sheriff in 1601 and mayor in 1604 and 1616, despite the fact his wife and eldest son were Recusants.[7]

It is not possible to determine in any exact way the frequency or extent of success the Catholic gentry enjoyed in escaping the penalty of Recusancy through their neighbors' charity, embarrassment, or lethargy, but we do know that Mrs. Lawson's success was no exception. There is, for example, evidence in a letter from the *Montagu Musters Book*[8] of leniency toward Sir Thomas Brudenell, afterwards Lord Brudenell of Dene. Wrote the justices in 1613:

> Sir Thomas Brudenell beinge divers times beefore us himselfe, his wife and many of his familie to the number of fifteen Recusantes; when if there had not beene too much regard had of him by some of us, there had passed a conviction before this time.

Not only did many squires and their ladies preserve their status and wealth; under James many of these rich Catholic gentry, like Dorothy's own uncle, Sir Robert Dormer, even rose to peerages in spite of their religion. These men were, of course, on the whole of a nature and stamp worldly-wise, ambitious, engaging, diplomatic, and sufficiently pliant in their religious perceptions to satisfy James' requirements. Sir Robert Dormer had paid the sum of £10,000 in 1615 for the title of Baron Dormer.[9] Such wealth might at once arouse the greedy instincts of James and his favorites and at the same time provide, by judicious employment, the influence to stave off official Recusant status, and therefore heavy fines, for many years. A notable example of this nimbleness was Dorothy Lawson's own brother Sir Henry Constable of Burton Constable, who had inherited great estates in Yorkshire in 1607 at the death of his father. Sir Henry was a suave, extravagant youth—at one time losing £3,000 in one sitting of gaming—and a determined one. Knighted at London in 1614, he began his skillful manipulation of court favoritism, through Buckingham, to procure for himself a Scottish peerage in 1620 as Baron Constable and Viscount Dunbar.[10] Henry

Constable managed with dexterity to stave off formal Recusancy charges until 1629, and even then obtained from the King a letter of immunity, so that it was not until 1630 that Viscount Dunbar paid any heavy fine as a Recusant. He was then ordered to pay £250 a year, an amelioration of a far heavier assessment, brought about through royal favor.[11] Lord Fauconberg, a very wealthy man, successfully evaded conviction for Recusancy all his life though secretly a Catholic since 1615.[12]

But above and beyond all the technicalities of fines and laws, there continued to exist, especially in the women of the households, a serene conviction of the unarguable truth of their ancestral Faith, a tough confidence, and a matter-of-fact determination to assure its ultimate triumph. An attitude of calm assumption that this would come shines through the terms of a trust formed in the early years of the reign of Charles I by Elizabeth Tarleton:

> But if Catholic times come upp, the black suit of church stuff shall goe to Herkerk Chapell if one be, or else to the parish church of Sefton, and the silver guilded chalice shall go into Sefton Church so shall the white suite also goe with the chalice.[13]

In Dorothy Lawson's life and achievements, this temperament and attitude reign supreme.

Born at Winge in Buckinghamshire in 1580 at the home of her grandfather Sir William Dormer, as second daughter of Sir Henry Constable of Burton Constable in Holderness and of Margaret Dormer, sister of Sir Robert Dormer, created a baronet and elevated to the peerage by the title of Baron Dormer of Winge in 1615, Dorothy from the first had the comfortable security of a powerful Yorkshire lineage, as well as a devoutly Catholic one.[14] Her mother suffered much persecution and a long imprisonment under Elizabeth on account of her refusal to conform to the Anglican religion.[15] She is a notable example of a factor that cannot be overlooked in evaluating the intangible forces that kept a Catholic minority alive—the influence of the women of the households. The Bishop of Winchester stated in 1580 that notwithstanding his success in persuading diverse persons of his diocese to come to church, many of their wives "do not only contynue obstinate by refusing . . . but also do use at their ordinary meetings among themselves unreverende speaches of the Relligion nowe established defacing the same as much as in them lieth."[16] These ladies were especially to the fore in the Recusant counties of Yorkshire and Lancashire. The same Bishop of Winchester, protesting against the release from prison of Mrs. Pitts of Alton—"a very obstinate person" whose "return to Winchester would do more harm than ten sermons would do good"—enunciated wisely "no man is sound himself whose wife is a recusant."[17]

It was among such quietly determined, stubborn women that the beautiful Margaret Dormer took her place and it was in just such a strong atmosphere of religious adherence that Dorothy grew up and in which she was educated. Margaret Constable, even in times of greatest danger, managed to keep a chapel and chaplains and to make them accessible to her Catholic neighbors, as did so many great houses of that time, notably the Vaux family of Harrowden.[18] Strikingly similar background is to be found in the life of Lady Magdalen Montague who came of the family of the Dacres of the north, was daughter of the third Lord Dacre of Graystock and Elizabeth, daughter of George Talbot, fourth Earl of Shrewsbury. Both families had strong Catholic traditions. At thirteen Lady Magdalen was sent to be educated at the house of Anne, Countess of Bedford, another staunch Catholic.[19] And there was the famous Mary Ward, founder of the first uncloistered order of English nuns, the Institute of the Blessed Virgin Mary. Daughter of Marmaduke Ward of Mulwith Manor and Ursula Wright Ward, Mary had been brought up in a well-to-do, deeply committed Catholic household. Her Grandmother Wright of Ploughland Hall in the East Riding of Yorkshire had been imprisoned some fourteen years for her faith and her mother Ursula Ward had been brought up in a hard school of suffering. Yet as wife to Marmaduke Ward she proved herself a careful mistress, loving mother, and gracious hostess who kept her home serene and normal despite the uncertain terrors of the day. Closely connected to the Percys at Alnwick Castle, Northumberland, and to the Babthorpe family, Mary was educated in adolescence at the home of Sir Ralph Babthorpe and Lady Babthorpe where she lived amid the splendor of one of the magnificent great Catholic homes of that time.[20]

Of striking good looks like her mother and "unexampled virtues," Dorothy Constable at marriageable age had no lack of suitors, and her family soon settled their choice upon Roger Lawson, son and heir of Sir Ralph Lawson of Brough Hall. Despite the strong Catholicity of the Constables they do not seem to have been averse to Dorothy's marriage to a conformist to the new religion, once they ascertained he was "well disposed in religion."[21] Apparently Mr. Lawson's honorable descent and his future inheritance of an estate worth yearly about three thousand pounds sterling was a consideration not to be overlooked! In the marriage settlement dated March 10, 1597, the manors of Burgh in York, Burn Hall in Durham, Byker, Cramlington, Scremerston, West Matsen, Camboise, and Blythe with lands in West Slickburne in Northumberland were bestowed upon the couple.[22] Such wealth, and the security of some conforming members of the family could be most helpful to the Catholic cause in the north, whether that had been the considered intention of her parents' choice or not. The Lawson family had been affluent merchant-adventurers of Newcastle-upon-Tyne for generations. In the confiscations and sales of Church property in the time of Henry VIII, James Lawson, Roger's great-grandfather, appears frequently in the *State Papers* as one of the aldermen of Newcastle most distinguished for his zeal and interest in the King's new ideas. As a faithful partisan of his royal master, James partook quite satisfactorily of the plunder. The fact that a number of womenfolk in his family presided over monastic lands helped provide him with priorities in the matter too. His sister Agnes, for example, had been prioress of St. Bartholomew's, Newcastle, and so, for £8 a year, he acquired the nunnery which included among other things thirty acres of pasture; for an additional £16 per annum, the "coal-mines of the late nunnery in Gateshead."[23] Nonetheless, this supposedly ardent reformist married his daughter Isabel into the homes of two ancient and loyal adherents of the old Catholic faith, first to Gerard Fenwick, also a merchant-adventurer of Newcastle, and then on his decease to Richard Hodgson of Hebburn, a "rank papist" and three times mayor of Newcastle.[24] His grandson—and Dorothy's father-in-law Ralph Lawson—also married into a Recusant home, for Elizabeth, daughter and heiress of Roger Brough of Brough, is entered upon the Recusant Rolls for March 1592–93.[25] This, no doubt, is why Margaret Constable felt fairly safe in entrusting her daughter into the hands of Elizabeth's son.

After their marriage, Dorothy and her husband resided for a while at the family seat at Brough. She had not been there a week before she was investigating the possibilities of finding a priest to whom she might go for the "refection of her soul."[26] Her cautious inquiries to Elizabeth Lawson elicited the fact that that good lady, though sympathetic, had no idea where one might be located, nor was she anxious to allow one to be brought to Brough because all her servants were "conformable to the times." Perhaps Elizabeth's spell on the Recusant Rolls had cured her of too much enterprise. But seventeen-year-old Dorothy, made of sterner stuff—or in her newly married state less under the pressure of long-established domestic compliance—answered that she knew how to find a priest and with her mother-in-law's permission would send for him and be responsible for his care.[27] Dorothy, having apparently gained Elizabeth's reluctant consent, secretly sent to Mr. Anthony Holtby, gentleman-waiter to her father living only four miles from Brough. Anthony was brother to Richard Holtby, Superior of the Society of Jesus in England.[28] Dorothy's zeal and courage, with Father Holtby's help, so reanimated her mother-in-law's spirit that she once more, on her own initiative, had a chaplain for religious services at least once a month at home. This was but the first of many such reconversions and conversions effected by Dorothy's quiet example. Within a very short period of time she had, for example, converted all of Sir Ralph's children, with the exception of her own husband. This included nine: six men and three women, plus their families and six servants.[29] She was so successful in her work of conversion that by 1604 the name of Lawson began more and more to be connected with other strong Recusant families, and one Lawson relative in particular, Henry, began to appear on Recusant lists, as did the Rokesby family; Thomas Rokesby having married Sir Ralph's daughter Margaret.[30] Henry Lawson appears with his wife Dorothy Marshall among those listed as not married in the Anglican Church though as "all these lyve together as man and wife they are suspected to be secretly marryed." The same Henry is listed as having children baptized privately "of late years."[31] In 1613 the Spiritual Court Books under Sedgefield complained against Alice Lawson, a sister-in-law of Dorothy, as an "outrageous papist."[32] In this regard, Dorothy again finds similar counterparts in many women of her time. It is recorded that Lady Montague by her example returned many lapsed members of her family to the Church and at her death left over thirty of her children, nieces, and nephews "constant professors of the Catholic faith."[33]

Dorothy herself realized the danger to which she exposed the entire Lawson family and so with her husband's apparent knowledge and with his consent, she established Anthony Holtby at Burn Hall as a seat and residence for his brother, Father Richard, separate from too obvious adherence to any household. Burn Hall remained "on loan" to the Holtbys until June, 1605, when it was sold by Dorothy's father-in-law.[34] The constantly enlarging family of Dorothy and Roger Lawson necessitated a more commodious residence by this time at any rate, so that they removed from Brough to Heaton in Northumberland near Newcastle.

As Roger Lawson came to spend more and more time as a barrister of the Inner Temple at London, he left the direction of repairs and improvements on their new home in the capable hands of his wife. She used this opportunity to provide a chapel in a little-used section of the house and had mass said there secretly once a month. Dorothy would let the priest in at night and usually while her husband was away on his business trips to London. Her next move, which was also of great necessity if she was to guard the secret of the chapel, was to acquire Catholic servants "which she did so dexterously by little and little, hiering one after another, and never two att once, that her husband between jest and earnest, tould her, his family was become Papists ere he perceived it."[35]

Dorothy and Roger Lawson were blessed with a large family—its reported size varying from twelve to nineteen, though fifteen seems to be the number most agreed upon.[36] All of these children were brought up and educated as Catholics; one girl, Mary, eventually entered the Benedictine Convent at Ghent,[37] and another Dorothy went to the Augustinians at Louvain.[38] The majority of them remained single,[39] except for the second son, Henry, who married Anne, daughter of their near neighbor and fellow Recusant, Robert Hodgson, while Dorothy's daughter Anne married Henry Widdrington of Buteland, and Elizabeth became the wife of John Yorke of Gothwayt, both Recusant families.[40]

In the busy years spent at Heaton, from 1605–1613, Dorothy by her charitable works of mercy among the sick and needy of the area discovered many opportunities for bringing new souls into her Faith, especially in the baptism of infants in danger of death at birth, as well as conversion of adults. Within a short space of time she had converted over a hundred.[41] Dorothy's skill in the art of physical healing was typical of the knowledge and charity of many great and wellborn women of that time. Anne Dacre Howard, Countess of Arundel, was equally famous for her knowledge of medicines, salves, plasters, and other remedies which she readily used

> to all kind of people who either wanting will, or means to go to doctors and chirurgeons, came to her for the curing of their wounds and distempers. And her charity herein was so famous that not only neighbours, but several out of other shires, twenty, forty and more miles distant did resort unto her to that end, and scarce a day passed in which many did not come, sometimes more than three score have been counted in one day. . . . She ordered divers kinds of drugs to be brought every year to make her salves and medicines, and herself in person would be present at the making of them to see and be more sure they should be well done and good.[42]

It is no wonder that she, like Mrs. Lawson, converted hundreds to her religion by the mere example of her gentle compassion.

In the midst of this activity, Dorothy suddenly received word, toward the close of the year 1613, that her husband was dying in London and wished to see her. The very night of her arrival she had the happiness of seeing her husband embrace her own Faith and receive all the last rites and ceremonies of the Catholic Church. After two weeks he died, leaving Dorothy the task of bringing up their large family, and of carrying on her work during the remainder of her life as a widow.[43]

Practicality, along with devoutness, seems to have been the keynote of this busy housewife and neighbor, for on her return from London to Heaton she immediately began to make arrangements, both for the present and the future, for the education of the majority of her children abroad, sending them "with sufficient maintenance" to various colleges and religious houses. In sending them to the English foundations in Flanders, she could reassure herself that they would be taught by and mingle with those of their own class, and often among their own kinsmen. The same family names occur over and over in the profession lists or death-bills of convents in the seventeenth century—names like Cary, Roper, Tempest, Blount, Knatchbull, Throckmorton, Lucy, Fermor, Sheldon, Blundell. Of a single generation of Poultons, six were Jesuits; of a single generation of Lawsons, one was a Benedictine monk, one a Jesuit, one a Benedictine nun, and four nuns of Mary Ward's Institute; while the record is probably held by an enormous family of Bedingfields, eighteen strong, of whom three became Augustianian canonesses, three Mary Ward nuns, two Poor Clares, two Carmelites, and one a Benedictine nun. By debarring the large body of Catholic gentry from many opportunities suitable to their position in life, the government actually promoted the cause of the religion it was their object to stifle. It perforce suggested to many of the gentry the possibility of offering their talents and services to religion since opportunity of serving the state was denied them. In this way, educated members of the socially acceptable classes continued to keep Catholicism alive among the gentry in an invaluable way.[44] Dorothy was thus preparing to follow the usual stream of events at that time by providing the proper "climate" for nourishing any possible vocations in her family. Henry, who had become the heir only the year before (1612), when her eldest son Ralph died while away at school in Douai, was kept at home as the future preservation of the estate now devolved upon him.

At the death of her husband, Mrs. Lawson also made arrangements for a permanent resident chaplain at her home, and with the appointment of Father Legard, S.J., to the post, there began the series of chaplains, mostly Jesuit, in the Lawson home, first at Heaton and later at St. Anthony's, which was to last the remainder of her life.[45] Dorothy Lawson's home, due to the number of conversions she had already achieved in the neighboring area, now became the headquarters for an ever-widening Jesuit enterprise in and about Newcastle-upon-Tyne. When Father Legard first arrived, there were no altar furniture or vestments available beyond those belonging to Mrs. Lawson; by the time of her death there were in the same district six missionary stations like that of the Lawsons.[46] In 1615 Bishop James Durham wrote to Archbishop Abbot of "the flocking of priests even in a walled town like Newcastle, where a few years ago there was not one recusant" and warned of danger from the King's lenity toward priests.[47] The activities of Father William Southern in Newcastle, for example, indicates that there was some truth to the Bishop of Durham's suspicion of increasing Recusancy.[48] Newkirk's account in 1615 of his meeting with Father Southern conjures up a vivid picture of the conditions under which a seminary priest lived and meetings took place in the "walled town," and also highlights the large part widowed women of all classes played in this work.[49] Father Southern's mission among the poor of the Sandhill and around the castle and river bank of Newcastle complemented the work of Mrs. Lawson and her Jesuit chaplains.

> I was informed to find him [Fr. Southern] at Newcastle in Pilgrim Street, at a widow's house called Mrs. Pynner or at Mrs. Watson's . . . . the next day Clesbie carried me to a widow's house on Sandhill, where a woman dwelleth wearing daily on the working day's a 4 corner cap, selling some small commodities in her shop, as Ropes, Red herrings and some salt fishes, and many small trifles. . . .
>
> Then came a right fair young woman (I suppose her daughter) upon the stairs standing. Asked who was coming up Friends says Mr. Clesbie. So up we went another pair of stairs; on the right hand is his [Southern's] chamber. . . . at last it was determined that I should come the next day to my Confession, so I promised to do, and did, and heard a Mass in company of six persons, 3 women, Sutheran's [*sic*] brother for one, who was Clerk to Mr. Sutheran, I myself the 2nd, Clesbie the 3rd and a gentleman with a red head whose name I do not know, the woman and daughter in the house, and 2 women more, whose names I do not know. . . .[50]

In 1616, three years after her husband's death, Mrs. Lawson's work at Heaton Hall was transferred to its new seat at St. Anthony's. Her father-in-law, having been offered a good price for Heaton, proposed to her that he exchange it for a place in an adjacent neighborhood but "more advantageous for her designs." There was, for Dorothy, considerable sacrifice entailed in the exchange, for while the new site was incomparably more pleasant, better secluded for her purposes and, to her mind, "holy" because it had been dedicated in Catholic times to St. Anthony, it had one great drawback—there was no house already built on the property. She had to undertake the erection of a home at her own expense "for which she was ill provided, her purse ebbing low at present by the discharge of . . . debts contracted by her husband."[51] Nonetheless her resourcefulness, and her many friends, made possible the erection of a large imposing mansion on the highest point of the bank overlooking the river. It was so situated that the busy plying of coal ships to and from Newcastle passed in full view of the house, yet "Catholics may resort there with such privacy, that they are not expos'd to the aspect of any." In those days St. Anthony's could still boast of the beautifully green and well-wooded slopes that clothed the higher portions of the still rich and renowned river Tyne before the Industrial Revolution destroyed all this. "Att the end of the house opposite to the water, shee caused to be made the sacred name of Jesus, large in proportion and accurate for art, that it might serve the mariners."[52] It was especially intended for those of other nations who might thus know it to be a Catholic house and come here, as they did "in swarms" for spiritual care. Though she was glad to live a little remote from Newcastle, Dorothy Lawson took no great pains to hide her Catholicity, yet in her lifetime remained entirely unmolested.

In this respect, St. Anthony's was to the north what Lady Montague's houses at Battle Abbey and Cowdray, Sussex, and her town house at St. Mary Overies (over-the-water) on the Thames side near London Bridge, were to the south of England. With the same indifference to possible consequences, Lady Magdalen built a chapel at Battle and boldly erected an altar of stone with stairs leading to the altar and enclosed with rails, a choir for singers and a pulpit for sermons! In short, it contained all the regalia of the Catholic Church open for all who visited her home to see.

Here almost every week was a sermon made, and on solemn feasts the sacrifice of the Mass was celebrated with singing and musical instruments . . . and such was the number of Catholics resident in her house, and the multitude and note of such repaired thither, that even the heretics, . . . gave it the title "Little Rome."[53]

Like Mrs. Lawson, Lady Montague made few efforts to conceal her religion. "When she walked abroad by her beads or cross which she used to wear about her neck, she professed herself a Catholic and so manifest was her religion that scarce any in England had heard her name who knew her not also to be a Catholic."[54] One can envision the stir the great lady must have made and the awe she inspired, for Lady Montague even in her advanced years was tall and straight of carriage and though very stout, not without dignity and grace. She was noted for her remarkably good sight ("she could discern a tower 15 miles off") her sharp wit and excellent memory, and respected for her common-sense judgments and spirited courage.[55] However, her courageous, or foolhardy, profession of faith brought her before the public assizes for not observing the law. In fact, she was the first of the nobility under James accused in public judgment. But Lady Montague refused to be either terrified or forced into submission. She said: "If the king will have two-thirds of my Estate I will joyfully live with the rest, and I thank God who hath permitted me to enjoy it and now permitteth that it be taken from me for profession of His Faith."[56] Actually the end result was to provide for her greater immunity in the future, for the King's Council by public letters addressed to the Attorney General, April 16, 1607 commanded no sentence should proceed against her, for "it pleaseth the King's Majesty [that by reason of her fidelity in the time of Queen Elizabeth] that her old years should be free from molestation."[57]

From the beginning Dorothy Lawson had planned and intended St. Anthony's for spiritual purposes more than as her private residence, and therefore she invited Father Richard Holtby, S.J., the superior of the district, to lay the foundation stone. This was early in 1623, and from that date it actually became a Retreat House for hunted priests.[58] At least half a dozen of the Society made their yearly spiritual exercises there for the space of eight days, provided with everything necessary for masses, silence, and true community life.[59]

In Father Holtby, "a little man, with a reddish bearde,"[60] of robust constitution and indefatigable energies, Dorothy had an invaluable lifelong friend. He had all the qualities and talents requisite for his position and work—prudence, industry, firmness, charity, as well as being an able gardener, mason, carpenter, or turner. A man of such versatility could be and was an invaluable help in directing the devout aspirations and advising in difficult situations a widow with a large family to bring up.

Shortly after Father Holtby had presided over the dedication of St. Anthony's, he was notified by a sorrowful Mrs. Lawson of the death of her chaplain and spiritual director Father Legard, who had been with her for nine years. Father Henry Morse, though he had not yet entered the Society of Jesus, was the replacement sent by Father Holtby. Unfortunately for the new chaplain, his arrival coincided with one of those sporadic fears in Newcastle concerning the increase of papists in that town. Perhaps it sprang from the general fear of the plague then raging, for Newcastle was "so infected, so ill-fortified, so ill-neighboured," that is, surrounded by Catholics, that Lord Clifford, the Lord Lieutenant, nervously calculated that five hundred men could ransack the town, a fact which suggested possibilities of a Catholic uprising, especially as he gloomily reported to Secretary Conway that the "Papists are so powerful . . . that His Majesty cannot find one man in ten to do him service."[61] Undoubtedly, too, animosity was the reaction among many to the breaking down of the Spanish marriage negotiations at this time, making further gesture of toleration unnecessary. At any rate the aldermen of Newcastle seized the opportunity to feign alarm from a papist assault, especially from the Lawsons at St. Anthony's. Most probably it was an indirect excuse for re-enforcing the fines against Recusants, rather than exacting a further levy from all the burghers for fulfilling the recent order of the King to Newcastle to fit, victual, and furnish with ordnance a hundred ships for the King's service. The authorities reasoned that by reducing the resources of the Catholics they also reduced the possibilities of an armed uprising.[62] Father Henry Morse fell victim to this general unrest although he had not been with the Lawsons more than a year when he was apprehended and imprisoned at Newcastle. Ironically, Father Morse had been attempting to return to the Jesuit novitiate at Watten in Flanders for his thirty-day Spiritual Exercises when he was taken from the ship Seahorse at Tynemouth Castle as a suspect. A pair of rosary beads found in his pocket led to his examination before the mayor and aldermen and his imprisonment as a Roman Catholic, although his priesthood could not be proven against him.[63]

Arrangements had thus already been made to supply Mrs. Lawson with a successor in a young Jesuit, Father John Robinson alias Taylor, and sometimes called Collingwood. Father Robinson was doubly acceptable to Mrs. Lawson for he came from a staunchly Recusant Yorkshire family which had lost all its property in Elizabethan times. His mother had been imprisoned for years for having had priests discovered in her house.[64] But Mrs. Lawson was destined for another disappointment, for before her new chaplain ever set foot on shore, the ship was boarded by searchers, and he was committed to the same jail as Father Morse. The two priests must have known one another fairly well as they had both been students at the English College in Rome at approximately the same time, and Father Morse eagerly utilized the opportunity this Jesuit friend offered to enter the Society. Under Father Robinson's tutelage he made his novitiate in his prison cell and took his simple vows into the Society in his presence[65]—an extraordinary scene, but so were the times.

Mrs. Lawson did not neglect her two imprisoned priests but with her usual serene courage she supplied them

> with church stuff, washed their linen, provided with all necessaries for clothes and victuals and though Mr. Morse was known to belong to her, nevertheless, preferring his conveniency before her own safety she adventured to visit him in gaol, and suited the magistrate he might enjoy the liberty of the town for his health.[66]

Mrs. Lawson was a veritable angel of mercy to the ailing Father Morse. Even the most robust must have quailed before a prison notorious for constant deaths due to lack of light or ventilation in cells, not to mention the terrible dampness. When the river flooded, many of the rooms were partly under water. The cost of supplying food and clothing must have been a considerable drain on the widow's already heavily taxed resources, for nothing could be brought into the prison without the payment of exorbitant funds to the keeper, Samuel Hale, who had been granted the office in February of 1617 for a period of sixty years.[67]

In the first year of the priests' imprisonment, Mrs. Lawson undoubtedly dared more, for Sir Thomas Liddell, known to be sympathetic to the Catholics was mayor at the time. Evidence of this support comes through in a letter November 19, 1625, from Mayor Liddell to Mr. William Smith, secretary to the Bishop of Durham:

> Sir, I received your letter dated yesterday, whereby I understand my Lord of Durham desires to be satisfied concerning the danger of Sir Robert Hodgson and Mrs. Lawson's houses, and of the recourse of each other by boats over the river. I and the aldermen my brethern, hearing of such report, made inquiry touching the same, and could find no matter thereof but idle reports, other than their keeping of boats for crossing the river. [68]

Actually Mrs. Lawson and the Hodgsons owed much to this neighborliness of Mayor Liddell and his aldermen for their own avoidance of danger in the recent imprisonments of the two priests. Their names were constantly involved in the incidents, and suspicion on the part of the Bishop of Durham was therefore understandably great. That Mrs. Lawson remained untouched and uninvestigated in any really annoying way, and without listing on the Recusant Rolls is certainly evidence of the strong local support she enjoyed.

The incidents of *The Flying Hart* and *The Good Fortune* (a ship which certainly belied its name) occurring in the same weeks in which Mrs. Lawson's chaplain had been taken prisoner, supported the sense of uneasiness over Catholic audacity and law evasion, and points up even more sharply Mrs. Lawson's fortunate protection. In the course of disembarking from the collier *Flying Hart* at Hankebill[69] opposite St. Anthony's, the Flemish servant named Vandenhaupt of Mr. Thomas Fairfax, Dorothy Lawson's nephew, had an argument with the Master of the ship over the agreed payment of passage money. The upshot was that Vandenhaupt's personal belongings and "fardel," a large case, were taken into custody by the Master, Mr. Hart, until payment was made. Having procured the necessary money from Mrs. Lawson's ever generous purse, the Flemish servant hastened next day to secure his goods. In the meantime, the fardel, addressed to Mr. North (Father Holtby's assumed name) had been seized by the chief customs officer, William Swan. Upon investigation the fardel yielded some eighty-two books destined for the priests' library at St. Anthony's, including among them the newest devotional and liturgical books and a special missal printed abroad *pro sacerdotibus Itinerantibus in Anglia*. It was the nucleus of a reference library Father Blount expected to provide eventually in the principal house of each district[70] and was to make available in the north more of the great flood of Counter-Reformation writings coming from printing presses abroad. Though Vandenhaupt disclaimed knowledge of the fardel's contents, he was imprisoned. Sir Thomas Liddell might be willing to be severe to foreigners who tried to smuggle in books and relics contrary to law, but when he discovered that the Bishop of Durham wished to use the evidence collected to convict Mrs. Dorothy Lawson, the Hodgsons, and others of his neighbors he reneged.[71] Despite the uproar, which included the seizure of several papists at Shields and the reports to the Privy Council concerning these alarming matters, Mrs. Lawson was not molested. The Council chose to ignore the accusations, even though the lady's sympathy with these persons, and the shelter she offered them, must have been a matter of common knowledge.

Apparently her reputation could provide protection for others under her roof as well, for when her nephew, young Thomas Fairfax, second Viscount Fairfax of Emly, returned from Brussels in 1621, an ardent convert to Roman Catholicism,[72] his father, alarmed and angered, ordered him out of his house and cut him out of his will. He therefore went to live with his mother's sister, Dorothy Lawson, until about 1629 when he married the granddaughter of the convert Lord William Howard, settling down at Naworth Castle. While he lived at St. Anthony's, amidst all the furor in which Vandenhaupt was implicated, Fairfax himself "does not seem to have been noticed by juries."[73]

In the midst of both increased vigilance and public excitement over the seized materials and persons from ships, as well as the triple loss of her three chaplains by death and imprisonment, life at St. Anthony's continued imperturbably.[74] At long last a chaplain with "staying power" appeared in the guise of Father William Palmes, S.J., Mrs. Lawson's director for the last seven years of her life, and her admiring biographer as well.[75] A Yorkshire man, he had been a missionary in England some eight years before assignment to the Lawsons, although he was not solemnly professed in the Society until November 11, 1631, a year before his benefactress's death and while he was still chaplain at St. Anthony's.[76]

This zealous chaplain has left us an amazing account of the rich liturgical life that went on undisturbed year after year at St. Anthony's. It is a testament in itself to the growing tolerance and peaceful life allowed the politically disinterested groups of Catholic gentry and their servants in the early Stuart period. Her chapel— "neat and rich" with its altar always "vested in the various habiliments, according to fashion in Catholick countrys"[77]—was the scene of daily mass, vespers at four, and evening services from eight to nine at night "at which all her servants were present."[78] In Holy Week the full solemnity of all ceremonies was observed and —if we are to judge from the good Father's description—with an emotionalism quite foreign to the Anglo-Saxon temperament of modern times though typical of the new emotionalism and dramatic tone of the Mediterranean Counter-Reformation ideas in which the Jesuits were trained. Catechism classes were held most afternoons, which the neighbors' children attended with her own household. Here again, the impact of the post-Tridentine emphasis on instruction of the young, utilizing the new Catechism of the famous Jesuit, Peter Canisius, is clearly evident.

Though Dorothy showed herself in all this a woman of serious and devout qualities, this by no means created in her a dour and stiff nature, but rather one noted for sweetness and affability, which often won to her faith those "whome schollars could not gain by learning and subtilty of argument."[79] A retainer of her father-in-law once told Father Palmes that he was converted to the Catholic religion by the many stories she recounted out of the Old Testament, as he rode before her on trips; and he added to the priest that "he never had before or since, such content in any journey."[80] She loved music and dancing, in this a true English woman, and at Christmas especially hired musicians for hall and dining chamber for her friends and servants. One gets a glimpse of her ability to enjoy thoroughly all legitimate recreations in the fact that she played games for an hour after dinner and supper and at Christmas she even stretched this to two hours after each meal and at that time would play for a shilling.[81] Her biographer epitomizes this Pauline widow in one pen stroke: "her authority, prudence, sweetness, and gravity was such, that every one lov'd her with fear, and feared her with love."[82] She fulfilled the spiritual and corporal works of mercy with utmost exactitude so that

> when any fell into travail or sickness, no occasion of business, weather, or time, were it night or day, detain'd her. . . . To women in travail shee never went without comfort of both sorts: relics for the soul, and, if they were poor, cordialls for the body. For these offices, shee gained so much on the opinion of neighbours, that they would generally say, they feared not if Mrs. Lawson were with them. None of her parish, man or woeman, departed this life without help, or infant without baptism.[83]

Nor was she merely a religious visionary or doer of good works who, busy in the affairs of others, forgets to lay up goods for her own household. Rather, she kept all her servants and children in excellent order. She arranged with justice and prudence for the work of her servants, according to their abilities, as well as their fair pay, although she frequently personally visited their domains to see that she in turn received just due. Each night she carefully went over the accounts and had a report from her steward as to the accomplishments of the day, as any practical, careful woman would do. In many ways it was a picture of the average busy life of any woman of a great household in the seventeenth century. True, there were difficulties, sacrifices, and some danger brought by her religion, but on the whole it was a calm existence. Nor was the Lawson home at all unusual in this. A summary of Lady Arundel's household, for example, is so akin to it that one cannot help being struck by the similarity of character, life, and outlook:

> Religious austerity was the key-note of the household. Lady Arundel rose early, and the day was punctuated by regular attendance at the services in the chapel, while many intervals were spent in devotional reading and private prayer. The utmost order and regularity prevailed in her household. Her servants, and doubtless her children, were schooled to the strict observances of Catholic orthodoxy. Yet through all the stern discipline imposed upon her by her faith, there shone a large and gracious personality, that never failed to earn for her, affection and respect. Her charities were unbounded; and in spite of infirmities of health, she would,

at any time, go considerable distances on foot, to relieve a case of urgent distress, and personally tend the sufferer. . . . Many was the hunted priest to whom she stretched out a helping hand. The Jesuit Fathers were the objects of her special munificence . . . Her liberality was not, however, restricted to members of her own creed. Neighbors of all denominations had reason to praise her bounty; while her unaffected piety and kindly disposition won her friends in many and varied quarters.[84]

Richard Smith, first Bishop of Chalcedon for England in 1629, and former chaplain to Lady Montague, leaves an equally similar impression of her devoted service:

She maintained three priests in her house [at Battle, Sussex] and gave entertainment to all that repaired to her, and very seldom dismissed any without the gift of an angel. . . . Her alms distributed every second day at her gates, unto the poor, were plentiful. . . . When she desisted from her prayers, she accustomed to spend much time in sewing shirts or smocks for poor men and women . . . visited the poor in their own houses and sent them either medicines or meat or wood or money as she perceaved their need.[85]

Nor did all the labors of her own generation go for naught. Dorothy, for one, lived to see the start of the marriage of her son Henry with Anne Hodgson, a marriage which was to prove fruitful in the continuation of religious vocations, though the grandmother did not live to see this fulfillment. Still, she undoubtedly had a hand in the earliest instruction of young Henry, who was to die in 1644 at the battle of Melton Mowbray in the service of Charles I; of John, who became a baronet at the Restoration; and of Francis and Mary, future Benedictines.[86] The constant union of Catholic families through intermarriage can be seen too in the fact that her grandson Henry married Catherine, eldest daughter and heiress of Sir William Fenwick of Meldon, while her granddaughter Dorothy became the wife of the Recusant William Blakeston of Sheildraw, a distant cousin.[87] The whole development of the post-reformation Catholic community is a continuing history of the linking together of leading families into a complicated network. By the 1630s this long criss-crossing of relationships had resolved itself into several main groups, as far as the wealthier gentry and peers were concerned. The Lawsons found themselves, for example, in the whole linkage of Dormers with Lords Worcester, Montagu, Molyneux, Dunbar, and Fairfax. Lord Worcester's sisters in turn were married to Lords Windsor and Petre and to the eldest son of Lord Arundel of Wardour, whose sisters were the wives of the heirs of Lords Eure and Baltimore.[88]

Her house well set in order for its future, like a tired general Dorothy Lawson died March 26, 1632, when still comparatively young (she was fifty-two) after a long and painful illness. Her private obsequies were celebrated late the night she died at St. Anthony's, with about a hundred Catholics "who spiritually depended of her"[89] attending. The description of her funeral the following day bears witness to the affection in which she was held by all Newcastle, and in this single instance is certainly an extraordinary manifestation of local toleration by all Protestants concerned, from the minister of All Saints Church to the Newcastle magistrates. It would have been impossible in a Puritan stronghold, but unlike most larger towns in the seventeenth century, an Anglican and Romanist preponderance then existed in Newcastle.[90] Father Palmes describes the amazing scene graphically:

Divers boats full of people came in the afternoon from Newcastle, all plentifully entertain'd with a banquet; and when their civil respects were ended, we carried the corps in the evening to Newcastle, in her own boat, accompanied with at least twenty other boats and barges, and above twice as many horses, planting them on both sides of the shore, till their arrival at the city. They found the streets shining with tapers as light as if it had been noon. The magistrates and aldermen with the whole glory of the towne, which for state is second only to London, attended at the landing place to wait on the coffin, which they received cover'd with a fine black velvet cloth, and a white satin cross, and carried it but to the church door, where with a ceremony of such civility as astonish'd all (none, out of love of her, and fearing of them, daring to oppose it), they deliver'd it to the Catholicks only, who with another priest (for I was not worthy of the honour), laid it with Catholick ceremonies in the grave. In the interim, a gentleman was appointed

to conduct the ladies and magistrates to a sumptuous banquet . . .
till all was ended in the church. Then her son . . . with more tears
than courtship . . . rendered many thanks for their noble civilities.[91]

This was but one of many gestures of kindliness from neighbor
to neighbor which, in a time and setting that was "out of joint"
with the inner religious convictions and external practices of Catholics, made possible for literally scores of women, of great and low
estate, lives of courageous serenity and unruffled normalcy at home
in their own England. However, amidst the uncertainties and shift-
ings of the hour, the accent was on the word "courage." It must
be remembered with due respect these were but women who thus
dared their times and dared to live according to their consciences.

N O T E S

1. Stonyhurst MS., Angliae A. 3 (100) as printed in Charles Dodd,
   Church History of England (1841 ed.), Vol. IV, part 5.

2. Robert Persons, S. J., *Three Conversions of England* (St. Omers,
   1603).

3. Recusancy was the Elizabethan term for the refusal (Lat. *recusare*)
   to attend in one's "parish church, chapel or usual place of common
   prayer," the services of the Church of England as established by
   the Act of Uniformity in 1559 (1 Eliz., cap. 2). By the statute of
   1581 the shunning of the aforesaid services in the case of persons
   above the age of sixteen was an indictable offense, triable as a
   misdemeanor at any of the criminal courts. By the statute of 1586
   the Recusant who failed to pay his fine of £20 a month is forfeiture
   to the crown of two thirds of his lands and all his goods and
   chattels. Remarks Hugh Bowler, O. S. B., in "Some Notes on the
   Recusant Rolls of the Exchequer," *Recusant History*, Vol. 4, no. 5
   (April, 1958), p. 183: "The long-term policy of treating recusancy
   as a source of state revenue had begun."

4. Brian Magee, *The English Recusants* (London, 1938), pp. 48–49, citing a Survey of Thomas Ogle, 1625. *Household Books of Lord William Howard,* Surtees Society, LXVIII (London, 1878), p. 432. "Chorographia: Or a Survey of Newcastle upon Tine (1649)," *Harleian Miscellany,* III, pp. 282–83, lists all of these as "Ancient families and names of gentry which have continued from William the Conqueror, unto these late days."

5. The family of the Grayes, mentioned in *Cecil Papers* 192/63, HMC, Vol. XIX, p. 3, is an excellent example of this intermarriage: "Sir Ralph Graye of Chillingham, not thought to be forward in religion, cometh seldom to Church, his lady being lately deceased, a recusant, in her tyme divers seminary priests secretly intertayned in his house, divers of his principall servants, recusants. His eldest daughter, a recusant, married to the chief of the Forsters. His second daughter married to young Mr. Huddleston of Westmoreland, neither of them come to Church. One of his sisters married to Mr. Ratcliff of Dilston, both he and she recusants, their children being many of both sexes, brought up in papistry, the other of his sisters wif to Mr. Collingwode of Eslington, deceased, both recusants. . . . Thomas Collingwode, eldest son (of Cuthbert) deceased, a recusant, his wif who yet liveth, a recusant, sister of Sr. Raph Gray. Ceorg Collingwode, second sone to Sr. Cuthbert a recusant, his wif a recusant, sister to Mr. Swinborne, a recusant. One sister married to Mr. Carnaby of Hatton both recusants. One sister a recusant married to Mr. Thomas Salvin. . . . [The document ends on a disgusted note] some Church papists, not one good protestant."

6. C. H. Hunter Blair, *The Mayors and Lord Mayors of Newcastle-on-Tyne 1216–1940 and the Sheriffs of the County of Newcastle 1399–1940,* Society of Antiquaries of Newcastle, Archaeologia Aeliana, series 4, Vol. XVIII (1940), pp. 50–51.

7. Sydney Middlebrook, *Newcastle upon Tyne, Its Growth and Development* (Newcastle, 1950), p. 71.

8. John Wake, ed., *Montagu Musters Book,* Northamptonshire Records Society, VII (Peterborough, 1935), p. 228. See also many interesting instances of this recorded in M. D. R. Leys, *Catholics in England* (New York, 1961), pp. 60–62. M. J. Havran's remark in the article on "The Bankes Papers" (*Recusant History,* Vol. 5, no. 6 [October, 1960], pp. 248–49) is well-taken: "There is solid ground for the thesis that the enforcement of the Penal Laws

and the resultant amounts of money collected from recusants, were contingent upon the whim, zeal, and religious fervour of the justices, constables, and churchwardens who were charged with the operation of the recusancy laws rather than upon royal proclamations or parliamentary petitions.

9. Thomas Birch, *Court and Times of James I,* ed. R. F. Williams, I (London, 1849), p. 365.

10. DNB, IV, 961.

11. C. S. P., *Dom., Charles I,* I (1628–29), p. 522.

12. Hugh Aveling, O. S. B., "The Catholic Recusancy of the Yorkshire Fairfaxes," *Recusant History,* Vol. IV (April, 1957), p. 63.

13. Eyre MSS., f. 78, Ushaw College Papers, as cited by David Mathew, *The Jacobean Age* (London, 1938), p. 245.

14. William Palmes, S. J., *The Life of Mrs. Dorothy Lawson of St. Antony's near Newcastle-on-Tyne,* 1646, G. Bouchier Richardson, ed., with footnotes by Sir Henry Lawson and his nephew Sir William Lawson (London, 1855), pp. 5–6. Sir William Dormer, Margaret's father, was made a Knight of the Bath at the coronation of Queen Mary. He married a Catesby. One already sees this early that interweaving of Catholic alliances. Margaret Constable's grandnephew Robert, Lord Dormer, was created Earl of Caernarvon in 1626.

15. Actually Elizabeth herself seems to have disliked the idea of imprisoning women. Father Weston, S. J., records that when the prisons of Wisbech, Ely, and Reading were being filled with highborn men "the Queen was asked to make the same provision for women; she is said to have answered, 'You have had your way with the men. Would you have me shut the women up too—like nuns in a convent? A fine thing that would be!' and she withheld her consent. Nevertheless in Yorkshire there were public gaols in which the wives of several men of rank were imprisoned." (William Weston, *Autobiography from the Jesuit Underground,* trans. from the Latin by Philip Caramen, New York, 1955, p. 33.)

16. *Acts of Privy Council,* n.s., Vol. XII, p. 244.

17. C. S. P., *Dom., Elizabeth,* (1581–90), CLXXV, 17. *The York Civic Records* are filled with similar allusions to outspoken and spirited replies from women in all walks of life. In All Hallows on the Pavement Parish, Elizabeth Wilkinson, wife of a milner

"sayeth she cometh not to the church because there is neither priest, altar or sacrifice." Margaret Taylor, wife of a tailor "sayeth she cometh not to church because there is not a priest as there ought to be." *York Civic Records,* Yorkshire Archaeological Society, Vol. VII, pp. 130–31.

18. Godfrey Anstruther, O. P., *Vaux of Harrowden* (Newport, Mon., 1953), see for example chap. IV.

19. A. C. Southern, ed., *An Elizabethan Recusant House,* comprising the life of Lady Magdalen Viscountess Montague (1538–1608), trans. from the original Latin of Dr. Richard Smith, Bishop of Chalcedon by Cuthbert Fursdon, O. S. B., in the year 1627 (Glasgow, 1954), p. vii.

20. Cf. Mary Oliver, I. B. V. M., *Mary Ward 1585–1645* (New York, 1959), for a delightfully written account based upon original sources.

21. Palmes, *op. cit.,* p. 8.

22. *Ibid.,* p. 9. The marriage settlement document is now located in Newcastle Public Library.

23. Richard Welford, *Men of Mark,* Vol. III (London, 1895), pp. 16 and 17; Palmes, *op. cit.*

24. Richard Welford, *History of Newcastle and Gateshead,* III (London, 1887), pp. 33–34.

25. "Recusant Rolls," *Catholic Record Society,* XVIII, 99.

26. Palmes, *op. cit.,* p. 13.

27. Her admiring hagiographer could not refrain from injecting a typical masculine observation at this point, for he suggests "it is innate to that sex to covet things that are most difficult, . . . a little water sprinkled upon hot coles makes them hotter" (*ibid,* p.13).

28. Richard Holtby, alias Richard Duckett, of Fraiton, Yorkshire, was a convert to Catholicism and was led to join the Society of Jesus in 1583 through the influence of his good friend Edmund Campion. He succeeded Father Henry Garnet as head of the English Mission, Dr. George Oliver, *Collectanea, S. J.* (London, 1845), p. 10s; Henry Foley, *Records of the English Province of the Society of Jesus,* III (London, 1877–84), p. 5.

29. Palmes, *op. cit.*, p. 15; Foley, *ibid.*, V (ser. XII) 716n lists Sir Ralph Lawson and his son as schismatics—bad Catholics, yielding to the times and attending occasionally the Protestant service; however, by December 3, 1608, Ralph Lawson's recusancy fines had become part of a grant to Thomas Marbury, along with that of Anne and Mary Yaxley of Suffolk, Katherine Brewdnell of Huntingdonshire, Elianor Lacon of Kinley, etc., C. S. P., *Dom.*, *James I*, VIII, 472.

30. Edward Peacock, ed., *A List of the Roman Catholics in the County of Yorkshire in 1604* (London, 1872) p. 79.

31. *Ibid.*, p. 100.

32. *Proceedings* of the Society of Antiquaries, Newcastle, n.s., X (1901), p. 95.

33. Southern, *op. cit.*, p. 46.

34. Welford, *Newcastle and Gateshead*, III, p. 167.

35. Palmes, *op. cit.*, p. 17.

36. *Ibid.*, pp. 21–22, mentions fifteen. The family pedigree at Brough Hall, nineteen; Foley, *op. cit.* V (ser. XII) 709 lists fifteen; *History of Northumberland*, ed. Committee of North, XIII, 393, lists eight boys and six girls. It also adds George, December 30, 1605, to those registered for baptism in All Saints Church.

37. Foley, *ibid.*: professed June 24, 1631, as Dame Benedicta. Mary was probably a twin, for Palmes, *ibid.*, says she "sent one of her twins to Gant."

38. Professed November, 1618. Adam Hamilton, O.S.B., ed., *Chronicle of St. Monica's*, Vol. I (1906), p. 134.

39. Palmes, *op. cit.*, p. 21, says she sent all but three to religious houses with vocations—but we do not have sufficient evidence for this.

40. *History of Northumberland*, XIII, p. 393.

41. Palmes, *op. cit.*, p. 19. Some appreciation of her wonderful kindliness which exerted so powerful an influence on her neighbors can be seen in her quietly heroic care of one of her husband's brothers who had "contracted a disease so contagious and noisome, that neighbor nor stranger would entertain him." She not only accommodated him in her own home, but for nearly three months undertook personally his complete care "without troubling any servant" (p. 23).

42. *Lives of Philip Howard and Anne Dacre His Wife* (ed. 1857), pp. 212–14. Anne Dacre was married in 1571 to Philip Howard, Earl of Arundel; after her husband's imprisonment in 1585 she lived much of the time at Arundel House, London, where Robert Southwell was her chaplain.

43. Palmes, *op. cit.*, p. 20.

44. William Blundell, *Cavalier's Notebook* (London, 1880), p. 69.

45. Palmes, *op. cit.*, p. 21. Father Legard may have been a son of Thomas Legard of Newcastle, merchant, whose daughter Mary married Mark Shafto, the recorder of Newcastle. On the other hand, Legard may have been merely an alias, common at that time. If so, there is no record of his true identity. Cf. Joseph Gillow, *A Bibliographical Dictionary of English Catholics*, IV, p. 162.

46. *Ibid.*, p. 23.

47. *Memoirs of the Life of Mr. Ambrose Barnes*, Surtees Society, Vol. L (1867), pp. 303–4.

48. Ann M. C. Forster, "Ven. William Southerne: Another Tyneside Martyr," *Recusant History*, Vol. IV, no. 5 (April, 1958), pp. 199–216. William had received the typical Jesuit education abroad, but not in the usual English Colleges in the Low Countries, Italy, or Spain. He had been sent rather to the Jesuit College at Vilna, Poland, probably in one of the ships of his merchant relatives. Here William Southern studied for six years until, having contracted tuberculosis, he went to Douay in 1596 and Valladolid in 1598, C. R. S., *Valladolid Diary*, XXX (1930), p. 51.

49. C. S. P., *Dom., James I*, IX, 301 and 302. Christopher Newkirk, a spy of William James, Bishop of Durham, was said to be a surgeon of Polish nationality; "a pretended Catholic and much courted by the priests."

50. Forster, *op. cit.*, pp. 206–7, citing S. P. 14, 54 iv.

51. Palmes, *op. cit.*, p. 26

52. *Ibid.*, p. 27

53. Southern, *op. cit.*, p. 44.

54. *Ibid.*

55. *Ibid.*, p. 63.

56. *Ibid.*, p. 45.

57. *Ibid.,* p. 54.

58. A. C. F. Beales, "Popish Schools under James I," *The Month,* Vol. CXCIII (April, 1952), p. 206. No trace of this interesting building remains. During the Civil War it was the property of Dorothy Lawson's grandson John, a royalist, and under the act of sale, 1652, St. Anthony's was sold for the use of the navy. In 1663 William Bonner was the owner ("History of Northumberland," XIII, pp. 262–63). Foley, *op. cit.,* V (series XII), p. 717, says it was destroyed in later times for fear the Scots would use it as a garrison.

59. Palmes, *op. cit.,* p. 41.

60. Foley, *op. cit.,* III, p. 6, citing C. S. P. *Dom., Elizabeth,* Vol. CCXLV, no. 24, 1593. Father Holtby was in England between 1589 and 1640.

61. C. S. P., *Dom., Charles I,* I, 102: Henry Lord Clifford to Sec. Conway, September 10, 1625, Appleby Castle.

62. Philip Caramen, *Henry Morse, Priest of the Plague* (New York, 1957), p. 39.

63. *Ibid.,* pp. 45–48, for an extended treatment of details.

64. Foley, *op. cit.,* III, p. 49.

65. *Ibid.,* I, p. 507.

66. Palmes, *op. cit.,* p. 41.

67. Anthony W. Twyford and Arthur Griffiths, *Records of York Castle* (London, 1880), pp. 138–39, citing a letter of Mr. John Wortham, 1642, to His Majesty's Judge of Assizes for county of York complaining of hardships of prisoners; cf. also pp. 141–45 for similar accounts dated 1618 and 1652. While in prison neither priest admitted his priesthood. Robinson continued to imitate a Dutch trader from Damm and also spoke to Morse in Italian; Caramen *op. cit.,* p. 56.

68. Barnes, *op. cit.,* I, pp. 309–10.

69. Caramen, *op. cit.,* p. 43. Hankebill was the residence of another Catholic center in the family of John Dann. Even after the uproar over Vandenhaupt he continued to serve as Dorothy Lawson's trusted smuggler.

70. *Ibid.,* p. 44.

71. Welford, "History of Newcastle," Vol. III, p. 274.

72. Barnes, *op. cit.*, p. 312.

73. Aveling, *op. cit.*, p. 61.

74. Cadwallader J. Bates, *History of Northumberland* (London, 1895), p. 234.

75. The actual MS. was apparently written in 1646, as Palmes (*op. cit.*, p. 43) speaks of his fourteen-year silence since her death in 1632.

76. Foley, *op. cit.*, III, p. 48.

77. Palmes, *op. cit.*, p. 38.

78. *Ibid.*

79. *Ibid.*, p. 39.

80. *Ibid.*, p. 42.

81. *Ibid.*, pp. 39–40.

82. *Ibid.*, p. 42.

83. *Ibid.*, p. 40.

84. M. F. S. Hervey, *The Life, Correspondence and Collections of Thomas Howard, Earl of Arundel* (Cambridge, 1921), pp. 13–14. Anne, though older than Dorothy Lawson, conducted most of her "open Popery" and notable works of charity and influence among her neighbors at the same time as Dorothy, that is, under the more benign rule of James I as far as Recusants were concerned. Though her son Thomas abjured her Faith, he did marry Lady Althea Talbot, the greatest heiress of her generation, brought up also in a great Catholic household at Sheffield Manor by her ardent if rather unbalanced mother, Lady Shrewsbury. A number of their children and descendants became famous and loyal Recusants.

85. Southern, *op. cit.*, pp. 39–40: Lady Montague and her large Catholic household of some eighty persons mostly resided at Battle, four miles from Hastings. The three priests included Thomas More, great-grandchild and direct heir of St. Thomas More, and elder brother of Cresacre More. He resided at Battle twenty years. Another priest was Thomas Smith who had tutored Englishmen in Paris. Among his pupils was Robert Southwell.

86. Sir William Dugdale, *Visitations of Yorkshire in 1665–6*, ed. Robert Davies, Vol. XXXVI, Surtees Society (London, 1859), p. 90.

87. *Archaelogia Aeliana*, n.s., Vol. I (1857), p. 95. Dorothy Lawson's sister Mary had married into the Blakeston family.

88. Mathew, *op. cit.*, p. 240

89. Palmes, *op. cit.*, p. 51.

90. *Archaeologia Aeliana*, n.s., Vol. II (1858), p. 225.

91. Palmes, *op. cit.*, pp. 52–53: Who the officiant was we do not know, but in 1632 there were five seminary priests working in Northumberland, two Jesuits, two Benedictines, and one Franciscan (*Catholic Record Society*, XXXV, 200). With Dorothy's long connections with Jesuits, it was presumably one of this Society. The magnanimous courtesy and tolerance of the Rev. Samuel Barker of All Saints Church and Sir Lionel Maddison, the mayor, who made this amazing scene possible, certainly deserved the public thanks rendered by the scion of the Lawsons.

EUROPEAN REACTION
TO THE DEATH
OF CHARLES I

C . V . W E D G W O O D

W**hen Charles I was beheaded, Clarendon, the historian of the English Civil Wars, could hardly find words strong enough to convey his anger. Sweeping up the whole fateful year of 1649 in his loathing, he described it as**

a year of reproach and infamy above all years which had passed before it; a year of the highest dissimulation and hypocrisy, of the deepest villainy and most bloody treasons that any nation was ever cursed with or under; a year in which the memory of all transactions ought to be rased out of all records, lest, by the success of it, atheism, infidelity and rebellion should be propagated in the world. . . .[1]

Clarendon is noticeably inconsistent in hoping that the King's execution should be expunged from the record while not hesitating to record it himself, but, rhetoric apart, his personal grief was extreme and his anxiety over the effects this defiant and public king-murder would have on the existing order was shared by many thoughtful statesmen. The inviolability of sovereign power, of an authority widely believed to have divine sanction, appeared to be of the utmost importance in maintaining civil order. The belief that rebellion was a form of blasphemy might appear to some politicians and thinkers as a useful fiction, but it was to others a genuine article of faith. For this reason Clarendon, in common with other English Royalists, believed that the King's death would provoke a general outburst in Europe against the "incarnate devils" who had brought it about.[2]

Indeed, news of the execution was received with expressions of horror by the princes and rulers of Europe. Cardinal Mazarin said[3] that tears of blood would be shed for the murdered monarch, had such tears been possible in nature, and similar indications of abhorrence were uttered by the ministers of most European states. But Clarendon was to be disappointed. Almost immediately events in The Hague, where the young King Charles II was in exile, should have indicated to him the wide divergence between what people said, and what they were prepared to do to avenge the late King's death. The words of Clarendon's history reveal the opening fissure:

> There could not be more evidence of a general detestation than there was amongst all men of what quality soever. Within two or three days . . . the States presented themselves in a body to His Majesty to condole with him for the murder of his father, in terms of great sorrow and condolence, save that there was not bitterness enough against the rebels and murderers.[4]

Reports from the Spanish Netherlands described even greater caution on the part of the Dutch. It was said that in conveying their sympathy to the poor young King they had as far as possible avoided calling him "Your Majesty," had pronounced this form only once (and very indistinctly), and had refused to set it down in writing[5]— a sufficiently broad hint that they had not made up their minds to break off relations with the existing Republican government of England.

From Munster which, since the recent conclusion of the Peace of Westphalia, was still a center of European diplomacy, the Venetian ambassador wrote home that the murder of King Charles was a shame and a scandal to his fellow sovereigns, who could have intervened to save him had they been less concerned with quarrelling among themselves.[6]

The indignation provoked by the strange death of King Charles turned out in the end to be not so much an inspiration to action as a substitute for it. This pattern, not altogether unfamiliar in modern times, was most noticeable in France. Here Queen Henrietta Maria, widow of the murdered King and aunt of the young Louis XIV, had taken refuge. It was to France that the English Royalists looked most confidently for help. Here too the popular outcry against the murderers of King Charles was both widespread and vehement. Indeed, exiled Cavaliers were sometimes molested by the angry populace who saddled all Englishmen indifferently with the guilt of regicide.[7] In his letters Gui Patin freely compared the English to wolves while the diarist Jean Vallier condemned the execution as the "most horrible and detestable parricide ever to be committed by Christians," not least because they had arraigned their sovereign before the petty lawyer Bradshaw, "*un petit juge subalterne.*" Popular pamphlets and ballads also bewailed the King's death and called down vengeance on its perpetrators.[8]

But as the English Royalists noticed with growing disillusion, Mazarin did not break off relations with England and the Commonwealth government's resident agent in Paris was not "in any sort disquieted." At least in The Hague the Dutch populace, stimulated by the angry idle Royalist soldiers who abounded there, was plaguing the life out of Walter Strickland, the Commonwealth's emissary.[9]

Meanwhile the behavior of other European rulers to the new *de iure* King of England was nothing if not cautious. The Dutch Estates had set an example. Soon the Archduke Leopold, Governor of the Spanish Netherlands, was writing to the King of Spain saying that he had postponed sending a letter of condolence until he had word, either from the Emperor or from Philip IV, as to the form of address he was to use. The same embarrassment was felt in Spain, where the King's Council eventually decided not to offend the newly proclaimed English republic by acknowledging Charles II as King. The letter of condolence to the bereaved prince should be carefully ante-dated so that the royal title accorded to him could be explained away on the grounds that King Philip IV had sent the letter before hearing of the abolition of monarchy in England that had followed the execution of the King.[10]

Royalist hopes of assistance had been falsely raised by the conclusion of the Peace of Westphalia in October, 1648. They had believed that the treaties which brought an end to the Thirty Years' War in Germany and the Eighty Years' War between the Spaniards and the Dutch would free the resources and troops of some European princes to come to their aid. But the signatories of the treaty were by no means liberated from their own pressing needs by the re-establishment of a partial peace. The efforts of Charles II to raise money among the north German princes were not successful. His own first cousin, the newly restored Elector Palatine, who was actually in London when his uncle the King was tried and executed, was at the time more anxious to settle his war debts in Germany than to raise any protest against the English regicides.[11]

The Vatican was more concerned to denounce the religious clauses of the Peace of Westphalia than to object to the judicial murder of the heretic King of England whose agents had, over the last four years, repeatedly sought in vain for Papal help. King Charles, it was true, had been on very good terms with Rome in the days of his power, but he had disappointed their hopes for major religious concessions, and in his critical last weeks his cause had been damaged by the insidious belief, propagated by the Spanish ambassador in England, that the present government of extreme sectaries intended to introduce religious toleration for everyone, including Catholics.[12]

Even the Portuguese, who had been Charles's most consistent ally during the Civil War, acted cautiously after his execution. Their representative at Munster did indeed take the trouble to pay a visit of compliment to the new King of England but was careful to explain that he was acting as a private individual having as yet received no instruction from Lisbon.[13] The Danish Chancellor Ulfeldt, on the other hand, proclaimed himself ready on his King's behalf to offer financial aid to Charles II and actually did provide a small amount; but this source of revenue quickly dried up.[14]

The truth was that the Peace of Westphalia on which the English Royalists had placed too much hope did not adequately settle the quarrels of Europe or relieve most of the Continental rulers of their personal ambitions and fears. France and Spain, the two major monarchies, were still at war; the first was not able and the second was not willing to give a lead in the matter of the King of England. Yet the trial and execution of Charles was almost universally felt to have violated the most sacred and significant political beliefs in which all monarchies and most governments shared, and it was widely predicted that awful consequences must follow if the criminal English remained unpunished. Charles himself had believed until the eleventh hour that his fellow sovereigns must come to his aid in their own interests if not in his. The English newspapers reported him, within weeks of his execution and even after the prison doors of Hurst Castle had been shut upon him, as confidently averring that help would certainly come from France, the United Provinces, and Denmark.[15]

But France had been his chief hope and in the correspondence of Mazarin the gap between theoretical indignation and practical action is most clearly revealed. As early as January, 1647, before he was handed over to Parliament by the Scots at Newcastle, Charles had drawn up a memorandum for the French ambassador, then in attendance on him, to give to the Queen Regent Anne of Austria. His cause, the defeated King declared, was not his alone but that of all Christian Kings. If they did not wish disorder and rebellion to triumph everywhere, let them hasten to make peace among themselves and come to his rescue.[16]

The King's opinion of the general danger inherent in his defeat was shared by Cardinal Mazarin, the effective ruler of France. He had already instructed his ambassador that the establishment of a republic in England would be *"très dommageable"* to France and personally offensive to the Crown, owing to the close family relationship between Charles I and the boy King Louis XIV.[17] As soon as the Peace of Westphalia was concluded, and in spite of France's continued war with Spain, he wrote to his ambassador in England, the Comte de Grignan:

> The peace now concluded in the Empire, and the likelihood that this will facilitate peace with Spain, may contribute to a settlement between the King of England and his subjects, for they may well be apprehensive lest, once a general peace is made, his Majesty may receive help from France, Spain and other princes whose interest it is to prevent his defeat and the establishment of a republic in England.[18]

Cardinal Mazarin was too experienced in statecraft to imagine that successful rebels, who had made themselves masters of England at the head of a formidable army, would modify their attitude to the King on a mere apprehension that the rulers of Europe were belatedly about to help him. But at the time of writing, early November, 1648, the King's situation did not appear desperate. It was true that Royalist risings in different parts of England had been utterly crushed during the summer, but Parliament, apparently in control of the situation, was disposed for a treaty with the King and negotiations for a settled peace were actually in progress at Newport in the Isle of Wight. This looked like a breathing space.

Not until November 20 by English reckoning (November 30 in France) did the Army present to Parliament its Remonstrance denouncing the proposed treaty and calling for the trial of the King as the "capital and grand author of all our troubles."[19] The text of this document was known in France within a few days and startled Mazarin into expressions of the highest indignation. Writing to Grignan on December 6/16 he declared that he was beside himself —"*hors de moy*"—at this effrontery.

> It is inconceivable that subjects should imagine such extraordinary ideas against their King. . . . I have read with horror the demands of the Army, and I trust that God will not allow this unhappy Prince to fall into such great misfortune, nor do I believe that the English will bring themselves to carry out such dire intentions against him.[20]

But Mazarin had other interests in England more urgent than that of helping the King, and having thus piously hoped for a change of heart in the Army and commended King Charles to the care of God, he filled the rest of his letter with instructions about recruiting English troops for the war against Spain.

Throughout the English Civil Wars the French, the Spaniards, and the Venetians had all, from time to time, requested permission of Parliament to recruit men for their armies, sometimes from Royalist prisoners of war, sometimes from disbanded regiments. Quite apart from the usefulness of the troops in themselves, it was important for the French and the Spanish ambassadors each to hinder the other from acquiring too large a share of the available manpower. In this the French envoy was usually outmaneuvered by the Spaniard. French ambassadors in England had not been popular during the war; the close relationship between Charles I and Louis XIV, the fact that Queen Henrietta Maria had taken refuge in France, and the various ineffective efforts at mediation made earlier in the war by the French government had created a deep suspicion on the Parliament side and a disinclination to grant favors.

The Spanish ambassador, on the other hand, Don Alonso de Cardeñas, had shown great skill in conciliating the Puritan Parliament and had done virtually nothing to assist the King. The agents of France and Portugal, both of which countries were at war with Spain, had conveyed messages for King Charles to Europe during the wars, the Portuguese envoy getting himself into considerable trouble about this.[21] But the Spaniard throughout had cultivated the government in power so that, by 1649, an Anglo-Spanish alliance seemed a threatening possibility to the anxious French ambassador in London. It was thus more important for him to raise men for France and to block the activities of Cardeñas than to jeopardize French relations with the English by intemperately supporting the King. Between the end of October, 1648, and the middle of January, 1649, Mazarin wrote to his ambassador five times on the subject of recruiting; his instructions about the unfortunate King, though often expressed with great fervour, were no more frequent and far less explicit.[22]

On December 6/16, the day on which Mazarin expressed his horror at the suggestion of the King's trial, coupled with further requests for the raising of men in England, the Army under Fairfax and Cromwell surrounded Parliament and expelled all members who favored negotiating with the King. A week later Mazarin wrote once more to Grignan expressing his anxiety at the King's increasing peril, and a fortnight later he instructed his ambassador on the urgent request of Anne of Austria to omit no measures that could help him.[23] Precisely what these measures were he did not, and indeed could not, specify. The boy King of France had correctly appended his signature to a rhetorical declaration against the blasphemous conduct of Fairfax and his Army, calling upon "all neighboring Kings, Princes, and States" to join with him on behalf of Charles,[24] but the purpose of this document was evidently to save the French King's face rather than the English King's head.

The truth was that Mazarin had far too many domestic troubles on his hands to spare time, resources, or energy for the King of England. Since the unsuccessful attempt by the Queen Regent to intimidate the Paris *parlement* by the arrest of its leaders in the previous August, the unpopularity of Mazarin had become extreme and Paris was smoldering with revolt. The Cardinal was personally afraid, as his notes and correspondence reveal, and events in England only served to sharpen his fears. The troubles of King Charles had begun, as he was not slow to point out to Anne of Austria, with his fatal willingness to sacrifice his faithful first minister, Strafford, to appease the multitude. But yielding of this kind had only made matters worse; so, far from being appeased, Parliament had been encouraged to further revolt and now to this final excess of bringing the King to trial.[25] The analogy between his own position and that of Strafford was clear: so was the moral which Anne of Austria was to draw from this terrible example.

Early in January the French court secretly left Paris for Saint-Germain with the intention of reducing the city to order and obedience by force of arms. Inside Paris, now in a state of siege, Queen Henrietta Maria remained at the Louvre. Just before the city was cut off she had sent two letters—one to Fairfax and one to the Speaker of the House of Commons—requesting that she might at least be allowed to visit her dear lord the King. The Comte de Grignan in London transmitted these letters to Parliament and the Army without giving them the official support of his government. As he reported later, he did not wish at this very critical juncture for France, to make Anglo-French relations any worse than they already were. It is probable that whatever persuasions Grignan had seen fit to use, the fate of the poor Queen's letters would have been no different. They remained unanswered and unopened.[26]

From the moment the court left Paris, it was clear that nothing more could be done for the King of England, though there were rumors of intended help and some face-saving gestures. Talk of a force of forty thousand men under Condé was repeated and discounted in diplomatic circles, when everyone knew that Condé was fully occupied in blockading Paris.[27] Possibly the grotesque rumor was encouraged by the French court to enable them to say afterwards that an expedition to help the King of England had only been prevented by their domestic troubles. This was certainly the excuse that Grignan offered to explain why he had raised no official protest whatsoever against the trial and execution of the King.[28]

A special envoy, the Comte de Varennes, was indeed despatched toward London, but he did not arrive in time and may not have been intended to do so. There was a little more honest realism in the letters composed for the ten-year-old Louis to send to Fairfax and Cromwell when Charles was already on trial. They were dated 23rd January/2nd February—exactly a week before the execution —and in them Louis pointed out that solid rewards could be expected, not only from the King of England but from himself, if they would desist from their terrible purpose and restore Charles to his freedom and his throne.[29] The appeal to personal ambition, though wholly unacceptable to those to whom it was addressed, at least showed a more practical attitude than the official threats which had been issued a month before.

Meanwhile in England the newspapers, in what space they could spare from the King's trial, reported the disturbances in Paris with enthusiasm and equated the cause of the Frondeurs with that of the English Parliament. In this similarity, more apparent than real, the Spanish ambassador at once saw an opportunity of embarrassing the French government, and in his despatches to Madrid indicated that he was doing his best to link up the rebel government of England with the rebels in France.[30]

This possibility had also occurred to Mazarin. Writing from Saint-Germain on February 3/13, a date at which he still imagined Charles to be alive, he repeated his formal instructions to Grignan to exert himself, however uselessly, on the King's behalf. But the more important part of his letter was devoted to his anxiety lest any understanding be achieved between the regicides and the Frondeurs, an eventuality against which Grignan was urged to take every precaution.[31]

News of the King's death must have reached Saint-Germain very shortly afterwards, but not for a fortnight did Mazarin communicate again with Grignan, and then he contented himself with eloquent but hollow expressions of horror.[32]

He need not have been anxious lest the Frondeurs of Paris gain encouragement from the awful spectacle of a King's execution. The members of the Paris *parlement,* though they obstructed the court and hated the Cardinal, were firm in their loyalty to the King. They immediately denounced the "execrable regicide" and "mad fury" of the English. Indeed, the shock of the execution, so far from encouraging them in their rebellion, undoubtedly had a dampening effect.[33] Early in March terms were signed at Reuil and the court returned in triumph to Paris.

Meanwhile pamphlets denouncing the execution and appealing to the rulers of Europe to avenge King Charles came in considerable numbers from the French press. The Huguenots were particularly vehement in their repudiation of the act of regicide, so embarrassingly committed by Protestants, but so contrary to the current ideas and interests of the French Calvinists.[34]

Very few pamphleteers took an opposite view. The strongest of these was the anonymous author of *Avis à la Reine d'Angleterre,* who gave special praise to the English for executing their King in public. Traitors may act in the dark; the just do not fear the daylight.[35] These bold words seem almost to foreshadow the boast of the fanatic Harrison at his trial as a regicide in 1660: "I do not come to be denying anything but rather to be bringing it forth to light. . . . It was not a thing done in a corner."[36] In 1650 Leveller influence on the revolt in Bordeaux would show that Mazarin, though he was wrong in his estimate of the Parisians, was not wholly wrong in fearing a connection between the ideas of the English rebels and those of France.

With his domestic troubles temporarily at an end, the Cardinal was at last able to take stock of the English situation. If he did not like the new government of England he could see that unequivocal support of the Royalists, besides being expensive, might precipitate an Anglo-Spanish alliance. On the other hand he did not feel that it was consonant with the dignity of the French Crown to keep Grignan any longer in London. But he instructed the ambassador to find some plausible unofficial excuse for his return to France, and while avoiding all formal recognition of the Commonwealth government, to do nothing that could give cause for offense.[37] His chief secretary, Croullé, was left in London to represent French interests and—a matter of some importance to Mazarin—to send word of any bargains that came up when the pictures and tapestries of King Charles's famous collection were sold. But even in this matter, as with the recruiting, the French were outmaneuvered by the Spaniards: Alonso de Cardeñas sent eighteen wagonloads of works of art to delight his master in Spain.[38]

The French ambassador in London, though very cautious, at least considered the prestige of monarchy and went through the motions of sympathetic concern at the fate of the King. His Spanish colleague behaved with a cynical callousness that was subsequently reflected in the conduct and policy of Philip IV and his Council. They, too, like Mazarin, and indeed rather more urgently, had pressing troubles of their own. Revolt in Catalonia, revolt in Portugal, and the continual war with France had lowered the prestige of the Spanish government and brought it near the end of its resources. The King, or at least his councillors, felt also some justifiable bitterness against Charles I for the support he had given the Portuguese revolt by recognizing King John IV and receiving an ambassador from him.[39]

Alonso de Cardeñas, in England, had two guiding aims: to serve the interests of Spain in her war with France, and to protect the interests of Roman Catholics in England. As the Independents of the Army made religious toleration a principal part of their program he had in 1649 reason to hope better things of this government than of any of its predecessors. For the rest, it was evidently his cue to take advantage of the awkward predicament of the French ambassador and to make himself, as far as was consonant with his dignity, *persona grata* with the new government.

There were nonetheless many in London who looked to him, as the representative of the proudest monarchy in Europe, to do something for Charles. He was approached both by Royalists and by Presbyterians to intervene. But while he freely admitted that the King's trial and execution would be regarded with the utmost disapproval by his royal master, he blandly argued that, for so unusual an occasion, His Catholic Majesty would no doubt send an ambassador extraordinary if he wished to take action. In the meantime, he had no instructions.[40]

Madrid was a long way off; Brussels was a great deal nearer. Here the Archduke Leopold, Governor of the Spanish Netherlands, began to bestir himself. Three days before the King's execution he despatched a letter to Cardeñas asking him to protest in the strongest terms. Cardeñas was probably telling the truth when he subsequently stated that this letter had not arrived until after the King was dead. Once the tragedy was over, he knew the correct diplomatic procedure; he put his whole household into mourning.[41]

Five weeks later, receiving Cardeñas' dispatches in Madrid, the King's Council condemned the wicked action of the English in killing their King, but saw no cause to take action; King Charles was merely a heretic prince, and they could not recollect that Spain had ever found it necessary to interfere when previous Kings of England had come to grief. The minutes sound rather as though the ministers of Philip IV regarded the deposing and murdering of English Kings as a commonplace occurrence and saw no difference between this and previous occasions.[42] But among the dependent and allied Habsburg states a certain anxiety was felt about the indifference of Spain to the moral issues raised by the King's death. Both at Vienna and in Brussels doubts were expressed as to the wisdom of condoning the actions of rebels and encouraging an unholy alliance between the regicide government and the Frondeurs.[43]

But at Madrid friendship with England was thought advisable. A determined, though unsuccessful, effort was made to prevent Hyde and Cottington, the emissaries of Charles II, from completing their journey to Spain.[44] Their reception there was unsatisfactory, and by the end of 1650 the King of Spain was the first monarch in Europe to accord official recognition to the English Commonwealth.

The only state in Europe to make a formal intervention in favor of the King was, paradoxically enough, the Dutch Republic. Their relations with England were far closer than those of either France or Spain, but were confused by commercial and dynastic complications which in 1648–49 were rapidly coming to a crisis. As early as 1641 King Charles, in the hope of improving his financial position, had married his eldest daughter to the only son of the Prince of Orange, a match which at the time seemed a very fine one. Subsequent political developments in England had left the young Prince with a crowd of his wife's relations and dependents seeking help and asylum in Holland.

Meanwhile tension had been developing between the Prince of Orange as hereditary Stadholder, and the Estates of the United Provinces, especially those of Holland. The peace with Spain in

1648 left a discontented party in the Netherlands who believed that more could still be gained from a renewed prosecution of war. Prince William II of Orange, a high spirited young man, soon became associated with the war party, while the Estates of Holland above all were strongly for peace. In the autumn of 1648 the Prince was privately sounding out Cardinal Mazarin as to the prospects of French help and cooperation in a renewed war with Spain.[45] He was also both for personal and dynastic reason, very willing to link the cause of Charles I with his other martial plans.

Popular feeling in the United Provinces was divided between animosity toward the English, owing to commercial and maritime rivalry, and sympathy for the religious and political demands made by Parliament at the outset of the war. By 1648 this initial sympathy had been party estranged by the emergence of more extreme views in England and there was fluctuating support for the Royalists. It was thus possible for them to operate a small fleet, made up of ships revolted from Parliament, from the Dutch coast. They preyed on English shipping and sold their prizes in Dutch ports, in spite of the protests of the Parliamentarian representative at the Hague, Walter Strickland, who lamented in his letters home that the Royalists "bring in our merchants like slaves and captives" without any redress from the Dutch.[46]

On the news of his father's trial, the Prince of Wales appealed to the Estates General of the United Provinces, accompanied by Sir William Boswell, the much respected diplomatist and scholar who had represented the interests of King Charles I in The Hague for the past sixteen years. The Estates responded sympathetically and agreed to dispatch a special embassy without delay, to protest against the trial of the King and, if possible, to mediate a settlement that would at least save his life. They chose for the task their most experienced negotiator, Adriaen Pauw, who had recently led their delegation at Munster. He took with him the venerable Albert Joachimi, who had for many years been the resident representative of the Dutch Republic in England. He was now ninety years old, but still alert in mind and body. The two envoys were to travel overland as far as Calais, thus shortening the sea journey, so apt to cause delays in the wintry season.[47]

Walter Strickland knew the worth of these two ambassadors

and wrote at once to his masters in England urging them to treat them with all respect.[48] He need have felt no anxiety as to the diplomatic tact of the Army and the remnant of Parliament now in power; in their handling of foreign representatives throughout these critical weeks they displayed an ingenious mixture of courtesy and caution. They were not looking for trouble with any foreign power; they merely asserted their right to act independently of criticism and to be the best judges of their own affairs.[49]

Distinguished as were the two representatives that the Estates General had chosen to plead the King's cause, their conduct during their brief visit to England suggests that they had no real intention of interfering with the course of events. Given the confused state of domestic politics in the Netherlands, the tension between the young Prince of Orange and the Estates, his known dynastic ambitions and his entanglement with the House of Stuart, no experienced Dutch statesman was likely to commit the Republic to a whole-hearted intervention on behalf of King Charles or a total breach with the existing government of England.

The ambassadors who arrived on January 26 tamely accepted the decision of Parliament not to receive them until January 29. The reasons given were very simple: January 27 would be fully occupied with the King's trial and January 28 was the inviolate Puritan Sabbath. When the ambassadors realized that the King had been condemned to death on the Saturday, they were sufficiently perturbed to seek interviews on the Sunday with the Speaker of the House of Commons and Lord Fairfax. They achieved nothing by this, since both the Speaker and Fairfax (who was accompanied by Cromwell and other leading Army officers) declared that they were unable to take any action before Parliament reassembled on Monday.

Therefore on Monday, January 29, the Dutch ambassadors were formally received by Parliament, but were told that no answer could be given to their plea for the King until it was translated into English. The Commons then rose with somewhat unseemly haste and the ambassadors withdrew to prepare a translation. Only next morning did they realize that the execution of the King was about to take place—within a few hours. This provoked them into making one more appeal to Fairfax. He was alone this time, listened sympathetically to them, and hurried off to Whitehall to see what he could do.

They themselves went back to their lodgings to await events, though they judged, from the number of soldiers now on guard in the streets of Westminster, that there was no hope of saving the King. By the early afternoon he was dead. With a touch of personal kindness they stayed to pay a visit of condolence to the King's two young children at Sion House. Pauw then returned to Holland, while Joachimi remained behind to look after Dutch interests in England.[50]

As in France, so also in Holland, the news of the King's execution was received with the greatest indignation. But it soon became apparent that the link between the English Royalist cause and the House of Orange would inevitably throw the massive weight of the anti-Orange party onto the side of the English Republic. It was significant that within a month of the King's death the Royalists were complaining that, to please the Dutch Estates, they had now to relinquish some of their naval prizes and curb their piratical ventures in the Narrow Seas.[51] Popular feeling still ran high against the King-murderers. The envoys they sent over to seek the friendship of the Dutch Republic were hooted in the streets, and when one of them, Dr. Dorislas, was assassinated by Royalist soldiers, the Dutch authorities made little attempt to find the culprits. On the other hand the Estates, and more especially those of Holland, were unwilling to give financial aid to the young Charles II.[52] The ambitious scheme of William II of Orange to resume the war on Spain with French help and to link this offensive against Spain with a plan for restoring the King of England came to nothing, owing to William's premature death and the subsequent triumph of the peace party. Naval and commercial rivalry was, within eighteen months, to involve the English and the Dutch Republics in open war, but this explosion had nothing to do with the rights and wrongs of the English Royal Family.[53]

While disapproval and some genuine dismay were expressed by almost every European state on the news of King Charles's death, and historians have often referred to the "shock of horror" which it caused, it is necessary to look as far as Russia before meeting with any immediate and effective expression of hostility to the English government. Even here the expulsion of English merchants by the Tsar is now recognized to have been nothing more than the culmination of a long-standing policy, the King's death being used as an excuse for an action which had long been intended.[54]

Pamphlets in considerable numbers came from the presses of France, Germany, Holland, and, more occasionally, Denmark; the paper warfare was ferocious, the most famous engagement being that between Saumaise and John Milton. The story of the King's last days was translated or retold for the next five or six years in French, Dutch, German, Latin, Italian, and even Polish. Journalists heightened its effect by adding Christ-like details to the sufferings he was said to have endured, and by inventing last-minute intrigues and attempts at rescue, some of which were worthy of Alexandre Dumas *père*. Thus the King's death deteriorated with remarkable speed into a sensational story the political significance of which was obscured by the drama of the detail.[55]

Logically, the death of Charles I ought to have damaged the mystique, or at least the prestige, of royalty throughout Europe. But in spite of the anxiety expressed on this score by the King himself, by Mazarin and many others, it had no such effect. In the eighteenth century his fate would be rhetorically cited as an awful warning to George III in the American Revolution and to Louis XVI in the French Revolution, but the similarities were slight. In the latter half of the seventeenth century there is little evidence to show that the institution of European monarchy was in any way affected by it. It would seem that practical statesmen were right to pay lip-service alone to the idea of avenging the outrage, and to govern their conduct toward its perpetrators by purely practical considerations.

NOTES

1. Clarendon, *History of the Rebellion*, ed. Dunn Macray (Oxford, 1888), IV, p. 511.

2. Hyde (Clarendon) to Prince Rupert, February 8/18, 1649, British Museum, Additional MSS. 18982, fol. 177.

3. *Lettres du Cardinal Mazarin,* ed. Chéruel (Paris, 1883), III, p. 1092.

4. Clarendon, *op. cit.,* V, p. 2.

5. Guizot, *History of Oliver Cromwell,* trans. A. R. Scoble (London, 1854), I, p. 383.

6. *Calendar of State Papers, Venetian, 1647–52,* p. 88 (hereafter referred to as *C.S.P., Venetian*).

7. *Nicholas Papers,* ed. G. F. Warner for the Camden Society (London, 1886), Vol. I, p. 115.

8. Ascoli, *La Grande Bretagne devant l'Opinion Française au XVIIe siècle* (Paris, 1930), I, pp. 74 ff.

9. Carte, *A Collection of Original Letters,* (London, 1739), I, pp. 223–24, 227.

10. Guizot, *op. cit.,* I, appendix, pp. 383, 387.

11. M. C. Lundorp, *Acta Publica,* (Frankfurt, 1668), VI, pp. 443–45.

12. Guizot, *op. cit.,* pp. 373–77.

13. *C.S.P., Venetian,* p. 89.

14. *Ibid.,* p. 88; Gardiner, *History of the Commonwealth and Protectorate* (London, 1901), I, pp. 78, 211–12.

15. *Heads of a Diary,* December 20–27; *Moderate Intelligencer,* December 28–January 4. The first of these was Independent in politics, the second Presbyterian.

16. Ranke, *History of England,* (Oxford, 1875), V, appendix, pp. 505–6.

17. *Ibid.,* pp. 486–87.

18. *Lettres du Cardinal Mazarin,* III, p. 225.

19. *Old Parliamentary History,* XVIII, pp. 160 ff.

20. *Lettres du Cardinal Mazarin,* III, p. 247.

21. Prestage, *D. Antonio de Sousa de Macedo, residente de Portugal em Londres* (Lisbon, 1916).

22. *Lettres du Cardinal Mazarin,* III, pp. 247, 1068, 1072, 1073, 1085.

23. *Ibid.,* pp. 1077, 1079.

24. Carte, *Original Letters,* I, pp. 195–97.

25. Chéruel, *Histoire de France pendant la minorité de Louis XIV*, (Paris, 1880), III, p. 191.

26. Bigby, *Anglo-French Relations*, 1641–49 (London, 1933), p. 150; Cary, *Memorials of the Great Civil War in England* (London, 1842), Vol. II, pp. 101–2.

27. Guizot, *op. cit.*, pp. 371–72; *C.S.P., Venetian*, p. 86.

28. Bigby, *op. cit.*, p. 150.

29. Guizot, *op. cit.*, pp. 369–70.

30. *Ibid.*, pp. 377 ff.

31. *Lettres du Cardinal Mazarin*, III, p. 1090.

32. *Ibid.*, p. 1092.

33. Chéruel, *Histoire*, pp. 191–92; E. H. Kossmann, *La Fronde* (Leiden, 1954), p. 97.

34. Salmon, *The French Religious Wars in English Political Thought* (London, 1960), pp. 104–05.

35. Moreau, *Bibliographie des Mazarinades*, I, p. 149; Ascoli, *op. cit.*, p. 194. I am grateful to Miss Gertrude Huehns for drawing my attention to this remarkable pamphlet.

36. *State Trials*, V, p. 1190.

37. *Lettres du Cardinal Mazarin*, III, p. 1099.

38. Guizot, *op. cit.*, pp. 406–8; Clarendon, *op. cit.*, IV, p. 498.

39. Guizot, *op. cit.*, pp. 377 ff.

40. *Ibid.*, p. 372.

41. *Ibid.*, pp. 373 ff.

42. *Ibid.*, pp. 377–82.

43. *C.S.P., Venetian*, p. 90.

44. Guizot, *op. cit.*, p. 390.

45. *Archives de la Maison d'Orange-Nassau*, ed. Groen van Prinsterer, Third Series, IV (Utrecht, 1859), pp. 279 ff.

46. Cary, *Memorials*, II, p. 107.

47. *Ibid.*, pp. 104–6, 108–9; *C.S.P., Venetian*, p. 87; *C.S.P., Domestic, 1648–49*, pp. 345–46.

48. Cary, *Memorials*, II p. 107.

49. *C.S.P., Venetian*, p. 91.

50. Guizot, *History of the English Revolution* (Oxford, 1838), appendix to Vol. II; *The Moderate Intelligencer*, January 25–February 1, *C.S.P., Venetian*, pp. 90–91.

51. Robert Long to Prince Rupert, February 28/March 10, 1649. British Museum, Additional MSS. 18982, fol. 20.

52. *Archives de la Maison d'Orange-Nassau, loc. cit.*, p. 300.

53. C. H. Wilson, *Profit and Power* (London, 1957), gives an illuminating and succinct analysis of this development.

54. Inna Lubimenko, *Les Relations Commerciales et Politiques de l'Angleterre avec la Russie avant Pierre le Grand* (Paris, 1933), p. 210.

55. I have had the opportunity to investigate only the pamphlets in the British Museum. Further search would no doubt produce an even larger crop of foreign languages and of grisly or exciting additional inventions. The Italians seem to have been particularly fertile in the latter.

KINGSHIP AND REPUBLICANISM IN THE SEVENTEENTH CENTURY: SOME RECONSIDERATIONS*

H E R B E R T   H .   R O W E N

Rutgers University

Each field of human activity, and certainly each scholarly discipline, has its own characteristic sin. The sin to which historians are particularly prone is anachronism. It is easy for them to guard against such simple mistakes as having clocks ring the hours in ancient Rome; but it is not easy to maintain the virtue of being true to the time we are studying when we come to such things as institutions, attitudes, and beliefs—if you will, to the things that are not seen, and to the meanings of things. It might seem that anachronism would be most prevalent among historians whose fields of interest are most distant from the present—the present in time, the present in place. Yet there is no less danger of treating the near past as a kind of backward extension of the present. Familiarity can breed not contempt but inattentiveness and misunderstanding. It is my purpose in these pages to show that two of the most familiar historical institutions—kingship and republics—were sufficiently different in seventeenth-century Europe from what we mean by

* First given in slightly different form as a public lecture at Rutgers University, New Brunswick, New Jersey, on April 6, 1964.

these terms in our own day, that we can escape anachronism only by deliberate and precise analysis.

Ever since the final decade of the eighteenth century, at least until the rise of modern totalitarian dictatorship, "monarchy" and "republic" were the two recognized major types of state. They were treated as terms so obvious, so clear and distinct in meaning, that unlike Descartes' "clear and distinct ideas" they needed no explanation. That not all political structures fitted this two-part system was not hard to see, even by mid-nineteenth century; there was the nagging problem of explaining why the constitutional monarchies of Western and Northern Europe were among the sturdiest of democracies. But Bagehot's sardonically utilitarian defense of constitutional monarchy was so effective that further analysis of the basic problem was pretty much cut off. However, the "monarchy-republic" division is quite modern, and begins to take clear shape only in the seventeenth century.

I shall attempt to describe the emergence of our modern use of these terms by comparing the meanings they had in the seventeenth century with those they have now, and by observing more clearly what they meant and what they mean in practice. I shall also propose a new way of locating them in the history of political institutions by showing that they were not yet primary forms of political structure but were variations upon the "estates-state," the fundamental and characteristic political form of early modern Europe. (The term "estates-state" is awkward English, but I know no other way to translate the German *Ständestaat,* and I know no other word of equivalent meaning to use.) I shall use France and the Dutch Republic as my primary examples, but not to the exclusion of other significant cases.

Let us repeat the obvious by noting the modern uses of the term "monarchy." First, of course, it is used as a synonym for "kingdom" and "kingship"—the state and the status of a king—taken together. (Or of a queen, we must add in this the age of Elizabeth II and Juliana.) The key word is *king.* What do we mean by a "king" today? He is, first of all, *anyone* who bears that title, whatever powers and duties he has or does not have. Thus the figurehead kings and queens in the constitutional monarchies of today are given this title without question—although Elizabeth I would have been hard put to comprehend the status of Elizabeth II. Kingship in limited monarchy is not the same thing as this at all, for it is shared power and shared duties; but limited monarchy in this sense no longer exists, except for the residual role of constitutional monarchs who in times of crisis embody the national sovereignty, as in Holland, Denmark, and Norway during the German occupations of the Second World War. Different from either figurehead or limited monarch is the king as "absolute" ruler—the king who has all powers and over whom no one else has power, the king whose archetype we find in Louis XIV. The "absolute" king is often equated to a "divine right" monarch, a king who rules by the grace of God. Nor is any distinction usually drawn between a king by the grace of God and a hereditary, dynastic king.

We may contrast these present-day notions of what a king is with the seventeenth-century notions. First of all, "monarchy" was then not identical with either kingship or kingdom as such: it still meant what Aristotle meant by it—any rule by a single person. He might be a king or an emperor or a duke or count or even a mere lord of the manor, a *roi d'Yvetot*. But even this use was not pure, for it was not limited to Aristotle's famous six-part matrix of political forms; in the seventeenth century mixed forms were more common by far than Aristotle's pure types. But one feature of Aristotle's system retained its full force: that monarchy was *right* rule, government by right and for the right, rule not for the sake of the ruler but for the sake of the ruled, for the sake of the community. Tyranny —monarchy without right—meant either the reign of a usurper or the misrule of a legitimate king.

But Aristotle's conception, however extended and modified, did not exhaust the meanings which the seventeenth century gave to the word "king." The king was also—or rather, he was first of all and fundamentally—the holder of a title and a power which had evolved over the centuries from the Germanic institution of the war chieftain. In the process of the conquest of the western Roman empire by the Germanic tribes and the emergence of new forms of power in the early middle ages, the kingship was transformed from chieftainship into feudal monarchy, in which the king was the keystone of the pyramid of feudal relations of vassalage; and then during the early modern period the feudal monarchy itself grew over into a different kind of monarchy, a kingship of kings ruling over subjects but retaining many medieval characteristics. The feudal king, like the early modern king, could hold the crown by inheritance or by election; what distinguished him from the tribal chieftain was that he held his power for life and that it encompassed the full range of political action, not just its military aspect. There is a clear statement of these two kinds of royal power—hereditary and elective—in a Dutch pamphlet of the year 1672: ". . . all Princes are Princes either by birth or by the supreme sovereign power which they exercise over a people."

In this passage we can hear without difficulty the echo of Machiavelli. It can be heard in the use of the word "prince" for any wielder of power and maker of policy, for any sovereign ruler; and "prince" was, we will remember, the usual word in contemporary political theory for any sovereign ruler as such, whatever his title—though not for sovereign assemblies. We would do well to remember not only that Machiavelli's little book described a third kind of prince who was neither hereditary nor elective, but also that the Florentine in his very first chapter made the often forgotten point that both kinds of princedom, hereditary and elective, were far superior to the rule of the self-made prince in stability, durability, and ease of government.

How well do the conceptions of kingship held in the seventeenth century and today mesh? To put the question another way: How well do the modern ideas of kingship serve in the historical study of early modern monarchy? Can they be accepted, and if so, with what modifications? Or must they be rejected outright?

Let us first take the problem of absolutism and the absolute monarch. The emergence of totalitarian dictatorship during this present century has enabled us to see the immensity of the chasm between, say, the monarchy of Louis XIV and the rule of a Hitler or a Stalin. Louis XIV was nothing if not a legitimate ruler; his power arose from fundamental law, he maintained that law and very largely lived by it, and he passed it on intact. His policies may have been unwise, wrong-headed or impolitic; he may have fallen victim to the only too human fault of mistaking one's desires for the will of God—I think these things were true to a very large degree, and France and Europe paid and to some extent are still paying for his willfulness, his lust for power and glory, and his too easy recourse to war as the instrument of attaining glory and power. Yet his errors and misdeeds were aberrations of a system deeply and truly dedicated to the notions of law and justice—law and justice, let it be repeated, even when not precisely our idea of what they are or should be. Can we say the same of the enthroned lawlessness of the twentieth century?

Absolutism meant something much less than totalitarianism. It meant actually just the Aristotelian idea of "pure" monarchy, monarchy unmixed with either aristocracy or democracy. It was absolute in the same way that "absolute alcohol" is absolute, not in the way it is used, but in being 200 proof. Absolutism meant that the king held all the powers of the state, but not that the state held all powers in and over society. Such a notion was wholly foreign to it; it neither claimed nor had the power to tamper greatly with the great institutions of society, the family, the property system, the patterns of residence. Modify them it could, but only in limited degree—and how limited and how few these changes were, we can see better today from our longer perspective and our different experiences. Absolutism did not mean arbitrary rule, rule without rule, according to the vagaries of an irresponsible mind; it did mean that final decision belonged to one man and that authority emanated from him and only from him.

We may balk at the notion that personal power, unshared power, can still be responsible power. That may well be true, yet the seventeenth century did not think so; for it, all legitimate government, royal, aristocratic, or democratic, was responsible to God, because it was given by God to be used for the common welfare. This is what "divine right" meant; and we should not forget that the phrase "by the grace of God" literally means by the gift and favor of God. How effective a safeguard against misrule this doctrine was in practice is another thing. As in so many other cases, it is the extreme and unequivocal statement which is probably wrong. Too many rulers, and Louis XIV not the least, were held in rein by this sense of having to answer for their deeds, for us to affirm that it was never efficacious. Why else did Louis XIV finally allow the repentant and hapless La Vallière to stay safe behind the walls of a convent? A wisp of belief no less than a scrap of paper may prove stronger than steel and powder. On the other hand, we must also remember that beliefs are not only barriers in the way of our purposes and our passions; they can also be the instrument by which we assure ourselves of the rightness of our purposes and our own righteousness. Louis XIV's ability to persuade himself that God was with him was at least as powerful as his sense of the limitations that God placed upon his action.

Individual power, unshared power—this is personal power, and purely personal power becomes identified with the state itself. We think, of course, of the famous phrase *L'État c'est moi*. There is no evidence that Louis XIV ever uttered these words, although he said and wrote things very much like them at least a hundred times. But just what does this phrase mean? Its literal sense is nonsense, for the state is many things: a land and its people, a government and a mystic unity of them all; and the king can hardly be equated with all of them. But the phrase is not really nonsense. In the narrow sense, it is merely a reaffirmation of the sole sovereignty of the king, and this was the sense required on the occasion when Louis XIV is supposed to have used it. In the broader, more significant, sense, the phrase implies an awareness of the state as an institution, an idea, and asserts that the king is the embodiment of that institution and that idea.

There is a basic flaw, I think, in this conception of the state incarnate in a man. Institutions are not superorganic entities, things or forces independent of human beings, which by some mystical process can be embodied in a human being; institutions are our convenient intellectual shorthand for the repeated actions and the habitual attitudes of many human beings. The state as an institution is an instrument of men; in monarchy, specifically, of one man. When we say men serve the state, we really mean that they are serving other men, men who hold political power. I suppose idolatry of the state as such has been declining among historians, at least during the past two decades, and this is why the notion of the king as the state has not been so popular recently as before.

The allied conception of the king as the embodiment of the nation has not suffered so badly. It is still the fashion at the level of textbooks, college entrance examinations, and even among some professional historians who ought to know better, to speak of the

early modern period as the age when the nation-state triumphed;
and since most states in the early modern period were monarchies,
therefore it follows that the monarchs were the leaders, the embodiment even, of nations. QED. The syllogism is good, but is the
major premise true? Were the states of the early modern period
nation-states? I dare not undertake a full survey of this question
in these few pages; not only is it a major problem all in itself, but
it is one which has been studied very inadequately. Historical inquiry into the national factor in early modern Europe has been extremely spotty; even worse has been the loose and even careless
analysis of the structure of the problem. I will rush in unangelically
and suggest an approach useful to our present concern. Nations,
of course, were already in existence by the sixteenth century, but
there were two kinds of nation: the ethnic-linguistic "folk," and
the "people" as the subjects of a government. Each of these concepts is in turn complex and needs further historical study, but
we may take them as they are in our present considerations. If we
define the nation-state in general as the actual or the desired identification of the ethnic-linguistic nation and the political nation, then
we must say that in the early modern period, although the elements of the modern nation-state had emerged, their conjunction
took place only rarely, only incompletely and often only transitorily.
In any case, kings felt themselves to be in the first instance representatives of dynasties, and the subjects looked upon themselves
most strongly in terms of local identities. But, to repeat, the three
centuries of the early modern period were indeed the age out of
which modern nationalism did arise. Instances of nationalism,
nation-state patterns, can be found: but we must remember that
these were occasional and anything but dominant. The kings of the
early modern period had their national moments, their national
sides, but these were not their primary characteristics.

The nineteenth century taught us to study history not only in
terms of nations but also in terms of classes. And early modern
kingship is frequently presented to us in terms of the class for which
it presumably spoke, the class which it presumably led. One view
has it that the king was the leader of the nobility; another, that he
was the leader of the bourgeoisie. There is an obvious difficulty
about accepting both of these views at the same time, especially if

we assume the incompatibility of "nobility" and "bourgeoisie." Yet these are notions which, however inadequate, are not wholly false. The kings were indeed the leaders of the nobility; they were indeed sensitive to wealth and the needs of wealth. But the class structure of the early modern period was immensely more complex, more fragmented, more specific, than the ordinary five-party structure of nineteenth-century class analysis (aristocracy, bourgeoisie, petty bourgeoisie, proletariat, and peasantry). Here is another important area where we cannot safely project our own experience backward, and much more close-in study is required before we can speak with adequate clarity and definiteness of "classes" in the early modern period. But we must add that the narrative history of the times is replete with evidence that the kings not only led but also fought these very groups. The relationship itself was complex, changing and contradictory—much too much so to be summed up in a single neat formula.

I should like to be more than critic, however, and will suggest some positive notions as to the character of early modern kingship. First, we must remember that it was an evolved form of feudal monarchy and must be defined in terms of that evolution. Modern states may have evolved, and often did evolve, out of the early modern monarchies—but we cannot therefore explain the earlier by the later. In history, events do not happen backwards; results are not causes. The medieval elements in early modern kingship are more significant than the modern elements.

Second, the relation of the king to the other politically important groups in the state was an ambivalent one of domination and dependence. In general, this relation was expressed in some form of the "estates-state," although in France the role of the "estates" was increasingly assumed by the *parlements,* on the one hand, and the informal but hardly insignificant institutions of conspiracy and rebellion, on the other.

Third is the dynastic aspect of hereditary kingship. By "dynastic" I mean succession to the throne by right of birth. Two of the most thoughtful historians of early modern Europe, Jack Hexter and the late Garrett Mattingly, have suggested that dynasticism is the least studied though one of the most important elements in the history of this period. I have proposed elsewhere that the key factor in dynasticism is the proprietary character of the royal power. By this I mean that the state (or the crown or throne, by which the royal power was symbolized) was held by the king as a form of property. When we realize this, we cease to treat wars of succession as aberrations at worst, or at best as wars really fought for some other, national (and therefore more laudable) objective. But the state was a special kind of property, for it involved political power, the power of command over men's purses, liberties, and lives. Such power, as we have noted, was justified in law and theory by the doctrine that all political power was to be used for the general welfare, for the service of others. But property is held to be legitimately used for one's own interest—and it can hardly be denied that kings were not reluctant to use their power to their own advantage. The tension between service to self and service to others was a key factor in the political struggles and controversies of these, as of other, centuries.

This brings me to the other political form being discussed here —the republic of seventeenth-century Europe. One characteristic modern way of defining a republic is to call it the political structure in which the people rule and hence the state serves the general welfare. This is the equation of republic with democracy, especially with parliamentary democracy. But not all animals are horses, and we know that democracy may have the form of constitutional monarchy. This apparent paradox is explained away when we recall that a republic may also be defined as a state without a king or other hereditary titular ruler. The two definitions are obviously not equivalent, although I do not forget my fellow-soldier in the United States Army in Britain some twenty years ago, who insisted to me that if the English really believed in democracy they would not allow themselves to be ruled by a king . . . and I remember my futile efforts to explain Bagehot to him.

But let us go back to the seventeenth century and ask what men at that time meant by "republics." In the first instance, they used the word in the sense it was given in political theory, where it meant any formally organized and legitimate political power, that is, any state. This is the sense in which it was used in the title of Jean Bodin's famous treatise on the French monarchy, *The Six Books of the Republic*. This use emphasized the notion of sovereignty. It was such a use which Johan de Witt, the Grand Pensionary of Holland, had in mind when he warned a Dutch ambassador in England during the Protectorate not to permit use of the term "The Republic of the United Netherlands" in a treaty under negotiation. There were seven republics in the United Provinces, De Witt emphasized, not one—seven sovereign provinces united for mutual defense by the Union of Utrecht. De Witt happened then to be especially touchy about provincial sovereignty; at other times, he did not mind speaking of "this state" or "our common fatherland" when he meant the United Provinces as a whole, indeed as an entity in international affairs. But he never called it "the Dutch Republic," as we do.

The word "republic" was used in another sense akin to but not identical with our own. It had to be fitted into the Aristotelian political matrix, which knew aristocracy and democracy alongside monarchy but did not know "republic." This was done by giving both aristocracies and democracies (or "popular states," as they were more usually called) the name of "republic."

Finally, "republic" meant a state without a "prince"—a king or other sovereign ruler. The prime examples in the seventeenth century were the Venetian and Genoese republics, the Swiss Confederation and the city-state of Geneva, the Republic of the United Provinces and the English revolutionary republic of mid-century. Yet only the Swiss and Genevan examples fitted this definition perfectly. Venice was in form a duchy, in practice an aristocracy; while Genoa considered itself to be under the sovereignty of the Virgin Mary. The Dutch Republic actually possessed a quasi-prince in the person of the Prince of Orange and was purely republican in practice only during the two stadholderless periods of 1650–72 and 1702–47. As for the English Republic, did it really include the Protectorate? What did Oliver lack of kingship but the title, the crown, and the certitude of succession that comes of centuries of rule by one family? Nonetheless, the experience of all these states *was* largely republican, and they were all called republics.

Let us now look critically at these notions of "republic." Take the equation of republic and democracy. The republic is "the people's thing": but who are the "people"? The "people" meant at various times and places the body of all subjects, or a majority of them; the nobility; the commoners, or just the wealthy and learned part of them. The seventeenth-century distinction between "aristocracy" and "democracy" (or "popular states") is much more precise and useful. If we emphasize "republic" as government of the people, we had best hold tight rein on our tendency to see government of the people as being either direct democracy or parliamentary government—unless we use "parliament" in the historically legitimate sense for an "assembly of estates." The notions of "social contract" and "divine right" applied equally to monarchies and republics. The States of Holland repeatedly affirmed that they ruled over their subjects by divine right. Divine right belonged to government as such, and Bossuet knew this as well as the Dutch.

If we try to define the social content of republics, we are no better off. They were not characteristically popular or "middle class" (whatever that much-misused term may mean). They were not characteristically linked to any particular social class or group. There is no more common historical distortion than to speak of the "mercantile republic" of Holland. Merchants were important in Holland, but they were not *the* government. They participated in the government, along with nobles and members of two other groups which do not fit the usual class system—the "regents," or members of the governing bodies, and the professional government servants, of whom the greatest was the councilor-pensionary of Holland, or Grand Pensionary. What is significant about both of these groups is that they quite quickly lost their original quality as members of the merchant class—and sometimes were not and had never been members of it. Furthermore, they developed into semi-hereditary governing cliques of strongly oligarchical character. Curiously, it was just the regents and the professionals who became increasingly predominant in the government of the Dutch Republic. We should not forget that the Venetian merchants were similarly governed by a hereditary aristocracy and that egalitarian democracy was one of the first victims of the English Protectorate. Switzerland, of course, had few nobles in this age; but that was because it was so poor, not because it was republican.

We are driven back upon the notion which corresponds best with the modern notion. A republic (always disregarding the use of the word in political theory for all states) was fundamentally just a state without a king or prince. In practice this usually meant the "estates-state" without a prince, and hence the transformation of the role of the estates from being advisors and assenters to the kings to being the rulers of the state. This was, of course, precisely the kind of transformation that took place at the foundation of the American Republic.

In conclusion, I would emphasize first that monarchy and republic in the seventeenth century were alike in a number of ways. Both rested upon social systems characterized by privilege; seventeenth-century republicans seldom abolished noble titles or even proposed it. Both experienced an increasing dynastic element: what else should we call the emergence of hereditary ruling groups in the republics? And both were forms of the "estates-state."

But they were dissimilar in three important ways. They differed in the number of those who ruled. Republican regents in Holland might be a "plurality of Caesars," in the annoyed phrase of a French ambassador at The Hague trying to hold the United Provinces to a pro-French policy; but "plural Caesars" are not quite the same as "one Caesar." Second, different political theories tended to be formed in republics and monarchies. Monarchial doctrines gave greater emphasis to the virtue of obedience, while in the republics notions of representative power and responsibility to the people persisted. Third, although both republics and monarchies were usually forms of the "estates-state," it was opposite members of the "estates-state" structure which were lopped off, the king in the case of the republic and the estates in the case of absolute monarchy.

But the combined form, the pure or true "estates-state," provided an alternative form of development. It grew into modern constitutional monarchy and, more importantly, modern parliamentarism. Even when the Dutch state was reorganized after the fall of the Napoleonic regime in 1813, it was remodeled not on the old republican pattern of estates-with-stadholder but on the pattern of English constitutional monarchy.

In our own day, of course, the distinction between republics and monarchies has lost almost all fundamental significance. We are all "democrats," all "republicans," even in the constitutional monarchies. But the debate still goes on: now it is waged over the specific practical content we give to these terms.

ABOUT THE
CONTRIBUTORS

*Of the twenty contributors to this volume, ten
did their study and research for the doctorate
(some for the M.A. as well) under Professor
Mattingly's direction at Columbia University.
To avoid repetition, their names are
preceded by an asterisk.*

*THE REVEREND ROBERT I. BRADLEY, S. J., born in Spokane, Washington, in 1924, holds two degrees from Gonzaga University, one from the University of Louvain, and two from Columbia; he is Chairman of the Department of History at Seattle University. He has in progress a variety of studies on the ecclesiological side of seventeenth–century intellectual history; his various articles include seven in *The New Catholic Encyclopedia*.

*CHARLES H. CARTER, born in Baker, Oregon, in 1927, specializes in Western European political and diplomatic history, 1450–1660. He is author of *The Secret Diplomacy of the Habsburgs, 1598–1625* (1964), of articles in various journals, and editor of C. J. Burckhardt's *Richelieu: His Rise to Power*. He is currently writing a career biography of Gondomar and a study of Anglo–Spanish relations 1598–1625.

*SISTER JOSEPH DAMIEN HANLON of the Congregation of St. Joseph, a native New Yorker who holds degrees from St. Joseph's College for Women, Catholic University, and Columbia, has also studied at the University of Tunghai (Taiwan). Her numerous Reformation and Counter-Reformation articles include five in *The Catholic Youth Encyclopedia* and ten in *The New Catholic Encyclopedia*. In progress are an essay on Catholic nuns in Early Stuart England and a book on English Catholic women in the Counter-Reformation.

433

G. R. ELTON was born in Tübingen, Germany (1921), and his broad background includes schooling in Prague and Wales. He holds degrees from the University of London (Ph. D.) and Cambridge (Litt. D.). His many publications include *Tudor Revolution in Government* (1953), *England Under the Tudors* (1955), *Tudor Constitution* (1960), and *Reformation Europe* (1963). He is currently studying the social and economic program of the group working with Thomas Cromwell, enforcement problems in the Henrician Reformation, and the Early Tudor Council.

*Within the broad field of the history of ideas JOAN GADOL, of City College of the City University of New York, has done exhaustive research on Leon Battista Alberti, an important source of her views "on what unifies the various currents of Renaissance thought and culture." Her book on that "universal man" is forthcoming.

LEO GERSHOY, born in Russia in 1897, holds three degrees from Cornell (Ph. D., 1925). Especially noted for his work in the social and cultural history of seventeenth– and eighteenth–century Europe, his many publications include *The French Revolution and Napoleon* (1933), *From Despotism to Revolution, 1763–1789* (1944), and *Bertrand Barère: A Reluctant Terrorist* (1962). He is preparing a study of France in the Old Regime for the series "A History of Society" (J. H. Plumb, ed.).

The phrase "one of the world's most distinguished living historians" is indispensable to any note on PIETER GEYL (b. 1887). He is best known for his great *Geschiedenis van de Nederlandse stam* (in English: *The Revolt of the Netherlands* [1932], *The Netherlands Divided* [1936], *The Netherlands in the 17th Century* [2 vols, 1961–63]) and for his critical essays, including those collected in *From Ranke to Toynbee, Debates with Historians,* and *Encounters in History.*

JOHN R. HALE, born at Ashford, Kent, in 1923, is a Renaissance historian especially interested in matters of war and peace. Educated at Eastbourne College and Jesus College, Oxford, he is now at the University of Warwick. His publications include *England and the Italian Renaissance* (1954), *Machiavelli and Renaissance Italy* (1961), *The Evolution of British Historiography* (1964), and (Ed.) *Sir John Smythe's "Certain Discourses Military"* (1964). He is currently preparing a history of Renaissance fortification, and the Renaissance volume in the "Fontana History of Europe."

DENYS HAY, born in 1915 at Newcastle-upon-Tyne and educated at Newcastle Royal Grammar School and Balliol College, Oxford, served from 1958 to 1965 in the demanding post of Editor of *The English Historical Review*. His numerous works on Renaissance history and historiography include (ed.) Polydore Vergil's *Anglica Historia* (1950), *Polydore Vergil* (1952), *Europe: The Emergence of an Idea* (1957), and *The Italian Renaissance in its Historical Background* (1961). He is currently writing a general history of Europe in the later Middle Ages.

J. H. HEXTER was born in Memphis in 1910. After receiving his Ph. D. from Harvard in 1937 he soon (1941) published a milestone of Early Stuart studies, *The Reign of King Pym*. This and his *More's Utopia: The Biography of an Idea* reflect the complementary sides of his scholarship: political and intellectual history. Some of his many historical essays are collected in *Reappraisals in History* (1961), including "Storm Over the Gentry," perhaps the most incisive historiographical critique of recent times.

*DAVID L. HICKS, born in Kansas City, Missouri, in 1927, is a specialist in the political and social history of Renaissance Italy. He is co-author of *A History of the Western World* (S. B. Clough, ed.). His earlier Sienese studies in scholarly journals will be followed by *The Rise of Pandolfo Petrucci at Siena, 1480–1503*.

CHRISTOPHER HILL (b. 1912), educated at St. Peter's School, York, and Balliol College, Oxford—of which he is Master—is especially noted for his exhaustive examination of economic and social factors in sixteenth– and seventeenth–century English history. In addition to many articles his works include *Economic Problems of the Church* (1956), *Puritanism and Revolution* (1958), *The Century of Revolution* (1961), *Society and Puritanism in Pre-Revolutionary England* (1964), and, currently appearing, *Intellectual Origins of the English Revolution*.

MONSIGNOR PHILIP HUGHES, one of our pre-eminent church historians, was born in Manchester in 1895. His works include *The Catholic Question, 1688–1829* (1929), *History of the Church to 1517* (3 vols, 1946–47), and *The Reformation in England* (3 vols, 1950–54). He is currently preparing a critical edition of the correspondence of John Lingard.

*DE LAMAR JENSEN, born in Roseworth, Idaho, in 1925, is an authority on early modern European diplomatic history. His *Diplomacy and Dogmatism: Bernardino de Mendoza and the French Catholic League* (1963) will be followed by an examination of the French diplomatic establishment in the age of Catherine de' Medici. His editorial activities include *Machiavelli: Cynic, Patriot or Political Scientist?* (1960).

*ROBERT M. KINGDON, born at Chicago in 1927, is the author of *Geneva and the Coming of the Wars of Religion in France, 1555–1563* (1956) and some fifteen articles on the Reformation. He was co-editor of the two-volume *Registres de la Compagnie des Pasteurs de Genève au temps de Calvin* (1962–64), and editor of William Cecil's *The Execution of Justice in England* and William Allen's *A True, Sincere, and Modest Defense of English Catholics* (1965).

PAUL OSKAR KRISTELLER'S many publications on Renaissance intellectual history include *The Philosophy of Marsilio Ficino* (1943), *Studies in Renaissance Thought and Letters* (1956), *Renaissance Thought* I and II (1961, 1964), and *Eight Philosophers of the Italian Renaissance* (1964). His *Supplementum Ficinianum* (1937) and *Latin Manuscripts before 1600* (1960) are being followed by the four-volume finding list of uncatalogued Renaissance manuscripts, *Iter Italicum* (vol. I, 1963, vol. II currently appearing, vols III and IV to follow).

*HERBERT H. ROWEN was born in Brooklyn in 1916. A specialist in the Netherlands and France in the seventeenth century, he is the first (1951) of the line of professional historians who worked for the doctorate under Garrett Mattingly. He is author of *The Ambassador Prepares for War* (1957) and *A History of Early Modern Europe* (1960); his wide editorial activities include *From Absolutism to Revolution* (1963). He is currently preparing *Studies in the History of Dynasticism,* as well as a study of Amsterdam in the Golden Age and a life of Johan de Witt.

*FRANK SMOLAR, a native of San Pedro, California, and an Assistant Professor of History at Western Reserve University, may be counted as the last of the group of historians who did their graduate study and research under Garrett Mattingly. He is currently at work on the economic history of the Spanish Netherlands in the early seventeenth century.

*GERALD STRAUSS, born in Frankfurt am Main in 1922, holds a B.A. from Boston University and an M.A. and Ph. D. from Columbia. An authority on German humanism, his works include *Sixteenth Century Germany* (1959) and *Historian in an Age of Crisis: The Life of Johannes Aventinus, 1477–1534* (1963). He is currently at work on a comprehensive study of the expansion of knowledge in Renaissance Europe.

C. V. WEDGWOOD is especially esteemed for combining meticulous scholarship and evocative writing. Her many works include biographies of William the Silent, Richelieu, and the Earl of Strafford (recently revised), *The Thirty Years' War,* and more recently *The Trial of Charles I* (1964). The third volume of her authoritative "History of the Great Civil War" is soon to follow *The King's Peace* and *The King's War.*

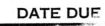

DATE DUE